Essentials of Buddhism

ESSENTIALS

Basic Terminology and

OF BUDDHISM

Concepts of Buddhist Philosophy and Practice

by
Kōgen Mizuno

translated by
Gaynor Sekimori

with a foreword by
J. W. de Jong

KŌSEI PUBLISHING CO. • *Tokyo*

This book was originally published in Japanese by Shunjū-sha under the title *Bukkyō Yōgo no Kiso Chishiki.*

Cover design by NOBU. The text of this book is set in a computer version of Palatino with a computer version of Optima for display.

First English edition, 1996

Published by Kōsei Publishing Co., 2-7-1 Wada, Suginami-ku, Tokyo 166, Japan.

ISBN 4-333-01683-5 LCC Card No. applied for

Contents

List of Charts 9

A Note on Indic and Other Foreign Words 11

Foreword, *by* J. W. de Jong 13

Preface 15

1. The Principal Branches of Buddhism 23

  The Two and Three Vehicles 24

    Hīnayāna, *24*

    Mahāyāna, *25*

    Points of Difference, *26*

    Pratyekabuddhayāna, *31*

  The Historical Sequence 33

    Primitive Buddhism, *33*

    Abhidharma Buddhism, *34*

    Mahāyāna Buddhism, *40*

  The Geographical Division 47

    Southern Buddhism, *47*

    Northern Buddhism, *49*

2. The Three Treasures 53

  The Buddha 55

    The Buddhas of the Past, *56*

    The Buddhas of the Three Periods and Ten Directions, *57*

Buddha Bodies, *57*
The Marks and Virtues of a Buddha, *61*
The Ten Epithets of a Buddha, *64*

The Dharma 68

Divisions of the Scriptures, *68*
The Teachings in Nine and Twelve Divisions, *68*
The Compilation of the Teachings, *75*
The Sūtra-piṭaka, *77*
The Vinaya-piṭaka, *79*
The Abhidharma-piṭaka, *82*
The Mahāyāna Tripiṭaka, *84*
The Dharma as Doctrine, *86*

The Saṅgha 89

The Composition of the Saṅgha, *89*
The Nature of the Saṅgha, *91*
The Functions of the Saṅgha, *92*

3. The Elements of Existence 95

The Five Aggregates 97

Form, *102*
Feeling, *104*
Perception, *104*
Mental Constituents, *105*
Consciousness, *106*
The Concepts of *Citta, Manas,* and *Vijñāna, 106*

The Twelve Sense Fields 108

The Internal and External Sense Fields, *109*
The Objects of Cognition, *110*
Sarvāstivādin *Dharma* Theory, *112*
The Nature of Truth, *114*

The Eighteen Elements of Existence 116

Mind and the Six Consciousnesses, *119*
Mind and *Manas* Consciousness, *119*

4. The Seals of the Law 121

Impermanence 124

Nonself 125

Nonself, Emptiness, and Nonbeing, *127*

Suffering 130
Nirvāṇa 132

5. Dependent Origination 135
General and Religious Dependent Origination 137
The Relationship Among Major Doctrines, *140*
The Yogācārin Three-Natures Theory, *140*
The Twelve-linked Chain of Dependent Origination 142
Relationships Among the Twelve Links, *143*
The Twelve Links, *146*

6. The Four Noble Truths 151
Canonical Statements 152
The Stages of Understanding, *152*
The Nature of the Four Noble Truths, *153*
Suffering 155
The Cause of Suffering 156
The Extinction of Suffering 157
The Way 158
The Eightfold Path, *158*
The Eightfold Path and the Threefold Practice, *160*

7. Religious Practice 163
The Thirty-seven Practices Conducive to Enlightenment 164
The Four Fields of Mindfulness, *164*
The Four Right Efforts, *164*
The Four Psychic Powers, *165*
The Five Roots of Emancipation, *165*
The Five Excellent Powers, *165*
The Seven Factors of Enlightenment, *166*
The Eightfold Path, *167*
The Threefold Practice 167
Morality, *168*
Concentration, *174*
Wisdom, *184*
The Stages of Practice 188

The Stages of *Arhat* Practice, *188*
The Types of Attainment, *191*
The Stages of Bodhisattva Practice, *196*
Doctrines of the Ten Stages, *199*
The First Stage of Enlightenment, *202*

8. The Defilements 203

The Concept of Defilements 203
The Defilements and Karma, *203*
Other Views of the Defilements, *204*
The Sarvāstivādin Theory of the Defilements 206
The Yogācārin Theory of the Defilements 208
The Fundamental Defilements, *208*
Auxiliary defilements, *212*

Notes 213
Indic Index 221
General Index 245

List of Charts

The Correspondence Between the Eightfold Path and the Six Perfections, 28
The Pāli Buddhist Listing of the Schools and Their Lineages, 36–37
The Sarvāstivādin Listing of the Schools and Their Lineages, 38–39
The Nikāyas and the Āgamas, 78
The Categories and Numbers of Offenses Applicable to Monks and Nuns as Recorded in the Vinayas of Major Schools, 80
Periods of Compilation of the Pāli Abhidhamma and the Sarvāstivādin Abhidharma, 83
The Pāli Tipiṭaka, 84
The Sarvāstivādin Theory of Seventy-five *Dharmas* in Five Categories, 98–99
The Yogācārin Theory of One Hundred *Dharmas* in Five Categories, 100–101
Classifications of Feeling, 104
Classifications of the *Dharmas* of Form, 111
The Relationships Among the Elements of Existence, 118
Dependent Origination, 141
Cause and Effect in the Past, Present, and Future, 144
The Four Noble Truths and Causality, 154
The Relationship of the Eightfold Path and the Threefold Practice, 161
Morality, 169

The Forty Subjects of Concentration, 181
The Stages of *Arhat* Practice, 194
The Sarvāstivādin Stages of Practice, 195
The Fa-hsiang Stages of Bodhisattva Practice and the Sarvāstivādin Stages of Practice, 198
The T'ien-t'ai Stages of Bodhisattva Practice, 199
The Yogācārin Defilements, 209

A Note on Indic and Other Foreign Words

This book is concerned with the Indian origins of Buddhism, and therefore Indic terminology is provided wherever possible. Initially, Buddhism was transmitted in Pāli, but by the end of the second century of the common era Sanskrit was preferred by some Abhidharma schools and by Mahāyāna adherents. Extant Buddhist works in Indic languages include texts in both Pāli and a form of Sanskrit known as Buddhist Hybrid Sanskrit, which unlike classical Sanskrit includes a relatively large number of vernacular elements. Pāli and Sanskrit, both Indo-Aryan languages, resemble each other substantially. One-quarter to one-third of all words are the same in both languages, and many other vocabulary items are simply variants of words in one or the other language.

In this book, the Sanskrit versions of Buddhist terms and of personal and place names are used in running text as a rule, since they are likely to be more familiar to readers of English than the Pāli equivalents. Exceptions include the titles of Pāli Buddhist texts, Indic terms embedded in quotations translated from Pāli texts, and the term *saṅgha*. Although *saṃgha* more closely reflects the Sanskrit orthography, in this book *saṅgha* is used because it is the spelling found in so many English-language books on Buddhism. When Indic terms are provided in parentheses, the Sanskrit is given first (*dharma, dhamma; nirvāṇa, nibbāna*). Occasionally only one Indic term is provided, either because it is the same in both Pāli and Sanskrit (*samādhi, vinaya*) or because it is specific either to Pāli Buddhism or to Abhidharma and Mahāyāna schools that used Sanskrit.

In running text Indic terms are pluralized as though they were English except in a few cases where long-standing convention dictates otherwise. When terms are given in parentheses, however, the orthography is not anglicized. A few Indic words that have come to be regarded as English are not italicized, such as sūtra, karma, and nirvāṇa—and, of course, buddha, which is capitalized only in reference to the historical Buddha.

The editors have also distinguished between Dharma referring to the Buddha's teachings and *dharma* referring to phenomena, and between Saṅgha referring to the Buddhist community as the third of the Three Treasures (the Buddha, the Dharma, and the Saṅgha) and *saṅgha* referring to a Buddhist monastic community. Every effort has been made to apply the same rule to Abhidharma (a branch of Indian Buddhism) and *abhidharma* (a commentary or treatise) and to Vinaya (the moral provisions of the Saṅgha as a whole) and *vinaya* (a specific code of monastic rules and regulations).

It should be noted, in connection with the romanization of Indic terms, that in quite a few cases more than one spelling is possible. The editors have done their best to ensure that orthography sanctioned by authoritative dictionaries is used, but the dictionaries themselves disagree. Any errors are the editors' responsibility. The hyphenation of Indic terms is another thorny area. The editors have tried to avoid end-of-line word divisions that clearly violate the rules of Indic syllabification, but the extreme length of some Indic phrases and the exigencies of English-language typography have made some compromises inevitable.

The handling of romanized Chinese and Japanese is less problematic. The Wade-Giles system is used for Chinese, and the components of compound terms are linked by hyphens (for example, *tu-wu-chi, tao-pi-an*). The romanization of Japanese follows the Hepburn system.

Foreword

Professor Kōgen Mizuno's name is not unknown in the West. Several of his books have been translated into English: *Primitive Buddhism* (1969), *The Beginnings of Buddhism* (1980), *Buddhist Sutras* (1982), and *Basic Buddhist Concepts* (1987). Without doubt *Essentials of Buddhism: Basic Terminology and Concepts of Buddhist Philosophy and Practice* will also be received with great interest by many readers because Professor Mizuno has a talent for explaining in a very lucid way the basic concepts and historical development of Buddhism. All his publications are based upon a profound knowledge of the Buddhist sources in Pāli, Sanskrit, and Chinese.

The above-mentioned books are intended for the general reader. The entire range of Professor Mizuno's scholarship can be appreciated only by readers of his Japanese publications. Professor Mizuno is one of the leading Japanese specialists in Pāli literature and has published a grammar, a reader, and a dictionary of Pāli. He has translated many Pāli texts and compiled a three-volume index of the sixty-five volumes of the Japanese translation of the Pāli scriptures. Buddhist philosophy has always been greatly interested in the mind and its functions. This topic has been studied by Professor Mizuno in a voluminous work of more than a thousand pages in which he compares the doctrines of the School of the Elders (Theravāda) with those of other schools. He has also written many articles on the different recensions of the famous *Dhammapada*. A collection of his articles on this subject appeared in 1981.

In the course of almost sixty years Professor Mizuno has published numerous articles on many aspects of Buddhist studies. His collected papers, which one hopes to see published in the near future, would fill several volumes. It would be of great benefit for Western scholars of Buddhism if a selection of his articles were to be published in English translation. It is a pity that the fruits of Japanese scholarship in the field of Buddhist studies are known to but a handful of Western specialists able to read Japanese.

In *Essentials of Buddhism* Professor Mizuno explains the basic concepts of Buddhist thought and practice which are found in the scriptures composed in India as Buddhism evolved from early Buddhism to the later schools and Mahāyāna. His book also takes into account the concepts of Chinese Buddhist schools, such as T'ien-t'ai and Hua-yen, which greatly shaped the development of Buddhism in China and later in Japan. As he remarks in his preface, Buddhism is not merely a field of academic inquiry. The perspective of a Japanese scholar brought up in the Japanese Buddhist tradition is different from that of a Western scholar of Buddhism. It will therefore be of special interest for the Western reader to see which topics Professor Mizuno has selected as the most essential ones in Buddhist doctrine and practice. His book will give the reader much important information which is not easily found elsewhere. It will also give very useful assistance in understanding Buddhist terms which the general reader encounters in studying books on Buddhism or translations of Buddhist texts. Japanese readers have at their disposal excellent and detailed dictionaries of Buddhism, but the same information is not available in English-language dictionaries. For this reason, too, many readers will undoubtedly welcome the publication of *Essentials of Buddhism*.

J. W. de Jong
Professor Emeritus
The Australian National University

Preface

Buddhism is the teaching expounded by the historical Buddha, Śākyamuni, during his forty-five-year ministry. Immediately after his death (around 480 B.C.E.) his sermons were compiled as scriptures, and the rules he had established for governing life in monastic communities (*saṅgha*) were organized as the regulations (*vinaya*). The scriptures eventually became the Sūtra-piṭaka (Sutta-piṭaka), or "Sūtra Basket," a collection of sūtras organized in four or five divisions called Āgamas; and the regulations became the Vinaya-piṭaka, or "Precepts Basket," a collection of regulations. Together these two collections of the Buddha's teachings make up the sacred works of primitive Buddhism.

About one hundred years after the Buddha's death the Buddhist religious community, until then a single body, split into two groups: the conservative Theravāda and the reformist Mahāsāṃghika. These two schools were further fragmented as Buddhism spread over a wider geographical area and differences in interpretation of doctrines and regulations arose. Because eighteen or twenty schools of Buddhism developed during this period, it is known as the age of Abhidharma, or sectarian, Buddhism.

Each school transmitted its own collections of sūtras and regulations and formulated its own collection of commentaries and treatises (*abhidharma, abhidhamma*), interpreting the scriptural teachings doctrinally. The canon of each school consisted of three collections—of sūtras, of regulations, and of commentaries—that were known collectively as the Tripiṭaka (Tipiṭaka), or "Three

Baskets." When we compare sectarian scriptures extant either in Pāli or in Chinese, we find considerable differences in the doctrines outlined in the various *abhidharma* collections but comparatively few differences among the sūtra and *vinaya* collections. That there are so few differences indicates that they predate the schism and that their origins lie in the teachings of the Buddha himself.

The sectarian emphasis on minute doctrinal distinctions gave rise to a reformist group around the beginning of the common era. Known as Mahāyāna, this group added its own doctrines to a number of theories adopted from various schools and created original Mahāyāna scriptures. Early Mahāyāna scriptures transmitted the true teachings of the Buddha, divorced from sectarian theory. Middle Mahāyāna scriptures, philosophical works that expounded the theory underlying the early Mahāyāna works, appeared around the fourth and fifth centuries C.E. and gave rise to such schools as Mādhyamika and Yogācāra. Mahāyāna began to follow the same course as the earlier schools, favoring philosophy over religious practice. To correct the abuses engendered by this academic focus, Esoteric Buddhism, a late Mahāyāna school, was expounded in the seventh and eighth centuries.

In India the development of Buddhism followed a course from primitive Buddhism to sectarian Buddhism, early Mahāyāna, middle Mahāyāna, and late Mahāyāna, although some Theravāda and Mahāsāṃghika schools continued to exist alongside Mahāyāna Buddhism. By the thirteenth century, after a history of nearly seventeen hundred years, Buddhism had virtually disappeared from India.

In the third century B.C.E. the Mauryan emperor Aśoka became a follower of Buddhism and, as the patron of missionaries, laid the foundations for the propagation of Indian Buddhism throughout the world. Buddhism entered Afghanistan and Iran via northwestern India and made its way as far west as Syria, Egypt, and Greece. It reached Burma to the east and was transmitted to Sri Lanka in the south. Sri Lankan Theravāda prospered mightily and from there was taken to Burma, Thailand, Cambodia, and Laos, where it flourishes today as Theravāda, or Pāli, Buddhism.

Buddhism also flourished in northwestern India, whence it was transmitted to China in the first century C.E. by way of Central Asia. For the next thousand years, via both the Silk Road and the southern sea route, Indian scriptures were taken to China and there translated. Chinese Buddhism was transmitted to Korea and Japan, where it continues to prosper. Various sects arose in China, where both Abhidharma and Mahāyāna doctrines were received from India and further elaborated. Japanese Buddhism then received Chinese Buddhist doctrines and developed them further. A number of the sects that emerged in China and Japan survive to this day. Beginning in the seventh century many Buddhist scriptures, chiefly Mahāyāna works but also the Vinaya and Abhidharma of the Sarvāstivāda, a pre-Mahāyāna school, were also transmitted to Tibet from India.

Today living Buddhism is centered on Theravāda Buddhism and Japanese Buddhism. There are followers of Buddhism in China, Korea, and Tibet, as well as in Southeast Asia, where Buddhism was taken by Chinese émigrés. Buddhism continues to be disseminated throughout the world by the Zen and Pure Land sects. Modern Buddhism thus encompasses the doctrines of every period of the religion's history, including those developed in China and Japan.

Because the doctrines of Indian Buddhism survive as the foundation of later doctrinal developments, *Essentials of Buddhism* is devoted to explanation of basic Buddhist terminology and concepts. Chapter 1 deals with the meaning of the term Buddhism and of terms associated with various schools that evolved during the religion's long history (in particular doctrinal terminology of the Hīnayāna and Mahāyāna schools), with the historical development of Buddhism in India, and with the development of Southern Buddhism. Chapter 2 centers on the structure of Buddhist faith and deals with the general and specific meanings of the Three Treasures—the Buddha, his teachings (the Dharma, or Law), and the Order (Saṅgha)—the symbols of faith and worship. So indispensable are the Three Treasures that Buddhism cannot be considered a living faith if they are not honored.

Chapter 3 introduces the three basic divisions of all physical and mental phenomena, "all that exists": the five aggregates, the twelve sense fields, and the eighteen elements of existence. From the beginning, primitive Buddhism was concerned with existence in terms of the phenomenal world—existence as we know it—and looked at ever-changing phenomena, in flux between existence and extinction, in terms of the law of causality, teaching followers how to regard phenomena in order to attain the ideal. Since subsequent chapters discuss the law of dependent origination and the importance of "being" as the essence of Buddhism, this chapter examines the formal categories of existence, which are the basis for further study, together with their classifications and definitions.

Chapter 4 discusses the Four and Three Seals of the Law, both in general terms and item by item. The Seals of the Law are basic to Buddhism: without them there would be no Buddhism. Chapter 5 considers dependent origination, a systematic doctrine based on the Seals of the Law, in general terms and then examines various aspects of the Twelve-linked Chain of Dependent Origination, a representative formulation of the doctrine.

In contrast to chapter 5, which examines the causes of the cycle of birth and death and suffering, chapter 6 deals with the Four Noble Truths, which elucidate the causes that lead from the state of delusion to the ideal of enlightenment. Reference to the Twelve-linked Chain of Dependent Origination enhances understanding of the Four Noble Truths. The Buddha's first discourse after attaining enlightenment was an exposition of the Four Noble Truths, which are of central importance to the understanding of Buddhism. Chapter 7 details methods of practice for attaining the Buddhist ideal that are described in the primitive sūtras. The most general of them are the thirty-seven practices conducive to enlightenment, but all are founded on the threefold practice (morality, concentration, and wisdom). Each of the thirty-seven practices conducive to enlightenment is described briefly, and each element of the threefold practice is discussed in depth. Finally, the various groupings of the stages of practice that were devised later are considered.

Chapter 8 deals with defilements, which hinder attainment of the ideal, and discusses briefly the various classifications of defilements devised within primitive and Abhidharma Buddhism. Buddhist enlightenment and the defilements are mutually exclusive: enlightenment cannot be attained unless the defilements are eliminated. There are said to be 84,000—that is, myriad—defilements; thus, to remove them the Buddha set out 84,000 "gates of the Law," or teachings. Of the vast number of defilements, ten are considered fundamental; of these the principal defilement is ignorance of basic Buddhist teachings, or egocentrism that interferes with learning Buddhist doctrine.

Buddhism is not merely a field of academic inquiry; it is a living religion of faith and practice whose way is personal experience and whose goal is supreme enlightenment. The connotations of experience and enlightenment cannot be fully understood through words, but only through experience. Comprehension even of logical explanations must be grounded in experience. A person can read about experience, but without personal experience will be unable to understand it fully. However many words are used to describe a religious concept, it can be understood completely only through religious practice. Nevertheless, this book attempts to give an understanding of the basic terminology and concepts of Buddhism. It is my hope that it will meet a need not satisfied by dictionaries.

Essentials of Buddhism

1. The Principal Branches of Buddhism

Buddhism refers to the teachings of the historical Buddha and, by extension, to the religion he founded. Buddha, or Enlightened One, is a title given to a person who has realized the universal truth. The historical Buddha is also known by the titles Śākya-muni (Sākyamuni), literally, Sage of the Śākya (Sākya) Tribe, and Bhagavat, or World-honored One. The epithet Bhagavat can be applied to any buddha, but Śākyamuni refers specifically to the historical founder of Buddhism, who according to the Theravāda tradition was born around 560 B.C.E. in the kingdom of the Śākyas in northern India and died around 480 B.C.E. In Pāli Buddhism the historical Buddha is known by his clan name, Gotama (Gautama in Sanskrit). The Japanese refer to him as Shakuson, "Śākyamuni the World-honored One."

Buddhism can also be defined as the religion that teaches the attainment of buddhahood. This is a Mahāyāna definition, based on the Mahāyāna doctrine that all sentient beings have the potential to become buddhas. Here Buddhism is understood as the teaching that points the way to personal perfection through its perception of the historical Buddha as a fully enlightened being.

Traditionally, three systems have been developed to account for the divergences that occurred during Buddhism's long history. The first is known as the two (sometimes three) vehicles and is based primarily on philosophical differences. The second divides Buddhism into three broad, historically consecutive movements within Indian Buddhism—primitive, Abhidharma (sectarian), and Mahāyāna. The third focuses on the geographical dispersal of Buddhism after it left India—Southern Buddhism and Northern Buddhism.

Japanese Buddhism has made wide use of two further classifications, based on whether the teachings are exoteric or esoteric and whether salvation depends on one's own strength or on that of another. Kūkai (774–835), the founder of the Shingon (True Word) sect in Japan, popularized the former, while the latter was adopted by the Pure Land Buddhism of Shinran (1173–1262) and others. Followers of Esoteric teachings believe it is impossible to express the true meaning of Buddhism in words, this being the secret attainment of the Buddha. That which cannot be so expressed is termed "hidden" or "secret," and that which can is called "revealed." Pure Land Buddhism teaches that rebirth in the Pure Land is possible through absolute faith in the lord of the Pure Land, Amida (Amitābha, Amitāyus) Buddha, a teaching that relies on the strength of another. The teachings of other Japanese sects, which stress self-perfection through individual effort and progress, are known as self-reliant teachings.

The Two and Three Vehicles

The term vehicle, a translation of the Indic *yāna*, is a metaphor for Buddhism, indicating the means by which people are conveyed from "this shore" of delusion to the "other shore" of enlightenment. The basic classification includes two vehicles, Hīnayāna and Mahāyāna, but a variant with three vehicles also exists. In this case Hīnayāna is divided into Śrāvakayāna (the vehicle of the hearers) and Pratyekabuddhayāna (the vehicle of the solitary buddhas), while Mahāyāna is termed Bodhisattvayāna (the vehicle of the bodhisattvas) or Buddhayāna (the vehicle of the buddhas).

Hīnayāna

Literally, the small, or inferior, vehicle, Hīnayāna was a designation used by the Mahāyāna schools to denote the perceived shortcomings of their predecessors. The Mahāyānists criticized

Hīnayāna principally for stressing benefits to the individual alone through its goal of self-perfection and release from the bonds of existence. Hīnayāna is also known as Śrāvakayāna, from its idea that enlightenment can be attained only by hearing the teachings of the Buddha directly. A *śrāvaka* (*sāvaka*), or hearer, is thus a disciple, and the term refers to all the direct disciples of Śākyamuni.

Both Hīnayāna and Śrāvakayāna are derogatory terms and thus are never used by the non-Mahāyāna schools themselves. The Mahāyāna T'ien-t'ai sect in China applied a less discriminatory designation, the teaching of the Tripiṭaka or Piṭaka, to non-Mahāyāna schools. Tripiṭaka, literally, the Three Baskets, refers to the canon upon which the teachings of the pre-Mahāyāna schools are based.

Up until the nineteenth century, Chinese and Japanese scholars included both primitive (presectarian) Buddhism and Abhidharma (sectarian) Buddhism in the Hīnayāna classification. Properly, however, Hīnayāna should be used to designate only those schools that developed as a result of Abhidharma scholasticism, not the Buddhism of the earliest period.

MAHĀYĀNA

Mahāyāna, literally, the great, or superior, vehicle, combines the two goals of self-perfection and the enlightenment of others. In the Mahāyāna view, it is not enough to attain perfection (buddhahood) oneself and thus win release from *saṃsāra*, the cycle of birth and death; this is worth nothing unless others are guided to enlightenment and release, as well. Mahāyānists consider this altruistic outlook, the view of the bodhisattva, to be the core difference between the two vehicles. It is because of its adherence to this ideal that Mahāyāna is also known as Bodhisattvayāna, the vehicle of the bodhisattvas, as well as Buddhayāna, the vehicle of the buddhas.

The Mahāyāna movement, which gained support in the first century B.C.E., about four hundred years after the Buddha's death, aimed to restore the spirit of Śākyamuni's teachings to a religion that had been reduced to a husk of its original form by overformalization. That process began in the fourth century B.C.E., about a hundred years after Śākyamuni's death, as schism divided the Buddhist movement and philosophy began to take precedence over practice. Mahāyānists were critical of the resulting sectarianism, which came to be known as Abhidharma Buddhism.

POINTS OF DIFFERENCE

Mahāyāna isolated six major areas of difference between itself and Hīnayāna. First, the ideal of the practitioner differed. Hīnayāna taught that the highest enlightenment for a *śrāvaka* was that of the *arhat* (*arahat;* an enlightened person on the level below buddhahood), not buddhahood itself. During the Abhidharma period Śākyamuni was, in effect, deified. He was thought to belong to a transcendent plane in both birth and personality. Thirty-two primary and eighty secondary distinguishing bodily marks and eighteen unique virtues were attributed to him. His attainment of buddhahood was considered to be the result of eons of accumulated practice as a bodhisattva, or aspirant to enlightenment, and it was this accumulated practice that set him apart. His disciples, by contrast, had merely heard his teachings and begun to practice in response to them.

Mahāyāna, on the other hand, asserted that all sentient beings possess the buddha-nature (*buddhagotra*), the disposition and capacity to attain buddhahood, and thus are capable first of becoming bodhisattvas through aspiring to enlightenment and then of attaining buddhahood itself by means of the bodhisattva vows,[1] self-awakening, and various practices, including the Six Perfections. Those who cannot achieve buddhahood in the present existence are assured of it sometime in the future, however many eons it may take. Self-awakening, resolution, and effort enable aspirants to persevere in their practice, never doubting the final outcome. This supreme confidence is a major difference between the outlooks of Hīnayāna and Mahāyāna.

The bodhisattva concept was broadened in Mahāyāna to include any being (*sattva*) aspiring to enlightenment (*bodhi*). A bodhisattva is thus a buddha-to-be, one who walks the path of enlightenment. One becomes a bodhisattva as a result of awakening within oneself the aspiration to enlightenment (*bodhicitta*) and embracing the four universal vows of the bodhisattva. Any being can become a bodhisattva. The designation bodhisattva presupposes that one is seeking to bring all others, not just oneself, to enlightenment.

Second, Mahāyāna stressed the importance of altruistic practice in this life, not the escape from the bonds of existence sought by Hīnayānists, who were primarily concerned with the question of karmic retribution and release from the suffering inherent in existence. The Hīnayāna *arhat*'s goal was to gain release from the cycle of birth and death and attain the tranquil, ideal state of nirvāṇa (*nibbāna*).

Saṃsāra, the cycle of birth and death, is sometimes translated as "transmigration" or "rebirth." In this cycle, which is grounded in delusion, sentient beings are governed by good and evil karmic retribution. Depending on the type of karma accumulated during a lifetime, sentient beings are reborn in one of six realms of existence. When good karma prevails, a person may be reborn as a human or heavenly being, whereas a preponderance of adverse karma brings rebirth in a hell or as a hungry spirit, an animal, or an *asura* (demon). This concept was inherited from pre-Buddhist Indian thought.

Nirvāṇa, the antithesis of *saṃsāra,* means "tranquillity," or the state in which the defilements binding one to *saṃsāra* have been extinguished. Hīnayāna considered it the condition of the highest enlightenment. Mahāyāna bodhisattva practice did not spurn the suffering of *saṃsāra,* nor did it have as its sole goal the tranquillity of nirvāṇa, since the bodhisattva's primary concern is to bring others to enlightenment even if his or her own practice remains unperfected. This concern is inherent in the first universal vow of the bodhisattva: "However innumerable sentient beings are, I vow to bring about their release." The bodhisattva is not preoccupied with concern over suffering or tranquillity, karmic retribution or rebirth. Far from avoiding suffering, the bodhisattva, compelled to relieve those who are in pain, voluntarily embraces the adverse destinations of rebirth to share the distress of their inhabitants. In short, the primary goal of Mahāyāna was to fulfill the bodhisattva vow to bring all sentient beings to enlightenment, not to attain nirvāṇa for oneself alone.

Third, as a corollary of this goal, Mahāyānists considered that Hīnayāna placed undue stress on the personal benefits of practice; in reaction, they emphasized altruistic practice. Dissatisfied with what they saw as an exclusive focus on self-perfection in the fundamental Hīnayāna doctrine of the Four Noble Truths and the Eightfold Path,[2] the Mahāyānists evolved a new doctrine, the Six Perfections, as the core of bodhisattva practice. By incorporating provisions for service to others in this doctrine, they compensated for an apparent lack in the method of practice set forth in the Eightfold Path. The concept of altruistic practice was further clarified with the formalization of the four means by which a bodhisattva leads sentient beings to release.[3] Donation, the first of the Six Perfections and the pivot of the practice of compassion, is the foundation for each of the four means.

The Six Perfections (*ṣaṭ-pāramitā*) are the six kinds of practice a bodhisattva undertakes to attain enlightenment and buddhahood. They are the perfections of donation (*dāna-pāramitā*); morality, or observing the precepts (*śīla-pāramitā*); forbearance, or patience (*kṣānti-pāramitā*); effort, or endeavor (*vīrya-pāramitā*); meditation (*dhyāna-pāramitā*); and wisdom (*prajñā-pāramitā*). As the chart below shows, the Six Perfections not only encompass all the practices of the Eightfold Path but also add two practices that have a social dimension, donation and forbearance. These prac-

The Correspondence Between
the Eightfold Path and the Six Perfections

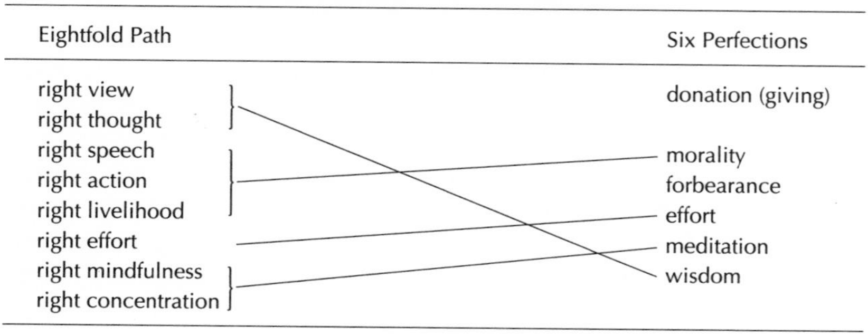
Eightfold Path
Six Perfections
right view
right thought
right speech
right action
right livelihood
right effort
right mindfulness
right concentration
donation (giving)
morality
forbearance
effort
meditation
wisdom

tices are characteristic of the Mahāyāna concern for altruistic practice. In particular, by making donation the first of the perfections, Mahāyāna stressed the necessity of mutual support among all members of society. The practice of donation enables bodhisattvas to deepen their compassion and gain the merits inherent in this practice.

Pāramitā (perfection) was originally translated into Chinese as *tu* (crossing over), *tu-wu-chi* (reaching the limitless), or *tao-pi-an* (reaching the other shore). These translations are derived from traditional interpretations of the term as *pāram-ita* (*pāram*, "to the other shore," and *ita*, "reached"). By means of *pāramitā* practice, a person leaves this shore of birth and death and reaches the other shore of nirvāṇa. Modern scholars, however, favor the interpretation *pārami-tā*, *pārami* being derived from *parama*, "supreme," a meaning close to the old Chinese translation "reaching the limitless." The abstract noun *pāramitā* can mean "perfection," as in *dāna-pāramitā*, the perfection of donation.

The Flower Garland Sūtra (*Avataṃsaka-sūtra*) later broadened the concept of the Six Perfections by relating them to the ten stages of bodhisattva practice.[4] For this purpose a list of ten perfections (*daśa-pāramitā*) was given, the original six and a further four: skillful means (*upāya-pāramitā*), vows (*praṇidhāna-pāramitā*), force of purpose (*bala-pāramitā*), and transcendental knowledge (*jñāna-pāramitā*). Pāli Buddhism compiled its own list of ten perfections (*dasa-pāramī*). Differing considerably from the Mahāyāna version, it consists of donation (*dāna-pāramī*), morality (*sīla-pāramī*), release from the world of delusion (*nekkhamma-pāramī*), wisdom (*paññā-pāramī*), effort (*viriya-pāramī*), forbearance (*khanti-pāramī*), truth (*sacca-pāramī*), determination (*adhiṭṭhāna-pāramī*), benevolence (*mettā-pāramī*), and equanimity (*upekkhā-pāramī*).

Classical commentators of both the Mahāyāna and the non-Theravāda Hīnayāna traditions generally held that it takes a bodhisattva three *asaṃkhyeyas* and one hundred great *kalpas* to perfect his or her practice of the perfections, while Pāli Buddhism held that a bodhisattva needs four *asaṃkhyeyas* and one hundred thousand *kalpas* to perfect his or her practice. An *asaṃkhyeya* (literally, "uncountable") is an incomprehensibly long period of time. A *kalpa* is an eon, thousands of billions of years, and is the period during which a universe arises, endures, decays, and disintegrates. The basic unit is a small *kalpa*. Eighty small *kalpas* make a great *kalpa* (*mahā-kalpa*), and one hundred great *kalpas* multiplied by an *asaṃkhyeya* are an *asaṃkhyeya kalpa*.

Although Mahāyāna criticized the *śrāvakas* for seeking only their own enlightenment and taking no thought for the world around them, this seems somewhat unjust. *Arhats*, through perfecting themselves by means of the Four Noble Truths and the Eightfold Path, must be considered ready to be active for the sake of others. They should not be thought of as self-righteous people striving merely for their own welfare but as individuals who teach others and guide them to enlightenment. This implication is inherent in the literal meaning of *arhat*, "worthy of respect."

The fourth point of difference concerned ontology, the metaphysical study of the nature of existence (*bhava*) and emptiness (*śūnyatā*). Śākyamuni had expressly forbidden ontological discussion, popular in the non-Buddhist philosophical schools of his time, reasoning that such speculation contributed nothing to actually solving the problems of human life. What should be studied, he said, was not existence itself but the phenomena surrounding it. The only questions worthy of attention were the conditions of such phenomena, how to deal with them, and one's correct attitude toward them. This is the law of dependent origination. All the basic doctrines of Buddhism, including the Four Noble Truths, the Eightfold Path, and the Twelve-linked Chain of Dependent Origination, are derived from this standpoint.[5]

As schools developed within Buddhism, however, concern turned increasingly to theoretical rather than practical matters, and many commentaries and treatises (*abhidharma, abhidhamma*) discussed ontological subjects, particularly the idea of existence. Mahāyānists criticized this focus on existence as a deviation from original Buddhism. In an endeavor to revive Śākyamuni's teachings, they emphasized the actual state of existence and what it should be in light of the emptiness of wisdom (*prajñā*). In doing so, they restored the original doctrine of dependent origination.

It is clear from the above that Mahāyānists stressed the practical over the theoretical—the fifth point of difference. The Abhidharma schools devoted themselves to studies that were so specialized and concerned with theory as to be comprehensible only to specially trained scholar-monks. Mahāyānists viewed this as a degeneration, a turning away from religious practice. Although early Mahāyānists did engage in theoretical discussion, they remained within the bounds of the original doctrine and concerned themselves only with matters necessary to clarify the foundation of practice. Moreover, the Abhidharma schools' preoccupation with increasingly abstruse philosophical studies led to many controversies, whose resolution became more important than religious practice. Mahāyānists reacted by emphasizing faith and practice in an effort to correct what they saw as the harmful influence of scholasticism and argument for argument's sake.

The sixth area of contention concerned the roles of the laity and the monkhood. The convoluted academic studies of the Abhidharma schools, too specialized for general comprehension, did nothing to further the faith and religious practice of believers as a whole. Having shut themselves away in monasteries to devote themselves to doctrinal studies, the monks were unable to fulfill their role as religious leaders of the community of lay believers.

In an effort to remedy this defect, the Mahāyānists devised the practice of the Six Perfections to provide an easily understood way of faith and practice. Donation, in particular, can be practiced by anyone, lay believer or monk, and teaches deep compassion and unselfish action. Donation was conceived as a selfless, unconditioned act in which there is no consciousness of being either the giver or the receiver and no thought of reward or merit from the act of donation. The perfection of donation having been achieved, the other perfections can be performed with the same supreme detachment of a mind rooted in emptiness, or *śūnyatā*. Furthermore, Mahāyāna taught that the ultimate truth of Buddhism lies in the day-to-day actions of the lay believer, so that everyday life itself is the place of enlightenment (*bodhi-maṇḍa*), the place of the bodhisattva practice of attaining enlightenment and helping others do so.

PRATYEKABUDDHAYĀNA

When Hīnayāna is divided into two vehicles, Pratyekabuddhayāna, the vehicle of the *pratyekabuddhas,* or the solitary buddhas, is the second vehicle, with Śrāvakayāna being the first vehicle. (The third vehicle is Bodhisattvayāna or Buddhayāna [Mahāyāna].) A *pratyekabuddha* gains enlightenment not by hearing the teaching of others, as a *śrāvaka* does, but as a result of personal realization of the doctrine of dependent origination. Unlike a bodhisattva or buddha, a *pratyekabuddha* is not concerned with bringing about the deliverance of others; the goal is individual enlightenment, and to hasten it the *pratyekabuddha* lives apart from the world, in forests or mountains.

Although the concept of the *pratyekabuddha* has no basis in historical fact, it existed in very early Buddhism and can be traced to pre-Buddhist sources. The *Isigili-sutta,* one of the earliest Buddhist writings, contains a reference to five hundred *pratyekabuddhas* who lived long ago on Mount Isigili. Abhidharma Buddhism inherited the concept and devised two categories of *pratyekabuddha:* those who practice in a group and those who practice alone.

Mahāyāna associated certain basic doctrines with each of the three vehicles. The practice of the *śrāvaka* was said to be based on the Four Noble Truths and the Eightfold Path, that of the *pratyekabuddha* on the doctrine of the Twelve-linked Chain of Dependent Origination, and that of the bodhisattva and buddha on the Six Perfections. These associations, however, were merely convenient conventions. Certainly no figure in Buddhist history can be regarded as a *pratyekabuddha,* and there was never an independent teaching intended for *pratyekabuddhas.* All the teachings cited here are basic Buddhist doctrines, and there seems little purpose in coupling them with the three vehicles in any way.

The concept of the *pratyekabuddha* is implicit in the traditional account of Śākyamuni's enlightenment under the *bodhi* tree. Realizing the nature of the law of dependent origination, the Buddha attained enlightenment and then spent several weeks in deep meditation, contemplating his understanding. At that time, having decided against teaching others because he considered the law of dependent origination too complicated for ordinary people's comprehension, Śākyamuni was in a state that could be likened to that of a *pratyekabuddha.* But the great deity Brahmā then appeared before him and pleaded with him to teach the Dharma (truth) both to succor suffering humankind and to prevent the world from becoming even more degraded. Brahmā urged the Buddha to temper his teaching to the capacity of his hearers to ensure that some at least would understand. On Brahmā's pleading, Śākyamuni resolved to attempt to teach and thereupon began his long ministry. In the view of the Mahāyānists, he could no longer be called a *pratyekabuddha* but was a perfectly enlightened buddha, or *samyaksaṃbuddha* (*sammā-sambuddha*).[6]

The Historical Sequence

Buddhism can also be categorized on the basis of the historical development of its doctrines, which occurred principally in India. According to this system, there are three broad divisions: primitive, Abhidharma, and Mahāyāna Buddhism.

PRIMITIVE BUDDHISM

Primitive Buddhism is the designation applied to the earliest period of Buddhism, from the time of Śākyamuni to around 350 B.C.E., roughly one hundred years after his death. No sectarian divisions were apparent during this interval; Buddhism was transmitted in its original form by a single group.

Some scholars subdivide the period into two phases, original Buddhism (the Buddhism of Śākyamuni and his direct disciples, extending to about thirty years after the Buddha's death) and primitive Buddhism in the narrowest sense (covering the subsequent period, up to the sectarian schism around 350 B.C.E.). This division is correct in theory, since it is logical to assume that the Buddhism of Śākyamuni himself was different from that experienced and interpreted by his direct disciples, but extant documents do not support such a division.

The Āgamas are the earliest extant collections of sūtras, or discourses of the Buddha. Together with the collections of monastic regulations called Vinaya-piṭakas, they were transmitted independently by each of the schools born of the schism. Although the Āgamas and the Vinaya-piṭakas originated in the time of Śākyamuni, their final form was not established until after the growth of sectarianism. Since sectarian doctrines color the extant writings, it is virtually impossible to extract directly from these materials the exact teachings of primitive Buddhism. Generalizations about the period of primitive Buddhism can be made, however, by comparing the Sūtra-piṭakas and the Vinaya-piṭakas of the various schools and identifying the points on which all agree.

ABHIDHARMA BUDDHISM

Around 350 B.C.E. the Buddhist community (*saṅgha*) was divided by controversies over the interpretation of doctrines and monastic regulations. A progressive group, the Mahāsāṃghika (Great Assembly), challenged the formalized traditionalism of the conservatives, known as the Theravāda (Sthaviravāda in Sanskrit), "Those Supporting the Teaching of the Elders."

Ancient Pāli Buddhist histories and commentaries offer two interpretations of the initial schism. The first interpretation holds that when pragmatic progressives among the monks proposed the observance of ten disputed practices in the monastic regulations, adapting traditional rules to the exigencies of time, local customs, and geography, the elder monks convened the Second Council.[7] These practices were condemned as heretical by the elders of the conservative group, and the controversy led to the split between the Mahāsāṃghikas and the Theravādins. The second interpretation holds that the split occurred as a result of a dispute over five theses deprecating the *arhat* raised by a monk named Mahādeva.[8] The theses were opposed by the conservative elders but supported by many younger monks.

Whatever actually happened, it is apparent that there was great friction in the Buddhist community over the interpretation of the doctrines and regulations recorded in the Sūtra-piṭakas and the Vinaya-piṭakas. As Buddhism spread throughout India and beyond as a result of the patronage of the Mauryan emperor Aśoka (r. ca. 273–ca. 232 B.C.E.), communication among local communities declined, ties among groups weakened, and a spirit of independence developed. Geographical distance coupled with doctrinal differences fostered the development of schools. The initial schism, which resulted in the establishment of Mahāsāṃghika and Theravāda, did not resolve all questions, and two or three hundred years later Buddhism was divided into eighteen (or twenty) schools. It is the sectarianism following the first schism that is termed Abhidharma Buddhism.

Understandably, the Sūtra-piṭakas and the Vinaya-piṭakas transmitted from the earlier period were revised as they entered the canons of individual schools. In addition, each school developed an Abhidharma-piṭaka, a compendium of doctrinal commentary, which was also included in its canon. The purpose of the *abhidharmas* (literally, "that which is about the Dharma") was to explain and define terminology and concepts appearing in the Āgamas (the Dharma, or the Buddha's teaching) and to record the results of the philosophical and doctrinal studies that emerged from the classification and organization of the Vinaya and of the doctrines of the sūtras. Since the *abhidharmas* appeared after the rise of the schools, they differ completely from school to school.

With the completion of the Abhidharma-piṭakas, the three divisions of the canon, or Tripiṭaka (Three Baskets), were complete. The Sūtra- and Vinaya-piṭakas, dating to the period of primitive Buddhism, are on the whole fairly similar from school to school, but the Abhidharma-piṭakas, having been completed independently, offer the clearest exposition of differences among the schools. The *abhidharmas* are too formalized and complex to be of much use to the average person, however.

Each school also had its own tradition about the names of the eighteen or twenty schools that made up Abhidharma Buddhism after the Mahāsāṃghika-Theravāda split. Of more than ten extant listings of the schools and their lineages, the most important are those of Pāli Buddhism and of the Sarvāstivādins (Those Who Hold the Doctrine That All Exists), one of the most influential of the pre-Mahāyāna schools, given in the charts on pages 36–37 and 38–39.

Later, Mūla-Sarvāstivāda (Root Sarvāstivāda, an orthodox group that broke away from the Sarvāstivādin mainstream in the fourth or fifth century C.E.), placed all the schools in four groups: Sarvāstivāda, Mahāsāṃghika, Saṃmatīya, and Sthaviravāda. This division is important, for it is the one that the Chinese priests Hsüan-tsang (ca. 600–664) and I-ching (634–713) used in

The Pāli Buddhist Listing of the Schools and Their Lineages

The broken line indicates that the Cetiyavāda of southern India subdivided into five schools, including the Cetiyavāda itself, after the formation of the eighteen schools.
(Sanskrit equivalents are given in parentheses.)

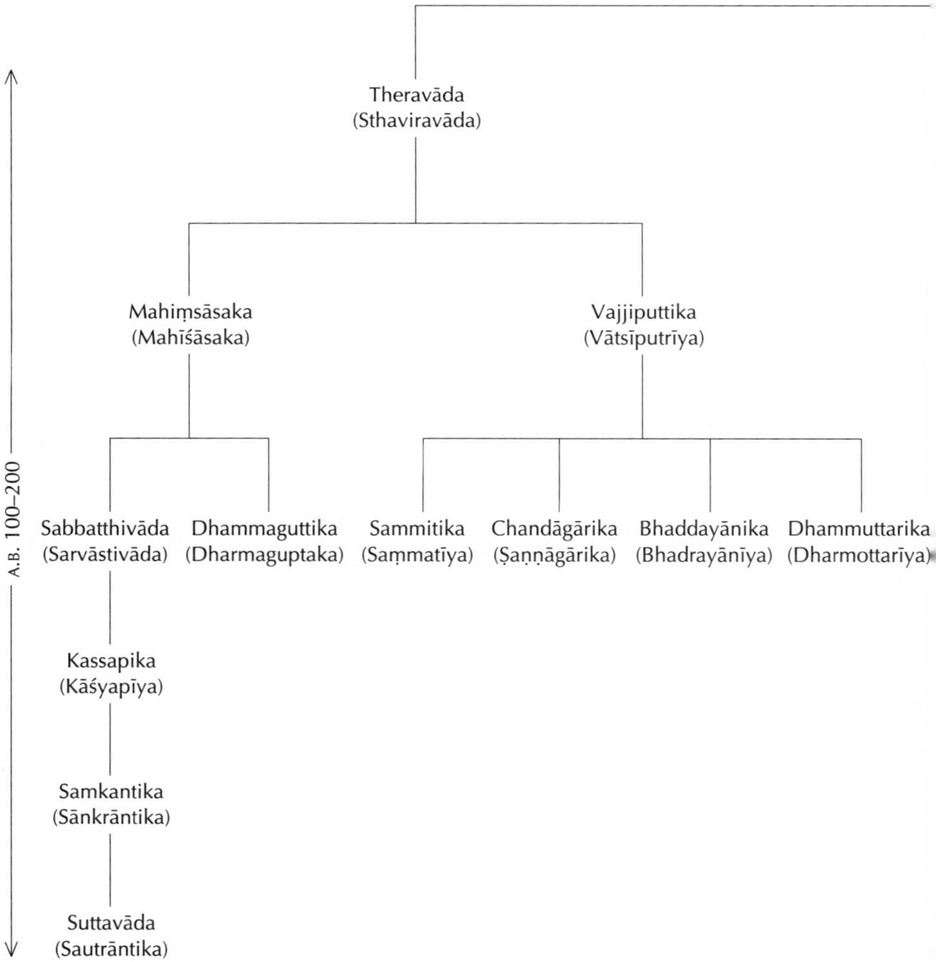

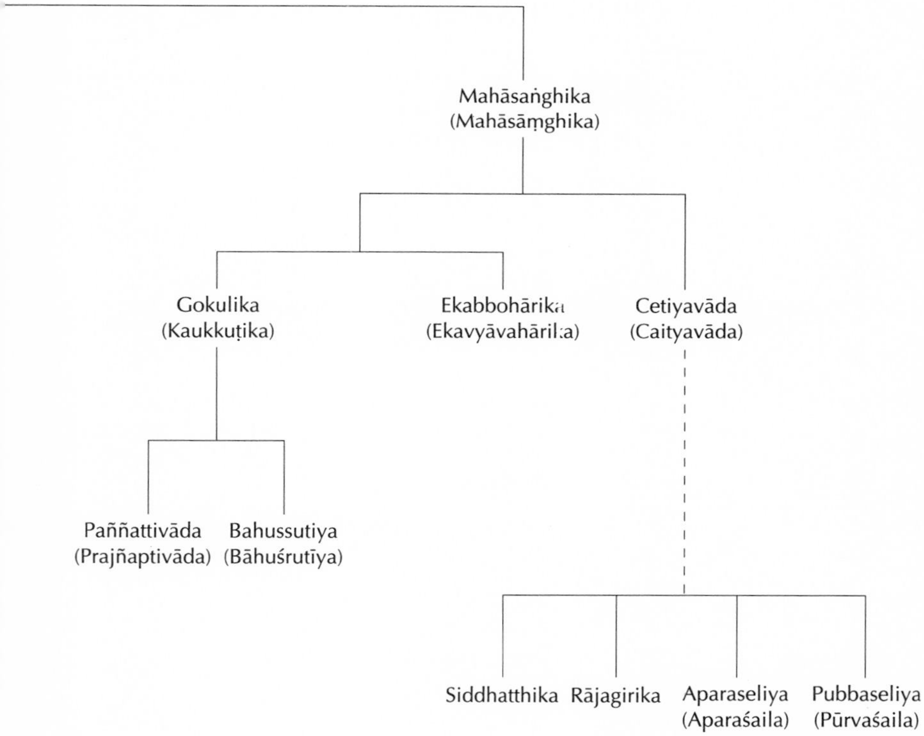
Mahāsaṅghika
(Mahāsāṃghika)
Gokulika
(Kaukkuṭika)
Ekabbohārika
(Ekavyāvahārika)
Cetiyavāda
(Caityavāda)
Paññattivāda
(Prajñaptivāda)
Bahussutiya
(Bāhuśrutīya)
Siddhatthika
Rājagirika
Aparaseliya
(Aparaśaila)
Pubbaseliya
(Pūrvaśaila)

A.B. = After the Buddha

The Sarvāstivādin Listing of the Schools and Their Lineages According to the Treatise on the Principles of Different Schools (*Samayabhedoparacanacakra*) by Vasumitra, Translated by Hsüan-tsang in 662

The Haimavata is usually omitted from the Sarvāstivādin listing, leaving twenty schools, because the Haimavata belonged to the Sthaviravāda (Theravāda) and nothing is known of its activities.
(Names are given in Sanskrit only.)

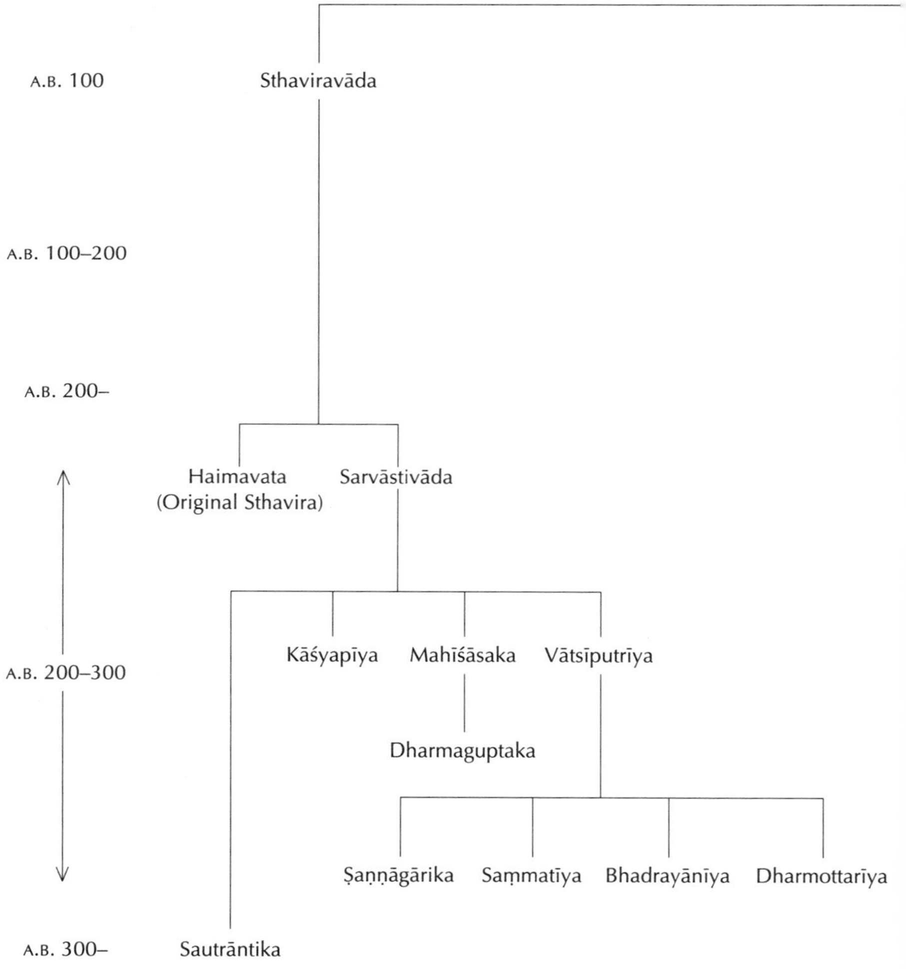

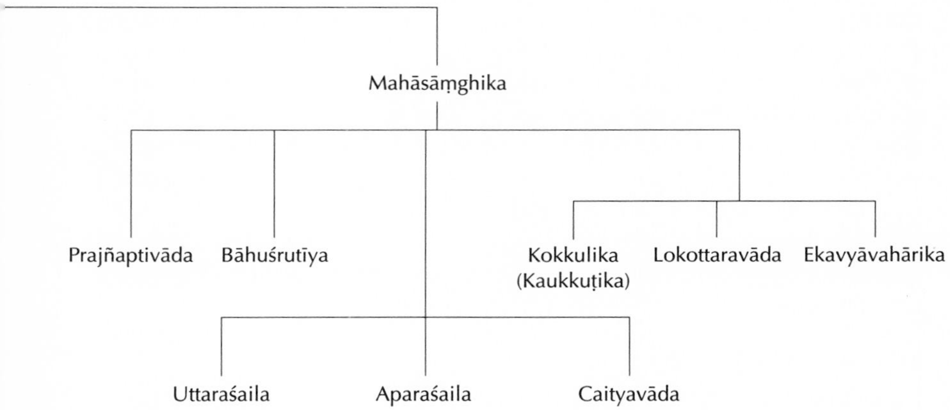

A.B. = After the Buddha

elucidating contemporary Indian Buddhism after returning to China. When Hsüan-tsang and I-ching made their journeys to India, only the schools of northwestern India (the area that is present-day Pakistan) did not follow this fourfold division. They preferred a fivefold categorization for the schools active in that area: Sarvāstivāda, Mahīśāsaka, Dharmaguptaka, Kāśyapīya, and Lokottaravāda.

According to the historical sequence considered here, the Abhidharma schools per se occupy only about three hundred years, the period following primitive Buddhism and preceding the rise of Mahāyāna. Sequential categories chronicle only the rise of the schools, however; after the beginning of the common era, Abhidharma schools existed side by side with Mahāyāna Buddhism in various parts of India and maintained their influence. According to Hsüan-tsang, who left for India in 629 and returned to China in 645, Hīnayāna followers appeared to outnumber those of Mahāyāna, judging by the numbers of temples and monks adhering to each.

MAHĀYĀNA BUDDHISM

Mahāyāna was a reform movement that arose around the first century B.C.E. in reaction to the formalized, academic Buddhism of the Abhidharma schools. In setting out to restore the original religious spirit of Buddhism, it rejected Abhidharma Buddhism, branding it as either the inferior vehicle (Hīnayāna) or the vehicle of the hearers (Śrāvakayāna). New scriptures, attributed to the Buddha, were composed by anonymous authors who believed that if Śākyamuni had been teaching his Law in their age, he would have preached what the Mahāyāna sūtras contained. The compilers of these sūtras did not set out deliberately to forge scriptures; they believed they were transmitting the true teaching of the Buddha and that their sūtras reflected the spirit of Śākyamuni more accurately than those of the Abhidharma schools.

The Abhidharma schools apparently claimed that the new Mahāyāna sūtras were the teachings of devils, not the Buddha. This assertion was revived in Japan in the latter part of the nineteenth century, when Western historical research methods were first applied to Buddhology. As a result, some scholars considered that Mahāyāna was not the direct teaching of the historical Buddha. If the Buddha's teaching is defined strictly as the actual words of Śākyamuni, however, then even the teachings recorded in the Āgamas are not original: the Āgamas did not take their present form until several hundred years after the Buddha's death, and in the course of their oral transmission both conscious and unconscious changes were introduced. Modern scholars agree that it is justifiable to regard as the Buddha's teaching whatever expounds the Law accurately and transmits its spirit. From this point of view, Mahāyāna scriptures must be accepted as part of the Buddha's teaching.

As it received growing support from former adherents of the Abhidharma schools, Mahāyāna spread quickly to various parts of India. This rapid growth stimulated the Abhidharma schools to reconsider their position and to initiate reforms. Though initially there were confrontations and disputes between the two groups, they gradually moved toward greater cooperation, heralding an age of prosperity for Buddhism as a whole. Buddhism's golden age, in terms of its influence and number of adherents, lasted from the third century B.C.E. to the fifth century C.E. During this period Buddhism was easily able to hold its own against the newly influential Brahmanical philosophical schools. Nevertheless, it is an exaggeration to call it, as some Western scholars have, the Age of Buddhist India. However much Buddhism flourished, it provided only a spiritual superstructure for the people. It could not change the infrastructure of Hindu society, nor did it attempt to do so. This inability to influence society as a whole was the principal reason Buddhism did not take deep root in India.

After the fourth or fifth century, orthodox Brahmanism revived, in the process absorbing Indian folk beliefs and adopting some doctrines and precepts from Buddhism. Even as the deep spirituality of Buddhism was influencing Hinduism, however, Buddhism itself was becoming more scholastic and neglecting religious practice. This tendency became pronounced after the seventh or eighth century, following the first Islamic invasions of northwestern India. As the followers of Islam gained power, they used military strength to suppress rival religions. They dealt the death blow to Buddhism, burning sūtras, destroying statues and temples, and killing monks. By the early thirteenth century Buddhism had all but disappeared from the Indian subcontinent.

Early Mahāyāna Early Mahāyāna spans the period from about the first century C.E. to about the end of the third century and is Mahāyāna in its purest form, most clearly manifesting the true spirit of Śākyamuni in its concern for faith and practice. This purity is evident in the sūtras and treatises produced during that time.

The principal early Mahāyāna sūtras reflect the development of a new current of thought concerning the nature of the Buddha, the practice of the bodhisattva, and the concept of emptiness (*śūnyatā*) as the essence of all things. Perhaps the oldest of these texts are the Perfection of Wisdom (*prajñāpāramitā*) sūtras, a related group of works of varying lengths. The prototype of the group is thought to be the Perfection of Wisdom Sūtra in Eight Thousand Lines (*Aṣṭasāhasrikā-prajñāpāramitā*). Expanded versions of this sūtra, containing basically the same text but with differing amounts of repetition, are numerous. The most important are the Perfection of Wisdom Sūtra in Twenty-five Thousand Lines (*Pañcaviṃśatisāhasrikā-prajñāpāramitā*) and the Perfection of Wisdom Sūtra in One Hundred Thousand Lines (*Śatasāhasrikā-prajñāpāramitā-sūtra*). Shorter summaries of the basic text were also compiled to transmit only the essence of the teaching. Two well-known sūtras of this type are the Diamond Wisdom (or Diamond) Sūtra (*Vajracchedikā-prajñāpāramitā-sūtra*) and the Heart of Wisdom (or Heart) Sūtra (*Prajñāpāramitā-hṛdaya-sūtra*). Another Wisdom sūtra of the period is the Sūtra of the Advancement Toward Truth (*Adhyardhaśatikā-prajñāpāramitā-sūtra*).

In addition to the Wisdom sūtras, one of the most important early Mahāyāna sūtras is the Vimalakīrti Sūtra (*Vimalakīrti-nirdeśa-sūtra*), which points out that lay believers can aspire to enlightenment just as ordained people do. Other important texts are the Flower Garland Sūtra—extant in Chinese versions of forty, sixty, and eighty fascicles—with its teachings of the stages of bodhisattva practice and of the interdependence of all phenomena;

the Lotus Sūtra (*Saddharma-puṇḍarīka-sūtra*), which reflects the Hīnayāna-Mahāyāna conflict in its teaching of the One Vehicle and the one true Buddhist Law and expounds the nature of a *tathāgata*, a fully enlightened being; and the Sūtra of Infinite Life (the Larger *Sukhāvatī-vyūha-sūtra*), which teaches pure faith in Amitābha (Amitāyus) Buddha, the buddha of the Pure Land.

The major writers of commentaries in this period were Nāgārjuna (ca. 150–ca. 250), the putative founder of the Mahāyāna Mādhyamika (Middle Way) school, and Āryadeva (also known as Kāṇadeva), a disciple of Nāgārjuna. Works attributed to Nāgārjuna include the Treatise on the Middle (*Mādhyamika-śāstra* or *Mūla-madhyamaka-kārikā*), the Treatise on the Transcendence of Controversy (*Vigraha-vyāvartanī*), and the Treatise on the Twelve Gates (*Dvādaśamukha-śāstra*), all of which are primarily critical examinations of other schools, as well as the Treatise on the Great Perfection of Wisdom Sūtra (*Mahā-prajñāpāramitā-śāstra*) and the Commentary on the [first two of the] Ten Stages (*Daśabhūmika-vibhāṣā-śāstra*). Āryadeva's chief works are the Treatise in One Hundred Verses (*Śata-śāstra*) and the Treatise in Four Hundred Verses (*Catuḥśataka*).

Middle Mahāyāna Middle Mahāyāna lasted from about 300 to the mid-seventh century, coinciding with a period of great intellectual activity in the non-Buddhist schools, particularly the six orthodox schools of Hindu philosophy (Pūrva-mīmāṃsā, Vedānta, Sāṃkhya, Yoga, Nyāya, and Vaiśeṣika). To compete with them, Buddhism was forced to develop a philosophical and logical foundation, and thus a shift toward philosophical debate was apparent in both Hīnayāna and Mahāyāna schools. As a result, the sūtras and treatises of this period read more like philosophical tracts than documents of faith. While this was a decadent period for Buddhism in terms of spirituality, as a philosophy Mahāyāna exhibited some of the most outstanding thought of all time, whether within Buddhism or within Indian philosophy as a whole. In fact, non-Buddhist schools adopted many philosophical premises from Buddhism.

Mahāyāna now emphasized the aspiration to enlightenment

(*bodhicitta*) and the buddha-nature (*buddhagotra*) or *tathāgata*-embryo (*tathāgata-garbha*)—that is, the potential for attaining buddhahood inherent in all sentient beings—as the source of this aspiration. Mahāyāna also expanded the traditional Hīnayāna concept of the nonself of sentient beings by positing the nonself of sentient beings and of *dharmas*. As interest in the nature of the mind deepened, Mahāyānists added a theory of dormant stages of consciousness, the *manas* consciousness and the *ālaya*, or storehouse, consciousness, to the traditional theory of the six consciousnesses.[9] Finally, there was thorough research into theories concerning the bodhisattva, the bodies of a buddha, the buddha realms, and nirvāṇa.[10]

The major Mahāyāna schools of this period were the Mādhyamika (Middle Way) and the Yogācāra (Yoga Practice), also known as the Vijñānavāda (Consciousness Only). The Mādhyamika, based on Nāgārjuna's Treatise on the Middle, was very influential. It eventually split into two streams, the Prāsaṅgika and the Svātantrika. The central doctrine of the school was emptiness (*śūnyatā*). The Yogācāra school, founded by Asaṅga and Vasubandhu, was concerned with the nature of mind (*manas*) and is best known for its doctrine of consciousness only (*vijñaptimātratā*). It too split, and later a syncretic school combining elements of Mādhyamika and Yogācāra evolved.

The most influential of the Abhidharma schools were Sarvāstivādin offshoots, the Vaibhāṣika and the Sautrāntika (Those Who Consider the Sūtras Alone Authoritative). In China the Sarvāstivādins were considered paradigmatic Abhidharmists, and many of their works were translated, including the Great Commentary (*Abhidharma-mahāvibhāṣā-śāstra*), the *Abhidharmakośa-śāstra*, the Expanded Treatise on the Essence of Abhidharma (*Saṃyuktābhidharma-hṛdaya-śāstra*), and the Treatise Following the True Teachings of the Abhidharma (*Abhidharma-nyāyānusāra-śāstra*).

Mahāyāna sūtras of the middle period fall into three broad groups. First, there are those sūtras that center on the concept of the buddha-nature or *tathāgata*-embryo, such as the Sūtra of the *Tathāgata*-Embryo (*Tathāgata-garbha-sūtra*), the Śrīmālā (or Queen of Śrīmālā) Sūtra (*Śrīmālādevī-siṃhanāda-sūtra*), and the Mahāyāna Sūtra of the Great Decease (*Mahā-parinirvāṇa-sūtra*). The second group, comprising such works of the Yogācāra school as the Sūtra of Profound Understanding (*Saṃdhinirmocana-sūtra*) and the no longer extant Sūtra on Mahāyāna Abhidharma (*Mahāyāna-abhidharma-sūtra*), expounds the teaching of the storehouse consciousness. The third group, represented by the Sūtra of the Appearance of the Good Doctrine in [Sri] Lanka (*Laṅkāvatāra-sūtra*), consists of works combining the teachings of the first two groups. Other important middle-period sūtras are the Golden Light Sūtra (*Suvarṇaprabhāsottama-rāja-sūtra*), the Sūtra of the Great Accumulation of Treasures (*Mahā-ratnakūṭa-sūtra*), and the Great Collection of Sūtras (*Mahā-saṃnipāta-sūtra*).

The greatest treatise writers of this period came from the Yogācārin stream. Maitreyanātha (or Maitreya; ca. 270–ca. 350) wrote the Treatise on the Stages of Yoga Practice (*Yogācārabhūmi-śāstra*), on which much of the thought of the Yogācāra school was based. His disciple Asaṅga (fourth to fifth century) expounded the teachings of yoga practice and consciousness only in the Comprehensive Treatise on Mahāyāna Buddhism (*Mahāyāna-saṃgraha*) and the Treatise on the Adornment of Mahāyāna Sūtras (*Mahāyāna-sūtrālaṃkāra*). Vasubandhu, Asaṅga's younger brother and student, was the author of works concerning the doctrine of consciousness only, including the Twenty Verses on the Doctrine of Consciousness Only (*Viṃśatikā-vijñaptimātratā-siddhi*) and the Thirty Verses on the Doctrine of Consciousness Only (*Triṃśikā-vijñaptimātratā-siddhi*).

Later Yogācārin writers include the scholar Dharmapāla (ca. 530–ca. 561), head of the great Nālandā monastic university, who wrote the Treatise on the Establishment of the Doctrine of Consciousness Only (*Vijñaptimātratāsiddhi-śāstra*), an authoritative commentary on Vasubandhu's work. Others were Sthiramati (ca. 510–ca. 570) from the Yogācāra center at Valabhī, in northwestern India, who wrote a commentary on Vasubandhu's Thirty Verses, and Sāramati (fourth to fifth century), who wrote on the immanence of the Absolute. Another member of Vasubandhu's lineage was the scholar Dignāga (ca. 480–ca. 540), the founder of a new school of epistemology.

Treatises in the buddha-nature and *tathāgata*-embryo tradition include the Treatise on the Buddha-nature (*Buddhagotra-śāstra*), attributed to Vasubandhu, and the Treatise on the Jewel-nature (*Ratnagotravibhāga-mahāyānôttaratantra-śāstra*). The Treatise on the Awakening of Faith in the Mahāyāna (*Mahāyāna-śraddhotpāda-śāstra*) combines elements of both Yogācāra doctrine and buddha-nature philosophy. This treatise has been attributed to the second-century priest Aśvaghoṣa, although many scholars hold that it was actually composed in China.

Late Mahāyāna The late period of Mahāyāna Buddhism lasted roughly from the mid-seventh century to the early thirteenth century, when Buddhism virtually disappeared from India. This was a period of religious revival, in reaction to the earlier preoccupation with philosophical and scholastic concerns. In general, there was a strong tendency to present the Buddhist ideal through symbols, thus making the scholastic achievements of the preceding period easier to understand. In part, this practice arose under the influence of the rich symbolism found in the Tantric literature then popular throughout India.

Esoteric, or Tantric, Buddhism (represented in Japan by the Shingon, or True Word, sect) symbolized the indescribable "secrets" of the buddha's body by mudrās (symbolic hand gestures), of his speech by mantras (mystical incantations; literally, "true words"), and of his mind by contemplation of the buddha as symbolized in the letters of his "seed syllable" (*bīja*). These three practices are called the Three Secrets. Symbol-laden Esoteric Buddhism was particularly popular in the region of Buddhism's origin, northeastern India. Eventually it fused with decadent folk beliefs and its true ideals were lost. As Buddhism declined, it proved unable to weather the challenge of Islam and Hinduism and became moribund in India.

Many sūtras of the late Mahāyāna period contain mystical verses (*dhāraṇī*) and rules for rituals and ceremonies. The most influential of these texts are the Great Sun Sūtra (*Mahā-vairocana-sūtra*), the Diamond Peak Sūtra (*Vajraśekhara-sūtra*), and the Sūtra of Good Accomplishment (*Susiddhikara-sūtra*). While many Esoteric works were translated into Chinese, a great quantity are known only in Tibetan translation. Tibetan Buddhism, or Lamaism, incorporated many elements of Esoteric Buddhism, and its scriptures are invaluable for the study of both late Indian Mahāyāna and the commentaries of the middle period.

THE GEOGRAPHICAL DIVISION

Beginning around the first century C.E., both Abhidharma and Mahāyāna works were transmitted to China by way of Central Asia and Southeast Asia. Later, Chinese Buddhism was transmitted to the Korean Peninsula and Japan. Buddhism reached Tibet around the seventh century and was taken from there to Mongolia and Manchuria. Meanwhile, by the fourth or fifth century Buddhism was well established in Sumatra, Java, and Borneo, all situated along the southern sea route from India to China.

Most of this transmission was Mahāyāna, although Abhidharma schools were influential in Sri Lanka, Burma, Thailand, Cambodia, and Laos. The division of Buddhism into Northern and Southern tends to separate the northern (Mahāyāna) regions from the southern (Theravāda) regions, but this classification is no more than a convenience, being imprecise both geographically and doctrinally. For instance, the Buddhism of ancient Sumatra and Java, which are geographically southern, is closer doctrinally to that of the Northern tradition.

SOUTHERN BUDDHISM

Southern Buddhism is the Buddhism of Sri Lanka, Burma, Thailand, Cambodia, and Laos. Doctrinally derived from Abhidharma Buddhism, it is generally known as Theravāda, or Pāli, Buddhism. Pāli, meaning "scriptures," refers to the language in which the canon of Southern Buddhism was recorded. Pāli provided a common language for communication among monks as Theravāda spread from Sri Lanka to Burma and Thailand.

Although use of the term Pāli to identify a linguistic entity has been disputed, modern Western scholars have consistently used the word this way in their studies of Southern Buddhist scriptures. Pāli is derived from an ancient western Indian vernacular, or Prākrit, related to Paiśācī, a Middle Indo-Aryan Prākrit.[11] It also contains some elements of Old Māghadī, the vernacular in which Śākyamuni delivered his discourses, in preference to the ancient Sanskrit preserved in the Brahmanic scriptures. Since Southern Buddhism emerged from the Theravāda of western India, which was transmitted in Paiśācī, the Māgadhī elements in Pāli probably reflect reverence for Śākyamuni and his actual words. Of the known Prākrits, Pāli is the closest to classical Sanskrit. The only language closer is Buddhist Hybrid Sanskrit. Pāli is preserved today only by Theravāda Buddhism, and its Pāli works outnumber those in any other Prākrit. Pāli was never used for any other body of literature in India.

The initial transmission of Buddhism beyond India was to Sri Lanka in the third century B.C.E., during the reign of the Mauryan emperor Aśoka, who then ruled almost the entire subcontinent. A devout Buddhist, he was eager to propagate the religion throughout the known world. The Pāli tradition relates that in his time missionaries were sent to nine places, both within India and abroad, and that Aśoka's son Mahinda took Theravāda Buddhism to Sri Lanka.[12]

In Sri Lanka, Buddhism prospered with the protection and active support of a succession of rulers and is still virtually the national religion. It faced periods of decline, however, and experienced persecution when the island was occupied by invaders, notably the Hindu Tamils and the Christian Portuguese, Dutch, and British. The Christian oppression, beginning early in the sixteenth century and continuing for more than four hundred years, was especially severe, and the Buddhist community suffered unremitting hardship throughout the period of European occupation.

Although at times other Abhidharma schools and Mahāyāna Buddhism prevailed in Sri Lanka, it is Theravāda that has continued to hold the trust and devotion of the people. In fact, in terms of its scriptures and religious community, Theravāda is today one of the purest forms of Buddhism anywhere. Only the Pāli canon of Theravāda Buddhism has been preserved in its entirety.

Buddhism was transmitted from Sri Lanka to Burma around the eleventh century, and from there to Thailand, Cambodia, and Laos in the thirteenth century. It is still the national religion in both Thailand and Burma.

It was the Theravāda of Sri Lanka that first became widely

known in Europe. Western scholars had begun studying it early in the nineteenth century, and through their work Southern Buddhism came to the attention of Japanese scholars after the Meiji Restoration of 1868, which effectively opened Japan to the West. Until that time nothing of Southern Buddhism was known in Japan. Japanese scholars have now made comparative studies of the Pāli and Chinese canons, and the Pāli scriptures have become indispensable for the study of primitive Buddhism. Translations of the Pāli canon have been made into English, French, German, and Japanese.[13]

NORTHERN BUDDHISM

Northern Buddhism is the Buddhism transmitted to China, either from northwestern India via Central Asia or via the southern sea route. The term also refers to the Buddhism transmitted from China to Korea and Japan, to Vietnamese Buddhism, and to the Buddhism transmitted directly to Tibet from India. Although some Abhidharma works were translated in these countries, the vast majority of translations were of Mahāyāna texts, so that to all intents and purposes Northern Buddhism is Mahāyāna. Since the original language of most of its scriptures is Sanskrit (Buddhist Hybrid Sanskrit), it might also be called Sanskrit Buddhism.

Buddhism arrived in China around the first century C.E., and Chinese translations of the scriptures began appearing in the second century. The oldest extant translations are those of An Shih-kao (d. ca. 170), a Parthian who is said to have arrived in Lo-yang in 148, and of Lokakṣema, an Indo-Scythian who was active between 150 and 190. Later translators included both monks from India and Central Asia and Chinese monks who had studied in India. By the second century of the T'ang dynasty (618–907), the Chinese Tripiṭaka amounted to more than one thousand works in well over five thousand fascicles; today it numbers over seventeen hundred works. In both quality and quantity, the Chinese canon surpasses all other extant collections of Buddhist scripture, making it invaluable as source material for Buddhist studies. While the Pāli canon is very old and pure, the Chinese canon is extensive and profound.

Buddhism in Tibet dates from roughly the seventh century, and until the thirteenth century scriptural translation there was undertaken on a scale equaling that in China. The numerous works of middle and late Mahāyāna Buddhism preserved in Tibetan translation and found nowhere else provide invaluable sources for scholars. The Tibetan Tripiṭaka consists of 6,453 works in the Peking edition, published in 1411, and 4,569 in the Derge edition, published around 1730. The numbers of works in these Tripiṭakas far exceed those in the Chinese Tripiṭaka, but because of duplicate translations and the large number of short works, the actual volume is less than that of the Chinese canon.

Buddhism was transmitted from India to Nepal during the twelfth and thirteenth centuries, when Buddhists retreated to the Himalayas to escape annihilation at the hands of the Islamic conquerors of India. Many Sanskrit manuscripts survived in Nepal thanks to those refugees. The first such manuscripts discovered in modern times were found by Brian H. Hodgson (1800–1894) when he was the British resident in Nepal, and his discovery was published in the Calcutta journal *Asiatic Researches* in 1826. Including duplicates, Hodgson found a total of 381 works, which he donated to libraries in Calcutta, London, and Paris. In 1844, after some ten years of research on Hodgson's manuscripts, Eugène Burnouf (1801–52) of the Collège de France published his *Introduction à l'histoire du Bouddhisme Indien* (Introduction to the History of Indian Buddhism). His translation of the Sanskrit Lotus Sūtra (*Le Lotus de la bonne loi*), published posthumously in 1852, marked the first appearance of a Buddhist sūtra in a European language. Daniel Wright (1833–?), a medical officer at the British Residency in Nepal who collected Sanskrit sūtras on behalf of Cambridge University, discovered 325 works between 1873 and 1876. Manuscripts continue to be found, and their collation and publication are still underway. Many of the manuscripts found by Japanese scholars are now in the possession of the University of Tokyo and Kyoto University.

The history of Buddhism in Central Asia is evidenced by the many fragments of Sanskrit texts that have been discovered there, in particular by British, French, German, Japanese, and Russian explorers who made their way to the area in the late nineteenth and early twentieth centuries. Sanskrit manuscripts have also been found in India and Tibet. Five Sanskrit palm-leaf manuscripts taken to Japan around the seventh or eighth century have been discovered: two versions of the Heart Sūtra and copies of the Diamond Sūtra, the Sūtra of Infinite Life (the Larger *Sukhāvatī-vyūha-sūtra*), and the Amitābha Sūtra (the Smaller *Sukhāvatī-vyūha-sūtra*). Transliterations and translations of these manuscripts were published by the Clarendon Press, Oxford, in the Sacred Books of the East series, under the editorship of Max Müller (1823–1900).

Northern Buddhism also entered Indonesia. Both the Abhidharma and the Mahāyāna traditions were transmitted to that area from India between approximately the third and the thirteenth centuries. From about the seventh century onward, the center of Buddhist scholarship in the region was the Śrīvijaya empire (whose capital became modern-day Palembang, on Sumatra). Buddhist statuary and other remains attest to the former vitality of Buddhism throughout this area.

2. The Three Treasures

The Three Treasures (*tri-ratna, ti-ratana; ratna-traya, ratana-ttaya*) are the Buddha, his teachings (the Dharma, or Law), and the Order (Saṅgha, or community of believers). Buddhism can exist only when all three are present, and taking refuge in them—the "three refuges"—is the believer's most important act, regardless of time, place, or sectarian tradition.

Scholars have traditionally defined the Three Treasures in historical, symbolic, and metaphysical terms. Usually, however, the Three Treasures are discussed in the context of the historical definition: Śākyamuni is the Buddha-treasure, his teachings are the Law-treasure, and his disciples are the Order-treasure. Defined more broadly, the Buddha-treasure is the object of believers' faith and veneration, the Dharma-teaching lord who brings release from suffering. Thus buddhas other than the historical Śākyamuni can be regarded as the Buddha-treasure. In the Lotus Sūtra (chapter 16, "Revelation of the [Eternal] Life of the Tathāgata"), for example, Śākyamuni is venerated as the Eternal Buddha who dwells in perpetuity on Vulture Peak. The Pure Land Buddhists put their faith in Amitābha (also known as Amitāyus), while Esoteric Buddhists call Mahāvairocana (Great Sun, the cosmic buddha) the Buddha-treasure. The teachings of the Buddha, which liberate people from anxiety and suffering and direct them toward the ideal of nonsuffering and tranquillity, are the Law-treasure. Buddhist faith and practice developed from these teachings. The Order, or Saṅgha, is the community of ordained men and women who guide and teach in the Buddha's stead, transmitting Buddhist theory and practice.

Defined symbolically, the Buddha-treasure can be statues or drawings of the Buddha venerated as objects of faith; the Law-treasure is the canon, the scriptures, written or printed; and the Order-treasure is the community of believers—originally, the monks and nuns. Even before the historical Buddha was depicted in human form in art, he was worshiped through symbolic association with the sites of the four great events of his life. His birthplace, Lumbinī Garden, near Kapilavastu, in Nepal, was symbolized by a footprint left when he walked at birth; Buddhagayā, in the kingdom of Magadha, where he attained enlightenment, was represented by the *bodhi* tree beneath which he had meditated; the wheel of the Law stood for Mṛgadāva, or Deer Park, in Varanasi, the scene of his first discourse, celebrated as "setting the wheel of the Law in motion"; and the stūpa, or relic tower, symbolized Kuśinagara, in the kingdom of Malla, where he died. His relics (*śarīra*), or ashes, were also venerated as the Buddha-treasure, and stūpas were built in many places to house them. This practice eventually gave rise to a widespread stūpa cult. Later, the teeth and hair of the Buddha were also worshiped, as were personal articles, such as his alms bowl. Collectively, these relics are termed *dhātu,* and places where they are stored are known as *dhātu-gabbha* in Pāli. The pagodas of Burma, for example, have their origin in Sri Lankan relic stores.

Metaphysically, the Three Treasures can be considered a single entity. The Law was discovered and elucidated by the Buddha; it exists as part of him, since it first took shape as his teaching. The Buddha could not exist without the Law, however, since it was by discovering the Law, realizing its significance, and mastering it that Śākyamuni attained buddhahood. The Law is thus the essence of the Buddha. The Order, which teaches the Law on behalf of the Buddha, cannot exist without both the Buddha and the Law. Since the value and meaning of the Buddha and the Law are revealed by the Order, and the Buddha and the Law can be effective only with the help of the Order, the Order is inseparable from the Buddha and the Law.

The significance of the Three Treasures as objects of faith is explained succinctly by the great Japanese Zen master Dōgen (1200–1253) in the "Kie Buppōsō-hō" (Taking Refuge in the Three Treasures) chapter of his *Shōbōgenzō* (Eye Storehouse of the True Law):

> We take refuge in the Buddha because he is our great teacher. We take refuge in the Law because it is good medicine. We take refuge in the Buddhist community because it is composed of excellent friends.[1]

The Flower Garland Sūtra gives another version of the formula for taking refuge in the Three Treasures:

> We take refuge in the Buddha. May we with all the living realize the Great Way and aspire to the unsurpassable intention.
>
> We take refuge in the Law. May we with all the living enter the sūtra-store and make our wisdom wide as the sea.
>
> We take refuge in the Saṅgha. May we with all the living lead many people to freedom from all hindrances.

Also recited is the following formula:

> I take refuge in the Buddha, the peerless, honored one. I take refuge in the Law, the uncontaminated, honored one. I take refuge in the Order, the harmonious, honored one.

The Pāli version of the formula for taking refuge in the Three Treasures is as follows:

> *Buddhaṃ saraṇaṃ gacchāmi.* (I go to the Buddha for refuge.)
> *Dhammaṃ saraṇaṃ gacchāmi.* (I go to the Law for refuge.)
> *Saṇghaṃ saraṇaṃ gacchāmi.* (I go to the Order for refuge.)

THE BUDDHA

Literally, buddha means "enlightened one." When a distinction must be made between a buddha, a *śrāvaka,* and a *pratyekabuddha,* all of whom are enlightened beings, a buddha is referred to as "the supreme, perfectly enlightened one" (*anuttara-samyaksaṃbuddha*). What distinguishes a buddha from other enlightened beings is that he has attained perfect enlightenment and brought others to enlightenment, as well. Although Western scholars—influenced by Pāli Buddhism, which venerates Gotama (Śākyamuni) alone as the Buddha-treasure—have tended to use the word buddha to refer only to the historical Buddha, the term is actually far more inclusive.

THE BUDDHAS OF THE PAST

Even primitive Buddhism held that numerous buddhas had preceded Śākyamuni, teaching the Law and leading people to release. The Sūtra of the Story of the Great Ones (*Mahā-apadāna-suttanta*) in the Dīgha-nikāya, or Collection of Long Discourses, of the Pāli canon lists seven Buddhas of the Past: Vipassin, Sikhin, Vessabhū, Kakusandha, Koṇāgamana, Kassapa, and Sākyamuni.[2] The Sūtra on the Preaching of the Wheel-rolling King (*Cakkavatti-sīhanāda-suttanta*), also in the Dīgha-nikāya, mentions a buddha of the future, Metteyya (Maitreya). A buddha, then, is any perfected being, past, present, or future, who bears witness to the truth and eternality of the Law.

Although there is no evidence for the historicity of the seven Buddhas of the Past, except for Śākyamuni, various Abhidharma schools expanded the early lists of these buddhas, their names and numbers varying from one list to another. For example, the Lineage of the Buddhas (*Buddhavaṃsa*), the fourteenth section of the Pāli Khuddaka-nikāya, or Collection of Minor Works, cites twenty-five Buddhas of the Past (with eighteen buddhas preceding the above-mentioned seven Buddhas of the Past), as well as twenty-eight Buddhas of the Past.[3] The Great Account (*Mahāvastu*), a Sanskrit text of the Lokottaravāda, in the Mahāsāṃghika lineage, also contains two lists: the first gives an aggregate of over four billion buddhas who bear just seventeen different names, and the second gives an additional one hundred twenty-nine names, excluding duplications.[4] One series of fifteen names in the second list ends with the seven Buddhas of the Past cited in the Pāli canon.[5] An almost identical series is found in the Sūtra of Great Compassion (*Mahākaruṇā-puṇḍarīka-sūtra*). Sūtra Stories of Deeds of the Buddha (surviving only in a Chinese translation, *Fo-pen-hsing-chi-ching*) includes two lists similar to those in the Great Account, the first giving vast multiples of buddhas who share seventeen names and the second citing an additional one hundred buddhas.[6]

The Mūla-Sarvāstivādins related the Buddhas of the Past to Śākyamuni's long practice as a bodhisattva, saying that he venerated seventy-five thousand buddhas in the first *asaṃkhyeya kalpa* of practice, seventy-six thousand in the second, seventy-seven thousand in the third, and six in the final one hundred great *kalpas*. The Great Commentary and the *Abhidharmakośa-śāstra* mention similar figures. Additional lists are given in the Detailed Narration of the Sport of the Buddha (*Lalitavistara*), both in the Sanskrit original and in the Chinese translations by Dharmarakṣa (231–308?) and Divākara (612–87), as well as in the Superior Sūtra of the Buddha Treasury (*Buddhapiṭaka-nirgraha-sūtra*).

THE BUDDHAS OF THE THREE PERIODS AND TEN DIRECTIONS

Many Abhidharma schools posited innumerable buddhas of the present and future in addition to the Buddhas of the Past. The three Sūtras of the Names of Three Thousand Buddhas (*San-ch'ien-fo-ming-ching*), for example, name one thousand buddhas each in the past *kalpa* of constellations (*tārā-kalpa*), the present *kalpa* of sages (*bhadra-kalpa*), and the future *kalpa* of adornment (*alaṃkāra-kalpa*). Moreover, the Lokottaravādins asserted that many worlds other than this world, the one in which Śākyamuni appeared, exist in the ten directions and that buddhas can appear simultaneously in all of them.[7]

By positing different worlds, the Lokottaravādins allowed for the existence of multiple buddhas, overturning the original Buddhist belief that only one buddha can appear in only one world and that it is impossible for several buddhas to exist at the same time. Mahāyāna expanded this new theory to accommodate innumerable buddhas in both space and time.

BUDDHA BODIES

Mahāyāna Buddhism brought a firmer philosophical foundation to buddha theory, postulating doctrines of two, three, and four aspects, or bodies (*kāya*), of a buddha. The two-body doctrine separates the ideal and physical aspects of a buddha, calling the former the Law-body (*dharma-kāya*) and the latter the birth-body (*rūpa-kāya*). Here the Law-body is the Law itself, which is the essence of a buddha; in other words, the Law-body is the ideal buddha body in the concrete form of the Law. The birth-body refers to Śākyamuni, a man born of earthly parents. The three-body doctrine has many variants. Two of the best known are Law-body (*dharma-kāya*), reward-body (*saṃbhoga-kāya*), and manifest-body (*nirmāṇa-kāya*), and substantial-body (*svabhāva-kāya*), enjoyment-body (*saṃbhoga-kāya*), and transformed-body (*nirmāṇa-kāya*). The four-body doctrine results from dividing the manifest-body into two aspects, manifest-body and transformed-body, or the enjoyment-body into self-enjoyment-body, a body reserved for the buddha's own use, and a body for others' enjoyment, that is, a body used for the spiritual benefit of others.

The Law-body The Dharma, or Law—the teachings of the Buddha—is believed to have been embodied in the Buddha. In primitive and Abhidharma Buddhism the Law-body was equated with five attributes (*pañca-dharma-kāya*): morality, concentration, wisdom, emancipation, and perfect knowledge of the state of emancipation. Here *dharma-kāya* means the accumulation (*kāya*) of the teachings (*dharma*), and the Buddha used the term in that sense in the following passage from the Sūtra of the Teachings Left by the Buddha (*Fo-i-chiao-ching*):

> If, from this time on, my disciples transmit my teachings and practice them, the Law-body of the Tathāgata is always existing and not extinct.

Mahāyāna went even further, personifying the ultimate truth of the universe (Dharma, Law) as the ideal body of a buddha. Here "buddha" refers not to one who has attained buddhahood but rather to a fundamental buddha, the original state of all things. The Mahāyānists distinguished three aspects of the Law-body: the teachings, truth idealized as a buddha body, and wisdom working within that ideal—action without repercussion.

When the Law-body is the focus of faith and devotion, usually the aspect of noumenal wisdom is venerated. This is exemplified by worship of Mahāvairocana Tathāgata in the Shingon sect of

Japan and of Śākyamuni Buddha dwelling in perpetuity on Vulture Peak as related in chapter 16 of the Lotus Sūtra, "Revelation of the [Eternal] Life of the Tathāgata." Adherents of Japanese Zen sects chant the names of buddhas as part of their liturgy and follow the Tendai sect's practice of naming Vairocana as the Law-body (Birushana Butsu in Japanese) and the reward-body (Rushana Butsu in Japanese) and Śākyamuni as the transformed-body.[8] Vairocana is spoken of as the Law-body in the Sūtra of Meditation on the Bodhisattva Universal Virtue (*Kuan-p'u-hsien-p'u-sa-hsing-fa-ching*) and as the reward-body in the Sūtra of the Brahma Net (*Brahmajāla-sūtra,* extant only in Chinese as the *Fan-wang-p'u-sa-chieh-ching*). In the latter aspect Vairocana incarnates billions of great and small Śākyamunis in the Lotus universe described in the Sūtra of the Brahma Net. Here Śākyamuni signifies the transformed-body.

The Reward-body The reward-body (*saṃbhoga-kāya*) is also called the enjoyment-body. Another name is homogeneous-body (*niṣyanda-kāya*), the ideal buddha body of the Dharma realm (*dharma-dhātu*). The reward-body is considered the reward of buddhahood, attained as the fruit of practice of the bodhisattva vows and the perfections (*pāramitā*). The enjoyment-body is the buddha body that accepts and enjoys the reward for virtuous acts.

There are two forms of the enjoyment-body: the body for a buddha's own enjoyment and use and the body used for the spiritual benefit of others. The first form is a buddha who accepts and enjoys the buddhahood attained through his own practice and whose acceptance and enjoyment of the Law are inner directed. The second form is a buddha who teaches and guides sentient beings by causing them to accept both the result of enlightenment and the majesty of the Law. This buddha's teaching, however, is only for bodhisattvas who have embarked on the ten stages of the bodhisattva, since the profound doctrine he expounds is beyond the comprehension of lower-ranking bodhisattvas and ordinary human beings. One theory holds that only the first form is the reward-body and that the second is actually the manifest-body.

Amitābha and Bhaiṣajyaguru are examples of the enjoyment-body as an object of faith and veneration. Amitābha made forty-eight vows as the bodhisattva Dharmākara, and after long practice achieved buddhahood in the western realm of Sukhāvatī. He is called both the Buddha of Infinite Life (Amitāyus) and the Buddha of Infinite Light (Amitābha), suggesting that his teachings are limitless in both time and space. Since Amitābha is able to save all sentient beings through his vows, his teachings are not intended only for bodhisattvas who have attained the first of the ten stages of the bodhisattva. Bhaiṣajyaguru, *tathāgata* of the eastern realm of Pure Emerald Light, made twelve great vows as a bodhisattva. Fulfilling those vows and attaining buddhahood as the reward-body, he is said to save all sentient beings from mental and physical sufferings, and from ignorance in particular. Thus in Bhaiṣajyaguru's case, too, the use of the body for the sake of others is stressed.

The Manifest-body The manifest-body (*nirmāṇa-kāya*)—also called the transformed-body—is the appearance of a buddha in the same form as those he teaches. Such a buddha belongs to a specific time and place and thus differs from the perfected reward-body, which exists throughout the three periods and the ten directions. The historical Buddha, Śākyamuni, is a manifest-body, as are Maitreya (the buddha of the future) and the Buddhas of the Past.

The manifest-body has two aspects, superior and ordinary. The superior aspect is the buddha who preaches the Law to bodhisattvas who have advanced to the first of the ten stages of the bodhisattva, while the ordinary aspect is the buddha who preaches the Law to all other sentient beings. Practically speaking, the superior aspect of the manifest-body is virtually indistinguishable from the enjoyment-body.

The transformed-body is the aspect in which a buddha assumes any manifestation appropriate to bring salvation to all sentient beings. The manifest-body refers specifically to the buddha body characterized by the thirty-two primary and eighty secondary marks, a body that appears in a specific time and place. The transformed-body, on the other hand, does not display these marks of a buddha; it can be manifested as an ordinary human being, the gods Brahmendra or Indra, a demon king, or an animal. Such a buddha teaches the Law to beings in the five realms of existence: gods, human beings, hungry spirits, animals, and inhabitants of hell.

Though Avalokiteśvara (Regarder of the Cries of the World) is a bodhisattva, he displays characteristics of the manifest-body and transformed-body of a buddha. He is said to assume thirty-three forms in order to save sentient beings. Except for the first (a buddha), all are manifestations of the transformed-body: a *pratyekabuddha,* a *śrāvaka,* Brahmendra, Indra, Īśvara, Maheśvara, a great divine general, Vaiśravaṇa, a minor king, an elder, a householder, a minister of state, a Brahman, a monk, a nun, a layman, a laywoman, the wife of an elder, the wife of a householder, the wife of a minister of state, the wife of a Brahman, a young boy, a young girl, a god, a *nāga,* a *yakṣa,* a *gandharva,* an *asura,* a *garuḍa,* a *kiṃnara,* a *mahoraga,* a diamond-holding god, and so on.[9] This variety of manifestations explains the iconographic diversity of representations of Avalokiteśvara in art. Commonly seen representations include Avalokiteśvara holding the *cintāmaṇi,* or gem of satisfaction, with which he saves all sentient beings; with the head of a horse or a horse-head crown, the horse symbolizing the trampling underfoot of evil; with eleven heads, ten of which are small and can symbolize either ten additional manifestations or the ten stages of the bodhisattva; and with a thousand arms and holding a thousand objects in his hands, symbolizing the innumerable ways in which he aids sentient beings.

THE MARKS AND VIRTUES OF A BUDDHA

A buddha is distinguished by both unique physical marks and extraordinary virtues. As a result of practicing good through one hundred great *kalpas* as a bodhisattva, a buddha is born with thirty-two primary and eighty secondary marks (*lakṣaṇa* and *vyañjana*) not found on ordinary human beings.[10] An interest in distinguishing marks seems to have existed in India during Śākyamuni's time. Such marks were thought to identify an ideal human being—in spiritual terms a buddha, in worldly terms a wheel-rolling king (*cakravartin*).

A large number of virtues are intrinsic to a buddha, the most characteristic being the eighteen unique virtues of a buddha (*aṣṭādaśa āveṇika-buddha-dharmāḥ*) cited by Sarvāstivādins and other Abhidharma schools: the ten powers, the four kinds of fearlessness, the three types of equanimity, and great compassion. These virtues are unique to a buddha; they are not found in a *śrāvaka,* a *pratyekabuddha,* or a bodhisattva. Of the various codifications of the eighteen unique virtues, the best known are those of the Sarvāstivādins and the Mahāyānists.

The Ten Powers The ten powers (*daśa-balāni*) of a buddha are those of distinguishing right and wrong in every situation; knowing the karmic relations of all acts, past, present, and future; comprehending all stages of *dhyāna* (meditation), *vimukti* (emancipation), and *samādhi* (concentration); judging the superiority or inferiority of the mental capabilities of all sentient beings; knowing the inclinations and motivations of all sentient beings; knowing the differences in faculties and conditions of all sentient beings; knowing all the paths that sentient beings will follow, whatever the stage of their practice; knowing all former existences of oneself and of others; knowing the future existences of all sentient beings; and knowing one's own enlightenment and the eradication of all hindrances of defilements.

The Four Kinds of Fearlessness A buddha is also endowed with four kinds of fearlessness (*catvāri vaiśāradyāṇi*), giving him supreme self-confidence and assurance in addressing any person or topic. Thus a buddha feels no fear or hesitation when dealing with criticism or censure. His confidence springs from four sources: he has supreme wisdom; he has rid himself of all defilements and delusions; he is able to teach the nature of karma and the defilements; and he is able to teach the threefold practice (morality, concentration, and wisdom), which eliminate defilements and suffering.

The Three Types of Equanimity Being endowed with three types of equanimity (*trīṇi smṛtyupasthānāni*), a buddha maintains proper mindfulness in all situations. In particular, there are three instances in which he exhibits farseeing wisdom: he does not rejoice in the veneration of believers; he does not grieve over others' lack of belief; and he neither rejoices in nor grieves over others' belief or slander.

Great Compassion The last of the eighteen unique virtues of a buddha is great compassion (*mahā-karuṇā*). A buddha's mind is one of constant benevolence and compassion; he is always seeking to save sentient beings from suffering.

The Eighteen Unique Virtues of the Mahāyāna Mahāyāna texts record differing series of eighteen unique virtues, both the virtues and their order varying from one source to another. One of the best-known lists is that in the Great Perfection of Wisdom Sūtra (*Mahā-prajñāpāramitā-sūtra*) and in Nāgārjuna's treatise on this sūtra, the Treatise on the Great Perfection of Wisdom Sūtra. The first six virtues in this series are fruits of the practice of morality, or precepts, and cause the attainment of nirvāṇa without fixed abode.[11] These virtues are the perfection of action, speech, and thought; impartiality toward sentient beings; elimination of distraction and mental instability in sentient beings; and omniscience, whereby nothing is forgotten or ignored.

The next group of six virtues emerges from the practice of concentration and also leads to the attainment of nirvāṇa without fixed abode. A buddha's belief in his nirvāṇa without fixed abode is pure and incorruptible; his practice is aided by unflagging resolution to attain his goal; and his effort is constant in every situation. He retains unfailing wisdom for the benefit of sentient beings, is constant in causing them to attain Mahāyāna emancipation, and never flags in causing them to attain nirvāṇa without fixed abode.

The final six virtues emerge from the practice of wisdom and are the embodiment of nirvāṇa without fixed abode. A buddha's actions, speech, and thought constantly reveal his perfect wisdom; and, having perfect knowledge of all things past, present, and future, he shatters sophistry. His knowledge is detached and unhindered, totally free.

Other lists of the characteristics of a buddha survive. For example, the Great Commentary and the Treatise on the Stages of

Yoga Practice cite one hundred forty characteristics: the thirty-two primary marks, the eighty secondary marks, the four absolute purities,[12] the ten powers, the four kinds of fearlessness, the three types of equanimity, the three actions that need not be guarded against,[13] great compassion, continual awareness of faults, the elimination of all residue of the defilements, and perfect knowledge of all things past, present, and future.

THE TEN EPITHETS OF A BUDDHA

Other terms expressing the nature of a buddha are the ten epithets that can be. used when referring to a buddha. They are Tathāgata, Worthy of Respect, Omniscient, Perfect in Knowledge and Conduct, Well Departed, Understander of the World, Unsurpassed, Controller of Humans, Teacher of Gods and Humans, Buddha, and World-honored One. Although there appear to be eleven epithets, as this list shows, there are actually only ten, because some versions omit the epithet Tathāgata and some combine two in the epithet Buddha and World-honored One. Primitive sūtras, for example, usually omit the epithet Tathāgata. In general, the Āgamas, the earliest sūtra collections, use the ten epithets as a formulaic reference to the Buddha-treasure. All eleven of the epithets used are explained below.

Tathāgata *Tathāgata* can mean "thus come" (*tathā-āgata*) or "thus gone" (*tathā-gata*). Signifying one who has reached, or has come from, Thusness, or absolute Truth (*tathatā*), it is a synonym for a buddha, one who has come from absolute Truth, taught it to others, and returned to it. The term is also found in pre-Buddhist sources, where it refers to a person who has achieved emancipation from the cycle of birth and death. *Tathāgata* entered Buddhism with this meaning; in primitive sūtras Śākyamuni often used it in the plural to indicate ideal people who have achieved liberation from the round of rebirth, but there is no instance in which he applied it to himself.

In primitive Buddhism the term buddha was used to indicate an extraordinary person, and *tathāgata* was restricted to a perfect, ideal being. Thus Śākyamuni refrained from including himself among the *tathāgatas*. In later times, however, *tathāgata* and buddha were used interchangeably; for example, Amitābha Buddha is also called the Tathāgata Amitābha, and the Buddha of Healing (Bhaiṣajyaguru) is also called the Tathāgata of Healing. There is one exception: Mahāvairocana, the cosmic buddha, is always styled Tathāgata, never Buddha.

Worthy of Respect According to Mahāyāna, an *arhat* is a supreme sage, a *śrāvaka* who has attained Hīnayāna enlightenment. This implies that self-enlightenment, not altruistic concern for the enlightenment of others, is the *arhat*'s objective. This connotation is not associated with the original meaning of *arhat,* literally, "worthy of respect or veneration." By virtue of being perfected, with all delusions extinguished, an *arhat* is able to teach others and lead them to good. By offering such a one clothing, food, and accommodation, the donor can expect the merit of donation to return a hundredfold. One epithet of an *arhat* is "field for planting merit" (*puṇya-kṣetra, puñña-khetta*), signifying that the *arhat* is like a rich field that will give a bountiful harvest. Just as seeds planted in such a field give high yields, that which is given the *arhat* will return, multiplied, as a great harvest of merit. Simply by existing, an *arhat* redeems the world and brings happiness to humankind. It is in this sense that *arhat* is used as an epithet of a buddha.

The direct disciples of the historical Buddha who achieved the highest stage of enlightenment are also called *arhats;* from this point of view, both the Buddha and his enlightened followers were *arhats.* Mahāyāna has distorted the original meaning of *arhat* by limiting its application to a Hīnayāna sage not concerned with teaching others.

Other terms used to describe an *arhat* are *aśaikṣa* (*asekha*), one who has no more to learn, and *kṣīṇāsrava* (*khīṇāsava*), one who has extinguished all delusions. Based on the folk etymology *ari* = bandit and *han* = kill, *arhat* has also been translated as "killer of bandits," that is, one who has vanquished the bandits of delusion.

It should be noted that Chinese Ch'an and Japanese Zen sects refer to groups of sixteen and five hundred *arhats,* all outstanding disciples of Śākyamuni. The sixteen *arhats* are important disciples of Śākyamuni, and the five hundred *arhats* are the five hundred monks said to have attended the First Council, at Rājagṛha, following the Buddha's death. This usage of *arhat* should not be confused with that of *arhat* as an epithet of a buddha.

Omniscient *Samyaksaṃbuddha* (*sammā-sambuddha*) can be translated as "omniscient" or as "one who is perfectly enlightened." This term is used to distinguish a buddha's enlightenment from that of a *śrāvaka* or a *pratyekabuddha.* It is frequently prefixed by the word *anuttara,* or supreme. Thus a buddha's enlightenment is often referred to as *anuttara-samyaksaṃbodhi* (*anuttara-sammāsambodhi*), supreme and perfect enlightenment. *Anuttara* is also translated "unsurpassed," and as such is another of the ten epithets.

Perfect in Knowledge and Conduct A buddha is perfect in both theoretical knowledge and practical conduct (*vidyācaraṇa-saṃpanna, vijjācaraṇa-sampanna*). Buddhist theory is rational, ethical, and religious, and is the basis of the practice of the Buddhist faith. In Buddhism, all theory is related to practice. Theory provides a foundation for practice and leaves no room for superstition or heresy. Both theory and practice are perfectly integrated in the person of a buddha.

Well Departed "Well Departed" (*sugata*) describes one who has truly departed for the other shore of enlightenment and who will never fall back into the sea of birth and death. A buddha is called Well Departed for four reasons: he treads the holy way of goodness and purity, he can attain immortal nirvāṇa (*amṛta-nirvāṇa, amata-nibbāna*), he is able to achieve supreme enlightenment through mastery of the perfections (*pāramitā*), and his words are always appropriate to the occasion.

Understander of the World Understander of the World (*lokavid, lokavidū*) means that a buddha has complete understanding of the world. Here, world (*loka*) refers both to the "receptacle world" (*bhājanaloka*), that is, the inanimate world, and to the world of sentient beings (*sattvaloka, sattaloka*). In primitive Buddhist writings, *loka* always refers either to the world of sentient beings or to sentient beings themselves, in contrast to *lokottara,* the supramundane world, the realm of enlightenment. *Loka* is thus the world of delusion, encompassing the six realms of existence and the three realms of existence (the realms of desire, form, and formlessness). Having complete understanding of the thoughts, character, and capabilities of all beings, a buddha helps sentient beings achieve release from delusion by teaching them through appropriate means and by knowing the nature of their suffering, its cause, the possibility of its eradication, and the means of eradicating it. Thus, by understanding the world, a buddha is able to teach sentient beings.

Unsurpassed A buddha is unsurpassed (*anuttara*), matchless among beings. No one can compare with him in the practice of morality, concentration, and wisdom or in his emancipation and his perfect knowledge of the state of emancipation.

Controller of Humans A buddha directs the training of all those possessing the buddha-nature, that is, all those capable of being trained and taught. He guides people according to their individual condition, at times using gentleness, at times strictness, and at times a combination of the two. He is called Controller of Humans (*puruṣadamya-sārathi, purisadamma-sārathi*) because he guides everyone to faith and to enlightenment attained through practice by using both gentleness and strictness.

Teacher of Gods and Humans As Teacher of Gods and Humans (*śāstā-devamanuṣyānām, satthā devamanussānaṃ*), a buddha emancipates all beings in all realms of existence, not gods and human beings alone.

Buddha An enlightened one, or buddha, is one who is enlightened and enlightens others as well.

World-honored One *Bhagavat,* usually translated as "World-honored One," means one who possesses (*vat*) auspicious virtue (*bhaga*). Auspicious virtue signifies a delusion-free mind, enlightenment, honor, auspicious marks, the aspiration to benefit both oneself and others, and the effort to do so. As the possessor of auspicious virtue, a buddha is respected by all the world. *Loka-*

nātha (lord of the world) is sometimes used with the same meaning as *bhagavat,* but it is the epithet *bhagavat* that is found most often in sūtras. In translations of the sūtras, "Buddha" has been used to render *bhagavat* in the formulaic opening lines of sūtras: "Thus have I heard. At one time the Buddha [*bhagavat*] was staying at . . ."

THE DHARMA

The second of the Three Treasures, the Dharma (Dhamma), or Law, is the doctrines taught by the Buddha. Dharma can refer to the teachings in the physical form of the canon, or it can refer to the doctrinal content of Buddhism.

DIVISIONS OF THE SCRIPTURES

The collected Buddhist teachings have traditionally been classified in either nine or twelve divisions, reflecting the literary forms of the sūtras, or in three divisions or "baskets" (*piṭaka*), the Tripiṭaka (Tipiṭaka; Three Baskets), based on doctrinal content. Since the nine or twelve divisions also depend on content to a certain extent, they are ambiguous classifications. Even so, they have been used extensively in both Hīnayāna and Mahāyāna Buddhism, though the composition of the divisions has changed with period and school. In the period of primitive Buddhism only the Sūtra-piṭaka was termed Dharma and classified in nine or twelve divisions. In the period of Abhidharma Buddhism the Vinaya and *abhidharmas* were added to the Dharma. The Mahāyānists added their own sūtras and commentaries to these works and tried to fit everything into the traditional divisions. The classification in the Tripiṭaka—Dharma, Vinaya, and Abhidharma—is based on the content rather than the literary form of the teachings.

THE TEACHINGS IN NINE AND TWELVE DIVISIONS

In presectarian Buddhism, only the Dharma was included in both the nine and the twelve divisions. The nine divisions of Pāli Buddhism are discourses (*sutta*), mixed prose and verse (*geyya*), predictions of buddhahood (*veyyākaraṇa*), verses (*gāthā*), utterances (*udāna*), the "thus said" narratives (*itivuttaka*), stories of former lives of the Buddha (*jātaka*), miracle narratives (*abbhutadhamma*), and expanded sūtras (*vedalla*). Chapter 2 of the Lotus Sūtra, "Tactfulness," presents one version of this list, demonstrating the way in which the Buddha accommodated his teaching to his hearers.[14] Though differing from the Pāli list in content, enumeration, and order, the list in the Lotus Sūtra was meant as a metonym for the Hīnayāna canon. The nine divisions cited in the Lotus Sūtra are discourses (*sūtra*), verses (*gāthā*), narratives of former matters (*itivṛttaka*), stories of former lives of the Buddha (*jātaka*), miracle narratives (*adbhutadharma*), introductory narratives relating the circumstances of a work (*nidāna*), heroic feats (*avadāna*), mixed prose and verse (*geya*), and explanatory discourses (*upadeśa*).

The twelve divisions were basically the same for all Abhidharma schools, with only slight differences in order and enumeration from one school to another. The following list is that of the Sarvāstivādins and of the Yogācārins, who inherited it from them: discourses, mixed prose and verse, predictions of buddhahood (*vyākaraṇa*), verses, utterances, introductory narratives relating the circumstances of a work, heroic feats, narratives of former matters, stories of former lives of the Buddha, expanded sūtras (*vaipulya*), miracle narratives, and explanatory discourses.

While some of the divisions are based on literary form (for example, the sūtra, the *gāthā*, and the *geya*), others are classified in terms of both narrative method and form (*udāna, itivuttaka, vedalla, vaipulya, upadeśa*), and still others by content alone (*nidāna, avadāna, jātaka, adbhutadharma*). Consequently, in theory a single sūtra can be assigned to two or three categories. Thus, it is thought that these classifications were probably not the basis of the initial organization of the canon.

***Sūtra* (*Sutta*)** Broadly speaking, as scriptures all the works in the twelve divisions can be called sūtras. The Chinese canon, composed of works translated from the Hīnayāna and Mahāyāna Tripiṭaka, is often called "the great sūtra store," and the Sūtrapiṭaka itself is sometimes called a sūtra, in the broadest sense of the word. Within the twelve divisions, however, the term *sūtra* is used in the narrowest sense, referring only to works composed in a particular literary form, that is, collected prose relating the essentials concisely. The term *sūtra* in this sense was used widely in India in both pre- and post-Buddhist times by non-Buddhist sects and schools to designate certain of their works. Examples of this usage are the Brahmanic Kalpa-sūtras, the Yoga-sūtras, and the Vedānta- or Brahma-sūtras.

Originally, *sūtra* meant "thread" or "line." As a long thread draws flowers together to make a garland, a sūtra joins prose in a simple fashion. In the nine and twelve divisions, a sūtra is a brief discourse of the Buddha in prose. In the same way, the *Prātimokṣa* (*Pātimokkha*), or Inventory of Offenses of Monks and Nuns, in the Vinaya, recorded in concise prose, could also be considered a sūtra and was in fact often called the *Prātimokṣa-sūtra* (*Pātimokkha-sutta*). Consequently, the commentary on the Inventory of Offenses of Monks and Nuns is known as the *Sūtra-vibhaṅga* (*Sutta-vibhaṅga*), or Analysis of the Sūtra.

***Geya* (*Geyya*)** *Geya* originally meant "that which should be sung." As a literary form, it indicates a discourse of the Buddha in which prose passages are repeated in or supplemented by verse (*gāthā*). The Chinese translations of the term bring this out clearly: *ying-sung* (verse corresponding to prose) and *ch'ung-sung* (verse added to prose).

***Vyākaraṇa* (*Veyyākaraṇa*)** The import of *vyākaraṇa,* or predictions of buddhahood, varies considerably in primitive and Abhidharma Buddhism on the one hand and in Mahāyāna Buddhism on the other. The term originally meant "explanatory prose in the form of questions and answers," and by extension "explanation and detailed narrative." Gradually it came to mean "predict and expound" or "analyze and predict." In Mahāyāna Buddhism it referred to content rather than a literary form and identified the Buddha's predictions to his disciples concerning their destinies, in particular their attainment of buddhahood. Thus, while the word originally meant "explanatory prose," it eventually came to mean "predictions of buddhahood." The Chinese translation, *chi-pieh,* can apply to either meaning.

Gāthā As a literary form, *gāthā* is verse. In the Sutta-piṭaka it is found in the Verses on the Law (*Dhammapada*), the Verses of the Elder Monks (*Theragāthā*), and the Verses of the Elder Nuns (*Therīgāthā*). The *Dhammapada* consists of 423 verses, each concerning an aspect of Buddhist life, and the *Theragāthā* and the *Therīgāthā* are collections of 1,279 and 522 verses, respectively, attributed to monks and nuns of the earliest Buddhist period who were renowned for their enlightenment.

Udāna The *udāna,* or utterances, comprise remarks made in response to some circumstance of interest. Though in some cases these remarks may be the opinions of disciples, in the main they are pronouncements of the Buddha himself. The *udāna* differ from sūtras in that they did not arise in response to requests. *Udāna* was not originally a literary form but meant "a discourse inspired by a particularly intense emotion." In form it is mixed verse and prose.

One of the sections of the Khuddaka-nikāya is the Solemn Utterances of the Buddha (*Udāna*), a collection of eighty utterances of the Buddha accompanied by legends relating the circumstances in which they were made. At the end of each is a summary, invariably preceded by the words "Thus the World-honored One, knowing the reason, made this utterance at this time."[15] It is very likely that the inclusion of this formula resulted in these narrative works being designated *udāna.* There are also a few non-narrative works in the Nikāyas that contain this formula, but they are not classified as *udāna.*

The Sarvāstivādin canon has a section called the Solemn Utterances of the Buddha (*Udāna-varga*), consisting of thirty-three short works in about 950 *gāthās*. It corresponds to the *Dhammapada* and contains verses from the *Dhammapada,* verses from the *Udāna,* and verses from other sources.

Nidāna *Nidāna* are introductory narratives relating the circumstances under which a certain discourse was delivered. *Nidāna* can concern the circumstances of statements in the sūtra as a whole, can be narratives of the circumstances in which a *gāthā* was expounded, or can be explanations of the background of offenses and regulations included in the Vinaya. The nine divisions of Pāli scripture do not include *nidāna,* but the introductions (*nidāna-kathā*) to *jātaka* tales can be considered *nidāna.* There, however, the *nidāna* are not part of the Buddha's discourse but later commentary.

***Avadāna* (*Apadāna*)** The meaning of the term *avadāna* changed with time and school. Originally it meant "tales of heroic feats," and *avadāna* told of karmic rewards by recounting the series of events, past and present, that explains the causal relation between a fortunate existence and the accumulation of good karma in the past. *Avadāna* in this sense can be interpreted as "moral tale." The tales of Śākyamuni's heroic feats in former lives as a bodhisattva, recorded in the *jātakas,* are a kind of *avadāna* and thus can be termed bodhisattva-*avadāna.* In true *avadāna,* however, the tales generally relate to former lives of the Buddha's disciples.

The Sūtra of the Story of the Great Ones (*Mahā-apadāna-suttanta*) in the Dīgha-nikāya relates the former lives of the Buddhas of the Past, and the Sūtra of the Heroic Deed of King Dīghīti (*Chang-shou-wang pen-ch'i-ching*) in the Madhyama-āgama (Medium-length Discourses) of the Chinese canon tells of long-lived kings and princes of the past; these are moral tales of heroic feats. Later the Sarvāstivādins and other schools produced *avadāna* in great numbers, such as the Story of Emperor Aśoka (*Aśokāvadāna*), the Heavenly Stories (*Divyāvadāna*), the One Hundred Stories (*Avadānaśataka*), and the Various Stories (*Saṃyuktāvadāna*).

Itivṛttaka* and *Itivuttaka Pāli Buddhism used the Pāli *itivuttaka* and the Sarvāstivādins used the Sanskrit *itivṛttaka* to mean quite different things. *Itivuttaka* literally means "thus it is spoken" (*iti-vutta-ka*), while *itivṛttaka* means "events of the past" (*iti-vṛtta-ka*). In the *Itivuttaka* ("Thus Said" Sūtras) section of the Khuddaka-nikāya, each sūtra begins with the formula "In truth I have heard that which was taught by the World-honored One, the Arhat" (*Vuttaṃ hetaṃ bhagavatā vuttaṃ arahatā ti me sutaṃ*), contains a verse summary introduced with the words "Thus the World-honored One spoke; in that place this was spoken" (*Etam atthaṃ bhagavā avoca, tatth'etam iti vuccati*), and ends with the phrase "I have heard that which was spoken by the World-honored One" (*Ayam pi attho vutto bhagavatā iti me sutaṃ*). These formulaic phrases distinguish this group of sūtras from others. Their literary form is mixed verse and prose.

Itivṛttaka, by contrast, refers to tales of past lives and events. Since divisions already exist for stories of Śākyamuni's and his disciples' former lives (*jātaka* and *avadāna*), the *itivṛttaka* rather vaguely include stories of the former lives of those who fit into neither category, such as the Buddhas of the Past and wheel-rolling kings (*cakravartin*). In view of this, it is likely that the Pāli interpretation (*iti-vutta-ka*) is correct.

Jātaka The *jātakas* are tales of Śākyamuni Buddha's earlier lives, when he accumulated merit through practicing the perfections (*pāramitā*) as a bodhisattva. During that time, say the stories, he lived in a variety of human conditions—*śrāmaṇera* (male novice), Brahman, king, minister, merchant, and so on—as well as in the forms of gods and animals. The *Jātaka* section of the Khuddaka-nikāya contains 547 tales, and a further 34 appear in the *Cariyā-piṭaka* (Collection Concerning Conduct), which is also in the Khuddaka-nikāya.

Only the *gāthā* element in the Pāli *Jātaka* is considered to be canonical, that is, the words of the Buddha. The actual tales are commentaries on the verses. The *Jātaka-atthakathā,* or Commentary on the *Jātaka,* separates each tale into five elements: the event in the present lives of the Buddha and his disciples; the tale of their former lives, centering on bodhisattvas; the verse concerning the *jātaka* tale (the only canonical element); a commentary on the terminology in the verse; and an explanation of which events in the tale of earlier lives coincide with events during the Buddha's lifetime.

Chinese translations of the *jātakas,* such as the Stories of Former Incarnations (*Sheng-ching*) and the Sūtra of the Collection of the Practices of the Six Perfections (*Liu-tu-chi-ching*), give only the tale of an earlier life itself; they contain neither verse nor elements connecting the past experience with present events. The Pāli *Cariyā-piṭaka,* on the other hand, uses verse alone and records only the practice of the perfections (*pāramitā*) in past lives.

Vaipulya* and *Vedalla The Sanskrit *vaipulya* and the Pāli *vedalla* have different meanings; thus the sūtras in these two divisions are quite different. Sūtras categorized as *vedalla* are cast in the form of questions and answers; two sūtras in the Majjhima-nikāya (Collection of Medium-length Discourses) fall into this category, the Greater Discourse of the Miscellany (*Mahāvedalla-sutta*) and the Lesser Discourse of the Miscellany (*Cūḷavedalla-sutta*). *Vaipulya,* translated into Chinese as "broad and wide," was generally used as a metonym for Mahāyāna. Literally, it means that which expounds broadly the profound and correct meaning of the teachings, and it originally referred to sūtras expounded widely by the Abhidharma schools. After Mahāyāna developed, *vaipulya* was adopted as an epithet for Mahāyāna sūtras. Thus the full title of the Flower Garland Sūtra is *Buddha-avataṃsaka-nāma-mahā-vaipulya-sūtra.*

Variants of *vaipulya* are *vaitulya* and *vetulla* (literally, "the doctrine equal everywhere"). Since *vetulla* closely resembles *vedalla,* the following sound shift is thought likely: *vedalla* —> *vetulla* (*vaitulya*) —> *vepulla* (*vaipulya*). The term *vaitulya,* too, is used to refer to Mahāyāna, as in the formal title of the Great Collection of Sūtras, *Mahā-vaitulya-mahā-saṃnipāta-sūtra.*

***Adbhutadharma* (*Abbhutadhamma*)** A great many of the works classified as *adbhutadharma* concern mysterious occurrences deriving from supernormal powers, miracles, and such events as natural disasters. Sūtras in this category include the Discourse on Wonderful and Marvelous Qualities (*Acchariya-abbhutadhamma-sutta*) in the Majjhima-nikāya and ten sūtras in the *adbhutadharma* section of the Madhyama-āgama in the Chinese canon. Various miracle narratives are also included in the Aṅguttara-nikāya (Collection of Discourses Treating Enumerations) in the Pāli canon.

Upadeśa The discourses classified as *upadeśa,* or explanatory discourses, are not necessarily discourses of the Buddha. For instance, Abhidharma treatises are also classified as *upadeśa.* The term *niddesa* (expositions), used in contrast to *uddesa* (general teachings) in primitive sūtras, refers to commentaries. *Niddesa* appear as commentaries on portions of the *Sutta-nipāta* (Collection of Suttas) in the Khuddaka-nikāya. In this use the term *niddesa* has almost the same meaning as *upadeśa.*

Upadeśa refers specifically to the scholarly commentaries and treatises called *abhidharmas,* suggesting that *niddesa* are the precursor of *abhidharmas.* Commentaries on some Mahāyāna sūtras are in fact titled *upadeśa,* for example, those on the Lotus Sūtra and the Sūtra of Infinite Life (the *Saddharma-puṇḍarīka-sūtra-upadeśa* and the Larger *Sukhāvatī-vyūha-sūtra-upadeśa*). In general, however, Mahāyānists used the terms *vibhāṣā* and *vyākhyā* to identify scholastic commentaries on *abhidharmas.* Reserving the designation *upadeśa* for commentaries on the Buddha's actual discourses, Mahāyānists included in their *upadeśa* only those *abhidharmas* that comment on the Dharma in the Āgamas expounded by the Buddha.

THE COMPILATION OF THE TEACHINGS

In Śākyamuni's time the Buddhist teachings consisted of the Dharma and the Vinaya. This designation was a simple reference to the Dharma—the discourses of the Buddha himself and the discourses of his lay and ordained disciples and of such beings as Brahmā and Indra, *yakṣas,* and other demons that he had heard and approved as correct teaching—and to the Vinaya, the daily regulations of Buddhist monastic communities; these rules can also be considered the Buddha's teachings in the broader sense, since they were formulated by him. The Dharma and the Vinaya, the corpus of the Buddha's teaching in the period of primitive Buddhism, are the foundation of the documents later organized as the Sūtra- and Vinaya-piṭakas of the Buddhist canon.

Soon after Śākyamuni's death in a grove of *śāla* trees near Kuśinagara around 480 B.C.E., his eminent disciple Mahā-Kāśyapa called a council to ensure the correct transmission of the Buddha's teachings to later generations.[16] In the three-month rainy season following Śākyamuni's death, five hundred *arhats* (enlightened disciples) gathered at the Cave of the Seven Leaves, on the outskirts of Rājagṛha, many days' journey southeast of Kuśinagara. There they compiled the Dharma and the Vinaya that the Buddha had taught them. This was the First Council, also known as the Council of Rājagṛha and the Council of the Five Hundred.

"Council" is a translation of *saṃgīti,* which means "chanting or reciting together." Although writing was already being used in commerce, Buddhists initially followed the ancient Indian custom of not recording their sacred works in writing but preserving them by oral transmission.[17] Thus at the First Council the disciples recited what they knew of the Dharma and the Vinaya to ensure that there were no discrepancies and to verify what was the Buddha's genuine teaching and what was not.

According to tradition, Mahā-Kāśyapa presided over the First Council, which he had convoked, and two important disciples, Ānanda and Upāli, recited the Dharma and the Vinaya, respectively. Though not an *arhat* at the time of the Buddha's death, Ānanda, a cousin of Śākyamuni, had been his personal attendant for twenty-five years and had heard and memorized all the Buddha's discourses during that time. In addition, he had heard discourses from the Buddha and from other disciples before becoming a personal attendant. He was known as foremost in hearing many teachings. Without Ānanda's participation in the First Council, it would have been impossible to compile a collection of the Buddha's teachings. The only participant who was not an *arhat* when the council was convoked, Ānanda wanted desperately to achieve enlightenment before it actually began and thus qualify to attend, but had no success. He stayed up late the eve of the opening, but finally, his goal unattained, lay down to sleep. It was then, legend says, before his head touched the pillow, that he became enlightened.

Upāli had been a barber, a member of a slave caste serving the Śākya clan. Having heard that young Śākya nobles were becoming monks, he begged Śākyamuni to ordain him, too. The Buddha administered the precepts to him first, thus making him senior to the Śākya youths in the community of monks. In doing this Śākyamuni aimed to forestall arrogance among the young nobles. Upāli developed a great interest in the Vinaya, memorizing and observing all the precepts and regulations that Śākyamuni had formulated. Being renowned for his knowledge of the Vinaya, he recited the regulations at the First Council.

This tradition concerning the recitation and collection of the Dharma and the Vinaya at the First Council is recorded in ancient texts and probably reflects a degree of historical truth. Later sources attesting that the entire Tripiṭaka—including the Mahāyāna writing—was compiled at that time are patently in error, since neither Abhidharma literature nor Mahāyāna works existed then. In fact, the Dharma and the Vinaya were not organized into the Sūtra- and Vinaya-piṭakas at that time. What was compiled was simply the core of the later collections.

THE SŪTRA-PIṬAKA

The Dharma compiled after the Buddha's death was gradually organized into the Sūtra-piṭaka, though its division into five Nikāyas in the Pāli canon and four Āgamas in the Chinese canon probably came about only later, as an aid to memorization. Exactly when this occurred is obscure, but some form of classification must have existed prior to the sectarian schism around 350 B.C.E., since all later schools transmitted the earliest sūtras in four or five divisions.

The Nikāyas Pāli Buddhism divides the sūtras into five collections (*nikāya*), grouping the discourses according to kind (see the chart on page 78). The first is the Dīgha-nikāya, or Collection of Long Discourses, containing 34 sūtras in three *vaggas,* or groups. The second is the Majjhima-nikāya, or Collection of Medium-length Discourses, containing 152 sūtras in fifteen *vaggas.* The third is the Saṃyutta-nikāya, or Collection of Grouped Discourses, containing 2,875 sūtras organized in fifty-six subgroups according to some unifying element.[18] The fourth group, the Aṅguttara-nikāya, or Collection of Discourses Treating Enumerations, contains 2,198 short sūtras arranged in eleven groups according to the number of topics discussed, which ranges from one to eleven.

The fifth division is the Khuddaka-nikāya, or Collection of Minor Works, which consists of 15 works in the Sri Lankan version. These are the *Khuddaka-pāṭha* (Short Readings), the *Dhammapada* (Verses on the Law), the *Udāna* (Solemn Utterances of the Buddha), the *Itivuttaka* ("Thus Said" Sūtras), the *Sutta-nipāta* (Collection of Suttas), the *Vimānavatthu* (Tales of Heavenly Palaces), the *Petavatthu* (Tales of Hungry Ghosts), the *Theragāthā* (Verses of the Elder Monks), the *Therīgāthā* (Verses of the Elder Nuns), the *Jātaka* (Tales of the Buddha's Former Lives), the *Niddesa* (Expositions), the *Paṭisambhidā-magga* (The Way of Analysis), the *Apadāna* (Stories of the Lives of Certain Monks and Nuns), the *Buddhavaṃsa* (The Lineage of the Buddhas), and the *Cariyā-piṭaka* (Collection Concerning Conduct).

The works in the Khuddaka-nikāya are a mixture of very old texts and comparatively new texts. For example, the *Sutta-nipāta* is older than any of the works in the other Nikāyas, and parts of it existed in the Buddha's time, since it was recited when he was alive and is quoted in the Āgamas. The *Dhammapada,* the *Udāna,* the *Theragāthā,* the *Therīgāthā,* the *Jātaka,* and the *Itivuttaka* are at least as old as the sūtras in the other Nikāyas, and therefore are important sources for the study of primitive Buddhism.

The Āgamas The Chinese canon classifies the early sūtras according to four divisions (*āgama*). The term *āgama* (literally, "transmission") was also used occasionally in Pāli Buddhism in lieu of *nikāya,* but was particularly favored in the Northern tradition. The Chinese Āgamas, which include different translations of individual works, are a random compilation of sūtras transmitted by a number of different schools. The four divisions are the Dīrgha-āgama (Long Discourses), containing 30 sūtras of the Dharmaguptaka (Those Who Are Protected by the Law) school; the Madhyama-āgama (Medium-length Discourses), containing 222 sūtras of a school in the Sarvāstivādin lineage; the Saṃyukta-āgama (Grouped Discourses), containing 1,362 sūtras of the main Sarvāstivādin lineage; and the Ekottara-āgama (Discourses Treat-

The Nikāyas and the Āgamas

Pāli	Chinese translation
Dīgha-nikāya (34 suttas)	Dīrgha-āgama (30 sūtras)
Majjhima-nikāya (152 suttas)	Madhyama-āgama (222 sūtras)
Saṃyutta-nikāya (2,875 suttas)	Saṃyukta-āgama (1,362 sūtras)
Aṅguttara-nikāya (2,198 suttas)	Ekottara-āgama (481 sūtras)
Khuddaka-nikāya (15 works)	[Kṣudraka-āgama or Kṣudraka-piṭaka]

ing Enumerations), containing 481 sūtras of an unidentified Mahāyāna school.

A fifth Āgama, the Kṣudraka-āgama, or Miscellaneous Discourses, is sometimes included; it contains a number of works from the Khuddaka-nikāya that are not found in the other four Āgamas. While the contents of the first four Āgamas are fairly similar from school to school, there are great differences in the fifth. Some schools did not include a fifth Āgama in their canons, having created instead a division separate from the Sūtra-piṭaka called the Miscellaneous Basket (Kṣudraka-piṭaka). Thus, although the complete Khuddaka-nikāya is extant, only portions of it survive in Chinese translation.

THE VINAYA-PIṬAKA

The monastic regulations compiled at the First Council were subsequently organized into the Vinaya collections handed down by the various schools. These regulations are of two general types: those concerning individuals (the prohibitions) and those concerning the organization of the monastic community as a whole (the regulations in the narrow sense).

The Vinayas of the different schools are divided into two sections, sometimes followed by an appendix. The first section, the Sūtra-vibhaṅga (Sutta-vibhaṅga), or Analysis of the Sūtra, is a commentary on the prohibitions for monks and nuns recorded in the *Prātimokṣa* (*Pātimokkha*), or Inventory of Offenses of Monks and Nuns, which was recited during the semimonthly confession ceremonies (*poṣadha, uposatha*), on the days of the new and full moon. The monks' code lists eight classes of offenses, with the number of regulations varying from 218 to 263, according to school or sect. The nuns' code contains only seven categories (the *aniyata*, involving sexuality, having been omitted) but cites from 279 to 380 offenses, depending on school or sect. The nuns' lists are inflated by rules applying specifically to women. The Chinese Lü and Japanese Ritsu (Vinaya) sects specified 250 prohibitions for monks and 348 for nuns, and Pāli Buddhism specified 227 for monks and 311 for nuns (see the chart on page 80).

Offenses are classified according to their gravity and the nature of their punishment; the following list is based on the code for

The Categories and Numbers of Offenses Applicable to Monks and Nuns as Recorded in the Vinayas of Major Schools

(Figures in parentheses are the numbers applicable to nuns.)

Category	Pāli	Dharmaguptaka	Mahīśāsaka	Sarvāstivāda	Mahāsāṃghika	Mūla-Sarvāstivāda
pārājika	4 (8)	4 (8)	4 (8)	4 (8)	4 (8)	4 (8)
saṃghāvaśeṣa	13 (17)	13 (17)	13 (17)	13 (17)	13 (19)	13 (20)
aniyata	2 (—)	2 (—)	2 (—)	2 (—)	2 (—)	2 (—)
naiḥsargika-prāyaścittika	30 (30)	30 (30)	30 (30)	30 (30)	30 (30)	30 (33)
prāyaścittika	92 (166)	90 (178)	91 (207)	90 (178)	92 (141)	90 (180)
pratideśanīya	4 (8)	4 (8)	4 (8)	4 (8)	4 (8)	4 (11)
śaikṣa-dharma	75 (75)	100 (100)	100 (100)	113 (106)	66 (77)	99 (99)
adhikaraṇa-śamatha	7 (7)	7 (7)	7 (7)	7 (7)	7 (7)	7 (7)
Total	227 (311)	250 (348)	251 (377)	263 (354)	218 (290)	249 (358)

monks. The most serious offenses, the *pārājika*—requiring expulsion from the monastic community—are killing, stealing, sexual activity, and lying. Offenses in the next category, the *saṃghāvaśeṣa* (*saṅghādisesa*), require suspension from the community.[19] The third category, *aniyata,* comprising offenses with no defined punishment, is applied when there is an accusation of sexual misconduct (the resulting charges are brought under one of the other categories). Members of the community who possess articles they should not commit offenses requiring forfeiture and expiation, or *naiḥsargika-prāyaścittika* (*nissaggiya-pācittiya*). Minor offenses requiring simple confession and repentance are called *prāyaścittika* (*pācittiya*).[20] The next category of offenses, *pratideśanīya* (*pāṭidesanīya*), concerns food and requires only confession. The seventh category, *śaikṣa-dharma* (*sekhiya-dhamma*), consists of rules of etiquette, and offenses here require self-reflection. The final category, *adhikaraṇa-śamatha* (*adhikaraṇa-samatha*), contains not offenses as such but formal procedures for preventing and settling disputes in the community.

The Skandhaka (Khandhaka), or Chapters, the second major section of the Vinaya, contains both the regulations for the organization of the community and a commentary on them. There are twenty-two parts altogether, including rules for admission to the community; the semimonthly confession ceremonies; residence during the rainy-season retreat, *vārṣika*, extending from the first day of the waning moon in the eighth lunar month to the full moon in the eleventh; the confessional ceremony of *pravāraṇā* (*pavāraṇā*) at the end of the rainy-season retreat; and the rules governing food, clothing, shelter, and medicines. The third section of the Vinaya, the Parivāra (Accessory), is an appendix and differs considerably from school to school, indicating that it was added later, after the rise of the Abhidharma schools. The first two sections, the oldest parts of the Vinaya, show great similarity from one school to another.

Of the seven complete Vinayas that survive, one is in Pali, five are in Chinese, and one is in Tibetan. All include the same three major sections. Extant in Chinese are the Five-Part Vinaya of the Mahīśāsakas, the Four-Part Vinaya of the Dharmaguptakas, the Vinaya in Ten Recitations (*Daśabhāṇavāra-vinaya*) of the Sarvāstivādins, the Vinaya of the Mahāsāṃghikas, and the Mūla-Sarvāstivādin Vinaya (*Mūlasarvāstivāda-vinaya*). This last also exists in Tibetan, and part of the original Sanskrit text has been discovered in a manuscript from Gilgit, northwestern Kashmir.

The Vinaya-piṭaka is essential for monastic communities. In Pāli Buddhism the life of the Saṅgha is still regulated by it, just as in the time of the Buddha. Though there were no Abhidharma schools in China, during the T'ang dynasty Tao-hsüan (596–667) founded a Vinaya sect based on the Four-Part Vinaya, so his sect was also called the sect of the Four-Part Vinaya. Mahāyāna precepts were later established both in China and in Japan, but they were never observed as strictly as the precepts of Pāli Buddhism.

THE ABHIDHARMA-PIṬAKA

With the organization and classification of the Dharma and the Vinaya in the period following the First Council, treatises defining difficult terms and systematizing doctrines and methods of practice began to appear. The very earliest treatises were incorporated into the Āgamas as sūtras, but later their content and form diverged too greatly from the sūtras to permit this treatment. These writings were known as *abhidharmas* (literally, "that which is about the Dharma"). When their volume and diversity increased to the point that they could no longer be included in the Sūtra-piṭaka, a separate division was created for them, the Abhidharma-piṭaka, or Treatise Basket. This is believed to have occurred with the development of the schools.

The Vinaya, too, was subjected to analysis, explanation, and organization, and these studies were termed *abhivinayas*, "that which is about the Vinaya." Unlike the *abhidharmas*, these treatises were added directly to the Vinaya-piṭaka as an appendix.

All schools had much the same Sūtra- and Vinaya-piṭakas, but there were great differences in their Abhidharma-piṭakas. This is because the Dharma and the Vinaya were based on a common body of material transmitted through the First Council, whereas Abhidharma literature grew out of study that was, on the whole, formulated and developed within individual schools. As a result, a school's characteristics are most evident in its Abhidharma-piṭaka.

Abhidharma-piṭakas of only three schools are extant: the Pāli Abhidhamma, the Sarvāstivādin Abhidharma, and the Śāriputra Abhidharma, attributed to the Dharmaguptakas. The seven treatises of the Pāli Abhidhamma and the Sarvāstivādin Abhidharma do not correspond closely, although they show similar stages in their development (see the chart below). They were probably developed between the third and second centuries B.C.E. and are the only such texts that are considered canonical.

The Pāli Abhidhamma consists of the Dhammasaṅgaṇi (Enumeration of Dhammas), an analysis of the physical and mental elements in terms of ethics; the Vibhaṅga (Distinctions), doctrinal explanations followed by questions and answers; the Puggalapaññatti (Description of Individuals), an analysis of personality types; the Kathāvatthu (Subjects of Discussion), an orthodox polemical treatise; the Dhātukathā (Discussion of Elements), an examination of the elements of existence; the Yamaka (Book of Pairs), definitions of ambiguous terms; and the Paṭṭhāna (Book of Relations), a discussion of dependent origination.

The divisions of the Sarvāstivādin Abhidharma are the Saṅgītiparyāya (Section for Recitation), an examination of doctrinal terms; the Dharmaskandha (Aggregate of Dharmas), a discussion of Sarvāstivādin doctrines; the Prajñapti (Book of Manifestation), a treatise on cosmology and psychological events; the Vijñānakāya (Group on Consciousness), a polemical treatise on the nonreality of self; the Dhātukāya (Group on Mental Elements), a psychological treatise; the Prakaraṇa (Treatise), an examination of the elements of existence; and the Jñānaprasthāna (The Course of

Periods of Compilation of the Pāli Abhidhamma and the Sarvāstivādin Abhidharma

Pāli		Sarvāstivādin
Dhammasaṅgaṇi Vibhaṅga Puggalapaññatti	early period	Saṅgītiparyāya Dharmaskandha Prajñapti
Kathāvatthu Dhātukathā	middle period	Vijñānakāya Dhātukāya
Yamaka Paṭṭhāna	late period	Prakaraṇa Jñānaprasthāna

Knowledge), a collection of definitions of key psychological terms and concepts.

The Śāriputra Abhidharma is basically a summary of the Pāli Abhidhamma and the Sarvāstivādin Abhidharma.

THE MAHĀYĀNA TRIPIṬAKA

No evidence suggests that a Mahāyāna Tripiṭaka existed in India. Early Mahāyāna Buddhism had no need for a Vinaya, since there were no Mahāyāna monastic communities. Only later, with the development of large-scale communities like the monastic university at Nālandā, the center of Indian Mahāyāna Buddhism, did such regulations become necessary. Instead of developing their own Vinaya, however, these communities seem to have adopted the Mūla-Sarvāstivādin Vinaya.

Another factor contributing to the lack of a Mahāyāna Tripiṭaka in India is that Mahāyāna sūtras and treatises were composed over many centuries, and there are enormous differences among works composed at different times and places. In fact, even the

The Pāli Tipiṭaka

Vinaya-piṭaka	Sutta-piṭaka	Abhidhamma-piṭaka
Sutta-vibhaṅga	Dīgha-nikāya	Dhammasaṅgaṇi
Mahā-vibhaṅga	Majjhima-nikāya	Vibhaṅga
Bhikkhunī-vibhaṅga	Saṃyutta-nikāya	Puggalapaññatti
Khandhaka	Aṅguttara-nikāya	Kathāvatthu
Mahā-vagga	Khuddaka-nikāya	Dhātukathā
Culla-vagga	*Khuddaka-pāṭha*	Yamaka
Parivāra	*Dhammapada*	Paṭṭhāna
	Udāna	
	Itivuttaka	
	Sutta-nipāta	
	Vimānavatthu	
	Petavatthu	
	Theragāthā	
	Therīgathā	
	Jātaka	
	Niddesa	
	Paṭisambhidā-magga	
	Apadāna	
	Buddhavaṃsa	
	Cariyā-piṭaka	

earliest works, such as the Perfection of Wisdom sūtras, exhibit clear differences in emphasis and terminology. This is true of the Perfection of Wisdom Sūtra in Twenty-five Thousand Lines, the Perfection of Wisdom Sūtra in Eight Thousand Lines, and the Diamond Sūtra, for example. Some texts, such as the Lotus Sūtra, the Flower Garland Sūtra, and the Sūtra of Infinite Life, display scarcely any common ground in either thought or language. With the rise of the Yogācāra and Mādhyamika schools, underlying consistency became even rarer. Consequently, in India (though not in China) no attempt was made to collect, codify, or organize Mahāyāna works.

The term *tripiṭaka* was ambiguous in China. On the one hand, Chinese Buddhism accepted the Lotus Sūtra's identification of the Tripiṭaka with Hīnayāna teachings and thus tended to use the term to refer to the Sūtra-, Vinaya-, and Abhidharma-piṭakas of the Abhidharma schools. On the other hand, the Chinese also used the term to refer to the canon as a whole and even used *tripiṭaka* as a title for a scholar-monk of superior merit. Thus, for instance, the monks Hsüan-tsang and I-ching were known as Masters of the Tripiṭaka (in Chinese *san-tsang-shih,* usually abbreviated to *san-tsang,* and in Sanskrit *tripiṭaka-dhara*).

Unlike Indian Mahāyāna, Chinese Mahāyāna did develop independent precepts, derived from the Sūtra of the Brahma Net and the Treatise on the Conduct of a Bodhisattva (*Bodhisattva-bhūmi,* in Chinese *P'u-sa-shan-chieh-ching*) and known as the Brahmajāla precepts and the Yoga precepts, respectively. The Sūtra of the Brahma Net was probably composed in China, but the Yoga precepts may have been taught in the Indian Yogācāra school. Since they are not regulations for monastic life, however, the Brahmajāla and Yoga precepts bear no resemblance to the precepts in the Vinaya of the Abhidharma schools. Therefore, these precepts cannot have been in use in Mahāyāna commentaries in India.

Indian Buddhist works were taken to China in the early centuries of the common era without regard for their origins, and when catalogues of canonical works were made in China, the traditional term *tripiṭaka* was used to identify all Hīnayāna works. The diversity of the works taken to China is indicated by the inventory of the Hīnayāna scriptures that Hsüan-tsang collected, as itemized in his account of his travels, Record of the Western Regions (*Ta-T'ang hsi-yü-chi*): fourteen works of the Sthaviravāda Tripiṭaka, fifteen works of the Mahāsāṃghika Tripiṭaka, fifteen works of the Saṃmatīya Tripiṭaka, forty-two works of the Dharmaguptaka Tripiṭaka, seventeen works of the Kāśyapīya Tripiṭaka, twenty-two works of the Mahīśāsaka Tripiṭaka, and sixty-seven works of the Sarvāstivādin Tripiṭaka. Of all these, only fourteen texts from the Sarvāstivādin Abhidharma and two Sarvāstivādin sūtras were translated; the other works, which existed only as fragile palm-leaf manuscripts, have been lost.

THE DHARMA AS DOCTRINE

Dharma can refer to Buddhist doctrine itself rather than to the physical canon. The main doctrinal teaching, or Dharma, of primitive Buddhism, for example, includes the five aggregates, the twelve sense fields, the eighteen elements of existence, the Four (or Three) Seals of the Law, the Twelve-linked Chain of Dependent Origination, the Four Noble Truths, the threefold practice, the thirty-seven practices conducive to enlightenment, and the eight stages of effort and attainment.[21] The Mahāyāna Dharma includes the Six Perfections, the ten stages of bodhisattva practice, the buddha-nature (*buddhagotra*), the *tathāgata*-embryo (*tathāgata-garbha*), the eight consciousnesses, the three natures of existence, the nonself of sentient beings and *dharmas*, the aspiration to enlightenment (*bodhicitta*), the six great elements, and the Three Secrets.[22] (Mahāyāna doctrine was further expanded in China and Japan.)

Primitive Buddhist texts define the Dharma as "the doctrine that has been well taught by the World-honored One, avails even in the present life, is immediate in its results, invites and is conducive to deliverance, and can be mastered by any intelligent person." As the good teaching of the World-honored One, "in the beginning it is good, in the middle it is good, at the end it is good, both in form and in content. It is the Dharma of noble action, pure, perfect, and complete." The Dharma is that which should be observed by each person who has the wisdom to perceive it, and the results of practice are immediately apparent. In this connection Dōgen pointed out that practice and result are identical, that practice is its own result. In other words, the Dharma is not something that can be learned secondhand; it must be experienced directly, so that it is actually seen and its results are actually felt. It is through the Dharma that people are led to the deliverance of nirvāṇa. If correctly practiced, the Dharma is comprehensible to any intelligent person.

In his commentary on the Dhammasaṅgaṇi, the fifth-century Theravāda philosopher Buddhaghosa added four further characteristics of *dharma* (*dhamma*) to those mentioned above: *pariyatti, hetu, guṇa,* and *nissatta-nijjīvatā*. First, *dharma* is the teachings (*pariyatti*) that express the religious nature of Buddhism, whose essence and religious ideal is holiness and spirituality. The Dharma comprises Śākyamuni's teachings, often referred to metaphorically as the eighty-four thousand teachings, which are necessary to extinguish the eighty-four thousand defilements with which human beings are burdened. There are manifold teachings because Śākyamuni taught in various expedient ways, just as a physician prescribes different medicines for different diseases.

Second, *dharma* is a cause (*hetu*). In the narrow sense, *hetu* means the cause that leads to enlightenment as the ideal of Buddhism (the teachings to be practiced). More broadly, it refers to the cause of every existence (phenomenon). Because the cause is related to its effect, the term *hetu* is considered to mean the correct relationship of cause and effect. Buddhism teaches the need to understand correctly how cause and effect work in society and life (phenomena). It also teaches the need for correct knowledge of the way, actual and ideal, to reach enlightenment and stresses the need to practice correctly to attain enlightenment. To know both the actual and the ideal and to put them into practice, it is necessary to trace those causal relationships that exhibit rational truth. Thus the causal antecedent (*hetu*) represents rational truth. This is the reason that *dharma,* in the sense of the Dharma, is called *tathatā,* or absolute Truth.

Third, *dharma* is spiritually salutary, possessing virtue (*guṇa*) in the sense of religious and ethical good. While Buddhism recognizes both a relative, or mundane, good (*āsava-kusala*) and an absolute, or sacred, good (*anāsava-kusala*), its ultimate purpose is the search for and realization of absolute good, transcending both good and evil in the relative sense. Relative good exists within the cycle of birth and death and is controlled by karmic retribution, so that doing good brings happiness and good fortune in future lives. Absolute good goes beyond cause, effect, and karmic retribution; it is the sacred good in the realm of enlightenment, free of the cycle of birth and death. Thus Buddhism is clearly focused on the ethical.

By positing the Dharma as the norm and ideal of life, these three points give Buddhism its universality and relevance as a world religion. What makes the Dharma the supreme teaching is its incorporation of both rational truth and ethical good. Buddhism's rational and ethical components make it accessible to any period, any region, and any person as the ideal. Buddhaghosa's fourth point, however, relates not so much to the Dharma as to all *dharmas* (*sabba-dhamma*), experiential elements of existence that are intrinsically devoid of self (*nissatta-nijjīvatā*), their individual existence being relative, that is, dependent on something else.

Dharmas include all elements of existence, good and bad, pure and impure, sacred and mundane, joyful and painful, true and transitory. Although primitive Buddhism limited the use of the term *dharma* to the phenomena of arising, change, and extinction, the usage was later expanded to include all existence. If we consider only the phenomenal world, which exists temporally and spatially, the elements of existence are limited to the five aggregates, twelve sense fields, and eighteen elements of existence of Abhidharma psychological analysis, which are the subject of chapter 3. Thus *dharmas* have no self, no absolute metaphysical existence.

Lack of self, however, also reflects Buddhism's fundamental principle and is equivalent to the Mahāyāna concept of *śūnyatā* (emptiness). No absolute, no permanence, should be sought in the *dharmas* of phenomenal existence, and religious practice should be free and unhindered, with no attachment, in accordance with the Dharma. Buddhism considers existence to be devoid of self. That is because existence is not substantial but constantly subject to arising, change, and extinction. This is the basis for not being attached to existence as absolute, permanent, and unchanging. Thus a basic tenet of Buddhism is that faith and practice must be based on nonself and nonattachment.

Nissatta-nijjīvatā, that is, nonself and nonattachment, is essential in the practice of *pariyatti, hetu,* and *guṇa.* The religious, rational, and ethical aspects of Buddhism are perfected through *nissatta-nijjīvatā.* The practitioner must go beyond both the sacred and the mundane, beyond cause and effect, beyond good and evil, to reach the highest truth. The Diamond Sūtra explains nonself and nonattachment this way:

> That which is called a good *dharma* is indeed not a good *dharma* [in the sense of nonself]; therefore the Tathāgata teaches a good *dharma.* That which is called a characteristic of the *dharmas* is indeed not a characteristic [in the sense of nonself]; therefore the Tathāgata teaches a characteristic of the *dharmas.*

The Diamond Sūtra's explanation of *dharma* offers four ways of looking at it. Their synthesis allows the true significance of *dharma* to be understood. Of the four, the idea of nonself, that is, emptiness, is unique to Buddhism and displays the characteristics of Buddhism most clearly.

The Saṅgha

The term *saṅgha,* meaning a group or a community, was used in pre-Buddhist India to refer to a merchants' or artisans' guild or to the ruling council of a royal family. It also designated a religious community, a usage that Buddhism adopted. In Buddhism the term denoted the community of ordained men (*bhikṣu-saṃgha, bhikkhu-saṅgha*) together with the community of ordained women (*bhikṣuṇī-saṃgha, bhikkhunī-saṅgha*).

THE COMPOSITION OF THE SAṄGHA

Traditionally, the term *saṅgha* designated only the community of ordained men and women, in which monks occupied the central position, nuns having a subordinate role. For the community of believers in the broadest sense, the term *pariṣad* (*parisā*) was used.

Two categorizations were used: the four groups, comprising laymen, laywomen, monks, and nuns, and the seven groups, consisting of the four groups plus three classes of novices.

A male lay believer who had taken refuge in the Three Treasures but remained a householder was called an *upāsaka.* He was required to observe the five lay precepts (not to kill, steal, commit adultery, lie, or drink intoxicants) all his life. A female lay believer (*upāsikā*) had the same obligations. Lay people were also expected to observe eight precepts on specified days of abstention each month, when their lifestyle approached that of the novice. The first five of these precepts are the same as the lay precepts (except that all sexual activity is prohibited); the additional precepts are to avoid personal adornment, singing, and dancing, not to use an elaborate bed, and not to eat after midday. When the sixth precept is divided into two (to avoid personal adornment and not to listen to music or watch dancing) and a final precept—the prohibition against receiving money—is added, we have the ten precepts for novices. (Different sets of precepts were drawn up in later periods.)

A fully ordained man was called a *bhikṣu* (*bhikkhu*). He had to be at least twenty and had to have received the full number of precepts for a monk (250 in the Dharmaguptaka tradition). An ordained woman, a *bhikṣuṇī* (*bhikkhunī*), was obliged to observe 348 precepts, according to the Dharmaguptaka tradition. She too had to be at least twenty to receive full ordination; but a married woman, even if under twenty, could become fully ordained if she had passed the probationary stage of *śikṣamāṇā.*

There were three types of novices. A *śrāmaṇera* (*sāmaṇera*) was a male candidate for *bhikṣu,* usually a youth under twenty, who was ordained but had not yet received all the precepts. (In Japan this term was applied to any adult male who had yet to receive all the precepts.) The novice had to follow ten precepts: the amended eight precepts of a lay believer, supplemented with a prohibition against receiving gold, silver, or any form of money. A female novice, a *śrāmaṇerī* (*sāmaṇerī*), had the same obligations. A second type of novitiate was possible for a married woman, who was called a *śikṣamāṇā* (*sikkhamānā*). Since a married woman might be pregnant, she had to pass through a probationary period of two years, long enough to bear and wean a child. Because of the burdens of pregnancy and child rearing, the *śikṣamāṇā* observed only six precepts: to refrain from killing, stealing, sexual activity, lying, drinking intoxicants, and eating at proscribed times.

Though the original intent of Mahāyāna was to dissolve the distinctions between lay and ordained believers by enabling all to aspire to enlightenment while leading secular lives, historically it is doubtful that this ever became a reality in Indian Mahāyāna, since there was a certain inconvenience in not having a specialist clergy. In later times, certainly, a clear distinction existed between lay and ordained believers, and East Asian Buddhism inherited this tradition, though without the strict monastic regulations of Pāli Buddhism.

THE NATURE OF THE SAṄGHA

The standard definition of the Saṅgha as one of the Three Treasures is found in the Dīgha-nikāya and the Aṅguttara-nikāya:

> The community of the Buddha's followers walks the Way well, honestly, truthfully, and correctly. Thus it is composed of those who have accomplished the eight *ārya* [noble] stages of effort and attainment to achieve sagehood. The community merits veneration, respect, donation, and respectful greetings from ordinary people, for it is a supremely rich field that yields a rich harvest to all people.

The Chinese Āgamas contain an almost identical passage, although some of them add five further items to the stages of practice: possessing the virtues of morality, concentration, wisdom, emancipation, and perfect knowledge of the state of emancipation.

This definition of the Saṅgha limits the original community to those disciples of the Buddha who have attained one of the eight *ārya* stages of effort and attainment but does not specifically exclude lay people. Since no mention is made of limiting the community to the ordained, lay sages can be included. Primitive sūtras agree that a lay person can attain *śaikṣa* (*sekha*) enlightenment, the stage below *arhat* enlightenment. The point here is that lay people, though sages, do not live the group life of the Saṅgha, and so in reality the community signifies only the Order of ordained sages, who merit the respect of all as part of the Order-treasure. We could say, however, that anyone worthy of such respect must be considered a member of the Saṅgha.

The traditional *saṅgha* of the Vinaya-piṭaka was solely the community of ordained people who had received all the precepts. Communities of four, five, ten, twenty, and more than twenty members were allowed, but not of fewer than four. The size of the community depended on the size of the secular community it served: a city could support a community of twenty or more, but a remote village or hamlet could support a community of only four or five. Two or three ordained people living together were termed a *gaṇa* (assembly) to distinguish their community from a *saṅgha.* Ideally, every community's members were supposed to have attained one of the eight *ārya* stages, but even in Śākyamuni's time communities accepted all ordained people, regardless of the level of practice they had attained. The ideal of having the community consist of people who had attained one of the eight *ārya* stages sprang from the meaning and the functions of the *saṅgha.*

THE FUNCTIONS OF THE SAṄGHA

The Saṅgha is considered to be "a supremely rich field" and merits respect and veneration because its purpose is to guide people in faith and practice and to bring about their release from the cycle of birth and death. In fulfilling this role, it takes the place of the Buddha, who is not physically present.

According to tradition, the Saṅgha originated when Śākyamuni delivered his first discourse in Varanasi, enlightening the five ascetics with whom he had practiced austerities earlier. The next convert, the youth Yaśas (Yasa), brought with him a large number of friends, raising the number of *arhats* in the Saṅgha to sixty.[23] As recorded in the Vinaya-piṭaka, the Buddha subsequently ordered these disciples to go separately to various parts of the country, preaching the Dharma:

> Monks! You and I have gained release from all the delusions and sufferings that are the destiny of gods and human beings. Monks! Go forth on your wanderings for the good of the many, for the happiness of the many, in compassion for the world, for the good, the welfare, the happiness of gods and human beings. Let not two of you go the same way. Monks! Proclaim the Law that is good in the beginning, good in the middle, and good at the end, endowed with truth and form. Reveal the holy life, which is perfect, complete, and pure.

This exhortation details the three functions of the Saṅgha. First, members of the Saṅgha are on the path of the eight *ārya* stages, released from the suffering of all defilements and karmic ties. They have faith in Buddhism and a correct understanding of its doctrine, and they have achieved a deep personal enlightenment through correct practice. They walk the Way "well, honestly, truthfully, and correctly."

A member of the Saṅgha guides people to faith and leads them to enlightenment to release them from suffering. This is the meaning of the metaphor "a supremely rich field." Thus the Saṅgha's second function is to bring happiness to people by proclaiming the Dharma, explaining its practice, and guiding them to it.

The third function of the Saṅgha is to transmit the Dharma correctly and in an unbroken flow to future generations. The Saṅgha members must maintain and pass on the teachings, and to do so they must practice the Buddha's Way. If Buddhism is to flourish, all three functions of the Saṅgha must be complete; without them Buddhism will wither and die.

These functions are elucidated in a list of the ten merits of the regulations, which appears in the Vinaya-piṭaka. According to the Pāli Vinaya, the regulations were established for the following reasons: for the good of the Saṅgha, for the happiness of the Saṅgha, to restrain the shameless, for the ease of good monks, for protection against the defilements of this world, to guard against the defilements of a future world, to bring unbelievers to faith, to deepen the faith of believers, to maintain the true Dharma, and to observe the regulations. The first six reasons pertain to the support and training of the ordained, the seventh and eighth to the guidance and teaching of others, and the final two to the maintenance and preservation of Buddhist teachings.

In the *Sutta-nipāta* the functions of the Saṅgha are also clarified by the definition of the four types of monks that Śākyamuni, the day before he died, gave to the smith Cunda:

> There are four kinds of monks [men of the path] and no fifth. [They] are the victor of the path, the preacher of the path, the man who lives by the path, and the one who pollutes the path.

The victor of the path is the *arhat*, who has achieved the highest enlightenment. His existence brightens the world, and he can bring about the release of all people. The preacher of the path is a monk at the *śaikṣa* stage, just before complete *arhat* enlightenment. He is characterized by faith, religious practice, and correct knowledge of Buddhist doctrine, and is best suited to teaching the Dharma. One who lives by the path is a monk who, though yet to attain enlightenment, lives according to the tenets of Buddhism, keeping the precepts and earnest in both study and practice. The polluter of the path is a monk who lacks correct faith and understanding, fails to observe the precepts, and neglects his practice. Buddhism flourishes when the first two types predominate and decays if monks of the fourth type prevail. With monks of the third type, at best Buddhism will maintain the status quo.

It is clear that the Saṅgha is not merely an assembly of believers but also the organ by which faith and practice of the Dharma are transmitted. As such, it should be the object of people's reverence, faith, and devotion. In Pāli Buddhism, all who are ordained and follow the regulations, however young or immature they may be, are revered and venerated by all lay believers, even kings and ministers, because the Saṅgha is a treasure endowed with the three functions discussed above.

3. The Elements of Existence

Unlike the Indian Brahmanic schools and Western philosophy, Buddhism does not describe existence in terms of noumenon or substance, for it holds that human beings do not have the cognitive power to recognize noumenon or substance as the eternal and unchanging existence of that which transcends both time and space and is not subject to arising, change, and extinction. Even if such existence is comprehended, the world of noumenon is not related to our world of phenomenon, and knowledge of it is thus of no benefit to religious practice and the quest for enlightenment. Therefore, it is held, Buddhism should not address the noumenal. It is the phenomenal—that which is temporal and spatial—that can be understood by means of sensation and perception; it is the phenomenal by which existence is recognized and judged. Consequently, Buddhism concerns itself exclusively with the phenomenal and refuses to address ultimately unanswerable questions of ontology.

In this Buddhism shares ground with modern science, which likewise focuses on phenomena alone. Like Buddhism, science holds that only the phenomenal world can be studied, whether in terms of natural science, the social sciences, or the humanities. Metaphysical existence cannot be verified by experiment and is therefore outside the purview of scientific inquiry. This shared outlook attests to Buddhism's modernity and rationality.

In general Buddhism defines all phenomena as the conditioned (*saṃskṛta, saṅkhata*), or *saṃskāra* (*saṅkhāra*) in the broadest sense, since the phenomenal world (*sarva-dharma, sabba-dhamma;* literally, "all *dharmas*") is one of constant change, full of pain and suffering as well as joy and contentment. What Buddhism clarifies is limited to this world. As mentioned in the previous chapter, Buddhism considers phenomena in terms of *dharmas,* elements of existence that embrace all components of existence. Whereas primitive Buddhism was content to identify as *dharmas* all things that were obviously objects of consciousness and defined existence as the phenomenal, the Abhidharma schools included in their definition of existence both the conditioned *dharmas* (*saṃskṛta-dharma, saṅkhata-dhamma*) and *dharmas* not subject to change (*asaṃskṛta-dharma, asaṅkhata-dhamma*).

Primitive Buddhism employed a threefold classification to describe material and mental existence: the five aggregates, the twelve sense fields, and the eighteen elements of existence. These were reinterpreted and their meanings expanded in the period of the Abhidharma schools, particularly with the growth of *dharma* theory.

The aggregates (*skandha, khandha;* literally, "heaps" or "bundles") divide all existence, individual as well as universal, into five psychophysical elements. Existence is further elucidated in terms of sensation and perception by the twelve sense fields (*āyatana*), that is, the six sense organs or faculties together with their objects. Adding the six consciousnesses to the twelve sense fields gives the eighteen elements of existence (*aṣṭādaśa dhātavaḥ, aṭṭhādasa dhātuyo*).

Being especially concerned with the nature of existence, both conditioned and unconditioned, the Abhidharma schools found the primitive Buddhist threefold classification of the elements of existence inadequate. In the early period of their history, however, they used it as the basis for interpretation and classification. As a result, the primitive classification tended to be adopted without change, which caused problems for later scholastics aware of its deficiencies.

By the late period of the Abhidharma schools, most had adopted a fivefold classification for the elements of existence and were using it in lieu of the earlier threefold division. The Sarvāstivādins, one of the most influential of the schools, classified all *dharmas* into seventy-five *dharmas* in five categories and asserted their characteristic reality in the three periods of past, present, and future, that is, their eternal reality. The Sarvāstivādins did not assert that what exists in the present is forever unchanging, however. They divided the *dharmas* into the conditioned and the unconditioned, the former consisting of seventy-two *dharmas* of phenomenal existence subject to arising and decay, divided into four categories, and the latter consisting of a single category of three *dharmas* considered to be unchanging (see the chart on pages 98–99). Originally interpreted as nirvāṇa in primitive Buddhism, unconditioned *dharmas* were understood by the Sarvāstivādins in terms of existence and included space (*ākāśa*) as the container of physical elements.

The Treatise on the Establishment of the Doctrine of Consciousness Only of the Yogācārins followed this basic classification but posited one hundred *dharmas* in five categories (see the chart on pages 100–101). Pāli Buddhism, however, used a different classification: one hundred seventy (or two hundred two) *dharmas* in four categories (material *dharmas*, mental *dharmas*, associated mental functions, and unconditioned *dharmas*), not acknowledging *dharmas* dissociated from mind.

The Five Aggregates

The five aggregates consist of psychophysical elements: form (*rūpa*), feeling (*vedanā*), perception (*saṃjñā, saññā*), mental constituents (*saṃskāra, saṅkhāra*), and consciousness (*vijñāna, viññāṇa*). Collectively they are called *nāma* (name) and *rūpa* (form). Thus the compound *nāma-rūpa* is a synonym for the five aggregates. Both the physical and the mental aggregates are characterized by impermanence, suffering, and nonself, and the purpose in teaching them is to emphasize these facts. This point is discussed in the Saṃyutta-nikāya:

> Monks! Form is impermanent. That which is impermanent is painful. That which is painful is [the result of a false idea] of

The Sarvāstivādin Theory of Seventy-five *Dharmas* in Five Categories

- (1) Unconditioned *dharmas* (*asaṃskṛta-dharma*)
  - space (*ākāśa*)
  - extinction of defilements through wisdom (*pratisaṃkhyā-nirodha*)
  - extinction and nonreproduction owing to lack of a productive cause (*apratisaṃkhyā-nirodha*)
- Conditioned *dharmas* (*saṃskṛta-dharma*)
  - (2) Form (*rūpa*)
  - (3) Mind (*citta*), or "mind ruler"
  - (4) Associated mental functions (*cittasaṃprayukta-saṃskāra*)
    - Basic (*mahābhūmika*)
    - Basic good (*kuśala-mahābhūmika*)
    - Basic defiled (*kleśa-mahābhūmika*)
    - Basic evil (*akuśala-mahābhūmika*)
    - Lesser defiled (*up-akleśa-bhūmika*)
    - Undetermined (*aniyata-bhūmika*)
  - (5) Functions dissociated from mind (*cittaviprayukta-saṃskāra*)

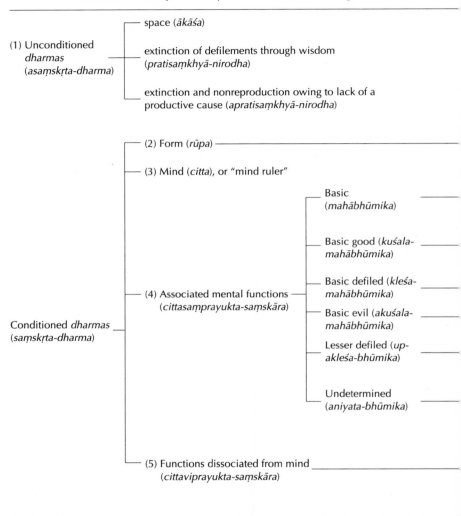

faculty of sight (*cakṣur-indriya*), auditory nerves (*śrota-indriya*), olfactory nerves (*ghrāṇa-indriya*), taste buds (*jihvā-indriya*), tactile nerves (*kāya-indriya*), objects of sight (*rūpa-viṣaya*), *sounds* (*śabda-viṣaya*), odors (*gandha-viṣaya),* tastes (*rasa-viṣaya*), palpables (*sparśa-viṣaya*), unmanifested form (*avijñapti-rūpa*)

feeling (*vedanā*), perception (*saṃjñā*), volition (*cetanā*), contact (*sparśa*), attention (*manaskāra*), desire (*chanda*), inclination (*adhimokṣa*), mindfulness (*smṛti*), concentration (*samādhi*), understanding (*mati*)

faith (*śraddhā*), diligence (*apramāda*), tranquillity (*praśrabdhi*), equanimity (*upekṣā*), shame (*hrī*), conscience (*apatrāpya*), noncovetousness (*alobha*), nonmalevolence (*adveṣa*), nonviolence (*ahiṃsā*), endeavor (*vīrya*)

ignorance (*moha*), indolence (*pramāda*), sloth (*kausīdya*), nonbelief (*āśraddhya*), languor (*styāna*), frivolity (*auddhatya*)

shamelessness (*āhrīkya*), lack of modesty (*anapatrāpya*)

wrath (*krodha*), hypocrisy (*mrakṣa*), parsimony (*mātsarya*), jealousy (*īrṣyā*), worry (*pradāsa*), causing injury (*vihiṃsā*), enmity (*upanāha*), deceit (*māyā*), trickery (*śāṭhya*), arrogance (*mada*)

discursive thought (*vitarka*), investigation (*vicāra*), drowsiness (*middha*), regret (*kaukṛtya*), greed (*rāga*), anger (*pratigha*), pride (*māna*), doubt about the teachings (*vicikitsā*)

acquisition (*prāpti*), nonattachment (*aprāpti*), species-shared qualities (*nikāya-sabhāgatā*), attainment of the fourth stage of the realm of form through the meditation of nonperception (*āsaṃjñika*), thoughtless trance (*asaṃjñi-samāpatti*), cessation of perception and feeling (*nirodha-samāpatti*), life (*jīvitendriya*), production (*jāti*), continuity (*sthiti*), decay (*jarā*), impermanence (*anityatā*), letters (*vyañjana-kāya*), words (*nāma-kāya*), phrases (*pada-kāya*)

The Yogācārin Theory of One Hundred *Dharmas* in Five Categories

- (1) Mind (*citta*)
- (2) Associated mental functions (*cittasaṃprayukta-saṃskāra*)
  - Universal (*sarvatraga*)
  - Limited (*viniyata*)
  - Good (*kuśala*)
  - Defiled (*kleśa*)
  - Auxiliary defiled (*upakleśa*)
  - Undetermined (*aniyata*)
- (3) Form (*rūpa*)
- (4) Functions dissociated from mind (*cittaviprayukta-saṃskāra*)
- (5) Unconditioned *dharmas* (*asaṃskṛta-dharma*)

the eight consciousnesses

attention (*manaskāra*), contact (*sparśa*), feeling (*vedanā*), perception (*saṃjñā*), volition (*cetanā*)

desire (*chanda*), inclination (*adhimokṣa*), mindfulness (*smṛti*), concentration (*samādhi*), wisdom (*prajñā*)

faith (*śraddhā*), endeavor (*vīrya*), shame (*hrī*), conscience (*apatrāpya*), noncovetousness (*alobha*), nonmalevolence (*adveṣa*), absence of ignorance (*amoha*), tranquillity (*praśrabdhi*), diligence (*apramāda*), equanimity (*upekṣā*), nonviolence (*ahiṃsā*)

greed (*rāga*), anger (*pratigha*), pride (*māna*), ignorance (*moha*), false views (*dṛṣṭi*), doubt about the teachings (*vicikitsā*)

wrath (*krodha*), enmity (*upanāha*), hypocrisy (*mrakṣa*), worry (*pradāsa*), jealousy (*īrṣyā*), parsimony (*mātsarya*), trickery (*śāṭhya*), deceit (*māyā*), arrogance (*mada*), causing injury (*vihiṃsā*), shamelessness (*āhrīkya*), lack of modesty (*anapatrāpya*), languor (*styāna*), frivolity (*auddhatya*), nonbelief (*āśraddhya*), sloth (*kausīdya*), indolence (*pramāda*), forgetfulness (*muṣitasmṛtitā*), distraction (*vikṣepa*), nondiscernment (*asaṃprajanya*)

regret (*kaukṛtya*), drowsiness (*middha*), discursive thought (*vitarka*), investigation (*vicāra*)

faculty of sight (*cakṣur-indriya*), auditory nerves (*śrota-indriya*), olfactory nerves (*ghrāna-indriya*), taste buds (*jihvā-indriya*), tactile nerves (*kāya-indriya*), objects of sight (*rūpa-viṣaya*), sounds (*śabda-viṣaya*), odors (*gandha-viṣaya*), tastes (*rasa-viṣaya*), palpables (*sparśa-viṣaya*), *dharmas* as objects of consciousness (*dharma-āyatanikāni*)

acquisition (*prāpti*), life (*jīvitendriya*), species-shared qualities (*nikāya-sabhāgatā*), inability to attain enlightenment (*pṛthagjanatā*), thoughtless trance (*asaṃjñi-samāpatti*), cessation of perception and feeling (*nirodha-samāpatti*), attainment of the fourth stage of the realm of form through the meditation of nonperception (*āsaṃjñika*), letters (*vyañjana-kāya*), words (*nāma-kāya*), phrases (*pada-kāya*), production (*jāti*), continuity (*sthiti*), decay (*jarā*), impermanence (*anityatā*), becoming (*pravṛtti*), distinction of causes and effects (*pratiniyama*), harmony (*yoga*), speed (*java*), order (*anukrama*), direction (*deśa*), time (*kāla*), number (*saṃkhyā*), concord (*sāmagrī*), discord (*asāmagrī*)

space (*ākāśa*), extinction of defilements through wisdom (*pratisaṃkhyā-nirodha*), extinction and nonreproduction owing to lack of a productive cause (*apratisaṃkhyā-nirodha*), extinction of pleasure and pain (*āniñjya*), extinction of feeling and perception (*saṃjñā-vedayita-nirodha*), Thusness, or absolute Truth (*tathatā*)

> self. One who is without self knows, "This is not mine, I am not this, this is not my self." Thus should it be rightly regarded and considered.
>
> Monks! Feeling is impermanent. . . . Perception is impermanent. . . . Mental constituents are impermanent. . . . Consciousness is impermanent. . . . Thus should it rightly be regarded and considered.

The enlightenment of an *arhat* can be attained through the correct understanding that the five aggregates are characterized by impermanence, suffering, and nonself, which enables the practitioner to reject both material and mental *dharmas* and thereby put aside greed and attain emancipation. It is said that following the opening of the Dharma Eye—initial enlightenment—after Śākyamuni's first discourse on the Four Noble Truths and the Eightfold Path, the first five disciples of the Buddha became *arhats* through comprehending his teaching of the nonself of the aggregates. He taught that because the aggregates are impermanent and devoid of self they engender suffering and are subject to change and decay and furthermore that there is nothing that one can consider "I" or "my self." Knowledge of the nature of existence helps practitioners rid themselves of the twenty false views of self.[1] The Heart Sūtra's declaration that the five aggregates are empty (*śūnya*) reiterates this concept: "Form is identical with emptiness, emptiness with form. It is the same for feeling, perception, the mental constituents, and consciousness."

FORM

Form (*rūpa*) is that which is physical, or material. The traditional definition of *rūpa* is that which has mass, occupies space, and therefore obstructs, since more than one physical object cannot occupy the same space; or that which can be transformed and thus decays. In its broadest sense, as the aggregate of form, *rūpa* is the generic term for all matter, incorporating the four great elements—earth, water, fire, and air—and their derivatives and the five physical sense organs (*indriya*) and their objects (*āyatana*). (In its narrowest meaning, as one of the twelve sense fields or one of the eighteen elements of existence, *rūpa* applies only to that which has color and shape and thus refers solely to matter that is the object of sight.)

As with Buddhist terminology in general, the meaning of *rūpa* underwent change in Abhidharma writings. In primitive Buddhism, concepts tend to be self-evident. Primitive sūtras give common-sense explanations of the four great elements, for example, according to which earth encompasses both biological matter (hair, nail, tooth, bone, and so on) and geological matter (stone, soil, metal, gems, and so on). In the Abhidharma period these simple definitions were expanded by infinitely detailed interpretations that rendered fundamental concepts incomprehensible to nonspecialists. The basic definition of *rūpa* was enlarged to include invisible qualities that are evidenced only through form, the earth being characterized by firmness, water by moisture, fire by heat, and air by motion. A hair, for example, was no longer merely part of the category earth; it was thought to contain attributes of each of the four great elements in varying degrees and to be a derivative of an element rather than an element itself.

Likewise, the scholastics minutely defined the sense organs. Regarded in common-sense terms, the eye is essentially the eyeball, and the ear, the outer ear and middle ear. The Abhidharma scholars, however, preferred to include the faculties of the organs in their definitions. Thus in their categorization of the *dharmas* the Sarvāstivādins considered both the organs and their objects to be *dharmas* of form: the eye and what is visible (form in its narrowest sense), the ear and what is audible, the nose and what can be smelled, the tongue and what can be tasted, and the body and what is palpable. To these ten *dharmas* of form the Sarvāstivādins and the Dharmaguptakas (the latter in the Śāriputra Abhidharma) added an eleventh, unmanifested form (*avijñapti-rūpa*). Unmanifested form encompasses the power of habit in word and action. Being potential form preserved in the physical body, it was considered a material *dharma*.

Form was also divided into infinitesimal particles called *paramāṇu*. There are many varieties of *paramāṇu*, and Abhidharma works, with much difference in points of detail, postulate the ways in which they are incorporated into physical organs and perceptible matter.

FEELING

Feeling (*vedanā*) is the receiving of impressions, either pleasant or unpleasant. It includes both physical feelings of pain and pleasure and mental feelings of suffering and ease. Feeling is thus both the action of receiving physical and mental impressions and the resulting emotion.

Six types of feeling are defined, according to the source of the contact with the external world: eye, ear, nose, tongue, body, or mind. Further classifications are made based on the nature of the feeling: painful, pleasant, or neither painful nor pleasant; and sorrow, joy, pleasure, pain, or indifference (see the chart below).

The physical sensations of pleasure and pain are experienced by any being having a nervous system. The mental feelings of joy and sorrow, however, seem to be felt only by human beings, though they are experienced differently by different people, depending on time and circumstance: the same object may sometimes cause joy, sometimes sorrow, and sometimes indifference.

PERCEPTION

Perception (*saṃjñā, saññā*) is not only the capturing of a mental image and the action of forming concepts but also the concepts themselves. When we look at red flowers or white cloth, for example, both sensation and perception come into play to bring about the cognitive function of the mind, and we create the concepts of color (red, white) and form (flower, cloth). Perception includes pain, pleasure, impermanence, impurity, and dislike.

Classifications of Feeling

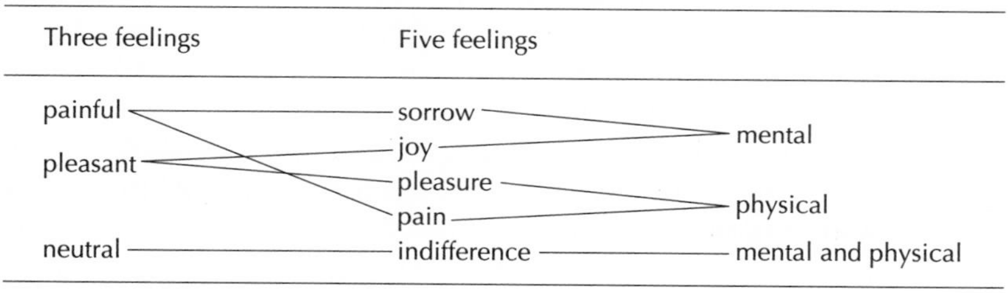
Three feelings
Five feelings
painful
pleasant
neutral
sorrow
joy
pleasure
pain
indifference
mental
physical
mental and physical

MENTAL CONSTITUENTS

Mental constituents (*saṃskāra, saṅkhāra*) are the working of the mind, that is, the mind in action. Mental constituents—all mental actions other than feeling, perception, and consciousness, which are separate aggregates—include such functions as attention (*manaskāra, manasikāra*), contact (*sparśa, phassa*), volition (*cetanā*), concentration (*samādhi*), mindfulness (*smṛti, sati*), and understanding (*mati* in Sanskrit). Volition, mental action either good or bad, is considered so representative of the mental constituents that *saṃskāra* has sometimes been translated as "volition," but "volition" is too limited to convey the meaning of *saṃskāra* adequately. In its broadest sense, *saṃskāra* means "all phenomena." Thus it is possible to consider *saṃskāra* in its broadest sense as referring to all the aggregates, not mental constituents alone.

Saṃskāra had different connotations in primitive and Abhidharma Buddhism. The Abhidharma schools defined *saṃskāra* in terms of various functions, collectively called associated mental functions (*cittasaṃprayukta-saṃskāra*), the third Sarvāstivādin category for classifying *dharmas.* The Sarvāstivādins also included a fourth category, functions dissociated from mind (*cittaviprayukta-saṃskāra*), nonmaterial and nonmental *dharmas* considered to be forces affecting both the mind and the body. The concept of functions dissociated from mind, found in neither primitive nor Pāli Buddhism, is indicative of the development of the concept of *saṃskāra* in the Sarvāstivādin school.

For scholars working with the Chinese Āgamas, a clear understanding of *saṃskāra* is further complicated by the way the term was translated into Chinese. The ideogram *hsing,* used for *saṃskāra,* was applied to a variety of Indic words. It was used for *caryā* or *cariyā* (religious acts) in the title *Cariyā-piṭaka,* for instance. *Hsing* was also used to translate *caraṇa* in "Perfect in Knowledge and Conduct" (*vidyācaraṇa-saṃpanna, vijjā-caraṇā-sampanna*), one of the epithets of a buddha, and *carita* (act) in the title of Aśvaghoṣa's biography of Śākyamuni, the Acts of the Buddha (*Buddhacarita*). Examples of other Indic words translated as *hsing* are abundant.

As the second link in the Twelve-linked Chain of Dependent

Origination (discussed in chapter 5), *saṃskāra* means "action." Used thus, it comes close in meaning to karma, the mental, verbal, or physical acts that result in good or bad conduct. In this sense, *saṃskāra* includes both overt behavior arising from volition and the tendency for such behavior to engender habit.

CONSCIOUSNESS

Consciousness (*vijñāna, viññāṇa*) encompasses analysis, judgment, and cognition arising from contact with an object. Etymologically, *vijñāna* means "what is known [*jñā*] through differentiation [*vi*]" plus the suffix *ana*, and its meaning seems to approximate "the cognitive function." Primitive sūtras, however, sometimes use *vijñāna* to refer to the mind as the subject of cognition, for example, consciousness as the third link in the Twelve-linked Chain of Dependent Origination.

Six types of consciousness have traditionally been described: visual, auditory, olfactory, gustatory, tactile, and mental. These are the six consciousnesses (*ṣaḍ-vijñāna, cha-viññāṇa*), or sensory perceptions, that complete the eighteen elements of existence. A seventh consciousness (*mano-dhātu;* literally, "mind realm") was added by the Abhidharmists to indicate a subtler type of mental functioning. Later the Yogācārins further refined the theory of consciousness by adding to the original six a seventh, *manas-vijñāna* (*manas* consciousness), and an eighth, *ālaya-vijñāna* (storehouse consciousness). In China a ninth, *amala-vijñāna* (undefiled consciousness), was also sometimes added.

THE CONCEPTS OF *CITTA, MANAS,* AND *VIJÑĀNA*

In primitive Buddhism the terms *citta* and *manas* (*mano*) were sometimes used interchangeably with *vijñāna* to refer to consciousness. The Abhidharma schools likewise made little distinction among the terms. It was the Yogācāra school that concerned itself with differentiating the terms in both name and meaning. The Yogācārins used *vijñāna* for the six consciousnesses or sensory perceptions, *manas* for the seventh consciousness, and *citta* for the eighth. Nevertheless, the definitions of these terms were not firmly fixed. In one theory all the eight consciousnesses were termed *vijñāna*, and in principle were not considered independent of one another.

Mind receives a great deal of attention in the primitive sūtras, since being free from delusion in order to attain enlightenment, a basic concern of Buddhism, is a function of the mind. It was considered important to discover the type of mind necessary for the attainment of enlightenment. In Pāli Buddhism, as among the Sarvāstivādins, consciousness was divided into three realms (desire, form, and formlessness) and the supramundane realm, was divided further into three moral categories (good, bad, and morally neutral), and was also divided into pain, pleasure, and neither pain nor pleasure. Pāli Buddhism eventually classified all the workings of the mind into eighty-nine or one hundred twenty-one states, or consciousnesses (*cittāni*), in which consciousness is combined with various mental factors.

The Abhidharma schools further postulated that the mind is composed of a core—*vijñāna* as the subject of the mind, the "mind ruler" of the Sarvāstivādin *dharma* categories—and a number of mental attributes (*caitta-* or *caitasika-dharma*), the associated mental functions of the *dharma* categories (see the chart on pages 98–99). The mind itself expresses its organizing force in terms of its attributes (conditions, qualities, and actions). The Sarvāstivādins categorized ten basic mental functions (*mahābhūmika*): feeling (*vedanā*), perception (*saṃjñā*), volition (*cetanā*), contact (*sparśa*), attention (*manaskāra*), desire (*chanda*), inclination (*adhimokṣa*), mindfulness (*smṛti*), concentration (*samādhi*), and understanding (*mati*). They developed a theory of associations (*saṃprayoga*) to discern what kind of mind is accompanied by what kinds and number of mental attributes.

These developments contrast with primitive Buddhist theory, which held that four aggregates (feeling, perception, mental constituents, and consciousness) are independent mental functions. There was no mention of a separate controlling force, the mind as subject; thus consciousness is no more than one of the aggregates. The Abhidharma theory of a subjective mind as the "mind ruler" and mental attributes, on the other hand, had no place for independent mental functions, since it was based on the idea that all mental attributes combine with a controlling mind. Thus the items that the aggregate theory ranked as equal with consciousness, that is, feeling, perception, and mental constituents, were relegated to a subordinate position as mental attributes.

Great as were the differences between primitive and Abhidharma Buddhist ideas concerning the mind, the ideas had common ground in that they dealt only with the conscious mind. Gradually, however, the theory of karmic retribution—according to which good and evil behavior leave a residue of habit in the mind—gained increasing attention, and the power of habit, reinforced through repetition, was thought to remain deep in the mind as memory, intellect, character, and prejudice and to exert great influence on cognitive judgment and behavior. Unless the power of habit was taken into consideration, it was difficult to explain adequately either everyday experience or the theory of karmic retribution. This led the Yogācārins to postulate a form of subconscious, the storehouse consciousness (*ālaya-vijñāna, ālaya* meaning "to be stored" or "to lie deep"). Each *dharma* arising from the power of habit stored in the storehouse consciousness is called a seed (*bīja*). Religious practice consists of ridding the mind of the tainted seeds, which hinder the attainment of enlightenment, and of increasing the number of untainted seeds, which lead practitioners closer to their goal.

Furthermore, selfishness and attachment arise instinctively and unconsciously because human beings are naturally self-centered, possessing a mistaken idea of self that gives rise to pride (*ātma-māna*), selfishness (*asmīti-chanda*), and attachment to self (*ātma-grāha*). That which holds continually to the idea of self is termed *manas*, and the Yogācārins eventually posited a *manas-vijñāna* and an *ālaya-vijñāna*. In many ways, the Yogācārin theory of eight consciousnesses accords with the concepts found in modern depth psychology and psychoanalysis.

The Twelve Sense Fields

The term sense fields is a translation of the Sanskrit and Pāli *āyatana*, composed of the elements *ā-yat* (entering) and the suffix *ana*. *Āyatana* can be interpreted as either "place of entry" or "that which enters." The place of entry refers to the six sense organs, or faculties: the eye, ear, nose, tongue, body, and mind (*manas*); that which enters refers to the six objects of cognition of the organs: visibles, sounds, odors, tastes, palpables, and mental objects.

THE INTERNAL AND EXTERNAL SENSE FIELDS

The six sense organs are the internal sense fields (*ādhyātmika-āyatana, ajjhattika-āyatana*), while their six objects of cognition are the external sense fields (*bāhira-āyatana*). Together they constitute the twelve sense fields. Sensation and perception occur through contact between an organ and its corresponding object. Like the aggregates, the twelve sense fields are intended to demonstrate that any element of cognition is subject to impermanence and suffering and is devoid of self; no permanent and unchanging substance can be found in elements of cognition. This doctrine is also found in the primitive sūtras.

Sense organ (*indriya*) refers to the faculty or the nervous system associated with it. The eye, for example, can be considered the place where visible objects enter (*cakṣur-āyatana, cakkhu-āyatana*) or the nervous system associated with the eye, which supports the faculty of sight (*cakṣur-indriya, cakkhu-indriya*). Ordinarily, by eye we mean the physical organ, the eyeball; but without the ability to see, that is, without the attendant nervous system that determines that ability, the eye in the sense of *indriya* (faculty or ability) is worthless. In the same way, the ear is the place where sounds enter (*śrota-āyatana, sota-āyatana*) or the auditory nerves (*śrota-indriya, sota-indriya*); the nose is the place where odors enter (*ghrāṇa-āyatana, ghāna-āyatana*) or the olfactory nerves (*ghrāṇa-indriya, ghāna-indriya*); the tongue is the place where taste enters (*jihvā-āyatana, jivhā-āyatana*) or the taste buds (*jihvā-indriya, jivhā-indriya*); the body is the place where one feels heat, cold, pain, smoothness, and roughness (*kāya-āyatana*) or the tactile nerves distributed all over the body (*kāya-indriya*). The Abhidharma scholastics differentiated the subtle and gross aspects carefully, terming the faculty "the surpassing organ" and the gross form "the organ aiding the senses."

The mind (*manas*) is not a physical sense faculty or organ but the means of perception. The mental faculty (*mano-indriya*) can be considered the mind that controls perception, and in many instances resembles the six consciousnesses in the eighteen elements of existence, discussed below. Mind as a point of entry for the objects of consciousness (*mano-āyatana*) is *manas*, and in this usage *manas* was not differentiated further in either primitive or Abhidharma Buddhism, being considered the same as *citta* or *vijñāna*.

THE OBJECTS OF COGNITION

Form Form (*rūpa-āyatana*) refers to sensory data received by the eye as the faculty of sight. Here form is used in its narrowest meaning and is limited to that which is seen by the eye. It is distinguishable by color and shape (blue, yellow, red, white, long, short, square, round). Unlike the aggregate of form, however, it does not include all that is material.

The Abhidharma schools recognized three categories of form in the broad sense. The first, visibles, is material form occupying space and visible to the naked eye. Only the objects of sight fall into this category. The second, invisibles, is material form occupying space but invisible to the naked eye. The remaining nonmental sense fields are included here. The third is invisible and intangible form, the Sarvātivādins' unmanifested form (*avijñapti-rūpa*), which is the power of habit for good or evil inherent in the body and included in mental objects (*dharma-āyatana*), one of the twelve sense fields. It is considered to be matter that does not occupy space. Unmanifested form, a Sarvāstivādin term, was unknown in Pāli Buddhism. In lieu of unmanifested form, Pāli Buddhism included fifteen intangible *dharmas* of form not occupying space (see the chart on page 111). This is a major point of difference between Northern and Southern Buddhism.

Sounds Sounds (*śabda-āyatana, sadda-āyatana*) are the objects of the ear as the faculty of hearing. They are classified as being made by humans and animals (voice) and by matter through touch and friction (noise). A distinction was made between sounds with meaning and those without meaning, and also between pleasant and unpleasant sounds.

Odors Odors (*gandha-āyatana*) are the objects of the nose as the faculty of smell and are classified as good or bad, beneficial or harmful.

Tastes Tastes (*rasa-āyatana*) are the objects of the tongue as the faculty of taste and are divided into salty, sour, bitter, sweet, spicy (hot), and bland.

Palpables Palpables (*spraṣṭavya-āyatana, phoṭṭhabba-āyatana*), that which is perceived tactilely by the body, consist of all that can be touched. The Sarvāstivādin scholars classified palpables as elemental, those that can be transformed (that is, the four great elements), and as derivative, those that are derived from transformation (such qualities as smoothness, roughness, heaviness,

Classifications of the *Dharmas* of Form

Pāli	Sarvāstivādin
four great elements	five sense organs
five sense organs	five sense objects
four sense objects	unmanifested form
three organic forces	
masculinity	
femininity	
physical life	
the physical basis of mind	
nutrition	
space	
two intimations	
body	
speech	
three conditions of physical fitness	
agility	
elasticity	
adaptability	
four phases of form	
production	
continuity	
decay	
disappearance	

lightness, cold, hunger, and thirst). Except for the four great elements, all *dharmas* of form, including the derivative palpables and the nine other nonmental sense fields, are derivatives (*upādāya-rūpa*). According to the Sarvāstivādins, unmanifested form is also a derivative. While their orthodox doctrine assigned color and shape to the objects of sight, another opinion favored assigning shape to the palpables, since shape was considered an object of the body (*kāya-āyatana*) rather than of the eye (*cakṣur-āyatana*).

Mental Objects As one of the twelve sense fields, *dharmas* (elements of existence) are mental objects (*dharma-āyatana, dhamma-āyatana*), incorporating all that can be considered mentally cognizable, such as existence and nonexistence, true and transitory *dharmas*. Any phenomenal element not included in the preceding sense fields falls into this category.

While primitive Buddhism regarded only the phenomenal, or conditioned, *dharmas* (*saṃskṛta-dharma, saṅkhata dhamma*) as objects of consciousness, the Abhidharma schools considered both conditioned and unconditioned *dharmas* (*asaṃskṛta-dharma, asaṅkhata dhamma*) to be mental objects. This categorization signaled a tendency toward ontology, a move away from the purely practical concerns of primitive Buddhism. Such concepts as associated mental functions, functions dissociated from mind, and unmanifested form, seen in Sarvāstivādin *dharma* theory, are related to this development and in many ways approach ontology, of which the Buddha had forbidden discussion. These shifts were factors in the Mahāyānists' attempt to return to orthodoxy in their doctrine that *dharmas* are devoid of self and are therefore empty (*śūnya*).

SARVĀSTIVĀDIN *DHARMA* THEORY

The Sarvāstivādins divided mental objects into four categories: unmanifested form (*avijñapti-rūpa*); associated mental functions (*cittasaṃprayukta-saṃskāra* or *caitasika-dharma*); functions dissociated from mind, elements both nonmaterial and nonmental (*cittaviprayukta-saṃskāra*); and unconditioned *dharmas* (*asaṃskṛta-dharma*).

Unmanifested Form Though categorized as a material *dharma*, unmanifested form actually refers to latent acts, either physical or verbal, originating in the power of habit for good or evil. The power for good arises from the practice of morality (*śīla, sīla*) and the Buddhist precepts (*saṃvara*) and that for evil from their opposites, immorality (*duḥśīla, dussīla*) and disregard of the precepts (*asaṃvara*). Moral rules and the Buddhist precepts are applicable both to the ordinary person and to the sage.

Another kind of unmanifested form is the result of unpremeditated evil, such as the action of a murderer who commits the crime without thinking about its moral implications. Also categorized as unmanifested form are the results of morally neutral actions, such as the practice of an art or the learning of a language.

Associated Mental Functions Associated mental functions are closely related to the mind and are the mental qualities associated with the mind in its central, organizing role. They are categorized under the aggregates of feeling, perception, and mental constituents. As shown in the charts on pages 98–99 and 100–101, in the *Abhidharmakośa-śāstra* the Sarvāstivādins cite forty-six associated mental functions in six categories, while the Yogācārins, in the Treatise on the Establishment of the Doctrine of Consciousness Only, give fifty-one (or fifty-five, depending on whether the five false views are considered a single function or are counted individually), also in six categories.

Functions Dissociated from Mind Functions dissociated from mind are the mental constituents remaining when the associated mental functions are excluded. Literally, *cittaviprayukta-saṃskāra* are mental constituents (*saṃskāra*) not corresponding to the mind and its attributes (*cittaviprayukta*), that is, *dharmas* that are neither material nor mental but affect both the mind and the body. The *Abhidharmakośa-śāstra* lists fourteen functions dissociated from mind, and the Treatise on the Establishment of the Doctrine of Consciousness Only lists twenty-four. Pāli Buddhism has no such classification as functions dissociated from mind and categorizes the items listed in the above works as *dharmas* of form or as *dharmas* of mental attributes. Since primitive Buddhism did not possess this concept at all, it is thought to have entered Buddhism later under the influence of Jainism and other non-Buddhist philosophical systems.

Unconditioned *Dharmas* Unconditioned *dharmas* are those elements whose existence is permanent and immutable. In primitive sūtras, the term unconditioned (*asaṃskṛta, asaṅkhata*) often appears as a synonym for nirvāṇa, with no ontological import. It refers simply to that which lies outside the cycle of birth and death, nirvāṇa being considered beyond transmigration, and thus describes a subjective state of mind rather than an objective fact. The Abhidharma schools, on the other hand, tended to interpret unconditioned as referring to phenomena that neither arise nor decay, contrasting it with conditioned existence. This, however, is a deviation from the original teaching of Buddhism.

The exact composition of unconditioned *dharmas* differs from school to school. Pāli Buddhism, like primitive Buddhism, considers only nirvāṇa to be unconditioned. The Sarvāstivādins posited three unconditioned *dharmas:* extinction of defilements through wisdom (*pratisaṃkhyā-nirodha*), extinction and nonreproduction owing to the lack of a productive cause (*apratisaṃkhyā-nirodha*), and space (*ākāśa*). A further three were added by the Yogācārins: extinction of pleasure and pain (*āniñjya*), extinction of feeling and perception (*saṃjñā-vedayita-nirodha*), and Thusness, or absolute Truth (*tathatā*).

THE NATURE OF TRUTH

In primitive Buddhism, existence (*bhava*) meant only the phenomenal and had this meaning in the five aggregates, the twelve sense fields, and the eighteen elements of existence. The Dharma, or Law, was the criterion of truth; Law was used in this sense in the theory of dependent origination and in the Four Noble Truths. The mechanisms of dependent origination did not depend on the Buddha's existence in the world but on the Dharma, the perpetual, unchanging Truth that is the real aspect of all things. Truth in this sense was denoted by such terms as *dharma-dhātu* and *tathatā*.[2] The Buddha realized the truth that he taught; he did not create it. Truth in this sense, being unchanging and eternal, can perhaps be considered unconditioned.

The primitive Buddhists, however, did not consider truth to be an element of existence, since existence was defined as that which is concrete. In later times, existence was defined as form (*lakṣaṇa*) or phenomenon (*vastu*) but not as noumenon or essence. In philosophical terms, existence was defined as that which has actuality and concrete form; that which has no actuality is not existence. This was a necessary concept, since Buddhism concerned itself with practice, not with theory for theory's sake.

Non-Buddhist religious and philosophical schools made no such distinction, and metaphysical argument was rife. Śākyamuni termed metaphysics morally neutral (*avyākṛta, avyākata*), neither helping nor hindering enlightenment. He forbade metaphysical discussion because existence is beyond description and explanation and because such discussion is of no use to practice. It was unthinkable for Buddhism to define existence as eternal and immutable yet related to metaphysical substance, as the non-Buddhist schools did, since actual existence comprises conditioned *dharmas*, which are subject to change. In the same way, Immanuel Kant refused to define ontological existence, since it is beyond understanding.

Existence as phenomenon is of two kinds: the *dharma* of delusion, belonging to the three realms of nonenlightenment (desire, form, and formlessness), and the *dharma* of enlightenment, belonging to the supramundane realm, beyond all defilements. The *dharma* of enlightenment is nirvāṇa, truth itself. No objective, immutable existence is implied for nirvāṇa, however.

There has been confusion over the concept of truth as the ideal. On the one hand, nirvāṇa is considered to be the ideal state and, therefore, truth. Nirvāṇa as the ideal state can be attained only by one who is perfectly enlightened. It is completely beyond the comprehension of the ordinary person. On the other hand, truth is truth as reason, existing perpetually in the realms of both delusion and enlightenment. Though both concepts have been termed truth, they are completely different. The two concepts were confused in the unconditioned *dharmas* of the Abhidharma schools, and this confusion was exacerbated by the ideas of metaphysical substance issuing from the non-Buddhist schools.

Any discussion of existence presupposes nonexistence, nothingness. The non-Buddhist schools thought the Buddhist concepts of emptiness (*śūnyatā*) and nonself (*nairātmya*) were no more than negations of existence; those schools failed utterly to understand the significance of the concepts in Buddhist thought. Buddhism defines nonexistence metaphorically as "the fur of a turtle" or "the horn of a rabbit."

Pāli Buddhism distinguishes between true *dharmas* (*bhūta*) and transitory *dharmas* (*paññatti;* literally, "derived concept"), defining as true *dharmas* the five aggregates and the twelve sense fields and as transitory *dharmas* the provisional combinations of the true *dharmas* and the *concepts* of the five aggregates and the twelve sense fields. Various classifications of transitory *dharmas* exist.

The whole question of truth and existence is very complicated in Buddhism, and it behooves Buddhist scholars to clarify the way in which the Mahāyāna concepts of *dharma-kāya* (Law-body of a buddha), *buddhagotra* (buddha-nature), and *tathāgata-garbha* (*tathāgata*-embryo) differ from the Brahmanic ideas of *brahman* (ultimate reality) and *ātman* (absolute Self).

The Eighteen Elements of Existence

The eighteen elements of existence (*aṣṭādaśa dhātavaḥ, aṭṭhādasa dhātuyo*) take sensation and perception into account in classifying the six sense organs, the six objects, and the six consciousnesses responsible for cognition. "Element of existence" is a translation of *dhātu* (difference, nature, or origin) that reflects the term's nuances. The first twelve elements are the sense fields. The corresponding six consciousnesses refer to elements of existence as subjects or functions of cognition: visual (*cakṣur-vijñāna-dhātu, cakkhu-viññāṇa-dhātu*), auditory (*śrotra-vijñāna-dhātu, sota-viññāṇa-dhātu*), olfactory (*ghrāṇa-vijñāna-dhātu, ghāna-viññāṇa-dhātu*), gustatory (*jihvā-vijñāna-dhātu, jivhā-viññāṇa-dhātu*), tactile (*kāya-vijñāna-dhātu, kāya-viññāṇa-dhātu*), and mental (*mano-vijñāna-dhātu, mano-viññāṇa-dhātu*).

The relationship of the eighteen elements of existence is explained as follows in the Discourse on the Six Sixes (*Chachakka-sutta*) in the Majjhima-nikāya:

Through the interaction of eye and form, visual consciousness is produced; through the interaction of ear and sound, auditory consciousness is produced; through the interaction of nose and odor, olfactory consciousness is produced; through the interaction of tongue and taste, gustatory consciousness is produced; through the interaction of body and touch, tactile consciousness is produced; and through the interaction of mind and mental objects, mental consciousness is produced.

The Pāli sūtras sometimes add further groups of six elements to the eighteen as extensions of mental activity: the six contacts (*cha-phassā*), the six feelings (*cha-vedanā*), and the six cravings (*cha-taṇhā*). Collectively these and the original eighteen elements of existence are termed the six sixes (*cha-chakka*). An additional extension brings the total number of groups to ten: the six perceptions (*cha-saññā*), the six volitions (*cha-cetanā*), the six reflections (*cha-vitakkā*), and the six investigations (*cha-vicārā*). The purpose of enumerating these supplementary groups is to show that all *dharmas* arise in response to conditions and therefore are impermanent and devoid of self. The eighteen elements of existence are thus the foundation for mental activity.

In the six consciousnesses, consciousness indicates both cognitive action and the subject of cognition. For example, in the statement "Through the interaction of eye and form, visual consciousness is produced," visual consciousness is regarded as a cognitive function. The Discourse on the Six Sixes also says, "Contact is the unity of organ, object, and consciousness," indicating that consciousness is viewed as the subject of cognition—the usual way of considering consciousness.

Mental objects (*dharma-dhātu*) in the eighteen elements of existence are the same as mental objects as one of the twelve sense fields (see the chart on page 118). Especially in China and Japan, there is considerable difference in the interpretation of *dharma-dhātu* from sect to sect. In Japan the Kegon (Flower Garland) sect, for example, posits four *dharma-dhātus,* while the Chinese T'ien-t'ai and Chen-yen (True Word) sects posit ten. These differences cannot be explained simply, since content and concepts differ.

The Relationships Among the Elements of Existence

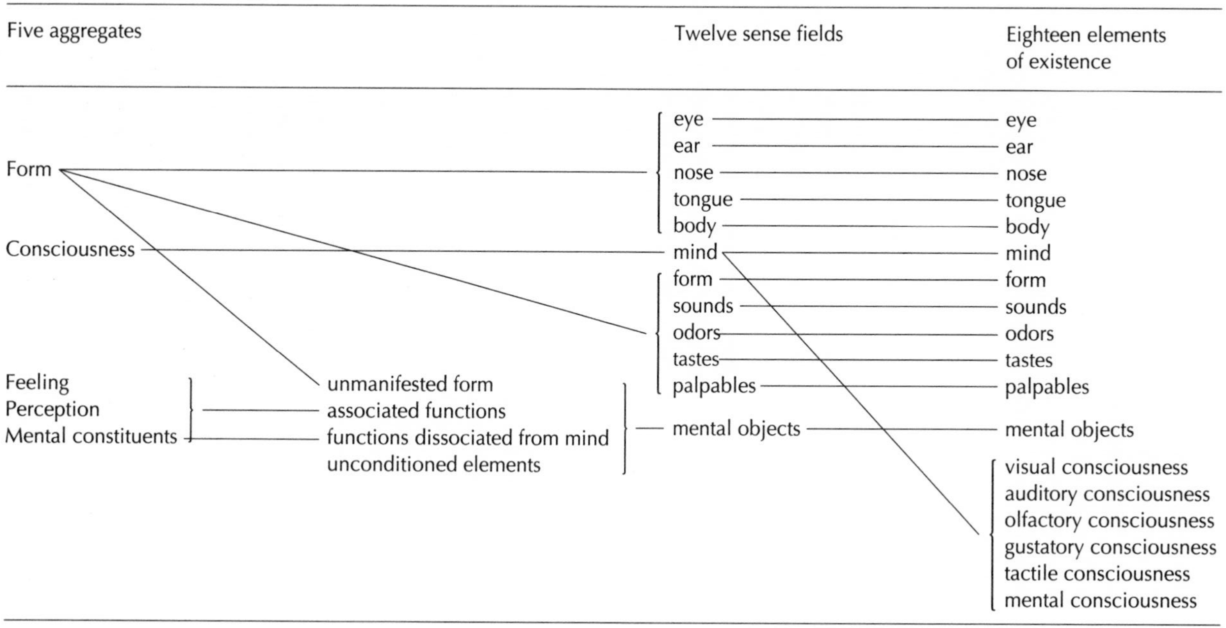

Moreover, the meaning of *dharma* itself is not the same from one sect to another.

The Āgamas give varying lists of six *dhātus,* as distinct from the eighteen elements of existence. The most common classification is the four great elements of matter (earth, water, fire, and air), space (which contains the material world), and consciousness (a general term for mental aspects). Other lists cite pleasure, pain, joy, lamentation, equanimity, and ignorance; and desire, anger, causing injury, lack of desire, lack of anger, and nonviolence. In later times, the first classification—beginning with the four great elements of matter—was called the six great elements. The Japanese Shingon sect in particular interpreted them as being the elements of which sentient beings and the universe are constituted and also developed a theory of dependent origination of the six great elements that holds that all existence evolves from their interaction.

MIND AND THE SIX CONSCIOUSNESSES

If all *dharmas* are subsumed under the twelve sense fields, mind (*manas*) is only the organ, or faculty, of perception (*mano-āyatana*), one of the sense fields. If the eighteen elements of existence are regarded as comprising all *dharmas,* mind spans seven elements of existence (*dhātu*): mind and the six consciousnesses. As one of the twelve sense fields, the perceptive organ embraces all that is mind; as one of the eighteen elements of existence, it is no longer the whole mind, since the six consciousnesses must also be considered.

Mind and the six consciousnesses are not separate. The six consciousnesses refer to the six consciousnesses in the present moment; when their action is completed, they become the six consciousnesses in the past. It is then that they are considered to be mind. Thus the difference between mind and the six consciousnesses is temporal alone, but this theory may have been developed because of the need to distinguish between them.

MIND AND *MANAS* CONSCIOUSNESS

In the period following that of the Abhidharma schools, there was great interest in the nature of mind. Mind was held to be the foundation of the six consciousnesses, which arise from it. As the basis of the six consciousnesses, mind is in the prior moment, instrumental in bringing forth the six consciousnesses in the present moment. In this sense, mind is the immediate condition (uninterrupted continuity) or foundation for inducing the six consciousnesses.

Pāli Buddhism proposed that the mind realm (*mano-dhātu*) lies outside the six consciousnesses. Mind was thought to function as the inducing cause (*āvajjana*) that brings about cognition through sensation (the five senses) and perception (the mental faculty). This inducing cause can be considered to have the same meaning as the foundation for inducing the six consciousnesses.

The Yogācāra school made mind a separate category outside the six consciousnesses, calling it the seventh, or *manas,* consciousness. Here mind is both the basis of the six consciousnesses and the fountainhead of a sense of ego. It possesses of itself defiled mental attributes: the placing of the self at the center of all things (*ātma-māna*), attachment to self, the illusion that there is a real self, and the belief that the self is permanent. Until release from adherence to the concept of self is gained and enlightenment attained, the *manas* consciousness is thought to continue, constantly spewing out thoughts of self. With enlightenment it becomes *samatā-jñāna,* the wisdom of regarding all things equally and universally, without distinction between self and other.

4. The Seals of the Law

The Seals of the Law (*dharma-mudrā* or *dharma-uddāna* in Sanskrit) are points of doctrine considered characteristic of Buddhism. In China, sūtras were judged to be the true teaching of the Buddha to the extent that they conformed with these tenets. Any discrepancy caused a sūtra to be rejected as spurious.

Four or three statements are recognized as the Four or Three Seals of the Law: all things (*dharma*) are impermanent; all things are devoid of self; all things are characterized by suffering; and nirvāṇa is tranquil. When the Three Seals of the Law are used, the statement that all things are characterized by suffering is omitted.

The Four Seals of the Law are recorded in a variety of sūtras. For example, the following formula is found in the Chinese Āgamas, in fascicle eighteen of the Ekottara-āgama:

> Whatever is phenomenal is impermanent;
> Whatever is phenomenal is suffering;
> Whatever is phenomenal is devoid of self;
> Nirvāṇa is eternally tranquil.

Similar expressions citing the same four points appear in both the Sanskrit originals and Chinese translations of the Treatise on the Stages of Yoga Practice and the Treatise on the Adornment of Mahāyāna Sūtras. It is from such passages that the traditional sequence of the Four Seals of the Law was derived.

Primitive sūtras did not mention the Four or Three Seals of the

Law as such, but the impermanence, suffering, and nonself of such *dharmas* as the five aggregates were considered to be aspects of nonself and were defined as the three aspects of conditioned *dharmas.* Pāli Buddhism preserved this teaching. Since the deep calm of nirvāṇa is attained through release from attachment to conditioned *dharmas,* together these four points can be considered the equivalent of the Four Seals of the Law.

Impermanence and nirvāṇa are mentioned in one of the most famous verses in Buddhism, the "verse of impermanence," which survives in both Indic originals and Chinese translations:

> All phenomena are truly impermanent,
> Subject to the *dharmas* of arising and decay;
> What has arisen ends in destruction.
> Their cessation is ease.

The terse Chinese rendering was elaborated in Japan in a well-known poem containing the entire Japanese syllabary:

> Colors are fragrant, but they fade away.
> In this world of ours, no one lasts forever.
> Cross the deep mountains of conditioned things today.
> There will be no more shallow dreaming,
> no more intoxication.

The "verse of impermanence" appears in the Sūtra of the Great Decease (*Mahā-parinibbāna-suttanta*) in the Dīgha-nikāya as the words spoken in sorrow by the deity Indra on the death of the Buddha. In the Mahāyāna Sūtra of the Great Decease (*Mahā-parinirvāṇa-sūtra*), however, the verse figures in the tale of the young ascetic of the Himalayas, the story of a former life of the Buddha.

In an earlier life, Śākyamuni was living in the Himalayas as a Brahman ascetic, and since no buddha then existed in the world, he was unable to seek out the Law. Indra appeared as a fearsome *rākṣasa,* a man-eating demon, to test the ascetic's will to pursue the Law even at the cost of his life. In this guise he recited the first half of the verse to the young man. Looking around, the ascetic saw only the horrifying demon but overcame his fear to ask whether it had indeed been the demon who had recited the superb lines. "It has been to hear such a teaching as this that I have been practicing austerities," he said. "If you know the remainder of the verse, please tell me. I will be your disciple as long as I live."

In reply, the *rākṣasa* stated that he depended on the warm flesh and blood of human beings for sustenance and that since he had not eaten for a long time he was growing desperate. Thereupon the young man offered himself as food, begging only that he be allowed to hear the second half of the verse before he died. The *rākṣasa* then chanted the remaining portion, to the ascetic's great joy. Wishing to leave the teaching for others, the young man inscribed the verse on the footpath before him and on stones, cliffs, and trees around him. This done, he climbed to the top of a tree and prepared to throw himself down to become the *rākṣasa*'s meal.

The *rākṣasa* then resumed his true form, as Indra, and caught the ascetic in midair. He knelt before the young man, praising him as a true bodhisattva, one willing to give up his life for the Law. Remorseful for having tested the ascetic in such a way, Indra prophesied the ascetic's future buddhahood and his role in bringing about the release of the people of the world.

The Mahāyāna Sūtra of the Great Decease thus presents the "verse of impermanence" as representing the Buddha's teachings. In China, however, Mahāyānists came to regard the idea of the Four or Three Seals of the Law as a Hīnayāna teaching. As the essence of Buddhism, they emphasized instead the "real aspect of all things," that is, the state of *tathatā*. The phrase "real aspect of all things" points out the real state of the elements of existence and by extension declares that the eternal truth is manifested in phenomena. Although this concept is found in the Perfection of Wisdom sūtras, it is the Lotus Sūtra, in particular the definitive Chinese translation by Kumārajīva (344–413), that develops the idea of the real aspect of all things. In Kumārajīva's translation, this is expressed in terms of the ten suchnesses: such an appearance, nature, substance, power, function, cause, condition, effect, retribution, and ultimate identity of beginning and end.[1] Since this list does not appear in the Sanskrit original, it is thought to have been added by Kumārajīva to clarify the meaning of the real aspect of all things by examining the nature of all *dharmas* from ten perspectives for the same reason that primitive Buddhism examined all *dharmas* in terms of impermanence, suffering, and nonself.

The Chinese T'ien-t'ai sect united the concept of the ten suchnesses with that of the ten realms of existence[2] to establish its basic teaching that all phenomena are contained in a moment of thought (literally, "three thousand realms in one thought").[3] Ultimately, from the point of view of truth itself, there is no contradiction between the Four or Three Seals of the Law and the real aspect of all things in terms of the ten suchnesses. Both teachings reflect basic Buddhist thought.

IMPERMANENCE

Impermanence is defined in Sanskrit as *anityā sarvasaṃskārāḥ* and in Pāli as *sabbe saṅkhārā aniccā,* meaning literally "all phenomena [*saṃskāra, saṅkhāra*] are without permanence." In this instance the term *saṃskāra* is used in its broadest sense to mean all phenomenal *dharmas,* subject to arising, change, and extinction, and has the same meaning as "conditioned" (*saṃskṛta*).

Nothing phenomenal ever comes to a complete standstill, never again to undergo change; therefore, nothing can be considered permanent. Even the atom, once thought to be the smallest particle of matter, fixed and permanent, is now known to be made up of electrons, neutrons, and other minute particles, all of which are in constant flux. Matter, being composed of atoms, thus undergoes change continually. Here modern scientific discoveries concur with the Buddhist theory of impermanence. Since impermanence is a part of our daily experience and is self-evident, it became the first of the Seals of the Law.

Buddhism teaches that impermanence is the source of suffering and the root of nonself. Although traditionally this teaching has implied a pessimistic outlook—stressing negative effects of impermanence, such as old age, sickness, and death—it also encompasses positive change. Sadness is the result of impermanence, but so is happiness, for impermanence means that suffering and pain can give way to joy. Thus it is the basic truth of impermanence that enables religion to teach the way to progress from imperfection to perfection.

The contemplation of impermanence is a meditation practice used in Buddhism with a threefold aim. First, the experience of impermanence, as through the death of a loved one, can arouse the mind to seek religion. Thus the mind opened to religion is defined as one that trembles with fear at the thought of impermanence. When everything is going well, people rarely devote time to self-reflection. It is when they experience disappointment that they engage in self-reflection, and through self-reflection they can begin to see their own faults and those of society. Thus contemplation of impermanence is said to kindle the religious mind.

Second, it is through the contemplation of impermanence that attachment and pride can be extinguished. Since everything is impermanent, we can lose our health, wealth, position, and reputation. Understanding of the true nature of impermanence helps us eliminate attachment to self and possessions and pride in them and instills humility and consideration.

A third effect of the contemplation of impermanence is that the importance of each moment is understood, with the result that each is lived fully. Time passes away instant by instant and cannot be recovered. Our present life is the sum of the good and bad effects of the past, and good is the key to further good. We make the best of life by giving our utmost attention to the actions of each moment. Because everything is impermanent, it is all the more important to act with the greatest effectiveness in the present. In Zen Buddhism this is called "one encounter, once in a lifetime." As recorded in the Pāli Sūtra of the Great Decease, Śākyamuni stressed this in his final instructions to his disciples as he lay dying: "All phenomena are impermanent and decay; work toward your final goal with diligence."

NONSELF

"All *dharmas* are devoid of self" (*anātmanaḥ sarvadharmāḥ, sabbe dhammā anattā*) means that nothing in the world exhibits any form of unchanging reality. Here *dharmas* are the elements of existence. They could be considered merely "things," except that the concept of "thing" in primitive Buddhism was limited to that which is intrinsically devoid of self (*nissatta-nijjīvata*). It would be more accurate to consider "all *dharmas*" as having the same meaning as *saṃskāra,* that is, as including all phenomenal existence.

Self, here, is *ātman,* or absolute Self: that unchanging substance which is not subject to arising, change, and extinction. Buddhism holds that there is no way of knowing unchanging substance, since it is beyond experience and beyond comprehension and proof. Thus it is classified as *avyākṛta,* or morally neutral, and forbidden as a topic of discussion. Buddhism stresses that all phenomena of the world are not substantial, that they are characterized by nonself rather than self.

While the idea of impermanence is readily understandable and widely held, the doctrine of nonself is unique to Buddhism. In Śākyamuni's time all the other philosophical schools recognized some form of unchanging substance, called *ātman* in terms of the individual reality and *brahman* in terms of the cosmic reality. Buddhism labels these concepts morally neutral, since they are susceptible of neither comprehension nor proof. Having no connection with the world of phenomena, they have no bearing on religious practice or release from the cycle of birth and death. It is because Buddhism concerns itself with the world of phenomena, not *ātman,* that the teaching "all *dharmas* are devoid of self" is unique. The Buddhist attitude toward ontological questions is clear in the Lesser Discourse to Mālunkyaputta (*Cūḷa-Māluṅkya-sutta*) in the Majjhima-nikāya.

Māluṅkyaputta, a young philosopher, had studied Brahmanic doctrines before becoming a disciple of the Buddha. He was greatly concerned with the ontological questions that were central to the non-Buddhist sects and schools of his time and asked Śākyamuni to elucidate his position on these questions. Saying that he did not feel he could begin practicing the Buddha's teaching before receiving satisfactory answers, he addressed four questions to the Buddha: Is the world eternal or not, is the world finite or not, are body and spirit identical or separate, and does the *tathāgata,* the person who transcends birth and death, exist after death or not?

In answer, Śākyamuni related the parable of the poisoned arrow. If struck with a poisoned arrow, he asked, does a person demand to know the name of the archer, the archer's clan and caste, or the type of bow and arrow used before agreeing to accept treatment for the wound? That person would die before the arrow could be removed and the poison neutralized. In the same way, a person who refuses to undertake religious practice to eliminate the defilements and attain release until such ontological questions have been elucidated would die and be subjected again to the suffering of transmigration, for such questions are inherently unanswerable. Māluṅkyaputta realized his error and committed himself to religious practice.

The Buddha spoke here of the fundamentals of religion and practice. The Law is profited by that which embodies truth, and practice is profited by that which helps practitioners attain the Buddhist ideal. Buddhist teaching therefore must both conform to truth and the true meaning and be useful for the attainment of enlightenment. Anything that is not useful for the attainment of enlightenment should be discarded, even if it conforms to truth and the true meaning. Anything that represents heresy or superstition should be rejected, even if it aids religious belief. Anything that contains neither truth nor the true meaning is, of course, not accepted.

NONSELF, EMPTINESS, AND NONBEING

Nairātmya (or *anātman*) has been translated into Chinese as *wu-wo* (no ego) and *fei-wo* (without ego). Mahāyāna Buddhism terms this concept *śūnya* (empty) or *śūnyatā* (emptiness). Ch'an (Zen) Buddhism uses the term *wu,* "nonbeing," in the same sense. As employed in Buddhism, emptiness and nonbeing do not mean simply nothingness or nihilism; rather, these terms indicate that all *dharmas,* as phenomena, are devoid of self, with no ontological connotation.

While Buddhism, unlike the non-Buddhist schools of philosophy, forbade discussion of any metaphysical self, it did not oppose mention of self in the ordinary sense of the word or of the perfected self that is the Buddhist ideal, and these two types of self are mentioned in primitive sūtras. Although the term that Buddhism used to refer to both the ordinary and the perfected self was used in an ontological sense by non-Buddhist schools, there was an important difference in its use in Buddhism. For example, the "I" of the usual opening line of sūtras, "Thus have I heard," is the ordinary self, which is also the subject of verse 160 of the *Dhammapada:*

> Self is the lord of self: for who else could the lord be? By a fully controlled self one obtains a lord, who is hard to gain.

Likewise, the self mentioned by the Buddha in his last instructions to his disciples before he died is the personal, not the eternal, self:

> Be an island [support] to yourself [*atta-dīpa*], be a refuge to yourself [*atta-saraṇa*], and take refuge in no other. Make the Dharma your island [*dhamma-dīpa*], the Dharma your refuge [*dhamma-saraṇa*], and no other.

These passages demonstrate that Buddhism does have the concept of an ordinary self, the self that is the subject of personality, although it denies self as a metaphysical substance.

When we come to the concept of soul, however, it is debatable whether Buddhism speaks of a soul. Buddhism certainly does not recognize the soul as an unchanging substance, but does allow for it as the subject of personality that maintains karma. This soul exists as the subject of transmigration throughout the past, the present, and the future but is nevertheless a conditioned *dharma,* subject to arising, change, and extinction in accordance with karma and experience. The Yogācārins postulated the *ālaya-vijñāna,* or storehouse consciousness, to fulfill this function.

Since Buddhism does not recognize a metaphysical self or soul, the concepts of nonself and emptiness refer to the state or condition of phenomena, not to the absence of substance. Theoretically, nonself and emptiness indicate "no self-nature" (*niḥsvabhāva*), meaning that there is nothing that is of itself unchanging, no metaphysical self. There is no element that is permanent, that has a fixed form subject to neither arising nor extinction. Something that is fixed exists independently, relying on no other thing. For humans and their society, nothing is absolute, existing in isolation, totally independent of all else. All things are relative and interrelated both in space and in time. Moreover, society does not proceed along a fixed course but develops in various ways in response to different conditions.

Practically, the concepts of nonself and emptiness appear in religious practice as the ideals of nonattachment (*aprāpti*) and nonhindrance (*anāvaraṇa*). A mind dwelling in nonattachment sees that nothing, neither ourselves nor our possessions, is fixed and permanent and that we cannot cling to any hope that anything in this conditioned existence is stable or unchanging. The attainment of nonhindrance comes with the perfection of nonattachment, so that no obstacles impede us and our minds are free and unhindered. In this state we are in harmony with the Law. This is the state of mind referred to in Confucius' maxim "By acting according to the dictates of the mind, the pattern is not violated." In Buddhism perfection of the personality is the ideal. Consequently, all facets of daily life must attain unhindered freedom. The Buddha's ability to act without hindrance in the three realms of desire, form, and formlessness demonstrates this state.

In the state of nonself or emptiness, there can be no self-centered greed, unreasonable fear of others, hate, flattery, boasting, insult, anger, jealousy, or envy. A person who has realized the nature of nonself cannot bring harm to others, since action is taken only after correctly considering both its immediate and its wider-ranging effects. This is expressed as compassion and pity for all beings. There is no conflict between self and others. As a result, the state of nonself has been defined as "great self," the state of mind of an enlightened person.

Theoretically, the understanding of nonself lets us see human life and society correctly, exactly as they are. Practically, perfected and fulfilled human life is gained from the attainment of nonself. The theoretical understanding of nonself and emptiness is the foundation of the attainment of nonself and emptiness, which is the ultimate goal of Buddhism. The Heart Sūtra's statement that the five aggregates are empty, that form is emptiness and emptiness form, should be understood in terms of both the theoretical and the practical aspects of nonself and emptiness.

Mahāyāna clarified the concept of nonself and emptiness by teaching two kinds of nonself and of emptiness: the nonself of sentient beings (*pudgala-nairātmya*) and the emptiness of the self, and the nonself of the *dharmas* (*dharma-nairātmya*) and the emptiness of the *dharmas*. The first points out that there is no permanent, unchanging being (*ātman*), and the second that phenomenal existence is subject to arising and extinction in which there are no substantial *dharmas*, such as the seventy-five *dharmas* in the five categories and the five aggregates. This clarification was devised to counter what Mahāyānists considered Sarvāstivādin heterodoxy in accepting the eternal existence of the *dharmas* and denying the nonself of sentient beings. The Mahāyānists did not originate this idea, however. Primitive Buddhism, though not actually positing the nonself of sentient beings, taught that all *dharmas* (such as the five aggregates, the twelve sense fields, and the eighteen elements of existence) are devoid of self, in effect affirming the two kinds of nonself and of emptiness.

Suffering

All things are characterized by suffering (*duḥkhāḥ sarvasaṃskārāḥ, sabbe saṅkhārā dukkhā*). Primitive sūtras refer to this, saying that phenomenal *dharmas* entail suffering because they are impermanent.

The concept of suffering is not as easy to grasp as the concepts of impermanence and nonself, which are more or less self-evident. Our experience tells us that while suffering does occur, there is also pleasure and sometimes neither suffering nor pleasure. Because they involve emotions, suffering and pleasure are to an extent individual and subjective, so that the same stimulus may be interpreted differently, according to the person or the occasion. What, then, is the meaning of the proposition "All things are characterized by suffering is objective truth"?

Three types of suffering were originally postulated. The first is ordinary physical suffering (*duḥkha-duḥkhatā, dukkha-dukkhatā*), such as that caused by injury, heat, or cold. This kind of suffering is objective, in that it is felt by any being with a nervous system. It is not permanent, however, and thus is not the type of suffering referred to in the statement that all things are characterized by suffering. The second type is mental suffering felt because of destruction or loss (*vipariṇāma-duḥkhatā, vipariṇāma-dukkhatā*). It is mental suffering arising from poverty, aging, disappointment, and discouragement—that is, from the deterioration or decay of things. Where the suffering of adversity exists, however, there is still the possibility of the pleasure of eventual prosperity, since decay does not exist without renewal and development. Purely mental suffering, too, does not fit the definition of phenomenological suffering.

It is to the third type that we must look to understand the import of the proposition. This is phenomenological suffering, the suffering due to conditioned states (*saṃskāra-duḥkhatā, saṅkhāra-dukkhatā*). Indian thought in general and Buddhist thought in particular hold that it is the life of delusion itself, the cycle of birth and death in the three realms of existence (desire, form, and formlessness) and the six realms of existence, that is in effect suffering. True ease, the absence of suffering, can be found only in the state of nirvāṇa, in which there is release from birth and death and from delusion.

For the ordinary deluded person all phenomena are equated with suffering, but for the enlightened sage phenomena cannot entail suffering. The nature of suffering, elaborated in the Four Noble Truths, is discussed more fully in chapter 6.

Buddhism places particular emphasis on the fact of suffering. It teaches that all things are characterized by suffering. The truth of suffering is the first of the Four Noble Truths, while the final link of the Twelve-linked Chain of Dependent Origination is old age and death, a metaphor for all suffering. All this has led many Western scholars to condemn Buddhism for what they perceive as renunciation of the world. In doing so, however, they overlook the fact that the Buddhist ideal is the state of nirvāṇa.

Religion originates in the urge to gain release from the suffering of this life and to achieve the ideal state of tranquillity. Thus, the starting point of religion is correct perception of the imperfection of this world. The starting point of Buddhism is suffering, impermanence, impurity, and folly, while that of Christianity, for example, is a sense of sin.

If people were satisfied with their lives and felt no discontent or suffering, there would be no search for the ideal, and probably no religion. People who have a strong sense of the ideal feel that the present is imperfect, defiled, and full of suffering. The awakening of religious awareness allows such people to gain release from the imperfect present and move toward the ideal by means of religious practice. Thus the teaching that all things are characterized by suffering is the starting point of Buddhism and the evocation of Buddhism's religious nature.

NIRVĀṆA

Feeling suffering means being conscious of an ideal free of suffering. Buddhism advocates as the ultimate ideal the teaching that nirvāṇa is tranquil (*śāntam nirvāṇam, santaṃ nibbānaṃ*). The word nirvāṇa means "to blow out" or "the condition of being blown out" (*nir-vā-ana*). In other words, nirvāṇa is the state in which the fire of the defilements has been extinguished.

Brahmanism names this state *amṛta* (sweet dew or ambrosia), the immortal. Primitive Buddhist sūtras define nirvāṇa as "the extinction of greed, the extinction of anger, the extinction of ignorance." The word tranquil (*śāntam, santaṃ*) is added when nirvāṇa is being regarded specifically as the ideal state of nonsuffering. Pāli Buddhism interprets nirvāṇa as "no forest" (*nir-vana*), indicating that the jungle of the defilements does not exist there.

Western scholars have long debated the meaning of nirvāṇa. One theory takes it to mean death, in the sense of the historical Buddha's physical death. Thus the Sūtra of the Great Decease, concerning the Buddha's death, has also been called the Nirvāṇa Sūtra. Moreover, graphic depictions of the Buddha's death are known as nirvāṇa statues, nirvāṇa drawings, and so forth, and the annual ceremony commemorating the Buddha's death is called the nirvāṇa ceremony. Nirvāṇa as used in all these examples is not an aspect of the concept discussed here but a reference to the death of an enlightened being, a usage adopted in later times.

Abhidharma Buddhism divided nirvāṇa into two types, with and without residue. Nirvāṇa with residue (*sopadhiśeṣa-nirvāṇa, saupādisesa-nibbāna*) is the state in which the defilements have been extinguished and release from future rebirth has been gained but the physical body remains as a result of past karma affecting the present. Thus this state cannot be called complete nirvāṇa. Nirvāṇa without residue (*nirupadhiśeṣa-nirvāṇa, anupādisesa-nibbāna*) is that in which nothing physical remains. All defilements have been overcome, and the physical body has been destroyed. This is complete nirvāṇa, the state into which the Buddha entered on his death (*parinirvāṇa, parinibbāna,* or perfect tranquillity). The theory of two kinds of nirvāṇa entered Buddhism under the influence of Jainism and other non-Buddhist schools, and incorporates a certain amount of ontological thought. No such division can be found in original Buddhism.

Mahāyāna Buddhism later added two further categories to the Abhidharma classification: nirvāṇa innately as pure as self-nature (*prakṛti-pariśuddha-nirvāṇa*) and nirvāṇa without fixed abode (*apratiṣṭhita-nirvāṇa*). Self-nature here refers to the buddha-nature (*buddhagotra*), the underlying essence, or mind, originally pure and characterized by permanence, ease, ideal self, and purity. Nirvāṇa without fixed abode refers to the true nirvāṇa, in which the mind is detached and nonclinging, dwelling within neither *saṃsāra* (birth and death) nor nirvāṇa. It is the state of mind in which a person acts voluntarily, through compassion, to bring all sentient beings to enlightenment, neither longing for nirvāṇa nor rejecting the cycle of birth and death. As explained in the *She-ta-ch'eng-lun-shih-ch'in-shih* (the Chinese translation of Vasubandhu's commentary on Asaṅga's Comprehensive Treatise on Mahāyāna Buddhism), "Through great wisdom, there is no abiding in birth and death; through great compassion, there is no abiding in nirvāṇa." This is the nature of the Buddha's nirvāṇa. It is the ideal nirvāṇa.

Primitive sūtras contain many synonyms for nirvāṇa, indicating what nirvāṇa meant in primitive Buddhism. The most common are the unconditioned, the final limit, nondelusion, truth, the other shore, subtle, extremely hard to see, ageless, firm and stable, indestructible, incomparable, inexpressible, tranquil, ambrosial, excellent, peaceful, restful, all craving extinct, rare, marvelous, without affliction, the state of no calamity, no anger or harm, free from desire, pure, release, nonabiding, island, lamp, shelter, place of protection, refuge, and reaching the other shore.

The word nirvāṇa was also used by the non-Buddhist schools. For example, the Jains used the term *nivvāṇa,* and *nirvāṇa* also appears in the great Indian epic the *Mahābhārata,* perhaps under the influence of Buddhism. Brahmanism preferred the term *amṛta* (ambrosial) to indicate the state of enlightenment beyond the cycle of birth and death, and this is one of the Buddhist synonyms for nirvāṇa. While many Indian religions and philosophies preached nirvāṇa as the ideal of human life, the connotations and conditions of this state varied from group to group.

Traditionally the Four Seals of the Law have been listed in the order impermanence, suffering, nonself, and nirvāṇa. In all likelihood this order derived from the importance primitive sūtras attach to a correct understanding of the first three items in order to attain release and nirvāṇa. Considering the logical construction of the Four Seals of the Law and their connection with the doctrines of dependent origination and the Four Noble Truths, however, I have amended the traditional order in my discussion here, using instead the sequence impermanence, nonself, suffering, and nirvāṇa. I have done this because the Four Seals of the Law are the foundation of the doctrine of dependent origination, and the amended sequence makes their close relationship easier to see. This relationship is discussed in the following chapter.

5. Dependent Origination

The doctrine of dependent origination (*pratītya-samutpāda, paṭicca-samuppāda*) is a synthesis of the Four Seals of the Law. This doctrine teaches that phenomena occur through conditions; all that comes into being is dependent on something else. A synonym for dependent origination is *idampratyayatā* (*idappaccayatā*), or "having its foundation in this." In short, dependent origination, or causality, refers to the interdependent relationships among phenomena.

Phenomena are impermanent, constantly undergoing change. This change is not arbitrary; given the requisite conditions, each cause produces an inevitable effect. This principle of change, called dependent origination, does not depend on the appearance or nonappearance of buddhas in the world,[1] for the interdependence of existence is a law itself.

Derived from the Four Seals of the Law, dependent origination is both a basic doctrine of Buddhism and the core of Buddhist truth. Indeed, it is the Law itself. Primitive sūtras point out that "one who sees dependent origination sees the Law; one who sees the Law sees dependent origination"[2] and that "one who sees dependent origination sees the Law, and one who sees the Law sees me [the Buddha]."[3]

The basic formula of dependent origination is "When this exists, that exists; with the arising of this, that arises. When this does not exist, that does not exist; with the cessation of this, that ceases."[4] The Dharma Eye (initial enlightenment) is also described in terms of causality: "The *dharmas* of origin are also those of extinction."[5] Phenomenal *dharmas*, which occur by means of conditions, are also capable of extinction when those conditions are eliminated.

All Buddhism, regardless of period, place, or school, considers dependent origination to be its central doctrine. Thus if dependent origination is fully understood, Buddhism itself will be understood. Dependent origination articulates Buddhism's unique views and distinguishes Buddhism from other religions and philosophies.

Before the introduction of Western Buddhology in the late nineteenth century, there were two principal streams of thought in Chinese and Japanese Buddhism: the theory of dependent origination and the theory of "real aspect." Chinese and Japanese Buddhism held that the theory of dependent origination explains the temporal relationships among phenomena and that the theory of "real aspect" clarifies their spatial relationships. Originally, however, the doctrine of dependent origination encompassed the totality of the relationships among phenomena, describing all things in both time and space and incorporating theoretical, logical relationships as well as factual relationships. Seen in this light, all Buddhist doctrine can be considered to be contained in the doctrine of dependent origination.

Theories of dependent origination include the following: the Sarvāstivādin theory that all phenomena arise by means of sentient beings' karma; the Yogācārin theory of dependent origination via the storehouse consciousness (*ālaya-vijñāna*); the theory in the Treatise on the Awakening of Faith in the Mahāyāna that all phenomena arise from the *tathāgata*-embryo through the action of dependent origination; the theory of the Chinese Hua-yen (Flower Garland) sect that the phenomenal world is produced by the endless mutual influence of all things;[6] and the Japanese Shingon-sect theory of dependent origination of the six great elements, which maintains that all existence evolves from their interaction.[7]

The theory of "real aspect" contrasts with the theory of the "real aspect of all things" held by the Chinese T'ien-t'ai and San-lun (Three Treatises) sects.[8] This theory, which emphasizes simultaneous, causal relationships rather than the sequential, temporal relationships of the doctrine of dependent origination, was preserved by the Japanese Zen and Pure Land sects.

The Hua-yen and Shingon theories of dependent origination deal not only with the temporal relationships among phenomena but also with their spatial and logical relationships. That the theory of real aspect also deals with temporal relations is seen in the teaching of the ten suchnesses (for instance, in cause, condition, effect, and retribution). Thus it is unreasonable to distinguish sharply between the two theories. Instead, both should be considered to be subsumed in the doctrine of dependent origination.

General and Religious Dependent Origination

The doctrine of dependent origination examines the workings of the universe and human existence in terms of spatial, temporal, and logical relationships. Buddhism, however, is not a philosophy or a science but a religion that concerns itself with the concrete resolution of the problems of human life. Thus it does not merely undertake an objective examination of the workings of human existence and the universe on a phenomenal level, but in addition analyzes them in terms of dependent origination in order to eliminate suffering.

Dependent origination encompasses two types of causality: general or physical (or external) and religious or mental (or internal). It is religious causality that is important to Buddhism. General causality, however, is taught as a foundation for religious causality and as a figurative explanation of it. The formulaic expression of dependent origination that begins "When this exists, that exists" teaches general causality.

Since human beings and their societies undergo constant change according to the law of causality, phenomena must be examined from a variety of aspects to be understood. Thus modern scholarship requires an interdisciplinary approach to the study of the law governing causal relationships among phenomena, taking into account the interplay of logic, psychology, the life sciences, the physical sciences, politics, economics, sociology, religion, and ethics. Buddhism teaches the doctrine of dependent origination not to clarify phenomenological relationships in the objective world but to elucidate the workings of religious and ethical phenomena (such as suffering, pleasure, delusion, and enlightenment) in society and people's lives. Yet precisely because societal phenomena and people's lives are so closely intertwined both temporally and spatially, it is difficult to discern the relationships among them. For the individual, the present is the sum total of all experience. Since birth he or she has existed in a particular environment, has been educated and socialized in a specific way, and has come into contact with a variety of people. These experiences are never erased but remain with the individual. Depending on the nature of these experiences, the personality changes for better or worse. Thus the intellect, the character, and the essence of the personality are the sum of all experiences since the individual's birth.

Just as causal relationships can be seen within the individual, so we can observe them between the individual and the environment. We exist in relationship to our immediate environment, receiving from and exerting on our surroundings both good and bad influences. We all exist and act within the orbits of family, school, society, regional groups, and nation and influence them, as we are influenced by them, for better or worse. These interdependent relationships are the causal connections that make for an organic, interactive relationship between the individual and his or her surroundings.

This is equally true of economic relationships. We depend on others for the basic necessities of food, clothing, and shelter. Through the processes of production, transportation, manufacturing, and commerce, a loaf of bread or a handkerchief passes through many hands before entering our possession. If people of the world did not work together, the economic system could not survive. At the same time, it is because we live and consume that production and commerce come about. Financial and communications institutions and all other social institutions are directly or indirectly related. Thus, Buddhism teaches, we are all mutually obligated and owe gratitude to society for sustaining us.

All the cultural riches of modern society—language, literature, philosophy, the arts, science, technology—have been handed down by the people of the past and further developed by the people of our own time. Through mass communications and education these riches are passed on to all. Without the information media and without language or script modern civilization would collapse. We are connected with world culture and, directly or indirectly, with all of human history.

Thus our present existence is made up not only of the sum total of our own past experiences—arising from character, ethics, politics, economics, culture, and the arts—but also of our close connections, both spatial and temporal, with the world around us. Our present could not exist without our past, or the environment in which we live, or the whole of history. In one instant of our present, then, is contained the entire past of both ourselves and our surroundings. Our present existence is an important factor in determining our future and has a crucial influence on our surroundings and their future. Buddhism expresses this network of interrelationships in the phrase "one is all, all is one." As individuals we act in the totality of the world, just as the whole world is closely connected with each of us as an individual. Both actively and passively, human and physical phenomena are intimately related, like the warp and weft of cloth. Hua-yen philosophy calls this relationship interdependent origination, the endless mutual influence of all things.

As we have seen, causality can have both general and religious import. The Four Seals of the Law apply to both types of causality, while the Twelve-linked Chain of Dependent Origination and the Four Noble Truths deal with religious causality. Religious causality can have a positive or a negative form: the positive is the state of enlightenment in nirvāṇa, and its conditions lead to nirvāṇa and release from the cycle of birth and death; the negative is the state of delusion and *saṃsāric* existence, whose conditions lead to transmigration.

THE RELATIONSHIP AMONG MAJOR DOCTRINES

The chart on page 141 demonstrates the relationship of general and religious causality to the components of causality (which include the Twelve-linked Chain of Dependent Origination), the Four Seals of the Law, and the Four Noble Truths. Of the Four Seals of the Law, "all things are impermanent" is concerned with temporal, sequential relationships. Although "all things are devoid of self" includes temporal relationships, it also involves the spatial, simultaneous connections and the theoretical, logical relationships not included in impermanence. In terms of general causality, when the simplified definition of causality is linked to impermanence and nonself, arising and cessation indicate temporal relationships, while existence and nonexistence indicate spatial and logical relationships.

"All things are characterized by suffering," being a state of delusion and transmigration, is a negative value, while "nirvāṇa is tranquil," the state of enlightenment, is a positive one. In its negative aspect, citing arising, the Twelve-linked Chain of Dependent Origination indicates the conditions leading to transmigration; and in its positive aspect, citing cessation, it shows the conditions leading to nirvāṇa. In the same way, the Noble Truths of suffering and its cause belong to the causal relationships of the world of delusion, leading to transmigration, whereas the Noble Truths of the cessation of suffering and the way to achieve this belong to the causal relationships of the world of enlightenment. Thus it is clear that the Four Noble Truths also teach the conditions that lead to both transmigration and nirvāṇa. In terms of religious causality, delusion and enlightenment are related to suffering and nirvāṇa, respectively, in the Four Seals of the Law.

THE YOGĀCĀRIN THREE-NATURES THEORY

The Yogācārin consciousness-only theory postulates three natures, or kinds, of existence: illusory, discriminating nature (*parikalpita-svabhāva*); dependent nature (*paratantra-svabhāva*); and fully accomplished, or true, nature (*pariniṣpanna-svabhāva*). There are many interpretations of what these actually signify.[9] In the interpretation based on the Flower Garland Sūtra—which holds

Dependent Origination

Type of causality	Components of causality	The Four Seals of the Law	The Four Noble Truths
General (physical)	(simplified definition) (*temporal*) With the arising of this, that arises; with the cessation of this, that ceases.	All things are impermanent.	
	(*spatial and theoretical*) When this exists, that exists; when this does not exist, that does not exist.	All things are devoid of self.	
Religious (mental)	(Twelve-linked Chain of Dependent Origination) (*conditions leading to rebirth*) From ignorance, actions arise; from actions, consciousness arises; from consciousness, name and form arise; from name and form, the six sense organs arise; from the six sense organs, contact arises; from contact, feeling arises; from feeling, craving arises; from craving, grasping arises; from grasping, becoming arises; from becoming, birth arises; from birth, old age and death and all suffering arise.	All things are characterized by suffering.	The existence of suffering The cause of suffering
	(*conditions leading to nirvāṇa*) On the cessation of ignorance, actions cease; on the cessation of actions, consciousness ceases; on the cessation of consciousness, name and form cease; on the cessation of name and form, the six sense organs cease; on the cessation of the six sense organs, contact ceases; on the cessation of contact, feeling ceases; on the cessation of feeling, craving ceases; on the cessation of craving, grasping ceases; on the cessation of grasping, becoming ceases; on the cessation of becoming, birth ceases; on the cessation of birth, old age and death and all suffering cease.	Nirvāṇa is tranquil.	The extinction of suffering The Way to the extinction of suffering

that the mind, the Buddha, and sentient beings are not different—the mind can be seen as dependent nature (which is beyond discriminating between pure and defiled); the Buddha, true nature (the positive value of the world of enlightenment); and sentient beings, discriminating nature (the negative value of the world of delusion). Thus dependent nature can be seen as general causality, discriminating nature the conditions leading to transmigration, and true nature the conditions leading to nirvāṇa.

THE TWELVE-LINKED CHAIN OF DEPENDENT ORIGINATION

Primitive sūtras speak frequently of religious causality. They deal with the way connecting items lead to transmigration or to nirvāṇa, and they contain lists of varying numbers of such items. The Four Noble Truths are in fact a description of the conditions that lead to transmigration and those that lead to nirvāṇa in terms of two items each. There are many such instances, in which sūtras speak of dependent origination without actually using the term.

Broadly speaking, three categories of causality are found in primitive sūtras. The first is general, based on the Twelve-linked Chain of Dependent Origination and abbreviations thereof. The second stresses causality derived from cognitive relationships in sequence from the six sense organs, their objects, and their consciousnesses to contact (the synthesis of the preceding items) and finally to feeling. The third consists of miscellaneous theories not included in the two preceding categories.

The best known of the categories is the Twelve-linked Chain of Dependent Origination, whose description in the primitive sūtras is virtually the same in both the Pāli and the Chinese versions. The following quotation is from the Saṃyutta-nikāya:

> Monks! What is dependent origination? On ignorance depend actions. On actions depends consciousness. On consciousness depend name and form. On name and form depend the six sense organs. On the six sense organs depends contact. On con-

tact depends feeling. On feeling depends craving. On craving depends grasping. On grasping depends becoming. On becoming depends birth. On birth depend old age and death, grief, sorrow, suffering, lamentation, and worry. Thus does the whole aggregation of suffering arise. Monks! This is called arising.

However, if there is no ignorance, actions cease. With the cessation of actions, consciousness ceases. With the cessation of consciousness, name and form cease. With the cessation of name and form, the six sense organs cease. With the cessation of the six sense organs, contact ceases. With the cessation of contact, feeling ceases. With the cessation of feeling, craving ceases. With the cessation of craving, grasping ceases. With the cessation of grasping, becoming ceases. With the cessation of becoming, birth ceases. With the cessation of birth, old age and death, grief, sorrow, suffering, lamentation, and worry cease. Thus does the whole aggregation of suffering cease.

RELATIONSHIPS AMONG THE TWELVE LINKS

There are many theories explaining the various relationships among the links of the Twelve-linked Chain of Dependent Origination. No detailed explanations are found in the primitive sūtras, but with the development of Abhidharma Buddhism came the theory of cause and effect in the three periods of past, present, and future. Ignorance and actions constitute the two causes of the past; consciousness, name and form, the six sense organs, contact, and feeling are the five effects of the present; and these together form cause and effect in the past and the present. Craving, grasping, and becoming are the three causes of the present; birth and old age and death are the two effects of the future; and together these constitute cause and effect in the present and the future. Taken together, the twelve links represent cause and effect in the three periods. These relationships are shown in the chart on page 144.

The general interpretation of the twelve links in terms of cause and effect in the three periods cites ignorance as a defilement of the past and actions as the good and bad karma of the past. Consciousness is the instantaneous arising of the five aggregates in

Cause and Effect in the Past, Present, and Future

The Twelve-linked Chain of Dependent Origination				
ignorance	delusion (contributory cause)	two causes of the past	Cause and effect in the past and present	Cause and effect in the past, present, and future
actions	karma (direct cause)			
consciousness name and form six sense organs contact feeling	suffering (result)	five effects of the present		
craving grasping	delusion (contributory cause)	three causes of the present	Cause and effect in the present and future	
becoming	karma (direct cause)			
birth old age and death	suffering (result)	two effects of the future		

the womb. Name and form are identified with the first four periods of an embryo: the first week after conception (*kalala*), the second week (*arbuda*), the third week (*peśī*), and the fourth week (*ghana*). The six sense organs signify the development of the organs and faculties of the embryo, then the fetus, during the fifth period (*praśākhā*), from the fifth week until birth.[10] Contact is the arising of the simple cognitive function after birth. Feeling is the arising of the simple functioning of impressions of pleasure and pain from childhood to puberty. Craving is attachment to wealth and lust after puberty. Grasping is the growth of this attachment. Becoming is the determining of future results as the power of habit grows through the good and bad karma of attachment. Birth is the emergence of future results. Old age and death are the development of name and form, the six sense organs, contact, feeling, and so on in the future, after rebirth.

This interpretation, found both in Pāli Buddhism and in Mahāyāna Buddhism, became the accepted theory of Buddhism in general. The Chinese Fa-hsiang and Japanese Hossō (Vijñānavāda) sects, based on the writings of the sixth-century Yogācārin philosopher Dharmapāla, however, interpreted the Twelve-linked Chain of Dependent Origination as existing in the present and the future only. The ten links from ignorance to becoming were defined as being of the present, while birth and old age and death were said to be of the future.

The Four Varieties of Causality While the Sarvāstivādins accepted the interpretation of the Twelve-linked Chain of Dependent Origination as cause and effect in the three periods, they taught four varieties of causality to explain its nature. The first is instantaneous (*kṣaṇika*) causality, in which the twelve links occur simultaneously and causality is a simultaneous and logical relationship. In the second, consecutive (*sāmbandhika*) causality, the twelve links, as psychophysical phenomena, change and develop moment by moment. The mental and physical actions of an individual's daily life are in accordance with this. The third is periodic (*āvasthika*) causality, that is, cause and effect in the three periods, in which the twelve links are dependent states in the past, present, and future. This is simply the traditional interpretation mentioned above. The final type, infinitely successive (*prākarṣika*) causality, points out that the connections among the twelve links are not confined to the three time periods (of an existence) but extend infinitely into the past and the future.

The Three Periods of Karmic Retribution When the chain of cause and effect is viewed temporally, karmic retribution is seen to occur at three different times. There is the retribution experienced in one's present life, the retribution experienced in the life following this one, and the retribution experienced in subsequent lives. The first can be equated with instantaneous causality and consecutive causality, the second with periodic causality, and the third with infinitely successive causality.

Modern Interpretations Modern Japanese and Western scholars have propounded various theories to explain the connections among the twelve links. Some hold to the traditional interpretation, others assert that the logical connection of simultaneous cause and effect is the true teaching of the Buddha, while still others favor an eclectic interpretation.

It must be remembered, however, that Śākyamuni tailored his teaching to fit the wisdom, capacity, and understanding of his hearers; the same doctrine could be taught either profoundly or simply, using easily understood examples and metaphors. This being so, the Twelve-linked Chain of Dependent Origination need not be viewed from one perspective alone. The Āgamas contain no embryological interpretation like the three periods, although the germ of that theory can be found in them. Today, consecutive causality is most easily understood, and even in the Āgamas many interpretations are expressed from this standpoint. Thus the examination of the twelve links that follows is based on consecutive causality.

THE TWELVE LINKS

The twelve links are dealt with in both the Pāli Nikāyas and the Chinese Āgamas, but there are minor differences in their interpretation of the links. Here the most germane of the interpretations are used.

Ignorance (*avidyā, avijjā*) Ignorance means unawareness of the Four Noble Truths and of dependent origination, that is, lack of understanding of the nature of the world and of human existence. It is a fundamental concept of Buddhist thought. Its opposite is right view, one of the items of the Eightfold Path.

Actions (*saṃskāra, saṅkhāra*) As one of the twelve links, actions refer to that which gives rise to deeds, words, and thoughts. Ignorance is a contributory cause of mistaken actions, which include not only mistaken behavior but also the power of habit that is the residual energy of such behavior. No behavior or experience is self-delimiting; some residual energy always remains, preserved and accumulated as such personal characteristics as intellectual capacity and personality.

Consciousness (*vijñāna, viññāṇa*) Consciousness can indicate both the function of cognition and the mind as the subject of cognition. As one of the twelve links, consciousness refers to the six consciousnesses in terms of the mind as the subject of cognition. Some Āgamas define consciousness as being of three kinds: the initial consciousness at conception, consciousness during gestation, and consciousness after birth. If only the initial consciousness is interpreted as the consciousness of the Twelve-linked Chain of Dependent Origination, then it is an embryological view, such as cause and effect in the three periods. Primitive Buddhism, however, considered consciousness to be operative in each of the three states cited above.

Name and Form (*nāma-rūpa*) Name and form refer to the six objects of consciousness. In the Saṃyutta-nikāya name and form are explained as follows: "That which is internal is consciousness; that which is external is name and form."

The Six Sense Organs (*ṣaḍ-āyatana, saḷāyatana*) As one of the twelve links, the six sense organs refer to the sensory and perceptual faculties.

Contact (*sparśa, phassa*) Contact is the synthesis of the six sense organs, their objects, and their consciousnesses. This synthesis establishes the conditions for cognition based on sensation and perception.

Feeling (*vedanā*) Feeling as one of the twelve links is the same as the aggregate of feeling, that is, the receiving of impressions of pain and pleasure. Feeling occurs at each of the six contacts and thus is also called the six feelings. The category of three feelings encompasses feeling that causes pain, feeling that results in pleasure, and feeling that does neither one nor the other. The feeling of pain or pleasure arises on contact. The same object may give rise to different feelings, so that one person may feel pleasure at something that causes another person pain. This happens because consciousness as the subject of cognition is not a tabula rasa but contains distinctive characteristics, such as greed and anger, according to an individual's past ignorance and actions.

Craving (*tṛṣṇā, taṇhā*) Craving can be likened to a thirsty person's desperation for water. There are six cravings, each originating in one of the six sense organs. There is also a category of three cravings: the craving for sensuous desires (*kāma-tṛṣṇā, kāma-taṇhā*), the craving for existence (*bhava-tṛṣṇā, bhava-taṇhā*), and the craving for nonexistence (*vibhava-tṛṣṇā, vibhava-taṇhā*). When impressions of pain or pleasure arise through cognition, they are followed by strong waves of revulsion and rejection or, alternatively, longing. These strong waves are craving, which can be defined as the arising of thoughts of love and hate in regard to pleasure and pain.

Grasping (*upādāna*) There are four kinds of grasping: sensuous desires, stubborn and egocentric views, attachment to heretical practices, and ideas arising from the concept of a self. Craving is mental; grasping is the longing or rejection that arises after craving. That which is loved is seized; that which is hated is cast away. Grasping thus signifies action that can lead to violation of the precepts, such as killing, stealing, adultery, and lying, and is the result of longing or rejection.

Becoming (*bhava*) Becoming is existence (*bhava*). Commentaries cite three realms of existence: the realm of desire (*kāma-dhātu*), the realm of form (*rūpa-dhātu*), and the formless realm (*ārūpya-dhātu, āruppa-dhātu*). In its broadest sense, becoming is phenomenal existence and, like mental constituents (*saṃskāra*) and the conditioned (*saṃskṛta*), encompasses the totality of existence. The twelve links as a whole are *bhava* (existence). Here, becoming has two aspects: karmic existence and retributive existence. The first is existence viewed in terms of good and bad karma; the second refers to the existence that is the result of that karma.

As one of the twelve links, becoming is the residual power of the act of longing or rejection, which arises from grasping. It is both the accumulated energy of past habit and the determinant of future actions. Fundamentally, it indicates that birth will follow.

Grasping and becoming correspond to the second link, actions, and craving is the equivalent of the first, ignorance. Actions arise from ignorance and contain both action and the residual power of habit, so that grasping, which arises from craving, in turn gives rise to becoming as a result of its residual power of habit.

Birth (*jāti*) Birth can refer either to the birth of a specific sentient being or to the arising of a specific experience in life. In the first instance, birth comes about as a result of the intellect, personality, and physical constitution formed as the residual power of past experiences. Therefore, each individual is born with certain characteristics. In the second instance, with these as a base new experiences arise. In both cases, birth arises from becoming.

Old Age and Death (*jarā-maraṇa*) The Saṃyutta-nikāya adds grief (*soka*), sorrow (*parideva*), suffering (*dukkha*), lamentation (*domanassa*), and worry (*upāyāsa*) to old age and death to indicate that old age and death, and all manner of suffering, arise through birth. Here, all forms of pain and distress are included under the rubric of old age and death.

Pain and distress are bound to follow mistaken thoughts and actions. All the suffering of transmigration in the three realms of existence is explained in terms of defilements (such as craving and ignorance) and of karma (such as actions, grasping, and becoming), for they are both the cause and the condition of suffering.

The Twelve-linked Chain of Dependent Origination emphasizes the conditions leading to transmigration and the way in which suffering arises. It says almost nothing about the conditions by which nirvāṇa is achieved—the elimination of suffering and the realization of enlightenment. It gives no concrete explanation of the means by which suffering is to be eliminated. For this one must turn to the doctrine of the Four Noble Truths, especially the fourth truth, which sets forth the Eightfold Path. Consequently, to understand fully the doctrine of dependent origination it is necessary not only to study the Twelve-linked Chain of Dependent Origination but also to study—and practice—the Four Noble Truths.

6. The Four Noble Truths

The Twelve-linked Chain of Dependent Origination has been termed "the doctrine of inner witness," an allusion to the enlightenment that Śākyamuni gained beneath the *bodhi* tree and his subsequent meditation on that enlightenment. Śākyamuni preached the doctrine of the Twelve-linked Chain of Dependent Origination to enable others to realize the basic truth of causality for themselves.

The Four Noble Truths, on the other hand, were expounded so that others could more easily understand causality, since the Twelve-linked Chain of Dependent Origination is essentially a theoretical statement. The Four Noble Truths offer explanations both practical and theoretical, with the practical predominating. For these reasons, dependent origination has been called the doctrine of self-enlightenment, and the Four Noble Truths the teaching for the instruction of others.

According to tradition, Śākyamuni took joy in his enlightenment but gave up the idea of trying to teach others, deeming the principle of dependent origination too hard for ordinary people to understand. At that point the deity Brahmā appeared before Śākyamuni and pleaded with him to teach so that the world might be saved from depravity, asserting that however difficult the teachings, there would be some people who could understand at least a part. Thus the Buddha devised the doctrine of the Four Noble Truths as the most effective means of elucidation.

It is said that he followed the physician's method of treating patients, prescribing the therapy that best cures the disease.

When the Buddha rose from meditation after several weeks, he went first to Deer Park, in Varanasi, where the five ascetics with whom he had practiced austerities were dwelling. Of all people, these five were best able to understand his teachings, and it was to them that he preached his first discourse, "setting the wheel of the Law in motion," in which he expounded the Four Noble Truths.

CANONICAL STATEMENTS

The section of the Saṃyutta-nikāya known as the Sūtra of the Turning of the Wheel of the Law[1] records the teaching of the Four Noble Truths to the ascetics in Deer Park as follows:

> Monks! Birth is suffering, old age is suffering, illness is suffering, death is suffering. To be united with what is hated is suffering. To be parted from what is loved is suffering. Not to obtain what is sought is suffering. In short, attachment to the five aggregates is suffering. This, then, is the noble truth of suffering.
>
> Monks! It is craving that leads to rebirth, is connected to joy and greed, and continually finds pleasure and delight now here, now there. It is the craving for sensuous desires, the craving for existence, and the craving for nonexistence. This, then, is the noble truth of the cause of suffering.
>
> Monks! Craving can be cast off and destroyed, abandoned and rejected. Release and nonattachment to craving [are possible]. This is the noble truth of the termination of suffering.
>
> Monks! This is the noble truth of the Way to the termination of suffering: right view, right thought, right speech, right action, right livelihood, right effort, right mindfulness, and right concentration.

THE STAGES OF UNDERSTANDING

After he had taught the Four Noble Truths, Śākyamuni spoke as follows. First, he had gained the theoretical knowledge that they were indeed truth, and not error. Second, he had practiced them appropriately, based on that knowledge. Third, as a result of truly accomplishing the practice and experiencing the unity of theory and practice, he had become conscious of being a buddha, a great teacher of gods and humans. Buddhist teachings thus begin with theoretical understanding, progress to correct practice based on this understanding, and finally find fulfillment in the perfection of practice, that is, in the oneness of theory and practice. When the perfection of practice is the basis of daily life, the ideal character has been formed.

These three stages are termed "the three turns of the wheel": the indicative (that which demonstrates each of the Four Noble Truths), the hortative (the encouragement to practice the Four Noble Truths), and the evidential (Śākyamuni's bearing witness that he had accomplished the second turn of the wheel). Abhidharma scholars refined these definitions. The first stage was considered to be that of the Way of View (*darśana-mārga*); the second, that of the Way of Practice (*bhāvanā-mārga*); and the third, the stage at which there is nothing more to be learned (*aśaikṣa-phala*). On hearing the teaching of the Four Noble Truths, the five ascetics gained theoretical awareness and their Dharma Eye was opened, enabling them to achieve theoretical understanding of the Four Noble Truths and dependent origination and to see human life and the world correctly. The opening of the Dharma Eye indicates the condition of faith in which no delusion remains and there is no more reliance on other belief systems. It is the first stage of enlightenment, the first step to gaining entry to the company of the sages.

THE NATURE OF THE FOUR NOBLE TRUTHS

As recorded in canonical accounts, the Four Noble Truths (*catvāri ārya-satyāni, cattāri ariya-saccāni*) consist of the truth of suffering, the truth of the cause of suffering, the truth of the extinction of suffering, and the truth of the Way to the extinction of suffering. Noble (*ārya, ariya*), the opposite of common or ordinary, indicates undefiled, supramundane enlightenment, a condition transcending the defiled existence of *saṃsāra*. The Four Noble Truths address both the conditions leading to transmigration and those leading to nirvāṇa. The truths of suffering and its cause explain the suffering of *saṃsāra* and its cause; the truths of the extinction of suffering and the Way to achieve it explain nirvāṇa, which is release from *saṃsāra,* and the method of practice necessary for attaining it. This relationship is shown in the chart below.

The Buddha taught the Four Noble Truths as the theoretical foundation for relieving pain and suffering, just as the physician treats physical illness on the basis of theoretical principles. Humankind's suffering is a spiritual sickness that can be cured according to the same principles applied to physical illness. For this reason, one epithet of Śākyamuni, recorded in the Saṃyukta-āgama, is Great Physician Who Cures All Pain and Suffering.

In that suffering is existential, it can be compared to physical illness. The cause of suffering is comparable to the cause of an illness. The extinction of suffering results in the ideal condition of ease, the condition of health in which disease no longer reigns. The Way is the means whereby this ideal is reached, and is like the treatment that the physician prescribes for a patient. To treat an illness, the physician must make an accurate diagnosis, ascertain the cause of the illness, and have a thorough knowledge of what constitutes a healthy physical state. The physician must then use all this knowledge in selecting the best treatment for the illness.

The ideal spiritual state can be reached in the same way. To cure the psychological ills of suffering and pain, we must understand the exact nature of suffering. Most important is understanding the root cause of suffering. In addition, we must have

The Four Noble Truths and Causality

The Four Noble Truths			
Suffering The uncomprehended actual world of suffering	Cause The reason for the origin of the actual world of suffering	Extinction The comprehended ideal world	Way The reason for the origin of the ideal world
effect	cause	effect	cause
conditions leading to transmigration		conditions leading to nirvāṇa	

knowledge of the ideal state, in which suffering no longer exists, and of the way to attain it. From this point on, actual practice brings the ideal closer step by step.

The theory of the Four Noble Truths is extremely logical, like medical theory and the scientific method. The first step in scientific research is to discover the principle of the workings of phenomena (that is, the connections between cause and effect) in regard to the object being studied. This approximates discerning the relation between suffering and its cause. The second step in research is to apply this principle to produce ideal goods or conditions for humankind. This is similar to understanding the causal relationship between the extinction of suffering and the Way and then practicing to achieve it.

The basic Buddhist doctrine of the Four Noble Truths is completely logical; it excludes anything that is illogical. The exclusion of the illogical is unique to Buddhism. The doctrine of dependent origination on which the Four Noble Truths are based is equally logical.

SUFFERING

It is necessary first of all to see our reality for what it is: viewed in terms of the absolute, it is incomplete and filled with contamination and suffering. This is the import of the truth of suffering (*duḥkha-satya, dukkha-sacca*).

The Four Noble Truths present eight kinds of suffering. To the basic four of birth, old age, illness, and death, a further four are added: contact with what we hate, separation from what we love, unattained aims, and the suffering inherent in attachment to the five aggregates. All these can be associated with the three types of suffering discussed in chapter 4: physical, mental, and phenomenological.

In the suffering inherent in birth, birth refers not to emergence from the womb but to the moment of conception. Since birth and rebirth among living beings are identified as suffering, the suffering inherent in birth can be considered to be phenomenological suffering.

To illustrate the suffering inherent in old age, illness, and death,

Buddhist tradition tells that on outings before he became an ascetic Śākyamuni encountered an old man, a sick person, and a corpse, thereby experiencing the suffering of human life. Those experiences prompted him to renounce secular life. The kinds of suffering Śākyamuni witnessed are usually considered physical, even though they are normally accompanied by mental suffering. Each results in anxiety for both the individual sufferer and his or her family. Suffering also arises from fears of loss of position, reputation, or influence. The concern of popular religions with healing sickness and remedying poverty is connected closely with such fears.

The suffering inherent in parting from what we love and coming into contact with what we hate includes lifelong parting, parting through death, and being with someone hated. Suffering becomes extreme in the event of passionate, self-centered clinging to the object of love or hate. Religion can resolve discord, since it can promote the removal of such suffering.

The suffering inherent in unattained aims arises from being unable to get what one wants. In a sense, all the forms of suffering discussed thus far occur because desires have not been fulfilled. The suffering of unattained aims is exacerbated by the nonfulfillment of excessive, self-centered desires.

The suffering inherent in attachment to the five aggregates summarizes the preceding seven forms of suffering, since the sūtras emphazise that attachment to the five aggregates is suffering. Suffering arises from self-centered attachment to the five aggregates, that is, all *dharmas.*

The Cause of Suffering

In the truth of the cause of suffering (*samudaya-satya, samudaya-sacca*), the Indic word translated as "cause" means "coming together and arising." The Sūtra of the Turning of the Wheel of the Law states that the cause of suffering is "craving that . . . continually finds pleasure and delight now here, now there." The sūtra distinguishes three cravings: for sensuous desires, for existence, and for nonexistence.

While the doctrine of the Four Noble Truths gives craving as the cause of suffering, the doctrine of the Twelve-linked Chain of Dependent Origination gives both ignorance and craving as the causes of transmigration and suffering. Buddhism considers ignorance to be the source of all defilements. Although craving alone is mentioned in the Four Noble Truths, we must remember that ultimately craving arises from ignorance; thus, by extension, ignorance can be thought of as the root cause of suffering in the Four Noble Truths. Moreover, craving can be considered representative of all the defilements. Here, however, we will examine the three cravings cited in the Sūtra of the Turning of the Wheel of the Law.

Craving for sensuous desires is the craving for the five desires, that is, desires arising from the objects of the five senses. It is craving for the sensuous pleasures of the world.

Craving for existence refers to craving for a superior existence, as in the heavenly realm, and thus is the desire for rebirth in some such state. This is nothing but self-centered craving, since both the heavenly realm and human life are part of the cycle of birth and death and thus cannot be considered ideal. To seek such a rebirth is the defilement of craving.

Craving for nonexistence is the desire for nothingness. In the India of Śākyamuni, it was believed there could be no absolute certainty or tranquillity in existence, and there grew up a belief in a realm of nothingness, or nonexistence, a condition of utter peace, like eternal sleep. Buddhism considers the craving for nonexistence to be self-centered. For Buddhism, nothingness (nihilism) is not the ideal; on the contrary, Buddhism recommends positive activity and an attitude of nonself to purify society in this life. Thus craving for nonexistence is also the defilement of craving. Craving for nonexistence has been widely interpreted as the desire for prosperity, *vibhava* having been translated as "prosperity." Although this is a possible translation, traditional commentaries have all interpreted *vibhava* as nonexistence.

THE EXTINCTION OF SUFFERING

The Sūtra of the Turning of the Wheel of the Law defines the truth of the extinction of suffering (*nirodha-satya, nirodha-sacca*) as the elimination of craving. Since craving is representative of all defilements, extinction is the state in which all defilements have been eliminated, that is, the state of nirvāṇa. Primitive sūtras define nirvāṇa as the elimination of defilements, the extinction of greed, anger, and folly. As discussed here, the extinction of suffering is also nirvāṇa, the ideal state in Buddhism.

THE WAY

The truth of the Way (*mārga-satya, magga-sacca*) refers to the extinction of suffering, to the course of practice for the attainment of nirvāṇa. This set of practices is called the Noble Eightfold Path (*ārya-aṣṭāṅgika-mārga, ariya-aṭṭhaṅgika-magga*), the noble way of eight parts. In the light of the definition of the extinction of suffering, it would seem necessary only to eliminate craving in order to achieve the extinction of suffering, but the truth of the Way sets forth eight necessary practices.

For instance, when treating a patient with tuberculosis, it is not enough to destroy the disease-causing organism. Along with direct treatment of the diseased organ, adequate nutrition, sleep, and exercise are prescribed, and mental stress and suffering alleviated. As a result, hope and peace of mind are attained, appetite increases, and health returns naturally. In short, medication alone will not make the mind tranquil or the body robust.

The approach is similar in treating mental suffering. The elimination of its cause, craving, is not enough. Since the body and the mind are organically related, good health, in this case nirvāṇa, cannot be achieved unless improvement is both physical and mental. This is the reason for the practices that constitute the Eightfold Path.

THE EIGHTFOLD PATH

As its formal name implies, the Noble Eightfold Path is the way of the sage (*ārya, ariya*), but it can also be followed in daily life in the secular world. Thus it will be discussed here from both the ordained and the lay perspectives. The eight practices of the Eightfold Path are examined separately for the sake of convenience; in fact, however, they are an organic whole and have no existence in isolation from one another.

Right View Right view (*samyag-dṛṣṭi, sammā-diṭṭhi*) refers to the correct way of looking at things. It is the wisdom that comes of understanding the Four Noble Truths and dependent origination. For one with little experience, who has yet to achieve this wisdom, right view consists of correct faith. In the secular world right view corresponds, for example, to the overall planning and estimates done by a company when undertaking a new project.

Right Thought Right thought (*samyak-saṃkalpa, sammā-saṅkappa*) is the thought or determination that precedes action or speech. An ordained person practices right thought with a mind that becomes increasingly gentle, compassionate, and pure. For a lay person right thought consists of always thinking correctly about his or her situation and determining to act accordingly.

Right Speech Right speech (*samyag-vācā, sammā-vācā*) is correct speech arising out of right thought. Right speech means refraining from lying, bad language, slander, and frivolous speech and using speech beneficially, in a way that leads to harmony, out of true love for others.

Right Action Right action (*samyak-karmānta, sammā-kammanta*) is correct action arising out of right thought. Right action is abstaining from killing, stealing, and adultery and, instead, practicing good deeds, such as the protection of sentient beings, philanthropy, and the observance of sexual morality.

Right Livelihood Right livelihood (*samyag-ājīva, sammā-ājīva*) is the correct conduct of our lives. The right way of earning a living allows us to conduct our lives correctly and spend our days in an orderly fashion. If we maintain regular habits of sleep, diet, work, exercise, and leisure, our health will improve, we will work more efficiently, and we will enjoy a harmonious family life and financial well-being.

Right Effort Right effort (*samyag-vyāyāma, sammā-vāyāma*) means exerting ourselves with valor. Effort refers to striving to achieve the ideals of religious faith, ethics, politics, economics, and health, producing and increasing that which is good and preventing and eliminating that which is bad.

Right Mindfulness Right mindfulness (*samyak-smṛti, sammā-sati*) ensures that with correct consciousness and awareness, the goal of attaining the ideal is never forgotten. In daily life it means acting without absent-mindedness or carelessness, for even momentary inattention can cause a disaster. From the Buddhist viewpoint, right mindfulness means maintaining constant awareness of impermanence, suffering, nonself, and so on.

Right Concentration Right concentration (*samyak-samādhi, sammā-samādhi*) refers to total concentration and here means specifically the four *dhyānas,* or meditational states, which are discussed in the following chapter. Even though the formal concentration of the four *dhyānas* is beyond the abilities of ordinary people, keeping the mind calm and concentrating are necessary even in everyday life in order to acquire true wisdom and to be able to act on it. Right concentration develops a mind that is unclouded, like a clear mirror or still water.

THE EIGHTFOLD PATH AND THE THREEFOLD PRACTICE

Abhidharma scholars constructed many different interpretations of the connection between the Eightfold Path and the threefold practice (morality, concentration, and wisdom), which is discussed in depth in the following chapter. The Pāli interpretation is shown in the chart on page 161.

Since all parts of the Eightfold Path can be thought of as existing simultaneously, we can say there is no specific sequence for its practice. It is equally possible, however, to say that there is a specific sequence, the one given in the chart. Likewise, with the threefold practice we can say that there is no specific sequence for its practice, but it is logical to think of the threefold practice in the traditional sequence of morality, concentration, and wisdom.

The sequence of the Eightfold Path corresponds to the sequence

The Relationship of the Eightfold Path and the Threefold Practice

Eightfold Path	Threefold practice
right view right thought	wisdom
right speech right action right livelihood	morality
right effort	all three categories
right mindfulness right concentration	concentration

Note: Some interpretations include right effort in concentration, while others include it in wisdom.

of wisdom, morality, and concentration of the threefold practice. When two more items are added to the Eightfold Path—right knowledge (*samyag-jñāna, sammā-ñāṇa*) and right liberation (*samyag-vimukti, sammā-vimutti*)—we have what are known as the ten *aśaikṣa dharmas,* which are attainments of those with *arhat* enlightenment. With these two items ending the list as a second category corresponding to wisdom, the progression of the expanded Eightfold Path is wisdom, morality, concentration, and wisdom, echoing the traditional sequence of the threefold practice except for the first instance of the category wisdom. That first category, corresponding to right view and right thought, is more properly termed faith, which the person beginning to practice the Eightfold Path must have. Thus the sequence of the expanded Eightfold Path could be stated more accurately as faith, morality, concentration, and wisdom.

7. Religious Practice

Buddhism concerns itself with both the actual state of people's spiritual development and the ideal state they can attain. Buddhism's ultimate purpose is religious practice that helps people attain the ideal state of development. Much of the content of primitive sūtras concerns methods of practice, since Śākyamuni taught many courses of practice, according to what best suited the environment and personality of each listener in terms of both faith and practice. As a physician prescribes the medication and other treatment most appropriate to a patient's illness, the Buddha taught in the way best suited to conquer the defilements of each disciple and advance that person on the road to enlightenment. Because of this, it has been said that Buddhism consists of eighty-four thousand (that is, myriad) teachings.

The Abhidharma scholastics classified thirty-seven practices, in seven groups, as being most representative of the numerous practices set forth in primitive sūtras, calling them the thirty-seven practices conducive to enlightenment. This classification ignored many other practices introduced in primitive sūtras, such as practice of the five and seven treasures, the eight qualities of *śrāvakas, pratyekabuddhas,* and bodhisattvas,[1] and the ten *aśaikṣa dharmas.*

Eventually the seven groups comprising the thirty-seven practices gave rise to independent systems, each of which was believed to lead to enlightenment. In time there evolved a further categorization of practice in which all methodologies were subsumed under three all-embracing categories, the so-called threefold practice: morality (*śīla*), concentration (*samādhi*), and wisdom (*prajñā*). Thus the thirty-seven practices could just as easily be described in terms of this threefold practice, which is, in fact, the simplest and most logical way to describe Buddhist practice.

The Thirty-seven Practices Conducive to Enlightenment

The thirty-seven practices conducive to enlightenment (*bodhi-pākṣika-dharma, bodhipakkhiya-dhamma*)—literally, "the parts (*pakṣika, pakkhiya*) leading to enlightenment (*bodhi*)"—are divided into seven groups: the four fields of mindfulness, the four right efforts, the four psychic powers, the five roots of emancipation, the five excellent powers, the seven factors of enlightenment, and the Eightfold Path.

THE FOUR FIELDS OF MINDFULNESS

The four fields of mindfulness (*catvāri smṛty-upasthānāni, cattāri sati-paṭṭhānāni*) correspond to right mindfulness in the Eightfold Path. The four fields are contemplation of the body (*kāya*), to be mindful of its impurity; of feeling (*vedanā*), to be mindful that it is suffering; of the mind (*citta*), to be mindful that it is impermanent; and of phenomena (*dharma, dhamma*), to be mindful that they are devoid of self. Thus the practice emphasizes the correct attitude to be taken toward all phenomena: the material (body), the mental (feeling, mind), and the objects of mind (*dharma*). This mindfulness is to be maintained at all times.

Primitive sūtras in the Saṃyutta-nikāya and the Saṃyukta-āgama define the four fields of mindfulness as *ekāyana-magga*, "a road leading to one place," that is, nirvāṇa; in short, this practice is considered a complete system of practice, suitable from the earliest stages through the highest enlightenment. The four fields of mindfulness are identical to the contemplation of the five aggregates, seeing each of the aggregates in terms of impermanence, suffering, and nonself.

THE FOUR RIGHT EFFORTS

The four right efforts (*catvāri samyakprahāṇāni, cattāri sammap-*

padhānāni) correspond to right effort in the Eightfold Path. In this practice, effort and striving are divided into four parts: eradicating evil that has already arisen, preventing the rise of evil, causing the rise of good, and improving and augmenting the good that has arisen.

Here, "good" is that which leads toward the ideal, and "evil" is that which leads away from it. From the Buddhist viewpoint, whatever furthers the way of the sage is good and whatever hinders it is evil. In the secular world, too—for instance, in ethics, politics, economics, and physical conditions—that which conduces to the ideal is good, and that which leads away from it is evil. With practice of the four right efforts, evil is overcome and good approached as the practitioner advances step by step toward the ideal. In Buddhism, exertion in the direction of evil cannot be termed endeavor (*vīrya, viriya*) but requires a special term—*kausīdya* (*kosajja*), meaning "sloth."

THE FOUR PSYCHIC POWERS

The practice known as the four psychic powers (*catvāra ṛddhipādāḥ, cattāro iddhipādā*) views the profound meditation (*dhyāna, jhāna*) necessary for the attainment of supernormal powers (*abhijñā, abhiññā*) in terms of four aspects: the will (*chanda*) to attain *dhyāna*, the endeavor (*vīrya, viriya*) to attain *dhyāna*, the mind (*citta*) to attain *dhyāna*, and the thought and investigation (*mīmāṃsā, vīmaṃsā*) through wisdom to attain *dhyāna*.

THE FIVE ROOTS OF EMANCIPATION

The five roots of emancipation (*pañcendriyāṇi, pañcindriyāni*) are faith (*śraddhā, saddhā*), endeavor (*vīrya, viriya*), mindfulness (*smṛti, sati*), concentration (*samādhi*), and wisdom (*prajñā, paññā*). Here "root" means "potential" or "ability." Thus the five roots are five potentials that lead people to enlightenment. They enable practitioners to proceed from delusion to enlightenment. Faith is cited first because it is the starting point for all Buddhist practice. From this sequence we know that this practice is one for beginners.

THE FIVE EXCELLENT POWERS

The five excellent powers (*pañca balāni*), developed together with the five roots of emancipation, correspond to the roots: faith, endeavor, mindfulness, concentration, and wisdom. The five excellent powers, however, signify greater advancement along the road of practice than the roots. All the powers can be practiced at every level, from that of the ordinary person to that of the sage. The various stages of practice are described in the discussions of concentration and wisdom below.

THE SEVEN FACTORS OF ENLIGHTENMENT

The seven factors of enlightenment (*sapta bodhyaṅgāni, satta bojjhaṅgā*) are to be practiced immediately prior to attaining enlightenment. Of all the thirty-seven practices conducive to enlightenment, they are considered the loftiest, especially those connected with *dhyāna.* In primitive sūtras dealing with practice, the practice of concentration on breathing (*ānāpāna-smṛti, ānāpāna-sati*), or "counting the breaths"—centering the mind by counting inhalations and exhalations—is followed by the practice of the four fields of mindfulness and then by the practice of the seven factors of enlightenment.

The seven factors of enlightenment make up a course for achieving transcendental knowledge (*vidyā, vijjā*)—that is, the wisdom of enlightenment—and liberation (*vimukti, vimutti*). The seven factors said to lead the practitioner to supernatural knowledge (*abhijñā, abhiññā*), perfect enlightenment (*saṃbodhi, sambodhi*), and nirvāṇa are as follows:

1. Mindfulness (*smṛti saṃbodhyaṅga, sati-sambojjhaṅga*), that is, remembering what was experienced in the distant past and maintaining excellent wisdom.
2. Investigation of the Dharma (*dharmavicaya saṃbodhyaṅga, dhammavicaya-sambojjhaṅga*), that is, studying and analyzing the Dharma, or doctrine, according to wisdom, maintaining mindfulness at all times.
3. Endeavor (*vīrya saṃbodhyaṅga, viriya-sambojjhaṅga*), that is, continuing to study and analyze the Dharma with wisdom, maintaining one's effort without flagging.
4. Joy (*prīti saṃbodhyaṅga, pīti-sambojjhaṅga*), that is, arousing joy in the Dharma through effort.

5. Tranquillity (*praśrabdhi saṃbodhyaṅga, passaddhi-sambojjhaṅga*), that is, cultivating the physical and mental comfort of one within whom joy has risen.
6. Concentration (*samādhi saṃbodhyaṅga, samādhi-sambojjhaṅga*), that is, attaining the concentrated mind of one whose body and mind are comfortable.
7. Equanimity (*upekṣā saṃbodhyaṅga, upekkhā-sambojjhaṅga*), that is, viewing the concentrated mind dispassionately, so that thoughts of attachment and desire are severed and the mind neither inclines to things nor wavers from calm.

THE EIGHTFOLD PATH

The Eightfold Path (consisting of right view, right thought, right speech, right action, right livelihood, right effort, right mindfulness, and right concentration) is discussed fully in chapter 6.

THE THREEFOLD PRACTICE

In the threefold practice (*trīṇi śikṣāṇi, tisso sikkhā*), which consists of morality (*śīla-śikṣa, sīla-sikkhā*), concentration (*samādhi-śikṣa, samādhi-sikkhā*), and wisdom (*prajñā-śikṣa, paññā-sikkhā*), the mind seeking enlightenment is analyzed in terms of will, emotion, and knowledge, respectively. This tripartite analysis is adopted merely as a convenience, since such a clear-cut psychological dissection of the mind is not actually possible. Morality, concentration, and wisdom must be considered together to gain an accurate view of the nature of the mind in terms of practice. The tripartite analysis is similar to examination of the Eightfold Path as eight individual practices, even though none of those practices exists independently of the others; all together form an organic whole. This stipulation of ultimate indivisibility applies to all methods of Buddhist practice.

Various sūtras speak of the threefold practice. The simplest explanation appears in the Sūtra of the Great Decease in the Dīgha-nikāya:

> Great is the fruit, great is the benefit of concentration when it is practiced together with morality. Great is the fruit, great is the

> benefit of wisdom when it is practiced together with concentration. The mind that is graced with wisdom is totally liberated from the afflictions [*āsrava, āsava*]—the affliction of desire, the affliction of becoming, the affliction of wrong views, and the affliction of ignorance.

A fuller explanation appears in the Aṅguttara-nikāya:

> Monks! There is the threefold practice: practice in the higher morality, practice in the higher powers of the mind, and practice in the higher wisdom.
>
> What, monks, is practice in the higher morality? Monks, here the monk receives the precepts and lives restrained by the code of precepts [*pātimokkha*]; he is endowed with right action and a good environment for such action; he views with fear the smallest misdemeanor; and he takes up and practices the rules of morality. This, monks, is called practice in the higher morality.
>
> And what, monks, is practice in the higher powers of the mind? Monks, here a monk separates himself from the desires and attains the first *jhāna* [*dhyāna*], the second *jhāna,* the third *jhāna,* and the fourth *jhāna.* This, monks, is called practice in the higher powers of the mind.
>
> And what, monks, is practice in the higher wisdom? Monks, here a monk deeply understands that there is suffering, that there is a cause of suffering, that there is cessation of suffering, and that there is a way leading to cessation of suffering. This, monks, is called practice in the higher wisdom.

The seven purities (*visuddhi*) and the seventeen stages of *arhat* practice (discussed on pages 189–90) are amplifications of the threefold practice. The first of the purities constitutes morality; the second, concentration; and the remaining five, wisdom. The first eight stages of *arhat* practice relate to morality, the next six to concentration, and the final three to wisdom.

MORALITY

Morality (*śīla, sīla*), the regulation of body and mind and the cultivation of good habits, encompasses not only the religious avoidance of evil but also the avoidance of activities inimical to the ideals of law, economics, physical health, and so on. The original meaning of *śīla* is the prevention of wrong and the restraining of evil. *Śīla* in the sense of restraining evil is also called *saṃvara* (precepts).

There is morality applicable to those still in a state of delusion and to those whose minds are free of delusion. According to the *Abhidharmakośa-śāstra,* morality applicable to the state of delusion includes the code of precepts governing behavior (*prātimokṣa-saṃvara*), which operates in the realm of desire, and the precepts (restraints) as meditation (*dhyāna-saṃvara*), which operate in the realm of form. Morality applicable to the state of nondelusion (*anāsrava*) is the precepts of nondelusion (*anāsrava-saṃvara*), which operate in the supramundane realm.

As shown in the chart below, the code of precepts obtains for both the ordained and the nonordained person. It is continually

Morality

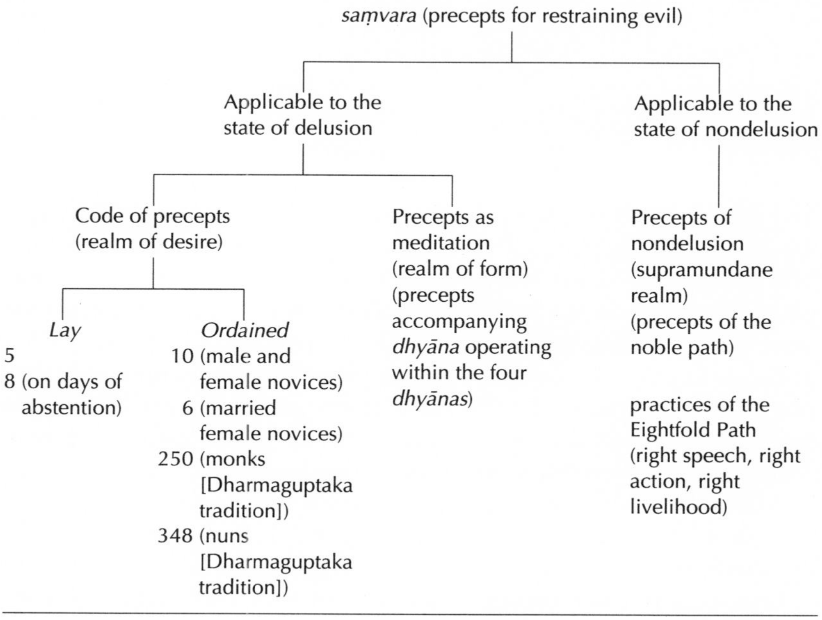

operative in those who have taken the vows, and is said to function independently of the mind. Its practice allows the accumulation of unmanifested form (*avijñapti-rūpa*), the power of habit for good or evil. There are five lay precepts, which increase to eight on days of abstention. For the ordained, according to the Dharmaguptaka tradition, there are 250 precepts for monks and 348 for nuns. Male and single female novices must observe ten precepts and married female novices six. (See the discussion of the Saṅgha in chapter 2 for a detailed explanation of these precepts.)

The precepts (restraints) as meditation operate in the realm of form as the practice of the four *dhyānas,* or meditational states, during which evil is automatically prevented. These precepts are also known as the precepts accompanying *dhyāna.* These and the precepts of nondelusion, which operate in the practice of an *ārya* (*ariya*), or sage, function together with the mind. It is only when the mind is free of delusion that evil will not occur.

Morality also includes the concept of promoting good. Besides the precepts for restraining evil there are precepts for creating good. The Vinayas of primitive Buddhism and the Abhidharma schools reflect this in recording certain precepts in their Sūtravibhaṅga (Sutta-vibhaṅga), containing the precepts for restraining evil, and others in their Skandhaka (Khandhaka), containing the precepts for creating good. (See the discussion of the Vinayapiṭaka in chapter 2 for a fuller discussion.)

The Mahāyāna Precepts With the development of Mahāyāna, the ideal of benefiting others through morality was emphasized. The precepts were no longer observed merely to prevent evil and promote good for oneself alone. This ideal is embodied in the three pure precepts (the Mahāyāna precepts).

The first of these, *saṃvara-śīla*—to do no evil—encompasses the precepts for the restraint of evil, in particular the code of precepts of primitive Buddhism governing behavior in the realm of desire, which were to be observed by both ordained and lay Buddhists. In Mahāyāna Buddhism, this precept refers to the restraint in the ten good precepts and the ten grave prohibitions (together with the forty-eight minor prohibitions).

The second pure precept, *kuśaladharma-saṃgrāhaka-śīla*—to do only good—incorporates the precepts for the promotion of good. This precept is thus the positive face of the ten good precepts and the ten grave prohibitions.

The third, *sattvārthakriyā-śīla*—to confer benefits on all sentient beings—is the precept for the practice of benefiting others. It is the compassionate, salvational expression of the ten good precepts and the ten grave prohibitions.

The ten good precepts. Primitive sūtras speak of the ten meritorious acts, but only after the rise of Mahāyāna were they made into precepts. They are not to kill, not to steal, not to commit adultery, not to lie, not to use bad language, not to slander others, not to speak frivolously, not to covet, not to give way to anger, and not to hold false views. The first three relate to physical acts, the next four to vocal acts, and the final three to mental acts.

The ten grave prohibitions. The violation of any of the ten grave prohibitions constitutes a *pārājika* offense of bodhisattvas, which requires expulsion from the *saṅgha* if the offender is ordained. The prohibitions are not to kill, not to steal, not to commit adultery, not to lie, not to sell intoxicants (or permit others to consume them), not to speak of the faults of others, not to praise oneself or disparage others, not to covet either the Law or property, not to give way to anger, and not to disparage the Three Treasures. They are almost the same as the ten good precepts. When forty-eight minor prohibitions are added to the ten grave prohibitions, we have what are known as the Brahmajāla (Brahma Net) precepts, which are set forth in the Sūtra of the Brahma Net.

The ten meritorious acts. The concept of the ten meritorious acts as Mahāyāna precepts originates in the Perfection of Wisdom sūtras and is also reflected in the Flower Garland Sūtra. The Perfection of Wisdom sūtras explain the perfection of morality (*śīla-pāramitā*) as the bodhisattva's practice of the ten meritorious acts and the encouragement of their practice in others. In the Flower Garland Sūtra, a bodhisattva in the second stage of practice (the stage of purity) practices the perfection of morality, keeping the ten good precepts and causing others to keep them. In addition, the bodhisattva cultivates compassion toward all sentient beings and observes the three pure precepts, all of which foster the arising of a deeply compassionate mind in the bodhisattva.

Thus the Perfection of Wisdom sūtras teach the ten meritorious acts from the perspectives of doing good and restraining evil, while the Flower Garland Sūtra adds a further dimension, enjoining the bodhisattva to benefit others through compassion. Together these teachings yield the three pure precepts. Because the names of the three pure precepts are found in the Treatise on the Stages of Yoga Practice, these precepts are also known as the Yoga precepts. The Treatise on the Stages of Yoga Practice does not interpret the first precept, to do no evil, as merely the nonviolation of the ten good precepts, as do the Perfection of Wisdom sūtras and the Flower Garland Sūtra, but equates it with the code of precepts observed by the seven groups of believers (laymen, laywomen, monks, nuns, male novices, single female novices, and married female novices).

Śīla-vinaya. Though common in Chinese and Japanese Buddhism, the compound term *śīla-vinaya* is not found in Indian Buddhism, since the two words have clearly different meanings. *Śīla* is a broad term encompassing spiritual and personally regulated matters, while *vinaya* is more restricted, applying to formal, externally regulated matters. In terms of general social concepts, *śīla* relates to ethical matters (such as morality) and *vinaya* (regulations) to legal matters (such as statutes). The two terms are sometimes used interchangeably, however. For example, the monks' and nuns' precepts, or *śīla,* are a part of the Vinaya (monastic regulations). Since the precepts can be called both *śīla* and *vinaya,* the combined form "precepts and regulations" (*śīla-vinaya*) came to be used in China.

The Mahāyāna Precepts in China and Japan Chinese Buddhism emphasized Mahāyāna precepts, a combination of the Yoga and Brahmajāla precepts. The Mahāyāna precepts are also known as the bodhisattva precepts, the *vajraratna* (diamond) precepts, and the *buddhagotra* (buddha-nature) precepts.

In China the Hīnayāna precepts of the Dharmaguptaka Four-Part Vinaya and the Mahāyāna precepts tended to be adopted together, especially after the seventh century. This practice was also followed in Japan after the Lü (Vinaya) sect was transmitted there (as the Ritsu sect) by the Chinese monk Chien-chen in 755.

In establishing the Tendai precepts (precepts for full and immediate enlightenment) at his temple on Mount Hiei, however, Saichō (767–822), the founder of the Tendai sect, eliminated the Hīnayāna element. Tendai, and the sects that emanated from it, follow Saichō's precepts.

In the Sōtō Zen sect, established by the thirteenth-century priest Dōgen, the bodhisattva precepts consist of sixteen items: the three refuges, the three pure precepts, and the ten grave prohibitions. It is interesting to note that the three refuges (taking refuge in the Three Treasures) became a precept. The precepts of the Rinzai Zen sect also consist of sixteen items.

In Japan the Shingon sect established its own *samaya* (equal and unobstructed) precepts, in which the three kinds of aspiration to enlightenment (*bodhicitta*) were made a precept. Apart from this, there is not a great deal of difference between the *samaya* precepts and the ten good precepts. In Japan some sects, such as the Jōdo Shin (True Pure Land), do not teach the precepts at all. As a rule, formalistic precepts do not appeal to the Japanese; Japanese Buddhism can be said to take the precepts more lightly than Indian and Chinese Buddhism.

The fact, however, that Japanese Buddhism, especially the sects that developed around the thirteenth century (for instance, Jōdo Shin, Nichiren, and Zen), did not make the precepts a central issue does not mean that morality was ignored. Rather, it was thought that deep faith would lead naturally to morality. Thus Japanese Buddhism of the Kamakura period (1185–1336) was characterized by the development of sects based on a single practice underpinned by pure faith—invoking the buddha Amida (Amitābha, Amitāyus), chanting the title of the Lotus Sūtra, or the *shikan taza* (just sitting) form of Zen meditation.

Absolute Pure Faith in the Four Imperishables Primitive Buddhism recognized the close relation between morality and faith and taught that morality springs naturally from faith. This is seen in primitive sūtras in the teaching of absolute pure faith in the four imperishables (*avetyaprasāda, aveccappasāda*) and in the "verse of commandment of the seven Buddhas."

There are four imperishables: the Three Treasures and the precepts. When one takes refuge in the Three Treasures and achieves absolute pure faith, the first stage of enlightenment has been attained. As a consequence, morality arises naturally from within. The precepts for the restraint of evil and for the promotion of good will be observed with no need for outside sanctions, since there will be no urge to violate the precepts. Absolute pure faith in the four imperishables, then, indicates that faith encompasses morality.[2]

The "verse of commandment of the seven Buddhas" (the seven Buddhas of the Past, including Śākyamuni) is one of the most famous verses in Buddhism:

> To do no evil,
> To do only good,
> To purify one's mind,
> This is the teaching of the Buddhas.

The possession of absolute pure faith—a faith that purifies the mind—and the keeping of the precepts (to avoid evil and to do good) are the essence of Buddhism in that they teach the means by which faith and morality are to be achieved. If faith in the Three Treasures is central, then the precepts will be followed naturally, and morality will become a function of faith. In the Eightfold Path, right view refers to faith, while right speech, action, and livelihood refer to morality.

CONCENTRATION

When the body and mind have been regulated by the precepts, concentration (*samādhi*) is practiced to focus the mind. The regulation of body, breath, and mind (required for the achievement of concentration) defines morality in the broad sense.

The Four *Dhyānas* Primitive sūtras define concentration, whether as part of the threefold practice or as an item of the Eightfold Path, exclusively in terms of the four *dhyānas* (meditational or trance states) because they are considered the most basic form of *samādhi*. A representative description in the Sūtra of the Recital (*Saṅgīti-suttanta*) in the Dīgha-nikāya states:

> The practitioner, free from sensuous desire, free from evil and blameworthy states of mind, but still exercising discursive thought and investigation, attains and abides in the first *jhāna*, which arises from seclusion and is characterized by delight and pleasure.
>
> With the cessation of discursive thought and investigation, the practitioner, serene of heart, concentrates the mind on one point and attains and abides in the second *jhāna*, which arises from concentration and is associated with delight and pleasure, but with the absence of discursive thought and investigation.
>
> With the renunciation of delight, the practitioner abides in equanimity, mindful and self-possessed, experiencing the pleasure in the body that the holy ones spoke of as living in equanimity, mindfulness, and pleasure, and thus attains and abides in the third *jhāna*.
>
> With the abandonment of pleasure and pain, and through the previous disappearance of delight and lamentation, the practitioner attains and abides in the fourth *jhāna*, which is neither painful nor pleasant, and because of equanimity mindfulness is completely pure.

Originally, concentration meant quieting the mind and focusing it. There are, however, many degrees of quieting the mind. That of the ordinary person in the everyday world is called the concentration of the realm of desire and is not true spiritual centeredness. True spiritual centering, called "fundamental concentration," is said to pertain to the concentration of the realm of form and of the formless realm. The four *dhyānas* are the fundamental concentration of the realm of form. The concentration of the formless realm is further quieting of the mind, approaching a state in which thought ceases.

The three realms of existence. Buddhism teaches that there are three realms of existence: the realm of desire (*kāma-dhātu*), the realm of form (*rūpa-dhātu*), and the formless realm (*ārūpya-dhātu, āruppa-dhātu*). In the realm of desire sensuous desire is rampant. In the realm of form there is no sensuous desire, only physical form. This realm indicates the state of *dhyāna* attained through the four *dhyānas*. In the formless realm there is no physical form at all, only a condition of utter calm, of pure spirit. This state of mind is known as the concentration of the formless realm. The original reason for positing the three realms was not cosmological but psychological.

According to the doctrine of karmic retribution, violation of the ten good precepts by an inhabitant of the realm of desire results in that person's rebirth in one of the undesirable realms (*durgati, duggati*): in a hell, in the realm of hungry spirits, or in the realm of animals. On the other hand, an inhabitant of the realm of desire who practices good, such as by keeping the precepts or through donation, will be reborn in one of the desirable realms (*sugati*), that is, as a heavenly or human being. One who still has defilements and practices the concentration of the realm of form will be reborn in one of the four *dhyāna* heavens, while one who still has defilements and practices the concentration of the formless realm will enjoy rebirth in one of the heavens of the formless realm. Originally the realm of desire, the realm of form, and the formless realm were mental states of people in this world. The concept of their physical counterparts as realms of retribution developed only later.

The three realms belong to the world of delusion, the world of birth and death. One who has gained release from the delusion of the defilements and has passed beyond the three realms is considered to have entered the supramundane world free of defilements. This realm of enlightenment is not a discrete world somewhere outside the three realms but a state of mind. Neither the world of the three realms (*loka*) nor the supramundane world beyond it (*lokottara*) is physical; they are mental states distinguished by the degree of delusion or enlightenment.

The doctrine of the ten realms. The T'ien-t'ai sect postulates ten realms of existence: hells, the realms of hungry spirits, animals, *asuras,* human beings, and heavenly beings, and the realms of *śrāvakas, pratyekabuddhas,* bodhisattvas, and buddhas. (The first six of these are realms in the world of delusion; the last four are the four noble realms of enlightenment.) Like the three realms, these ten realms are nothing more than categorizations of people's mental states. Within the reality of the mind, each realm has the potential to contain each of the other realms; this is the doctrine of the interpenetration of the ten realms.

The Four Formless Concentrations Just as there are four *dhyānas* in the realm of form, the formless realm has four stages of concentration, called the four formless concentrations (*ārūpya-samāpatti, āruppa-samāpatti*). When the mind achieves calm (*śamatha, samatha*) on attainment of the four *dhyānas,* it is ready to enter the formless concentrations. At this point there is no awareness of the material, of either one's body or one's surroundings. The four formless concentrations are four stages of increasing calm, termed the stage of the infinity of space (*ākāśānantyāyatana, ākāsānañcāyatana*), the stage of the infinity of consciousness (*vijñānānantyāyatana, viññāṇānañcāyatana*), the stage of nothingness (*ākiṃcanyāyatana, ākiñcaññāyatana*), and the stage of neither perception nor nonperception (*naivasaṃjñānāsaṃjñāyatana, nevasaññānāsaññāyatana*). They are defined in the Sūtra of the Recital as follows:

> The *samādhi* [concentration] of the realm of the infinity of space transcends the *jhānas* of the realm of form, and with the elimination of the objects of form and the raising of no conscious thoughts, the meditator concentrates exclusively on the infinity of space [that remains].
>
> The *samādhi* of the realm of the infinity of consciousness transcends the realm of the infinity of space. Here the meditator concentrates exclusively on the infinity of consciousness.
>
> The *samādhi* of the realm of nothingness transcends the realm of the infinity of consciousness, and the meditator concentrates exclusively on nothingness.
>
> The *samādhi* of neither perception nor nonperception transcends the realm of nothingness, and the meditator concentrates exclusively on that which is beyond the concept of nothingness and dwells in the realm of neither perception nor nonperception.

The first stage transcends all form, all that is material. Although sensuous desire is eliminated in the *dhyānas* of the realm of form, conscious thought about material form remains. In the formless realm, all ideas of form are transcended. This is achieved through concentration on the infinity of space. In this realm there is nothing material, no concept of the material, and no thought of good or evil.

The second transcends thought of external space and focuses on the infinity of the consciousness that perceives this space. The third goes beyond all thought of consciousness and focuses on nothingness, or emptiness. The mind is drawn by nothing at all.

The fourth discards the thought of nothingness and attains the condition of no thought at all. This does not mean that the mind has stopped functioning, as if the meditator were dead, but indicates an utterly peaceful state in which there is no thought of whether perception occurs. There is neither perception nor nonperception. This is the highest of the formless concentrations.

Terms Denoting Concentration *Samādhi* is the broadest, most general term for concentration. Thus it is used for concentration in the world of defilements, concentration in the supramundane world free of defilements, the concentration when active thought ceases, and the concentration of the three realms.

Dhyāna (*jhāna*) includes only the four *dhyānas* of the realm of form, not the concentration of the realm of desire and of the formless realm. *Dhyāna* refers to both the defiled and the undefiled states.

Samāpatti, attainment, encompasses only the fundamental concentration of the realm of form and the formless realm, not the concentration of the realm of desire. It refers to both the defiled and the undefiled states. The four *dhyānas* and the four formless concentrations are together called the eight *samāpattis.* In addition to these higher attainments there is a ninth, the concentration of the cessation of perception and feeling (*nirodha-samāpatti*). Of the nine *samāpattis* (*anupūrva-samāpatti, anupubba-samāpatti*), the first eight can be attained by anyone, but the ninth can be attained only by the *anāgāmin* (nonreturner, one who will not be reborn in the realm of desire) or the *arhat.*

Śamatha (*samatha*), calm or tranquillity, appears most often in conjunction with *vipaśyanā* (*vipassanā*), contemplation or insight, in the compound *śamatha-vipaśyanā* (calm and contemplation). *Śamatha* is usually included in the concentration of the formless realm, while *vipaśyanā* is seen largely in the realms of desire and form. The fourth *dhyāna* of the realm of form is called the state of balance between calm and contemplation, which coexist in equilibrium and moderation. The wisdom of enlightenment and the supernormal powers are attained from this *dhyāna*, which is considered the ideal *dhyāna*.[3]

Cittaikāgratā (*cittekaggatā*), or fixing the mind on one point, another synonym for *samādhi*, emphasizes the idea of concentration itself.

Yoga is a concentration practice used by Brahmans since before the time of the Buddha. In Buddhism *dhyāna* and *samādhi* refer to this practice. Even in primitive Buddhism the term *yoga* was used to mean *dhyāna*, and later the expressions *yogācāra* (*yoga* practice) and *yogācārya* (*yoga* adept) came to be widely used in Buddhism.

Other synonyms for concentration are *samāhita* (composed), *samāpanna* (in the state of fundamental concentration), and *dṛṣṭa-dharma-sukhavihāra* (*diṭṭhadhamma-sukhavihāra*), being perfectly composed and experiencing bliss of mind and body while in a state of concentration in this existence; this term is used especially of *arhats*.

Zen. Chinese *ch'an* and Japanese *zen* are not the same as Indian *dhyāna;* they are something more than meditation or concentration as a division of the threefold practice or as one of the Six Perfections. *Zen* is a combination of all three parts of the threefold practice and all the perfections. This is because *zen* is not simply a device for centering and calming the mind but also encompasses the wisdom of enlightenment. The declaration that the purpose of *zen* is to see one's true nature and to open and illuminate the mind indicates that *zen* is concerned with seeking the wisdom of enlightenment. *Zen* was introduced to the West with the Japanese term rather than the Sanskrit *dhyāna* to underscore the difference in connotation between the two.

The five kinds of zen. In the preface to the *Ch'an-yüan-chu-ch'uan-chi*, a collection of famous sayings of Ch'an masters and brief histories of various Ch'an sects compiled by the Hua-yen patriarch Tsung-mi (780–841), five types of *zen* are listed: non-Buddhist *zen,* ordinary people's *zen,* Hīnayāna *zen,* Mahāyāna *zen,* and the *zen* of the highest vehicle, or the *zen* of the *tathāgatas.* This categorization emphasizes the degree of enlightenment achieved in the type of *zen* practiced and the degree of wisdom contained in that enlightenment. It stresses the *zen* that includes wisdom emanating from the highest enlightenment, the *zen* of the *tathāgatas,* the *zen* of the patriarchs.

Methods of Practicing Concentration As can be seen, a great deal is encompassed by the terms *dhyāna* and *samādhi.* In the primitive sūtras alone, a wide variety of methods of practice are set forth for concentration. The Abhidharma schools codified and clarified these.

The forty subjects of concentration. Pāli Buddhism teaches forty subjects of concentration,[4] most of which appear in the primitive sūtras (see the chart on page 181). These subjects (*kammaṭṭhāna*), discussed below, are categorized according to the practitioner's personality type, with suggestions for the most suitable themes for concentration for each personality type and an indication of which of the eight *samāpattis* is attainable through each theme. Six personality types are recognized: personalities that are dominated by greed, anger, folly, distraction, faith, and intellect.

All eight *samāpattis* can be achieved by meditating on a physical object characterized by one of the ten universals (*dasa kasiṇa-āyatanāni*): earth, water, fire, air, blue, yellow, red, white, light, and space. The use of an object facilitates concentration.

The contemplation of the ten impurities (*dasa asubha-saññā*) is a meditation to overcome greed through concentrating on the ten stages of decomposition of a corpse: swollen, discolored, putrefied, dismembered, devoured by birds and animals, scattered, hacked and scattered, bloody, worm-infested, and skeletonized.

The ten states of mindfulness (*dasa anussatiyo*) begin with contemplation of the virtues of the Buddha, the Dharma, and the Saṅgha, contemplation of morality and almsgiving, and contemplation of the happy state of heavenly beings. These practices are suitable for people in whom faith is dominant, who are motivated to continue the practice of concentration as their faith strengthens. Mindfulness of death (contemplation of the inevitability of one's own death) is suitable for the intellectual type. Mindfulness of the body, practiced to overcome greed, comprehends the body as a receptacle filled with filth. Mindfulness of the breath is suitable for one dominated by folly or distraction. Cultivating awareness of one's inhalations and exhalations has a calming effect on

The Forty Subjects of Concentration

The subjects	Personality type
The ten universals	
earth, water, fire, air	all
blue, yellow, red, white	angry
light, space	all
The ten impurities	greedy
ten stages of decomposition of a corpse	
The ten states of mindfulness	
the virtues of the Buddha, the Dharma, and the Saṅgha	faithful
morality and almsgiving	faithful
the happy state of heavenly beings	faithful
death	intellectual
the body	greedy
the breath	foolish, distracted
calm	intellectual
The four Brahmā abodes	angry
kindness	
compassion	
sympathetic joy	
disinterestedness	
The four formless concentrations	all
the infinity of space	
the infinity of consciousness	
nothingness	
neither perception nor nonperception	
Contemplation of the loathsomeness of food	intellectual
Analysis of the four great elements	intellectual

the body and mind. Mindfulness of calm (contemplation of the calm of nirvāṇa) is suitable for the intellectual type.

The four Brahmā abodes (*cattāro brahma-vihārā,* also called *cattasso appamaññāyo,* the four immeasurable contemplations)—kindness, compassion, sympathetic joy, and disinterestedness—are practiced to counteract anger. Kindness is a feeling of friendship toward all beings. Because kindness can degenerate into attachment, compassion for the suffering of sentient beings is practiced as a preventive. Sympathetic joy, the ability to share the happiness of others, is cultivated to forestall spiritual pride, which can be generated by compassion. Disinterestedness is impartiality toward all beings.

The four stages in the formless realm—the infinity of space, the infinity of consciousness, nothingness, and neither perception nor nonperception—are discussed on pages 177–78. The concentration on them cultivates in the practitioner a pure, flexible mind divorced from the realm of form.

Contemplation of the loathsomeness of food (*āhāre paṭikūlasaññā*) is undertaken to quell sensuous desire. The practitioner meditates on the disgusting aspects of the preparation, ingestion, and elimination of food.

Analysis of the four great elements (*dhātu-[vavatthāna-]kammaṭṭhāna*) weans the practitioner from attachment to the body by emphasizing that it is nothing more than a chance union of elements.

The five meditations for settling the mind. Another set of meditations related to personality type is found in a Sarvāstivādin categorization of the subjects of contemplation. This is the five meditations for settling the mind to rid it of the five delusory states of greed, anger, folly, egoism, and distraction, which is an ancillary practice to prepare the mind for intensive meditation.

To overcome greed, practitioners meditate on the impurity of all things, contemplating the ten impurities. To overcome anger or hate, they meditate on compassion by concentrating on the four Brahmā abodes. To overcome folly, they meditate on the Twelve-linked Chain of Dependent Origination. To overcome egoism, they focus on analysis of the four great elements. To overcome distraction, they meditate on breathing, counting inhalations and exhalations. When all five of these delusory states have been overcome, a practitioner is ready to begin the contemplation of the four *dhyāna* stages.

Meditation on the five gateways, a variant of the five meditations for settling the mind, substitutes contemplation of the virtues of the Buddha for analysis of the four great elements. This meditation, considered suitable for all personality types, purifies the mind.

The twenty-five ancillary practices. T'ien-t'ai teaching on the practice of meditation sets forth twenty-five ancillary practices for *dhyāna*, divided into five groups of five. The first group consists of the five conditions necessary to create a suitable environment for meditation. The meditator should ensure purity by keeping the precepts, should possess sufficient food and clothing, should live in quiet, should recognize the need for concentration, and should recognize the need for a good teacher. The second group deals with repressing the five desires (for form, sound, odor, taste, and touch), and the third with removing the five hindrances to meditation (greed, anger, languor and drowsiness, frivolity and regret, and doubt or perplexity). The fourth is the regulation of the five physical needs (for food, sleep, body, respiration, and mind), and the fifth is the cultivation of the five attributes of *dhyāna* (desire to practice, effort in practice, mindfulness, bringing wisdom into action, and concentration) to create a steady, unswerving mind.

The Merits of Concentration Concentration is an integral practice of Buddhism because it focuses the mind, enables observation of the real aspect of all things with a mind that is like a clear mirror or still water (thus fostering the acquisition of true wisdom), and empties the mind so that prompt, appropriate action based on correct judgment can be taken. Wisdom is both acquired and activated by means of *samādhi*.

Pāli Buddhism lists five merits of *samādhi*. First, it brings about bliss of mind and body. Second, it allows the attainment of contemplation or insight (*vipassanā*), the enlightened wisdom of the *arhat*. Third, it enables attainment of the five supernormal powers: knowledge of the whereabouts of any being in the realm of form (*dibbacakkhu*), the ability to hear any sound anywhere (*dibbasota*), the ability to know the thoughts of all other minds (*cetopariya-ñāṇa*), the ability to perceive both one's own former lives and those of others (*pubbenivāsānussati-ñāṇa*), and the power to be anywhere or do anything at will (*iddhividhā-ñāṇa*). Fourth, it brings rebirth in an excellent realm of form or formless realm. (This is actually a non-Buddhist concept.) Fifth, it enables attainment of cessation of perception and feeling (*nirodha-samāpatti*)—a state higher than the fourth of the formless concentrations, a pure state achieved only by the *anāgāmin* and the *arhat*.

In addition, the Āgamas speak of eleven merits of meditation on compassion. The practitioner sleeps at ease; wakes at ease; has no bad dreams; is loved by other people; is also loved by animals and other nonhuman beings; is guarded by deities; is not harmed by fire, poison, or sword; can enter *samādhi* swiftly; has a serene countenance; dies unconfused; and, even though he or she may not have attained enlightenment, will at least be reborn in the first of the four *dhyāna* heavens.

The various practices spanning progress from concentration to wisdom cited in the Āgamas include contemplation of the five aggregates, contemplation of the Four Noble Truths, concentration (*samādhi*) on the three subjects (the three gates to liberation),[5] and the eight stages of mastery of the senses (*aṭṭhābhibhāyatanāni*).

WISDOM

Buddhism's ultimate goal is the attainment of the wisdom of enlightenment. Thus wisdom is the last item in the threefold practice, as well as in the ten *aśaikṣa dharmas* and the Six Perfections. Yet there are many aspects and degrees of wisdom. There is the mundane wisdom of the realm of desire; there is the wisdom inherent in the first stage of enlightenment; and there is wisdom in its highest form, the wisdom of the *arhat* (*śrāvaka*), of the *pratyekabuddha*, of the bodhisattva, and of the buddha.

Buddhism uses a wide variety of terms and metaphors to denote the concept of wisdom. The most important of these are discussed below.

Prajñā* and *Jñāna The most widely used terms for wisdom are *prajñā* (*paññā*) and *jñāna* (*ñāṇa*). Early Chinese translations used *chih-hui* for both. The seventh-century translator Hsüan-tsang, however, made a distinction between them, translating *prajñā* as *hui* and *jñāna* as *chih*. The transcendental wisdom of the threefold practice and the Six Perfections is always *prajñā*.

Prajñā is wisdom in its broadest sense. According to Abhidharma Buddhism, *prajñā* embraces all mentation—good, bad, and neutral—and encompasses all stages of wisdom, from the inferior wisdom of the ordinary person in the world of defilements to superior wisdom, free from all defilements. The term *prajñā* generally denotes the highest form of wisdom, but when used without the word *pāramitā* (perfection), it can denote even wisdom in the ordinary sense. *Prajñā-pāramitā*, the perfection of wisdom, is the highest, perfect form of wisdom.

Jñāna, transcendental knowledge, denoting chiefly the wisdom of enlightenment, is used in such expressions as "complete knowledge," "final knowledge," and "correct knowledge," which generally refer to the wisdom of an *ārya*, or sage. *Jñāna-pāramitā*, the perfection of knowledge, is the highest wisdom of a bodhisattva at the tenth stage of practice (as described in the Flower Garland Sūtra), while *prajñā-pāramitā* is the wisdom of a bodhisattva at the sixth stage of practice. Other expressions for the wisdom of enlightenment of a bodhisattva are the four forms of wisdom (perfecting wisdom, profound observing wisdom, impartial wisdom, and great mirror wisdom) and the five forms of wisdom (the four forms of wisdom plus the wisdom of the embodied nature of the *dharma-dhātu*, or Dharma realm). Also related to the wisdom of enlightenment are the three kinds of wisdom: *śrāvaka* and *pratyekabuddha* knowledge that all the *dharmas* are empty (*sarvajña-jñāna*), bodhisattva knowledge of everything to do with salvation (*mārgākāra-jñāna*), and buddha knowledge of all things in every aspect and relationship, past and present (*sarvajñatā-jñāna*).

In referring to mundane wisdom, *jñāna* is used in the same sense as *prajñā*. In the *Abhidharmakośa-śāstra* classification of the ten forms of knowledge, only the first, mundane knowledge, is the wisdom of the realm of defilements, the remaining nine being wisdom free from defilements.[6] The Vijñānavāda school created a classification of eleven forms of knowledge by adding to the *Abhidharmakośa-śāstra* list the knowledge of reality, which is the highest wisdom of the ordinary person in the realm of defilements, not a form of wisdom free from defilements. Mundane knowledge as wisdom in the realm of defilements is identified with the four kinds of wisdom (*prajñā*), that is, wisdom acquired through birth, through hearing or being taught, through thought, and through practice.

Synonyms for *Prajñā* *Vidyā* (*vijjā;* knowledge), *buddhi* (awakening), *medhā* (wisdom), and *bhūri* (wide)—as well as the metaphors *cakṣu* (*cakkhu;* the eye) and *āloka* (light)—can denote wisdom (*prajñā*). *Vidyā* refers in particular to the wisdom of a buddha, as in the epithet *vidyācaraṇa-saṃpanna* (*vijjācaraṇa-sampanna;* Perfect in Knowledge and Conduct).

Darśana (*dassana;* seeing) is used in such expressions as "to know by seeing." *Dṛṣṭi* (*diṭṭhi;* view) is most often used negatively—as in false views or heterodox views—and thus signifies evil views and opinions. In the Eightfold Path, however, *dṛṣṭi* is used in the sense of superior wisdom in the item right view.

Vipaśyanā (*vipassanā*), contemplation or insight, used in the compound term *śamatha-vipaśyanā*, indicates wisdom. *Anupaśyanā* (*anupassanā*), viewing or consideration, indicates the wisdom of observation in the four fields of mindfulness. *Parijñā* (*pariññā*), thorough knowledge, is the wisdom of correctly understanding suffering as one of the Four Noble Truths. *Abhijñā* (*abhiññā*), supernatural knowledge, is the wisdom of enlightenment and also indicates the five supernormal powers.

Ājñā (*aññā*), clear understanding, is the wisdom of the first stage of enlightenment, achieved through the opening of the Dharma Eye. *Ājñā* is an element in the name of Ājñāta-Kauṇḍinya, one of the five ascetics who were Śākyamuni's first disciples. Ājñāta-Kauṇḍinya, whose name has been interpreted as meaning "possessed of clear understanding [of nonexistence]," is said to have been the first person after Śākyamuni to attain enlightenment, that is, clear understanding of the Buddha's Law. *Samprajāna* (*sampajāna*), right knowledge, which is found in such expressions as "right mindfulness and knowledge," refers to correct consciousness.

Mīmāṃsā (*vīmaṃsā*), investigation, is the term used for wisdom in the four psychic powers. *Parīkṣā* (*parikkhā*), investigation, is the term used for both investigation and wisdom in the chapter of the Treatise on the Middle dealing with the contemplation of causes and conditions. *Pratyavekṣaṇa* (*paccavekkhana*), or thorough consideration, also means both investigation and wisdom.

Dharmavicaya (*dhammavicaya*), discrimination of true from false, denotes the wisdom that analyzes the Dharma and also denotes investigation of the Dharma, the second of the seven factors of enlightenment. *Pratisaṃvid* (*paṭisambhidā*), unhindered understanding or knowledge, is wisdom free of obstacles and free from delusion, such as a bodhisattva or a buddha possesses. The four *pratisaṃvids* (four kinds of unhindered understanding, knowledge, or interpretation) concern the doctrine, its meaning, its language or form of expression, and its eloquence or argument.

Bodhi (enlightenment) and *saṃbodhi* (*sambodhi;* perfect enlightenment) denote not only wisdom but also the state of enlightenment, in which morality, concentration, and wisdom have been perfected. *Bodhi* and *saṃbodhi* encompass both body and mind. The attainment of the experiential wisdom of *bodhi* and *saṃbodhi* is called *sparśana* (*phusana*), or contact, since enlightenment "touches" both body and mind through physical experience.

The Function of Wisdom Wisdom can be divided into discriminating wisdom (*savikalpa-jñāna*), wisdom that is conscious of its object, and nondiscriminating wisdom (*nirvikalpa-jñāna*), wisdom in which there is no consciousness of an object, wherein wisdom and its object are one. The latter is the wisdom of the highest enlightenment.

The Buddhist ideal is correct theoretical knowledge of the doctrine that all phenomena are devoid of self and without self-nature (*niḥsvabhāva*). This knowledge enables practitioners to achieve the unhindered state free from delusion, in which they are attached to nothing. Neither power nor mind is of use in the unhindered, nondelusory state. Nondiscriminating wisdom is that of the free, unhindered mind acting spontaneously within the realm of absolute Truth, or *tathatā*. This wisdom of supreme enlightenment is the perfection of wisdom (*prajñā-pāramitā*), the last of the Six Perfections.

The buddhas and bodhisattvas who attain this supreme, nondiscriminating wisdom do not rest there. Using this wisdom, they act compassionately to liberate sentient beings. Through their actions, this wisdom becomes discriminating in that it has an object, consciousness of sentient beings. Since this change occurs after supreme, nondiscriminating wisdom has been attained, however, this transformed wisdom is no longer merely discriminating wisdom but is termed "discriminating wisdom attained after nondiscriminating wisdom."

The five perfections that precede the perfection of wisdom are embodiments of discriminating wisdom attained after nondiscriminating wisdom. These five perfections are called *upāya*, skillful means, that is, correct ways of leading sentient beings to enlightenment. Thus the Six Perfections can be considered to be both *upāya* and *prajñā*. *Upāya* is the working of compassion through discriminating wisdom attained after nondiscriminating wisdom, and *prajñā* is the working of wisdom through nondiscriminating wisdom. The former is the great compassion (*mahā-karuṇā*) of the bodhisattva working to instruct sentient beings, and the latter is great wisdom, seeking enlightenment. To be endowed with great wisdom and great compassion is the ideal and goal of Buddhists.

The Stages of Practice

Śākyamuni said little in an organized fashion about the stages of religious practice, though even the oldest extant canonical works, the Āgamas, expound the process from the first stage of enlightenment to the stage of the *arhat*.

THE STAGES OF *ARHAT* PRACTICE

Differing processes are set forth in the Āgamas depending on whether the stage of the *arhat* is to be attained through faith, through theoretical understanding of doctrine, or through contemplation. Some sūtras in the Āgamas describe stages of practice from the level of the ordinary person to that of the *arhat*. Two representative conceptions of the stages of *arhat* practice are examined below.

The Seven Purities The Discourse on the Relays of Chariots (*Rathavinīta-sutta*) in the Majjhima-nikāya cites the seven purities (*visuddhi*) as stages of practice. These are purity of morality (*sīla-visuddhi*), purity of mind (*citta-visuddhi*), purity of views (*diṭṭhi-visuddhi*), purity of overcoming doubt (*kaṅkhāvitaraṇa-visuddhi*), purity of knowledge and insight into right and wrong paths (*maggāmagga-ñāṇadassana-visuddhi*), purity of knowledge and insight into the mode of progress (*paṭipadā-ñāṇadassana-visuddhi*), and purity of knowledge and insight (*ñāṇadassana-visuddhi*).

The seven purities are described in detail in the Path of Purity (*Visuddhimagga*) by Buddhaghosa, the most important Pāli Buddhist work on the philosophy of practice.

The Seventeen Stages of *Arhat* Practice The Greater Discourse at Assapura (*Mahā-assapura-sutta*) in the Majjhima-nikāya lists seventeen stages of *arhat* practice, from the beginning of religious practice to *arhat* enlightenment. These stages are as follows:

1. Feeling shame for both one's own misdeeds and those of society (*hirottappa-samannāgata*). This refers to correct mental attitude, the most important attribute of a monk.
2. Practicing purity of physical actions (*parisuddha-kāyasamācāra*), which is equivalent to right action in the Eightfold Path.
3. Practicing purity of speech (*parisuddha-vacīsamācāra*), which is equivalent to right speech in the Eightfold Path.
4. Purity of thought (*parisuddha-manosamācāra*), which is equivalent to right thought in the Eightfold Path.
5. Practicing purity of living (*parisuddha-ājīva*), which is equivalent to right livelihood in the Eightfold Path.
6. Protecting the doors of the senses from delusion (*indriyesu guttadvāra*). This refers to not clinging to objects.
7. Knowing what is sufficient for nourishment (*bhojane mattaññu*). (Stages six and seven can also be considered to be part of right livelihood in the Eightfold Path.)

8. Practicing intent effort (*jāgariyam anuyutta*), such as not allowing oneself to fall asleep during meditation. This is equivalent to right effort in the Eightfold Path.
9. Practicing right mindfulness and right knowledge (*sati-sampajaññena samannāgata*), which is equivalent to right mindfulness in the Eightfold Path.
10. Abiding alone in a quiet place suitable for meditation and abandoning the five hindrances (greed, anger, languor and drowsiness, frivolity and regret, and doubt or perplexity), which are a barrier to entering the *dhyāna* of the realm of form (*vivitta-senāsana, pañcanīvaraṇa-pahāna*). This is the preparation for entering the stage of meditation. Once the five hindrances have been cast aside, the practitioner can enter the next stages, the *dhyāna* stages of the realm of form.
11. Attaining the first *dhyāna* stage (*paṭhamajjhāna*), that is, the first of the four *dhyānas.*
12. Attaining the second *dhyāna* stage (*dutiyajjhāna*), that is, the second of the four *dhyānas.*
13. Attaining the third *dhyāna* stage (*tatiyajjhāna*), that is, the third of the four *dhyānas.*
14. Attaining the fourth *dhyāna* stage (*catutthajjhāna*), that is, the fourth of the four *dhyānas.*
15. Having insight into the past lives of oneself and others (*pubbenivāsānussati-ñāṇa*).
16. Having insight into the future lives of oneself and others (*sattānaṃ cutūpapāta-ñāṇa*).
17. Having nirvāṇa insight into suffering so as to be able to overcome all defilements and temptations in the present life (*āsavānaṃ khaye ñāṇa*).

Stages one through eight are concerned with morality, stages nine through fourteen with concentration, and stages fifteen through seventeen with wisdom. Through correct concentration the mind becomes centered and wisdom is attained. This is the final enlightenment of an *arhat.* With enlightenment, the three insights (*te-vijjā*), that is, stages fifteen through seventeen, are attained.

The seven purities and the seventeen stages of *arhat* practice elucidate the process whereby one attains enlightenment through the threefold practice, the process whereby the practice of the ordinary person becomes that of the *arhat*. Now let us consider the steps by which the *arhat* stage is attained.

THE TYPES OF ATTAINMENT

With the rise of Abhidharma Buddhism, works in the primitive canon dealing with practice were collected and codified. This codification resulted in the formulation of the eight stages of effort and attainment and the linking of the stages with eight types of attainment based on personality type (doctrinal, devotional, or contemplative).

The Eight Stages of Effort and Attainment The enlightenment of the *śrāvaka*, or disciple, consists of eight stages, four of effort and four of attainment, occurring in consecutive pairs. The first pair is the stage of the streamwinner. Here, the *śrāvaka* overcomes errors of view, which form a barrier between the secular and the sacred that must be surmounted in order to enter the first *arhat* stage. The lower stage of the streamwinner, that of effort, is *srota-āpatti-pratipanna*, and the higher stage, that of attainment, is *srota-āpanna*. The second pair is the stage of the once-returner, who is assured of only one more rebirth. The lower stage here is *sakṛdāgāmi-pratipanna*, and the higher *sakṛdāgāmin*. The third pair is that of the nonreturner; a person at this stage will never be reborn in the realm of desire. Here the lower stage, of effort, is *anāgami-pratipanna*, and the higher, of attainment, *anāgāmin*. The fourth pair is the stage of the *arhat*, which is the highest degree of *śrāvaka* enlightenment. The lower stage here is *arhat-pratipanna*, and the higher *arhattva*.

One who has reached the final stage of attainment is called *aśaikṣa*, one who has nothing more to learn. By contrast, people in the other seven stages still have more to learn and are termed *śaikṣa*. At the first stage, the stage of effort of the streamwinner, theoretical delusions are eliminated; thus this stage is called the Way of View (*darśana-mārga*). Stages two through seven, those in which the truth is cultivated, are termed the Way of Practice (*bhāvanā-mārga*). In the stages of the Way of Practice errors in habitual behavior—defilements relating to thought or practice—are eliminated. The final and highest stage is achieved only when all defilements have been extinguished.

Primitive Buddhism discussed the nature of the defilements that are extinguished in the course of the eight stages. During the first stage the three defilements known as the three fetters (*tīni saṃyojanāni*) are extinguished. The first of these is false views about a permanent self (*sakkāya-diṭṭhi*), or selfish and self-centered thinking. The second is doubt (*vicikicchā*) about such things as causality, karmic retribution, and the existence of good and evil. It is the same as perverse views (*micchā-diṭṭhi*), the denial of good and evil. Thus doubt also includes denial that retribution for good and evil karma extends throughout the past, present, and future. The third fetter, attachment to heretical practices (*sīlabbata-parāmāsa*), consists of being in error about the correct goal, or the ideal state, and about the method by which it is to be attained. It encompasses superstitious or heretical thought.

Until the three fetters are extinguished, it is utterly impossible for the practitioner to progress from the state of the ordinary person to that of the streamwinner. In short, the three fetters are the initial, basic obstructions to entering the *ārya,* or noble, stage. Having severed the three fetters, the practitioner enters the second stage as "one who has reached the first stage of enlightenment" and is known as a person resolved to attain the highest enlightenment (*sammatta-niyata-rāsi*). Such a person, who is sure to attain the highest stage, that of the *arhat,* can never retrogress from the *ārya* stage or turn to other religious beliefs. The second stage can be attained either through faith or through study of the Dharma.

At the sixth stage, that of the *anāgāmin,* two further defilements—anger (*vyāpāda*) and craving for the realm of desire (*kāmacchanda*)—are extinguished. Together these two defilements and the three fetters are known as the five lower fetters and represent all the defilements of the realm of desire. Having severed the five lower fetters, the *anāgāmin* is not reborn into the realm of desire but proceeds immediately to the highest enlightenment or is reborn into either the realm of form or the formless realm and there becomes a supreme *arhat*.

At the eighth stage, that of the *arhattva*, all the defilements of the realm of form and of the formless realm are extinguished. Known collectively as the five higher fetters, these defilements are craving for the realm of form, craving for the formless realm, frivolity (*auddhatya*), pride (*māna*), and ignorance (*avijjā*). Since at the *arhat* stage all defilements of the three realms have been extinguished, the *arhat* is said to be "one who has extinguished all delusions" (*khīṇāsava*) or "one who has exhausted all learning," that is, "one who has nothing more to learn" (*asekha*).

The Eight Types of Attainment Eight types of attainment are posited in the context of three stages of *arhat* practice. The attainment of the Way of View through faith is a practice suitable for a person with relatively dull mental faculties (*śraddhānusārin*). One who is relatively quick-witted (*dharmānusārin*), however, can attain the Way of View through observation of the working of the Dharma. The Way of Practice can be attained through faith (*śraddhādhimukta*) or through insight (*dṛṣṭiprāpta*). At both the stage of the Way of Practice and the *aśaikṣa* stage, sages can attain the realization of practice through contemplation (*kāyasakṣin*). At the *aśaikṣa* stage, the contemplative type attains a mind free from defilements and delusions (*citta-vimukta*), the doctrinal type attains freedom from all hindrances to emancipation through wisdom (*prajñā-vimukta*), and both the contemplative and the doctrinal types attain emancipation from all obstacles to understanding and contemplation (*ubhayato-bhāga-vimukta*).

The relationships between the *arhat* stages and types of enlightenment are shown in the chart on page 194. Although it has been included in the chart for the sake of clarity, *citta-vimukta* can be omitted if *kāyasakṣin* is included, since *kāyasakṣin* encompasses the *arhat* stages of both effort and attainment, which are reached through *dhyāna*. *Ubhayato-bhāga-vimukta* refers to the highest degree of *arhat*, one who has achieved both understanding and contemplation. Such a person is endowed with the six supernormal powers (the five supernormal powers plus nirvāṇa insight into suffering) and the three insights.

The Sarvāstivādin Stages of Practice The *Abhidharmakośa-śāstra* and other Sarvāstivādin works further systematize the stages of practice. These works generally recognize two broad stages of practice, the common and the *ārya* (see the chart on page 195).

The *ārya* stage is essentially the eight stages of effort and attainment. The common stage is divided into the three pure causes and the seven expedient degrees, that is, seven types of skillful means (*upāya*). The three pure causes are detaching body and mind, reducing desires, and the four holy ways (related to food, clothing, shelter, and medicine). The seven expedient degrees are subdivided into the external and the internal. The external, re-

The Stages of *Arhat* Practice

<table>
<tr><th>Three stages of arhat practice</th><th>Eight stages of effort and attainment</th><th>Eight types of attainment</th><th>Personality type</th></tr>
<tr><td rowspan="2">Way of View</td><td rowspan="2">Streamwinner (effort)</td><td>Through faith (śraddhānusārin)</td><td>Devotional</td></tr>
<tr><td>Through insight (dharmānusārin)</td><td>Doctrinal</td></tr>
<tr><td rowspan="3">Way of Practice</td><td rowspan="3">Streamwinner (attainment)
Once-returner (effort)
Once-returner (attainment)
Nonreturner (effort)
Nonreturner (attainment)
Arhat (effort)</td><td>Through faith (śraddhādhimukta)</td><td>Devotional</td></tr>
<tr><td>Through insight (dṛṣṭiprāpta)</td><td>Doctrinal</td></tr>
<tr><td>(all stages)
Through contemplation (kāyasakṣin)</td><td>Contemplative</td></tr>
<tr><td rowspan="3">Aśaikṣa-phala</td><td rowspan="3">Arhat (attainment)</td><td>Mind free of delusion (citta-vimukta)</td><td>Contemplative</td></tr>
<tr><td>Wisdom (prajñā-vimukta)</td><td>Doctrinal</td></tr>
<tr><td>Understanding and contemplation (ubhayato-bhāga-vimukta)</td><td>Contemplative, doctrinal</td></tr>
</table>

The Sarvāstivādin Stages of Practice

Common stage	Three pure causes		Detaching body and mind Reducing desires Four holy ways (food, clothing, shelter, medicines)		
	Seven expedient degrees	Three wise degrees	Five meditations for settling the mind (contemplating impurity, cultivating compassion, contemplating dependent origination, contemplating analysis of the elements, counting inhalations and exhalations)		*Sambhāra*
			Particular stages of mindfulness General stages of mindfulness	Four fields of mindfulness	
		Four good roots	*Uṣmāgata* *Mūrdhan* *Kṣānti* *Lokāgradharma*	Meditation on the Four Noble Truths in sixteen aspects	*Prayoga*
Ārya stage	Way of View	Streamwinner (effort)	Fifteen mind *kṣaṇas*		*Darśana-mārga*
	Way of Practice	Streamwinner (attainment) Once-returner (effort) Once-returner (attainment) Nonreturner (effort) Nonreturner (attainment) *Arhat* (effort)			*Bhāvanā-mārga*
	Aśaikṣa-phala	*Arhat* (attainment)			*Aśaikṣa-phala*

lated to mindfulness, consists of the three wise degrees; the internal, concerned with the deepening of meditation, consists of the four good roots, which enable comprehension of the Four Noble Truths.

The common and the *ārya* stages of practice are linked in the five stages leading to enlightenment: *sambhāra* (preparation), that is, the decision to practice, and the three wise degrees; *prayoga* (application), that is, realization of the four good roots, after which the practitioner enters the *ārya* stages; *darśana-mārga*, or the Way of View, the first *ārya* stage; *bhāvanā-mārga*, or the Way of Practice, the intermediate *ārya* stage; and *aśaikṣa-phala*, the final *arhat* stage, in which there is nothing more to learn.

THE STAGES OF BODHISATTVA PRACTICE

According to primitive Buddhism and the Abhidharma scholastics, the highest stage of practice attainable is that of the *arhat*. Primitive Buddhism and Abhidharma scholastics held that it is not possible to attain buddhahood, saying that the historical Buddha was a special person and that ordinary people cannot become such as he was. Mahāyāna Buddhism, however, teaches that all sentient beings are endowed with the buddha-nature, or potential for attaining buddhahood, and that they need only to resolve to attain enlightenment and to practice as bodhisattvas in order to achieve buddhahood through the perfection of practice.

While T'ien-t'ai doctrine acknowledges that all sentient beings are endowed with the buddha-nature and therefore have the potential to attain buddhahood, the Fa-hsiang sect posited five groups of sentient beings that differ in their potential for buddhahood according to their basic nature. These five groups are the disciple (*śrāvaka*), the *pratyekabuddha*, the bodhisattva, the undetermined (who have the potential to become *śrāvakas*, *pratyekabuddhas*, or bodhisattvas), and those with no potential for enlightenment at all (*icchantika*). Of the five groups, only the bodhisattvas and some of the undetermined can attain buddhahood. The *śrāvakas*, the *pratyekabuddhas*, and others of the undetermined can achieve only the enlightenment of their particular kind. The fifth group is said to have no chance of any kind of enlightenment. The categorization of the five groups pertains to differences in potential within a specific time frame, however. If the transformation of potential over a very long period is taken into consideration, it is clear that all sentient beings are endowed with the buddha-nature.

All Mahāyāna Buddhism posits stages of a bodhisattva's practice, but details differ from one sect to another. For example, the Fa-hsiang (Vijñānavāda) sect spoke of forty-one stages, including buddhahood (see the chart on page 198), while T'ien-t'ai teaches fifty-two, which are preceded by the degrees of the five classes of disciples.[7] These stages correspond to the six stages of enlightenment (see the chart on page 199).

The greatest difference between Fa-hsiang and T'ien-t'ai thought is that Fa-hsiang considered the first level of the first stage of the ten stages of developing buddha wisdom (*daśa-bhūmi*) to be the Way of View (the first of the *ārya* stages), while T'ien-t'ai—and also Hua-yen—considers the ten abodes (*daśa-vihāra;* see page 200) and above to belong to the *ārya* stage, with all practices up through the completion of the ten stages of faith (*daśa-śraddhā*) considered to be the common stage. T'ien-t'ai and Hua-yen hold that with the attainment of the semblance of enlightenment on completion of the ten stages of faith, the degree of the Way of View has been reached. Thus we see that even within Mahāyāna (especially in China and Japan) there are considerable differences in the doctrine of the stages of enlightenment.

The forty-one stages of bodhisattva practice of Fa-hsiang and the fifty-two of T'ien-t'ai and Hua-yen are not found in Indian or Tibetan Buddhism. In early Indian Mahāyāna the ten abodes were defined as the bodhisattva stages and were also called the ten stages; once the Flower Garland Sūtra had expounded the concept of ten stages ranging from joyfulness to the Dharma cloud (see page 201), however, Mahāyāna adopted the version in the Flower Garland Sūtra as the sole interpretation of the stages of bodhisattva practice.

The ten stages of faith, the ten stages of practice, the ten stages of transference of merit, and so forth, were never part of the stages of bodhisattva practice in India. Around the latter half of the fifth century Chinese Buddhism accepted the ideas set forth in the spurious sūtras composed in China, such as the Sūtra of

The Fa-hsiang Stages of Bodhisattva Practice and the Sarvāstivādin Stages of Practice

Fa-hsiang stages	Sarvāstivādin stages		
Ten abodes (*daśa-vihāra*) (the first abode includes the ten stages of faith) Ten stages of practice (*daśa-caryā*) Ten stages of transference of merit (*daśa-pariṇāma*) Stages 1–9		Three wise degrees	Resolution to attain enlightenment (*sambhāra*)
Stage 10		Four good roots	Realization of good roots (*prayoga*)
Ten stages of developing buddha wisdom (*daśa-bhūmi*) Stage 1 entry	Streamwinner (effort)	Way of View	Unimpeded understanding (*prativedha*)
abiding exit Stages 2–10	Streamwinner (attainment) Once-returner (effort) Once-returner (attainment) Nonreturner (effort) Nonreturner (attainment) *Arhat* (effort)	Way of Practice	Stage of practice (*bhāvanā*)
Stage of buddhahood	Buddhahood	*aśaikṣa-phala*	Supreme stage (*niṣṭhā*)

The T'ien-t'ai Stages of Bodhisattva Practice

	Six stages of enlightenment	
	Theoretical understanding of Buddhism Notional understanding of Buddhism	
Degrees of the five classes of disciples	Contemplation and practice	Common stage
(*Fifty-two stages of bodhisattva practice*) Ten stages of faith	Semblance of enlightenment	
Ten abodes Ten stages of practice Ten stages of transference of merit Ten stages of developing buddha wisdom Approximate supreme enlightenment	Partial enlightenment	*Ārya* stage
Supreme enlightenment of self and others	Perfect enlightenment	

Adornments (*Ying-luo-pen-yeh-ching*), and began speaking of varying numbers of stages of practice. Thus the forty-one and fifty-two stages of bodhisattva practice were Chinese accretions, not the authentic transmission received from Indian Buddhism.

DOCTRINES OF THE TEN STAGES

In the transitional period from Abhidharma Buddhism to Mahāyāna, ten stages of bodhisattva practice were generally cited. Various theories of the ten stages are recorded in the extant Indian Buddhist literature. The scope and variety of these theories are outlined below.

The ten stages set forth in the Great Account (*Mahāvastu*) are the teaching of the Lokottaravādins, an offshoot of the Mahāsāṃghikas. The ten stages in the Great Account are as follows:

1. Difficult to enter (*durāroha*)
2. Fastening (*baddhamāna*)

3. Adorned with flowers (*puṣpamaṇḍita*)
4. Beautiful (*rucira*)
5. Expansion of the heart (*cittavistara*)
6. Lovely (*rūpavatī*)
7. Difficult to conquer (*durjaya*)
8. Ascertainment of birth (*janmanideśa*)
9. Installation as crown prince (*yauvarājya*)
10. Coronation (*abhiṣeka*)

Early Mahāyāna initially taught that there were four degrees of enlightenment. Later the four degrees were expanded into ten stages, which are actually the ten abodes:

1. Setting the mind toward enlightenment (*prathama-cittot-pādika*)
2. Beginner (*ādikarmika*)
3. Practitioner (*yogācāra*)
4. Born into a noble family (*janmaja*)
5. Perfection of means (*pūrvayoga-sampanna*)
6. Endowed with merits in the previous life (*śuddhādhyāśaya*)
7. No backsliding (*avaivartya*)
8. Becoming a prince (*kumāra-bhūta*)
9. Installation as crown prince (*yauvarājyatā*)
10. Anointment as king [buddha] (*abhiṣekaprāpta*)

The four degrees of enlightenment, which survive in the ten stages, are setting the mind toward enlightenment (stage one), continuation of practice (stage three), no backsliding (stage seven), and becoming a bodhisattva who will attain buddhahood in the next life (stage ten).

Perfection of Wisdom (*prajñāpāramitā*) sūtras combine the three vehicles (Śrāvakayāna, Pratyekabuddhayāna, and Bodhisattva-yāna) into one (Buddhayāna). This is reflected in the definition of practice given in these sūtras:

1. The stage of dry knowledge (*śuṣkavidarśanā-bhūmi*)
2. The stage of [noble] lineage (*gotra-bhūmi*)
3. The eighth stage [streamwinner] (*aṣṭamaka-bhūmi*)
4. The stage of right view (*darśana-bhūmi*)

5. The stage of diminishing defilements (*tanu-bhūmi*)
6. The stage in which all defilements of the realm of desire have been eliminated (*vītarāga-bhūmi*)
7. The stage in which all defilements of the three realms have been eliminated (*kṛtāvī-bhūmi*)
8. The *pratyekabuddha* stage (*pratyekabuddha-bhūmi*)
9. The bodhisattva stage (*bodhisattva-bhūmi*)
10. The buddha stage (*buddha-bhūmi*)

Stages one and two are those of the common person, stages three and four are those of the streamwinner, stage five is that of the once-returner, stage six that of the nonreturner, stage seven that of the *arhat*, stage eight that of the *pratyekabuddha*, stage nine that of the bodhisattva, and stage ten that of the buddha.

Finally, there are the ten stages of bodhisattva practice (*daśa-bhūmi*) delineated in the Flower Garland Sūtra, which have become the stages of bodhisattva practice for Mahāyāna as a whole. The Flower Garland Sūtra specifies stages prior to the stages of bodhisattva practice: the ten abodes (*daśa-vihāra*), the ten stages of practice (*daśa-caryā*), and the ten stages of transference of merit (*daśa-pariṇāma*). Other works, such as the Sūtra of Adornments, also mention ten stages of faith (*daśa-śraddhā*). The ten stages of bodhisattva practice expounded in the Flower Garland Sūtra are as follows:

1. The stage of joyfulness (*pramuditā-bhūmi*)
2. The stage of purity (*vimalā-bhūmi*)
3. The stage of light giving (*prabhākarī-bhūmi*)
4. The stage of radiant wisdom (*arciṣmatī-bhūmi*)
5. The stage of conquering difficulties (*sudurjayā-bhūmi*)
6. The stage of being face to face (*abhimukhī-bhūmi*)
7. The stage of being far reaching (*dūraṃgamā-bhūmi*)
8. The stage of being immovable (*acalā-bhūmi*)
9. The stage of meritorious wisdom (*sādhumatī-bhūmi*)
10. The stage of the Dharma cloud (*dharmameghā-bhūmi*)

The first six stages are in fact the practice of the Six Perfections, leading the practitioner to wisdom. In the seventh stage, the practitioner is born into this world and cultivates skillful means (*upāya*) in order to bring about the salvation of all sentient beings. In the eighth, the practitioner works to transfer his or her merit to others by means of the bodhisattva's vows (*praṇidhāna*). In the ninth, the practitioner achieves complete expression of compassion and cultivates the power (*bala*) of overcoming hindrances. In the final stage, the practitioner attains buddhahood with transcendental knowledge (*jñāna*).

THE FIRST STAGE OF ENLIGHTENMENT

As we have seen in the discussion of the eight types of attainment above, primitive Buddhism spoke of two kinds of people who gain the stage of effort of the streamwinner: people who gain that stage through faith (*śraddhānusārin*) and those who gain it through insight (*dharmānusārin*). To attain enlightenment through faith, it is necessary to believe in the four imperishables (the Three Treasures and the pure precepts). Attaining enlightenment through intellectual insight is termed gaining the Dharma Eye, far removed from the dust and defilements of this world, meaning that the eye of wisdom is gained through understanding the Four Noble Truths and dependent origination. Attaining enlightenment through intellectual insight is also termed "present insight into the noble truth" (*sacca-abhisamaya*).

The first stage of enlightenment having been reached, there can be no more performing evil deeds or falling into the undesirable realms of rebirth as retribution for evil deeds. This state is termed "no more backsliding" (*avinipāta-dhamma*). There can be no retrogression from the *ārya* stage or delusion through non-Buddhist beliefs; continued progress toward supreme enlightenment is certain. A person at this first stage of enlightenment is termed *samyaktvaniyata-rāśi*, one who has achieved right confirmation.

8. The Defilements

Defilements (*kleśa, kilesa*) cause sentient beings mental and physical distress and agitation and obstruct achievement of the Buddhist ideal. The defilements hinder practice and thus prevent the attainment of enlightenment.

The Concept of Defilements

Defilements are usually not manifest but lie deep in the mind as inclinations or proclivities and only occasionally become apparent. In Abhidharma Buddhism the term residue (*anuśaya, anusaya*) refers particularly to this latent condition, when the defilements lie dormant in the mind. The manifest aspect is called bonds (*paryavasthāna, pariyuṭṭhāna*).

THE DEFILEMENTS AND KARMA

If the defilements are considered to have both latent and manifest aspects, the manifest aspect comes very close to negative mental karma (moral acts). A negative mind is defined as one totally possessed by the defilements, and like negative mental karma the negative mind is associated with the manifest mind. In this case, defilements and karma have almost the same meaning.

Like the defilements, karma has two aspects, manifest (*vijñapti-karman*) and nonmanifest (*avijñapti-karman*). The Sarvāstivādins defined nonmanifest karma as the elements of form (*rūpa*), or matter in general, but it can also include mental phenomena. An example of such mental phenomena is the depraved character in which the power of evil habit has taken hold. This depraved character is the manifestation of the defilements.

The individual links of the Twelve-linked Chain of Dependent Origination can be categorized as delusion, karma, or suffering (see the chart on page 144). The delusions—ignorance, craving, and grasping—are in fact defilements. These defilements are the cause of the generation of karma—actions, or mental constituents, and becoming—which result in suffering: consciousness, name and form, the six sense organs, contact, feeling, birth, and old age and death.

This categorization of the Twelve-linked Chain corresponds to theories of cause and effect in the past, present, and future. It seems more reasonable, however, to classify grasping with becoming, as karma. The combination of grasping and becoming yields actions, or mental constituents: grasping is the manifest working of actions, and becoming is the latent power of grasping.

OTHER VIEWS OF THE DEFILEMENTS

All mistaken concepts of attachment to self and all depraved personality traits harbored deep in the mind are defilements. The Sarvāstivādins and the Yogācārins considered the defilements to be either evil or neutral. Evil (*akuśala;* literally, "not good") defilements exist only in the realm of desire, while neutral (*avyākṛta*) defilements occur only in the realm of form and the formless realm. This interpretation contrasts with that of Pāli Buddhism, which considers all defilements to be evil and has no classification of neutral defilements. Unlike the Sarvāstivādins and the schools of Northern Buddhism, which constructed detailed theories about the defilements, Pāli Buddhism does not go into the subject very deeply.

According to the Sarvāstivādins, moral neutrality (*avyākṛta*) has two forms: impedimentary moral neutrality (*nivṛta-avyākṛta*) and nonimpedimentary moral neutrality (*anivṛta-avyākṛta*). The former refers not to evil but to the defilements that impede wisdom and obscure the pure mind. Evil, on the other hand, not only obstructs wisdom and clouds the pure mind but also brings about negative retribution, that is, misfortune in the next existence. All evils are, of course, defilements.

Nonimpedimentary moral neutrality is a pure form of neutrality that has nothing to do with defilements. The Sarvāstivādins distinguished four types of nonimpedimentary moral neutrality:

1. Heterogeneous result (*vipāka*), that is, the retribution and result of good and evil karma
2. Mode of deportment (*īryāpatha*), that is, deportment in walking, standing, sitting, and lying down
3. The arts and crafts (*śilpa-sthāna*), that is, fine art, crafts, and technology
4. The transformations (*nirmāṇa*), that is, the fruits of transformations effected through supernormal powers

Pāli Buddhism does not speak of impedimentary moral neutrality at all and posits only two kinds of moral neutrality: heterogeneous result (*vipāka*) and action itself (*kiriyā*), which is neither good nor evil, neither positive nor negative retribution. The latter includes the compassionate acts of an *arhat* moving among the three realms of existence in an unhindered state of nonself and nonattachment, or *anupalambha*.

The Defilements and Wisdom The defilements, which hinder practice and obstruct wisdom, can be destroyed by wisdom. The result of this destruction is liberation, by which the mind is released from the bonds of the defilements and is able to act freely in the ideal way according to the Dharma. The state in which all the fires of the defilements have been extinguished is called nirvāṇa. Ideal wisdom (*bodhi, sambodhi*) being both latent and manifest, this is the condition of enlightenment.

Synonyms for the Defilements There are many synonyms for the defilements, for example, delusion, dust, and contamination. Two—the residues and the bonds—have already been noted. Others are discussed below.

Fetters. There are various categories of fetters (*saṃyojana*). The three fetters, extinguished at the first stage of the *ārya* path, are false views about a permanent self, doubt or perplexity, and attachment to heretical practices. The five lower fetters, broken to achieve the stage of attainment of nonreturner, are greed in the realm of desire, anger, false views about a permanent self, doubt or perplexity, and attachment to heretical practices. The five higher fetters, destroyed when the stage of attainment of *arhat* is achieved, are greed in the realm of form, greed in the formless realm, frivolity, pride, and ignorance. The seven fetters are greed in the realm of desire, anger, false views, doubt or perplexity, pride, desire for existence, and ignorance. The nine fetters are craving, anger, pride, ignorance, false views, attachment to heretical practices, doubt or perplexity, jealousy, and parsimony. When craving is divided into two aspects—greed in the realm of desire and desire for existence—we have the ten fetters.

Hindrances. The five hindrances (*nivaraṇa*) are eliminated to gain the first *dhyāna* stage. They are greed, anger, languor and drowsiness, frivolity and regret, and doubt or perplexity.

Yokes. There are four yokes (*yoga*): sensuous desire, desire for existence, false views, and ignorance.

Outflows. The three outflows (*āsrava, āsava*) are sensuous desire, desire for existence, and ignorance. When we add false views to these, we have the four outflows.

Raging streams. The four raging streams (*ogha*) are sensuous desire, desire for existence, false views, and ignorance.

Ties. The four ties (*grantha, gantha*) are the same as the four yokes, the four outflows, and the four raging streams.

Other synonyms. Greed, anger, and folly (ignorance) are termed the three fires, the three impurities, and the three poisons. Further synonyms for the defilements are arrows (*iṣu*), jungle (*vana, vanatha*), tangle (*jaṭā*), and excess (*utsada, ussada*).

THE SARVĀSTIVĀDIN THEORY OF THE DEFILEMENTS

All the above synonyms are found in the Āgamas. Various Abhidharma scholars attempted to codify these synonyms, but it was the Sarvāstivādins who developed a detailed theory of the defilements.

Since defilement originally referred to that which hinders enlightenment, it was logical to associate certain of the defilements with various stages of practice. Thus it was said that as part of the effort to gain the stage of streamwinner, the three fetters must be broken. In like manner, attainment of the stage of nonreturner requires elimination of the five lower fetters, overcoming all the defilements of the realm of desire, while an *arhat* of the highest stage has eliminated the five higher fetters, overcoming all the defilements of the realm of form and the formless realm.

The three degrees of *ārya* attainment can also be associated with particular defilements. To gain the stage of the Way of View, one must have overcome the defilements of view; and to gain the stage of the Way of Practice, one must have overcome the defilements of practice. All defilements, theoretical and actual, must be overcome to reach the supreme stage, that of *aśaikṣa* (*arhat*).

The defilements of view are theoretical, intellectual delusions. In general, these defilements are acquired or cultivated, and they can be eliminated immediately through understanding of faultless theory; for this reason they are also known as the "sharp defilements."

The defilements of practice, or delusions of volition, are habitual, emotional delusions. Some of them can be considered innate. They are persistent habits or propensities and thus cannot be overcome merely by intellectual understanding. Only through dogged effort over a long period are they gradually eliminated, which is why they are also called the "dull defilements." There are five defilements of practice: greed, anger, folly (ignorance), pride, and doubt or perplexity.

Together the defilements of view and of practice are known as the fundamental defilements, which usually include six or ten items. The most basic of the fundamental defilements are greed, anger, and folly (ignorance)—the three poisons. The central defilement is folly (ignorance), just as ignorance is the first item of the Twelve-linked Chain of Dependent Origination. The six fundamental defilements are greed, anger, folly (ignorance), pride, doubt or perplexity, and false views. The ten fundamental defilements are identical to the six fundamental defilements except that the sixth item, false views, is separated into five false views.

The six and ten fundamental defilements can also be considered defilements of view. In addition, Abhidharma Buddhism included a classification of eighty-eight defilements of view, which are false views about the Four Noble Truths in each of the three realms of existence. This, however, is an overformalized categorization with little practical application.

The defilements of practice include only four of the ten fundamental defilements: greed, anger, folly (ignorance), and pride. The fundamental defilements of doubt or perplexity and the five false views are chiefly defilements of view. There are ten defilements of practice, four in the realm of desire and three each in the realm of form and the formless realm, in both of which anger is omitted. There is also a categorization of eighty-one defilements, all defilements of practice. In this categorization the three realms are divided into nine grades, and nine defilements are assigned to each grade. The ninety-eight defilements encompass the eighty-eight defilements of view and the ten of practice.

The eighty-eight defilements of view are overcome by the practice of the sixteen mental states of the stage of the Way of View, that is, the eight forms of wisdom and the eight forms of recognition that precede them.[1]

The Yogācārin Theory of the Defilements

The Sarvāstivādin codification of associated mental functions (*cittasaṃprayukta-saṃskāra*), discussed in chapter 3, proved inadequate in terms of the theory of associated mental functions that the Yogācārins evolved. Later the Yogācārin classification was revised into a logically consistent statement. The Yogācārin six defiled associated mental functions were considered to be fundamental defilements, and the twenty lesser defiled associated mental functions were considered to be auxiliary defilements, which were further categorized as major, intermediate, or minor auxiliary defilements.

THE FUNDAMENTAL DEFILEMENTS

As is clear from the chart on page 209, the Yogācārin fundamental defilements are the same as the six fundamental defilements of the Sarvāstivādins. And if the five false views are counted individually, the Yogācārin fundamental defilements are the same as the ten fundamental defilements of the Sarvāstivādins. Let us examine the Yogācārin fundamental defilements, as well as some of the minor auxiliary defilements.

Greed (*rāga*) or craving (*tṛṣṇā*) is desire for and attachment to an object of longing in the realm of desire. Greed of the realm of desire is distinguished from that of the realm of form and that of the formless realm.

Anger (*pratigha*) is the displeasure and revulsion felt toward an object of dislike. Aspects of anger are found among the minor auxiliary defilements: wrath (*krodha*), enmity (*upanāha*), and causing injury (*vihiṃsā*). *Krodha* is violent indignation and temper.

The Yogācārin Defilements

The fundamental defilements (*kleśa*)	The auxiliary defilements (*anukleśa*)
greed (*rāga*)	*Minor*
anger (*pratigha*)	wrath (*krodha*)
ignorance (*avidyā*)	enmity (*upanāha*)
pride (*māna*)	hypocrisy (*mrakṣa*)
false views (*dṛṣṭi*)	worry (*pradāsa*)
doubt about the teachings (*vicikitsā*)	jealousy (*īrṣyā*)
	parsimony (*mātsarya*)
	trickery (*śāṭhya*)
	deceit (*māyā*)
	arrogance (*mada*)
	causing injury (*vihiṃsā*)
	Intermediate
	shamelessness (*āhrīkya*)
	lack of modesty (*anapatrāpya*)
	Major
	languor (*styāna*)
	frivolity (*auddhatya*)
	nonbelief (*āśraddhya*)
	sloth (*kausīdya*)
	indolence (*pramāda*)
	forgetfulness (*muṣitasmṛtitā*)
	distraction (*vikṣepa*)
	nondiscernment (*asaṃprajanya*)

Upanāha is the long-term ill will that is closely linked with anger. *Vihiṃsā* is the fruit of anger, when the mind is filled with the urge to harm others. Cruelty is akin to *vihiṃsā.*

Ignorance (*avidyā*) is that which prevents a person from acquiring right understanding, or enlightenment. It is the same as ignorance in the Twelve-linked Chain of Dependent Origination; it is not knowing the teachings of the Four Noble Truths and dependent origination. Ignorance is the egocentrism that impedes knowledge of the truth. Ignorance is attachment to the self. It is the most basic of all the defilements.

Pride (*māna*) is the egoism of considering oneself better than others and others inferior to oneself. According to one categorization, there are three kinds of pride:

1. Pride in regarding oneself as superior to equals and equal to superiors (*atimāna*)
2. Pride in regarding oneself as superior to inferiors and equal to equals (*māna*)
3. Pride in regarding oneself as only a little inferior to those who far surpass one (*avamāna*)

A second categorization posits seven kinds of pride:

1. Pride in regarding oneself as superior to inferiors and equal to equals (*māna*)
2. Pride in regarding oneself as superior to equals and equal to superiors (*atimāna*)
3. Pride in feeling superior to manifest superiors (*mānātimāna*)
4. Pride in the belief that the aggregates are self and are possessed by self (*asmimāna*)
5. Pride in possessing the Truth, or enlightenment (*adhimāna*)
6. Pride in regarding oneself as only a little inferior to those who far surpass one (*avamāna*)
7. Pride in regarding oneself as possessing virtues, such as wisdom and enlightenment, although lacking them (*mithyāmāna*)

In a further categorization, that of the nine kinds of pride, each of the three kinds of pride is seen from the point of view of superior to equals and equal to superiors, superior to inferiors and equal to equals, and only slightly inferior to those who are far superior.

Something similar to pride is found among the minor auxiliary defilements. Arrogance (*mada*) is pride in one's family status, wealth, position, influence, prosperity, health, knowledge, good looks, or abilities. *Māna* and *mada* are distinctly different in meaning, however. *Māna* involves seeing oneself in a superior position when comparing oneself with others. *Mada* is simply thinking oneself superior, making no direct comparisons with others.

False views (*dṛṣṭi*) include all heretical thought and also signify deluded, that is, non-Buddhist, philosophies. Originally sixty-two false views were posited, but the Sarvāstivādins and others condensed these to five false views, which the Yogācārins adopted—sometimes considering the five collectively as a single defilement and sometimes considering them individually.

The first false view is belief that the aggregates are self and are possessed by self (*satkāya-dṛṣṭi*).

The second consists of extreme views (*antagrāha-dṛṣṭi*): that body and spirit are eternal, that death ends life, that there is eternal existence, that there is nonexistence, that body and spirit are the same, that body and spirit are different, that a *tathāgata* exists after death, and that a *tathāgata* does not exist after death. This category also includes false views of suffering and pleasure.

The third false view is perverse views (*mithyā-dṛṣṭi*), which, broadly speaking, include all ideas that reject the concept of cause and effect. As denials of cause and effect these views are known as the ten perverse views: that there is no giving, no offering, no rites, no retribution for good and evil karma, no present existence, no other existence, no mother, no father, no metamorphic rebirth, and no practitioner who has seen the fruits of practice. In short, these views constitute erroneous understanding of the working of karma in the three realms of existence. They also include denial of the Three Treasures, of the Buddha's teaching of dependent origination, and of the attainment of enlightenment through practice by the Buddha and the Saṅgha. This category of false views is considered to be the most abhorrent, since denial of cause and effect prevents comprehension of the Buddha's teachings.

The fourth is stubborn, perverted views (*dṛṣṭi-parāmarśa*): the view that one's own egocentric understanding is absolutely true and that all other doctrines are mistaken. This seems to correspond to modern exclusionist ideologies.

The fifth false view is attachment to heretical practices (*śīlavrata-parāmarśa*), referring to adherence to ascetic practices in the belief that they will bring release or heavenly rebirth.

Doubt or perplexity about the teachings (*vicikitsā*) is doubt about the Three Treasures, about retribution for good and evil karma, about cause and effect in the past, present, and future, and about the Four Noble Truths and dependent origination.

AUXILIARY DEFILEMENTS

Several auxiliary defilements have already been discussed in conjunction with the fundamental defilements. Here the most important of the remaining auxiliary defilements are examined.

Parsimony (*mātsarya*), a minor auxiliary defilement, is stinginess. There are five kinds of parsimony: monopolizing a dwelling, an almsgiving household, alms received, praise, and knowledge of the Law.

Shamelessness (*āhrīkya*), the first intermediate auxiliary defilement, is the lack of an inner, or personal, sense of shame, while lack of modesty (*anapatrāpya*), the second intermediate auxiliary defilement, is the absence of the external, or public, sense of shame that modulates one's public acts.

Languor (*styāna*), a major auxiliary defilement, is the sinking of the mind into depression.

Frivolity (*auddhatya*), a major auxiliary defilement, is giddiness that does not permit mental calm.

Sloth (*kausīdya*), a major auxiliary defilement, is the opposite of effort. It is lack of application toward the ideal, as well as active resistance to the ideal.

Indolence (*pramāda*), a major auxiliary defilement, is both action aimed solely at one's own benefit and thought and action that ignore the precepts.

Notes

Chapter 1. The Principal Branches of Buddhism

1. There are four universal vows of the bodhisattva (*praṇidhāna*): (1) However innumerable sentient beings are, I vow to bring about their release. (2) However limitless my defilements are, I vow to extinguish them. (3) However immeasurable the Buddha's teachings are, I vow to learn them. (4) However infinite enlightenment is, I vow to attain buddhahood.

2. The Four Noble Truths and the Eightfold Path are discussed in chapter 6.

3. The four means (*catvāri saṃgraha-vastūni*) are donation, kind words, conduct benefiting others, and compassionately assuming the form of the sentient beings to be benefited.

4. The ten stages of bodhisattva practice are discussed in chapter 7.

5. The law of causality, or the law of dependent origination (*pratītya-samutpāda*), is the nucleus of all Buddhist philosophy. In simple terms, the law of causality means that every effect has a definite cause and every cause a definite effect.

6. Hīnayāna scriptures teach that only men can attain buddhahood. Although certain Mahāyāna scriptures teach that women can become buddhas, they also make it clear that a woman must be reincarnated as a man in order to attain buddhahood. Thus all buddhas are male, and it is correct to use *he, him,* and *his* in statements about buddhas.

7. The First Council of Buddhist elders, comprising five hundred senior disciples of Śākyamuni, met shortly after the Buddha's death to compile the sermons and monastic precepts he had expounded. The Second Council—a conference of seven hundred *sthavira,* or elders—met about one hundred years after the Buddha's death to resolve disputes that threatened to sunder the community of Buddhist believers.

The ten disputed practices condemned by the elders are recorded as follows in Pāli sources: *sirigiloṇa-kappa,* or storing salt in a horn instead of eating it on the day it is received; *dvaṅgula-kappa,* or eating after midday, so long as the shadow is no more than two fingers wide; *gāmantara-kappa,* or begging for alms and eating in one village, and the same morning going to another village to beg for alms and eat; *āvāsa-kappa,* or holding more than one confession ceremony within the same monastic boundary; *anumati-kappa,* or obtaining ex post facto approval for ceremonies held without the entire *saṅgha* in attendance; *āciṇṇa-kappa,* or justifying acts by their customary performance; *amathita-kappa,* or drinking milk in the afternoon, so long as it contains no curds; *jalogipātuṃ-kappa,* or drinking liquor with a low alcohol content; *adasaka-nisīdana-kappa,* or using a sitting mat that has no border and is not of the prescribed size; and *jātarūparajata-kappa,* or accepting gold and silver, that is, money.

8. The five theses of Mahādeva stated that *arhats* are subject to temptation and may ejaculate in their sleep, may not achieve perfect knowledge, may have doubts about secular matters even though they have no doubts about the teachings, may not realize they have attained enlightenment until others tell them, and may aspire to enlightenment only after crying out in suffering.

9. The complex, interrelated theories of *manas* consciousness (*mano-dhātu*), storehouse consciousness (*ālaya-vijñāna*), and the six consciousnesses (*ṣaḍ-vijñāna*) are discussed in chapter 3.

10. Theories of the bodhisattva are discussed in chapter 7, those of buddha bodies (*buddha-kāya*) and buddha realms (*buddha-kṣetra*) in chapter 2, and those of nirvāṇa in chapter 4.

11. See Kōgen Mizuno, *Pārigo Bumpō* (A Grammar of the Pali Language), rev. ed. (Tokyo: Sankibō Busshorin, 1959), pp. 1–27.

12. The nine places to which Aśoka sent missionaries and the monks he dispatched are given in Pāli sources as northwestern India (Kasmīra and Gandhāra), Majjhantika; the eastern part of southern India (Mahisamaṇḍala), Mahādeva; the western part of southern India (Vanavāsa), Rakkhita; the coastal regions of western India (Aparantaka), Yonaka Dhammarakkhita; southwestern India (Mahāraṭṭha), Mahādhammarakkhita; the Hellenized areas of West Asia (Yona), Mahārakkhita; the Himalayan area (Himavanta), Majjhima; the coastal regions of Burma (Suvaṇṇabhūmi), Soṇa Uttara; and Sri Lanka (Tambapaṇṇī), Mahinda.

13. Translations of Pāli works are to be found in the Harvard Oriental Series (Cambridge, Mass.: Harvard University Press), the Sacred Books of the East series (Oxford: Clarendon Press), and the Sacred Books of the Buddhists and the Pali Text Society translation series (London: Pali Text Society). To honor the pioneering Japanese Buddhologist Junjirō Takakusu (1866–1945), a group of scholars translated the Southern Tipiṭaka into Japanese between 1935 and 1941. Their translation was published as sixty-five fascicles in seventy volumes.

Chapter 2. The Three Treasures

1. Yūhō Yokoi with Daizen Victoria, *Zen Master Dōgen: An Introduction with Selected Writings* (New York and Tokyo: John Weatherhill, Inc., 1976), p. 129.

2. These buddhas are also known by the Sanskrit renderings of their names: Vipaśyin, Śikhin, Viśvabhu, Krakucchanda, Kanakamuni, Kāśyapa, and Śākyamuni.

3. The twenty-five Buddhas of the Past, including Sākyamuni, are Dīpaṅkara, Koṇḍañña, Maṅgala, Sumana, Revata, Sobhita, Anomadassin, Paduma, Nārada, Padumuttara, Sumedha, Sujāta, Piyadassin, Atthadassin, Dhammadassin, Siddhattha, Tissa, Phussa, Vipassin, Sikhin, Vessabhū, Kakusandha, Koṇāgamana, Kassapa, and Gotama (Sākyamuni). The twenty-eight Buddhas of the Past are those given above, preceded by Taṇhaṅkara, Medhaṅkara, and Saraṇaṅkara.

4. The complete first list is 3 billion Śākyamunis, 800 million Dīpaṃkaras, 500 Padmottaras, 300 million Puṣyas, 8,000 Pradyotas, 18,000 Māradhvajas, 90,000 Kāśyapas, 15,000 Pratāpas, 2,000 Kauṇḍinyas, 1 Samantagupta, 1,000 Jambudhvajas, 84,000 Indradhvajas, 15,000 Ādityas, 6,200 Anyonyas, 64 Samitāvins, and 1 Suprabhāsa.

5. The fifteen names are Dīpaṃkara, Sarvābhibhu, Padmuttara, Atyuccagāmin, Yaśottara, Śākyamuni, Arthadarśin, Tiṣya, Puṣya, Vipaśyin, Śikhin Viśvabhu, Krakucchanda, Kanakamuni, and Kāśyapa.

6. The first list is 3 billion Śākyamunis, 800 million Dīpaṃkaras, 300 million Puṣyas, 90,000 Kāśyapas, 60,000 Pradyotas, 18,000 Māradhvajas, 10,000 Pāraṃgatas, 15,000 Ādityas, 2,000 Kauṇḍinyas, 6,000 Nāgamunis, 1,000 Jambudhvajas, 500 Padmuttaras, 64 Jaṭilas, 1 Samitāvin, 8.4 trillion *pratyekabuddhas,* 1 Suprabhāsa, and 1 Aparājitadhvaja.

7. In Buddhist cosmology the ten directions are the four cardinal directions, the four intermediate directions, zenith, and nadir.

8. The formula most often used by the Rinzai and Sōtō Zen sects is "Homage to the boundless *dharma-kāya* Vairocana Buddha; the complete *sambhoga-kāya* Vairocana Buddha; the manifest *nirmāṇa-kāya* Śākyamuni Buddha; the future buddha Maitreya; all buddhas, past, present, and future, in the ten directions; the Mahāyāna Lotus Sūtra; the great compassionate Avalokiteśvara Bodhisattva; the many bodhisattva-*mahāsattvas.*"

9. Īśvara and Maheśvara are epithets of the deities Brahmā and Śiva, respectively. Vaiśravaṇa, one of the four heavenly kings under Indra's jurisdiction, is ruler of the north. A *nāga* is a dragon king. A *yakṣa* is a demon in the retinue of Vaiśravaṇa. A *gandharva* is a celestial musician. An *asura* is a mighty demon who battles Indra. A *garuḍa* is a fabulous bird with golden wings, king of all birds and hunter of *nāgas.* A *kiṃnara,* half human and half animal, is a musician of Indra's. A *mahoraga* is a boa spirit, a kind of demon. A *vajrapāṇi* is a guardian deity; five hundred *va-*

jrapāṇis are in the retinue of a buddha to protect him. The seven beings from *nāga* through *mahoraga* are also known as protectors of Buddhism.

10. The Sūtra on the Distinguishing Marks (*Lakkhaṇa-suttanta*) in the Dīgha-nikāya gives the thirty-two primary marks as follows: flat feet; impressions of the wheel of the Law on the soles; broad heels; long fingers and toes; uncallused hands and feet; webbed fingers and toes; shapely ankles; slender lower legs like those of a deer; long arms; a concealed penis; a golden complexion; no dust adhering to the body; each pore containing a single hair; body hair curling upward and to the right; erect posture; well-fleshed thighs, arms, shoulders, and neck; a torso like a lion's; no furrow between the shoulder blades; body well balanced, like a banyan tree; breasts equally rounded; a keen sense of taste; lion-like jaws; forty teeth; straight teeth; no missing teeth; lustrous eyeteeth; a long tongue; a mellifluous voice; intensely blue eyes; eyelashes like those of a cow; a whorl of white hair between the eyebrows; and a protuberance on the top of the head. The eighty secondary marks are a more detailed version of the thirty-two marks.

11. Nirvāṇa without fixed abode (*apratiṣṭhita-nirvāṇa*) is the Mahāyāna conception of the ideal form of nirvāṇa, the state in which a person acts voluntarily, out of compassion, to bring others to enlightenment and neither strives for nirvāṇa nor rejects the cycle of birth and death.

12. The four absolute purities (*catasraḥ sarvâkāra-pariśuddhayaḥ*) are absolute purity of dependence (*āśraya*), of objects of perception (*ālambana*), of mind (*citta*), and of wisdom (*jñāna*).

13. The three actions that need not be guarded against (*trīṇy ārakṣyāṇi*) are the words, deeds, and thoughts of a buddha, for they are perfect and faultless.

14. "He causes them all to rejoice, / Preaching either sūtras, / Or gāthās, or former things, / Or birth stories, or the unprecedented, / And also preaching by reasonings, / By parables and geyas, / and by upadeśa scriptures" (Bunnō Katō et al., trans., and W. E. Soothill et al., revisers, *The Threefold Lotus Sutra* [Tokyo: Kōsei Publishing Co., 1975], pp. 62–63).

15. The Pāli formula is *"atha kho bhagavā etam atthaṃ viditvā tāyaṃ velāyaṃ imaṃ udānaṃ udānesi."*

16. Mahā-Kāśyapa (Mahā-Kassapa), chief among the disciples at the time of the Buddha's death, ignited the Buddha's funeral pyre. Considered the second patriarch of Buddhism (after Śākyamuni), he was succeeded by Ānanda.

17. According to the Pāli tradition, the scriptures were first recorded in writing in Sri Lanka in the time of King Vaṭṭagāmanī (r. 89–77 B.C.E.), using the Sinhalese script to transcribe the Pāli texts. The Northern tradition follows the Sarvāstivādin claim that the scriptures were first recorded in written form in northern India in the second century C.E.,

during the reign of the Kushan king Kaniṣka, when the Great Commentary was inscribed on copper plates. Whatever the historical truth, it is probable that Buddhism was the first Indian religion to break the mold of tradition and commit its sacred literature to writing.

18. The Saṃyutta-nikāya consists of five *vaggas*, subdivided into fifty-six smaller groups (*saṃyuttas*). Each *vagga* is organized on the basis of a unifying element: *Sagātha-vagga* (protagonists), *Nidāna-vagga* (causation), *Khanda-vagga* (the aggregates), *Saḷāyatana-vagga* (the six sense organs), and *Mahā-vagga* (the thirty-seven practices conducive to enlightenment).

19. Generally there are thirteen *saṃghāvaśeṣa* offenses for monks and seventeen for nuns. For monks, these offenses include masturbating, building living quarters exceeding the size permitted by the *saṅgha*, maligning an enemy, and injuring the faith of the laity. For nuns, they include encouraging a man to donate food and clothing and reviving a resolved quarrel.

20. *Prāyaścittika* offenses for monks include eating and drinking at proscribed times, viewing a military camp without reason, and knowingly traveling with a thief. Those for nuns include shaving body hair and repeating a master's words that one does not understand.

21. The five aggregates, the twelve sense fields, and the eighteen elements of existence are discussed in chapter 3; the Seals of the Law are the subject of chapter 4; the Twelve-linked Chain of Dependent Origination is discussed in chapter 5; the Four Noble Truths are the subject of chapter 6; and the last three doctrines are discussed in chapter 7.

22. The Six Perfections, the buddha-nature, the aspiration to enlightenment, and the Three Secrets are discussed in chapter 1; the eight consciousnesses, the nonself of sentient beings and *dharmas*, and the six great elements are discussed in chapter 3; the three natures of existence are discussed in chapter 5; and the ten stages of bodhisattva practice are discussed in chapter 7.

23. Influenced by Yaśas, four of his close friends became monks and eventually gained enlightenment, as did a further fifty friends. This brought the total number of *arhats* to sixty.

Chapter 3. The Elements of Existence

1. The twenty false views of self (*ātma-dṛṣṭi, sakkāya-diṭṭhi*) is a heretical doctrine that claims the self is real and permanent when it is in fact composed only of the five aggregates. About each of the five aggregates, this doctrine asserts: The aggregate is self; the aggregate is possessed by self; in self there is the aggregate; in the aggregate there is self.

2. *Dharma-dhātu* is the Dharma realm (the entire universe), the realm of *dharmas* (where the law of causality operates), or an object of the mind (one of the eighteen elements of existence, discussed in the next section).

Tathatā, Thusness, is the real aspect of all things, or absolute Truth, the underlying reality on which phenomenal existence depends.

Chapter 4. The Seals of the Law

1. The ten suchnesses characterize each *dharma* and are the factors common to the phenomenal existences in the ten realms of existence.

2. The ten realms of existence are hells, the worlds of hungry spirits, animals, *asuras,* human beings, and gods, and the worlds of *śrāvakas, pratyekabuddhas,* bodhisattvas, and buddhas. The first six realms are the realms of existence for ordinary people; the last four are the realms of enlightenment for *arhats,* who are not subject to rebirth.

3. The ten realms of existence interpenetrate (10 x 10 = 100). Each of these is characterized by the ten suchnesses (100 x 10 = 1,000), and these thousand items are each seen in terms of sentient beings, the aggregates, and space (1,000 x 3 = 3,000). "Three thousand realms in one thought" indicates the interpenetration of all *dharmas* within the mind, an understanding achieved through the practice of concentration.

Chapter 5. Dependent Origination

1. Both the Saṃyukta-āgama and the Saṃyutta-nikāya state that absolute Truth, being eternally unchanging, is not dependent on the appearance or nonappearance of buddhas in the world.

2. This formula is in the Majjhima-nikāya, in the Greater Discourse on the Simile of the Elephant's Footprint (*Mahāhatthipadopama-sutta*).

3. This formula is in the Saṃyutta-nikāya and in the Sūtra of the Rice Stem (*Śālistamba-sūtra*).

4. The Pāli formula, *"imasmiṃ sati idaṃ hoti, imass' uppādā idam uppajjati, imasmim asati idaṃ na hoti, imassa nirodhā idaṃ nirujjhati,"* is in the Saṃyutta-nikāya and in several sūtras in the Saṃyukta-āgama.

5. In Pāli the statement is *"yaṃ kiñci samudaya-dhammaṃ sabbaṃ taṃ nirodha-dhammaṃ."* It is found in the Vinaya-piṭaka, the Saṃyutta-nikāya—in the Sūtra of the Turning of the Wheel of the Law (*Dhammacakkappavattana-sutta*)—and elsewhere.

6. The Hua-yen sect held that the Sarvāstivādins (representing Hīnayāna in general) defined causality as the conditions leading to rebirth under the influence of karma, that early Mahāyāna defined it as the arising of all phenomena from the storehouse consciousness (the level of mind where the karmic process thrives), and that later Mahāyāna defined it as all phenomena arising from the *tathāgata*-embryo. As defined by mature Mahāyāna, that is, the Hua-yen sect, each phenomenon is a universal cause, so that *saṃsāra* is nirvāṇa and the phenomenal world is the only true existence in accord with the Law (the *dharma-dhātu,* or Dharma realm).

7. According to this theory, the six great elements (earth, water, fire, air, space, and consciousness) suffuse the universe and thus are contained even in a grain of sand. All that exists is formed from these elements, which coexist, so that one is in all, all are in one.

8. According to this theory, the reality underlying all things is the *tathatā* (absolute Truth). This doctrine is found in the Perfection of Wisdom sūtras and was inherited by the San-lun sect; it is also central to the Lotus Sūtra, the principal scripture of the T'ien-t'ai sect.

9. The three-natures theory, based on the Sūtra of Profound Understanding, was taught by the Indian Yogācāra school. It is one of the basic tenets of the Chinese Fa-hsiang and Hua-yen sects. Its exact interpretation depends on the sect. *Parikalpita-svabhāva* is the characteristic of mistaking the unreal for the real. *Paratantra-svabhāva,* the characteristic that occurs as a result of dependent origination, is perception of the world of phenomena, characterized by the Seals of the Law. This perception constitutes relative impure or pure knowledge. *Paratantra-svabhāva* is the foundation of both *parikalpita-svabhāva* and *parinişpanna-svabhāva. Parinişpanna-svabhāva* characterizes the fulfilled state of perfect knowledge, beyond all discrimination, which is the nature of *tathatā,* absolute Truth.

10. The theory of five periods of embryological development was derived from texts in the Dīgha-nikāya, Dīrgha-āgama, Majjhima-nikāya, and Madhyama-āgama explaining consciousness of the twelve links as *paṭisandhi-viññāṇa,* the initial consciousness on moving from the past to the present. Though these explanations were regarded as metaphorical, they were elaborated upon by Abhidharma scholars and became the basis for a biological explanation of causality.

Chapter 6. The Four Noble Truths

1. The Sūtra of the Turning of the Wheel of the Law is also found in the Vinaya-piṭaka.

Chapter 7. Religious Practice

1. The five treasures are faith (*saddhā*), morality (*sīla*), obedient hearing (*suta*), generosity (*cāga*), and wisdom (*paññā*); the seven treasures are these plus conscience (*ottappa*) and shame (*hirī*). The eight qualities (*aṭṭha mahāpurisa-vitakka*) of *śrāvakas, pratyekabuddhas,* and bodhisattvas are noncovetousness (*appiccha*), satisfaction (*santuṭṭha*), seclusion (*pavivitta*), unfailing effort (*āraddhaviriya*), right mindfulness (*upaṭṭhita-sati*), concentration (*samāhita*), wisdom (*pañña*), and avoidance of absurd reasoning (*nippapañca*).

2. Faith is, in fact, the only method of practice that primitive sūtras cite for lay believers, since with faith they cannot be diverted either from Buddhism or from their ultimate attainment of enlightenment.

3. According to the Pāli Sūtra of the Great Decease, the Buddha died after entering the fourth *dhyāna.* At the time of his death he had progressed through the first, second, third, and fourth *dhyānas* and then through the four formless concentrations and had attained the ninth *samāpatti,* the cessation of perception and feeling. From this state he returned through the eight *samāpattis* to the first *dhyāna* and from there once again progressed through the second, third, and fourth *dhyānas.* After attaining the fourth *dhyāna* he entered complete nirvāṇa, or *parinirvāṇa.* On progressing through the nine *samāpattis,* the Buddha's mind became pure and calm to the highest degree. Maintaining that state, he entered final nirvāṇa from the fourth *dhyāna,* in which tranquillity (the four stages of the formless realm) and insight (the four *dhyānas*) are balanced. (This equilibrium is also achieved at the time of initial enlightenment, but only at the time of final nirvāṇa does the practitioner progress through the nine *samāpattis* before entering nirvāṇa from the fourth *dhyāna.*)

4. The forty subjects are recorded in the Path of Purity (*Visuddhimagga*), the authoritative study of Buddhist doctrine and practice of concentration compiled by Buddhaghosa.

5. The three gates to liberation (*tīṇi vimokkhā-mukhāni*) are emptying the mind of thoughts of self (*suññata*), getting rid of ideas of form (*animitta*), and getting rid of desire (*appaṇihita*).

6. The ten forms of knowledge (*daśa jñānāni*) are common knowledge (*saṃvṛti-jñāna*), enlightened knowledge of the Four Noble Truths in the realm of desire (*dharma-jñāna*), enlightened knowledge of the Four Noble Truths in the realm of form and the formless realm (*anvaya-jñāna*), knowledge of the truth of suffering (*duḥkha-jñāna*), knowledge of the truth of the cause of suffering (*samudaya-jñāna*), knowledge of the truth of the extinction of suffering (*nirodha-jñāna*), knowledge of the truth of the way to the extinction of suffering (*mārga-jñāna*), knowledge of the minds of others (*paracitta-jñāna*), knowledge of extinction of all defilements (*kṣaya-jñāna*), and the wisdom that transcends the cycle of birth and death (*anutpāda-jñāna*).

7. The five classes of disciples are teachers who perform the five practices described in the Lotus Sūtra: receiving and keeping, reading, reciting, expounding, and copying the sūtra.

Chapter 8. THE DEFILEMENTS

1. The eight forms of wisdom are enlightened understanding of the Four Noble Truths in the realm of desire (the four *dharma-jñāna*) and in the realm of form and the formless realm (the four *anvaya-jñāna*). The eight forms of recognition (*kṣānti*) arouse enlightened understanding of the Four Noble Truths first in the realm of desire and then in the realm of form and the formless realm.

Indic Index

abbhutadhamma. See *adbhutadharma*
abhidhamma. See *abhidharma*
abhidharma (S; *abhidhamma*, P), 30, 35, 68, 75, 82
Abhidharma (S; Abhidhamma, P), 23, 25, 26, 33, 34–40, 47, 58, 68, 70, 82, 103, 107, 110, 132, 185, 191, 203, 208
Abhidharmakośa-śāstra (S), 44, 57, 113, 169, 185, 186, 194
Abhidharma-mahāvibhāṣā-śāstra (S), Great Commentary, 44
Abhidharma-nyāyānusāra-śāstra (S), Treatise Following the True Teachings of the Abhidharma, 44
Abhidharma-piṭaka (S; Abhidhamma-piṭaka, P), Treatise Basket, 35, 82–84, 85
abhijñā (S; *abhiññā*, P), 165, 166, 186
abhimukhī-bhūmi (S), 201
abhiññā. See *abhijñā*
abhiṣeka (S), 200
abhiṣekaprāpta (S), 200
abhivinaya (S), 82
avyākṛta (S), 126
acalā-bhūmi (S), 201
Acchariya-abbhutadhamma-sutta (P), Discourse on Wonderful and Marvelous Qualities, 74
āciṇṇa-kappa (P), 214 n. 7
adasaka-nisīdana-kappa (P), 214 n. 7
adbhutadharma (S; *abbhutadhamma*, P), 69, 74
adhikaraṇa-samatha. See *adhikaraṇa-śamatha*
adhikaraṇa-śamatha (S; *adhikaraṇa-samatha*, P), 80, 81
adhimāna (S), 210
[*adhimokkha*]. See *adhimokṣa*
adhimokṣa (S; [*adhimokkha*, P]), 99, 101, 107
adhiṭṭhāna-pāramī (P), 29
Adhyardhaśatikā-prajñāpāramitā-sūtra (S), Sūtra of the Advancement Toward Truth, 42
ādhyātmika-āyatana (S; *ajjhattika-āyatana*, P), 109
ādikarmika (S), 200
Āditya (S), 215 nn. 4, 6
adveṣa (S), 99, 101
āgama, 78
Āgama (S, P), 33, 35, 41, 75, 77, 78–79, 82, 91, 105, 119, 121, 146, 147, 184, 188, 206
ahiṃsā (S, P), 99, 101

ahirīka. See *āhrīkya*
āhrīkya (S; *ahirīka,* P), 99, 101, 209, 212
ajjhattika-āyatana. See *ādhyātmika-āyatana*
ājñā (S; *aññā,* P), 186
Ājñāta-Kauṇḍinya (S; Aññāta-Koṇḍañña, P), 186
ākāsa. See *ākāśa*
ākāśa (S; *ākāsa,* P), 97, 98, 101, 114
ākāsānañcāyatana. See *ākāśānantyāyatana*
ākāśānantyāyatana (S; *ākāsānañcāyatana,* P), 177
ākiṃcanyāyatana (S; *ākiñcaññāyatana,* P), 177
ākiñcaññāyatana. See *ākiṃcanyāyatana*
akuśala (S), 204
akuśala-mahābhūmika (S), 98
ālambana (S), 216 n. 12
alaṃkāra-kalpa (S), 57
ālaya (S), 44, 108
ālaya-vijñāna (S), 106, 108, 128, 136
alobha (S), 99, 101
āloka (S, P), 186
amala-vijñāna (S), 106
amata-nibbāna. See *amṛta-nirvāṇa*
amathita-kappa (P), 214 n. 7
Amitābha (S), Buddha of Infinite Light, 24, 43, 53, 59, 60, 65, 173. *See also* Amitāyus
Amitābha Sūtra (S). See *Sukhāvatī-vyūha-sūtra,* [Smaller]
Amitāyus (S), Buddha of Infinite Life, 24, 43, 53, 60, 173. *See also* Amitābha
amoha (S), 101
amṛta (S), 132, 134
amṛta-nirvāṇa (S; *amata-nibbāna,* P), 66
anāgāmin (S, P), 178, 184, 191, 192
anāgami-pratipanna (S), 191
Ānanda (S, P), 76, 216 n. 16
ānāpāna-sati. See *ānāpāna-smṛti*
ānāpāna-smṛti (S; *ānāpāna-sati,* P), 166
anapatrāpya (S; *anottappa,* P), 99, 101, 209, 212
anāsava. See *anāsrava*
anāsava-kusala. See [*anāsrava-kuśala*]
anāsrava (S; *anāsava,* P), 169
[*anāsrava-kuśala*] (S; *anāsava-kusala,* P), 88
anāsrava-saṃvara (S), 169
anātman (S), 127
anātmanaḥ sarvadharmāḥ (S; *sabbe dhammā anattā,* P), 125
anāvaraṇa (S), 129
Aṅguttara-nikāya (P), Collection of Discourses Treating Enumerations, 74, 77, 78, 84, 91, 168
animitta (P), 220 n. 5
āniñjya (S), 101, 114
anityā sarvasaṃskārāḥ (S; *sabbe saṅkhārā aniccā,* P), 124
anityatā (S), 99, 101
anivṛta-avyākṛta (S), 204
aniyata (S, P), 79, 80, 81, 100
aniyata-bhūmika (S), 98
aññā. See *ājñā*
Anomadassin (P), 215 n. 3
anottappa. See *anapatrāpya*
antaggāhika-diṭṭhi. See *antagrāha-dṛṣṭi*
antagrāha-dṛṣṭi (S; *antaggāhika-diṭṭhi,* P), 211
anukleśa (S), 209
anukrama (S), 101
anumati-kappa (P), 214 n. 7

anupādisesa-nibbāna. See *nirupadhiśeṣa-nirvāṇa*
anupalambha (S), 205. See also *aprāpti*
anupassanā. See *anupaśyanā*
anupaśyanā (S; *anupassanā*, P), 186
anupubba-samāpatti. See *anupūrva-samāpatti*
anupūrva-samāpatti (S; *anupubba-samāpatti*, P), 178
anusaya. See *anuśaya*
anuśaya (S; *anusaya*, P), 203
anutpāda-jñāna (S), 220 n. 6
anuttara (S), 66, 67
anuttara-samyaksaṃbodhi (S), 66
anuttara-samyaksaṃbuddha (S), 55
anvaya-jñāna (S), 220 nn. 1, 6
Anyonya (S), 215 n. 4
apadāna. See *avadāna*
Apadāna (P), Stories of the Lives of Certain Monks and Nuns, 78, 84
Aparājitadhvaja (S), 215 n. 6
Aparantaka (P), 214 n. 11
Aparaśaila (S; Aparaseliya, P), 37, 39
Aparaseliya. *See* Aparaśaila
apatrāpya (S; *ottappa*, P), 99, 101, 219 n. 1
appaṇihita (P), 220 n. 5
appiccha (P), 219 n. 1
apramāda (S), 99, 101
aprāpti (S), 99, 129
apratisaṃkhyā-nirodha (S), 98, 101, 114
apratiṣṭhita-nirvāṇa (S), 133, 216 n. 11
āraddhaviriya (P), 219 n. 1
arahat. See *arhat*
arbuda (S), 145
arciṣmatī-bhūmi (S), 201
arhat (S; *arahat*, P), 26, 27, 30, 34, 65, 66, 76, 92, 94, 102, 161, 168, 178, 179, 184, 188, 189, 190, 191, 192, 193, 194, 195, 196, 197, 201, 205, 206, 207, 214 n. 8
arhat-pratipanna (S), 191
arhattva (S), 191, 193
ariya. See *ārya*
ariya-aṭṭhaṅgika-magga. See *ārya-aṣṭāṅgika-mārga*
Arthadarśin (S), 215 n. 5
āruppa-dhātu. See *ārūpya-dhātu*
āruppa-samāpatti. See *ārūpya-samāpatti*
ārūpya-dhātu (S; *āruppa-dhātu*, P), 149
ārūpya-samāpatti (S; *āruppa-samāpatti*, P), 177
āruppa-dhātu. See *ārūpya-dhātu*
ārūpya-dhātu (S; *āruppa-dhātu*, P), 175
ārya (S; *ariya*, P), 91, 92, 93, 153, 158, 170, 185, 192, 194, 196, 202, 205, 207
ārya-aṣṭāṅgika-mārga (S; *ariya-aṭṭhaṅgika-magga*, P), 158
Āryadeva [also known as Kāṇadeva] (S), 43
aśaikṣa (S; *asekha*, P), 65, 191, 193, 195, 207
aśaikṣa-dharma (S), 161, 163, 184
aśaikṣa-phala (S), 153, 194, 195, 196
asāmagrī (S), 101
āsaṃjñika (S), 99, 101
asaṃjñi-samāpatti (S), 99, 101
asaṃkhyeya (S), 29, 30
asaṃkhyeya kalpa (S), 30, 57
asaṃprajanya (S), 101, 209
asaṃskṛta (S; *asaṅkhata*, P), 114
asaṃskṛta-dharma (S; *asaṅkhata-dhamma*, P), 96, 98, 100, 112
asaṃvara (S, P), 113

asaṅkhata-dhamma. See *asaṃskṛta-dharma*
Asaṅga (S), 44, 45, 133
āsava. See *āsrava*
āsava-kusala. See [*āsrava-kuśala*]
āsavānaṃ khaye ñāṇa (P), 190
asekha. See *aśaikṣa*
asmimāna (S), 210
asmīti-chanda (P), 108
Asoka. *See* Aśoka
Aśoka (S; Asoka, P), 34, 48, 214 n. 11
Aśokāvadāna (S), Story of Emperor Aśoka, 72
āśraddhya (S), 99, 101, 209
āsrava (S; *āsava,* P), 168, 206
[*āsrava-kuśala*] (S; *āsava-kusala,* P), 87
āśraya (S), 216 n. 12
[*assaddhiya*]. See *āśraddhya*
aṣṭābhibhāyatanāni (S; *aṭṭhābhibhāyatanāni,* P), 184
aṣṭādaśa āveṇika-buddha-dharmāḥ (S), 62
aṣṭādaśa dhātavaḥ (S; *aṭṭhādasa dhātuyo,* P), 96, 116
Aṣṭasāhasrikā-prajñāpāramitā (S), Perfection of Wisdom Sutra in Eight Thousand Lines, 42
aṣṭamaka-bhūmi (S), 200
asura (S), 27, 61, 176, 215 n. 9
Aśvaghoṣa (S), 46, 105
atimāna (S), 210
ātma-dṛṣṭi (S), 217 n. 1
ātma-grāha (S), 108
ātma-māna (S), 108, 120
ātman (S), 116, 126, 130
atta-dīpa (P), 128
atta-saraṇa (P), 128
aṭṭhābhibhāyatanāni. See *aṣṭābhibhāyatanāni*
aṭṭhādasa dhātuyo. See *aṣṭādaśa dhātavaḥ*
Atthadassin (P), 215 n. 3
aṭṭha mahāpurisa-vitakka (P), 219 n. 1
Atyuccagāmin (S), 215 n. 5
auddhatya (S; *uddhacca,* P), 99, 101, 193, 209, 212
avadāna (S; *apadāna,* P), 69, 72, 73
Avadānaśataka (S), One Hundred Stories, 72
avaivartya (S), 200
āvajjana (P), 120
Avalokiteśvara (S), 61, 215 n. 8
avamāna (S; *omāna,* P), 210
āvāsa-kappa (P), 214 n. 7
āvasthika (S), 145
Avataṃsaka-sūtra (S), Flower Garland Sūtra, 29. See also *Buddha-avataṃsaka-nāma-mahā-vaipulya-sūtra*
aveccappasāda. See *avetyaprasāda*
avetyaprasāda (S; *aveccappasāda,* P), 173
avidyā (S; *avijjā,* P), 147, 193, 209, 210
avijjā. See *avidyā*
avijñapti-karman (S), 203
avijñapti-rūpa, (S), 99, 103, 110, 112, 170
avinipāta-dhamma (P), 202
avyākata. See *avyākṛta*
avyākṛta (S; *avyākata,* P), 115, 126, 204
āyatana (S, P), 96, 102, 108

baddhamāna (S), 199
bāhira-āyatana (S, P), 109
Bāhuśrutīya (S; Bahussutiya, P), 37, 39
Bahussutiya. *See* Bāhuśrutīya
bala (S), 202

bala-pāramitā (S), 29
Bhaddayānika. *See* Bhadrayānīya
bhadra-kalpa (S), 57
Bhadrayānīya (S; Bhaddayānika, P), 36, 38
bhaga (S), 67
[Bhagavant]. *See* Bhagavat
Bhagavat (S; [Bhagavant, P]), 67, 68
Bhaiṣajyaguru (S), 59, 60, 65
bhājanaloka (S), 66
bhava (S, P), 30, 114, 149
bhāvanā (S, P), 197
bhāvanā-mārga (S), 153, 192, 195, 196
bhava-taṇhā. See *bhava-tṛṣṇā*
bhava-tṛṣṇā (S; *bhava-taṇhā*, P), 148
Bhikkhunī-vibhaṅga (P), Nuns' Analysis, 84
bhikkhu. See *bhikṣu*
bhikkhunī. See *bhikṣunī*
bhikkhunī-saṅgha. See *bhikṣunī-saṃgha*
bhikkhu-saṅgha. See *bhikṣu-saṃgha*
bhikṣu (S; *bhikkhu*, P), 90
bhikṣunī (S; *bhikkhunī*, P), 90
bhikṣunī-saṃgha (S; *bhikkhunī-saṅgha*, P), 89
bhikṣu-saṃgha (S; *bhikkhu-saṅgha*, P), 89
bhojane mattaññu (P), 189
bhūri (S, P), 186
bhūta (S, P), 116
bīja (S, P), 46, 108
bodhi (S, P), 26, 164, 187, 205
bodhicitta (S), 27, 44, 86, 173
bodhi-maṇḍa (S, P), 31
bodhipakkhiya-dhamma. See *bodhipākṣika-dharma*
bodhipākṣika-dharma (S; *bodhipakkhiya-dhamma*, P), 164
bodhisattva (S), 25, 26, 27, 29, 31, 32, 42, 44, 57, 62, 72, 171, 172, 173, 176, 184, 185, 188, 196, 198, 199, 200, 201, 202
bodhisattva-*avadāna* (S), 72
bodhisattva-bhūmi (S), 201
Bodhisattva-bhūmi (S; *P'u-sa-shan-chieh-ching*, C), Treatise on the Conduct of a Bodhisattva, 85
bodhisattva-*mahāsattva* (S), 215 n. 8. *See also* bodhisattva
Bodhisattvayāna (S), 24, 25, 32, 200
Brahmā (S, P), 32, 33, 75, 151, 181, 182, 215 n. 9
Brahmajāla (S), 85, 171, 172
Brahmajāla-sūtra (S), Sūtra of the Brahma Net, 59, [171]
Brahmendra (S), 61
Brahman (S), 61, 73
brahman (S), 116, 126
buddha (S, P), 23, 32, 33, 40, 41, 42, 44, 53, 54, 55–68, 69, 70, 71, 73, 74, 75, 76, 114, 126, 128, 132, 133, 135, 146, 176, 180, 181, 183, 184, 185, 186, 196, 198, 201
Buddha-avataṃsaka-nāma-mahā-vaipulya-sūtra (S), Flower Garland Sūtra, 74
Buddha[-*bhagavat*] (S), 68
buddha-bhūmi (S), 201
Buddhacarita[-kāvya-sūtra] (S), The Acts of the Buddha, 105
Buddhagayā (S, P), 54
Buddhaghosa (P), 87, 88, 189, 220 n. 4
buddhagotra (S), 26, 44, 86, 116, 133, 172
Buddhagotra-śāstra (S), Treatise on the Buddha-nature, 45
buddha-kāya (S), 214 n. 10
buddha-kṣetra (S), 214 n. 10

Buddhapiṭaka-nirgraha-sūtra (S), Superior Sūtra of the Buddha Treasury, 57
Buddhavaṃsa (P), The Lineage of the Buddhas, 56, 78, 84
Buddhayāna (S), 24, 25, 32, 200
buddhi (S, P), 186

cāga. See *tyāga*
caitasika-dharma, caitta-dharma (S), 107, 112. See also *citta-saṃprayukta-saṃskāra*
Caityavāda (S; Cetiyavāda, P), 37, 39
Cakkavattisīhanāda-suttanta (P), Sūtra on the Preaching of the Wheel-rolling King, 56
cakkhu. See *cakṣu*
cakkhu-āyatana. See *cakṣur-āyatana*
cakkhu-indriya. See *cakṣur-indriya*
cakkhu-viññāṇa dhātu. See *cakṣur-vijñāna-dhātu*
cakravartin (S), 61, 73
cakṣu (S; *cakkhu*, P), 186
cakṣur-āyatana (S; *cakkhu-āyatana*, P), 109, 112
cakṣur-indriya (S; *cakkhu-indriya*, P), 99, 101, 109
cakṣur-vijñāna-dhātu (S; *cakkhu-viññāṇa dhātu*, P), 116
caraṇa (S, P), 105
carita (S, P), 105
cariyā (S, P), 105
Cariyā-piṭaka (P), Collection Concerning Conduct, 73, 78, 84, 105
caryā (S), 105
catasraḥ sarvâkāra-pariśuddhayaḥ (S), 216 n. 12
cattāri ariya-saccāni. See *catvāri ārya-satyāni*
cattāri saṃgaha-vatthūni. See *catvāri saṃgraha-vastūni*
cattāri sammappadhānāni. See *catvāri samyakprahāṇāni*
cattāri sati-paṭṭhānāni. See *catvāri smṛty-upasthānāni*
cattāro brahma-vihārā (P), 182
cattāro iddhipādā. See *catvāra ṛddhipādāḥ*
cattasso appamaññāyo (P), 182
Catuḥśataka (S), Treatise in Four Hundred Verses, 43
catutthajjhāna (P), 190
catvāra ṛddhipādāḥ (S; *cattāro iddhi-pādā*, P), 165
catvāri ārya-satyāni (S; *cattāri ariya-saccāni*, P), 153
catvāri saṃgraha-vastūni (S; *cattāri saṃgaha-vatthūni*, P), 213 n. 3
catvāri samyakprahāṇāni (S; *cattāri sammappadhānāni*, P), 164
catvāri smṛty-upasthānāni (S; *cattāri sati-paṭṭhānāni*, P), 164
catvāri vaiśāradyāṇi (S), 62
cetanā (S, P), 99, 101, 105, 107
Cetiyavāda. *See* Caityavāda
cetopariya-ñāṇa (P), 184. See also *paracitta-jñāna*
cha-cetanā (P), 117
cha-chakka (P), 117
Chachakka-sutta (P), Discourse on the Six Sixes, 116
chanda (S, P), 99, 101, 107, 165
Chandāgārika. *See* Ṣaṇṇāgārika
cha-phassā (P), 117
cha-saññā (P), 117
cha-taṇhā (P), 117
cha-vedanā (P), 117
cha-vicārā (P), 117
cha-viññāṇa. See *ṣaḍ-vijñāna*
cha-vitakkā (P), 117

cintāmaṇi (S), 61
citta (S, P), 98, 100, 106, 110, 164, 165, 216 n. 12
cittaikāgratā (S; *cittekaggatā*, P), 179
cittāni (S), 107
cittasaṃprayukta-saṃskāra (S), 98, 100, 105, 112, 208
citta-vimukta (S), 193, 194
cittaviprayukta (S), 113
cittaviprayukta-saṃskāra (S), 98, 100, 105, 112, 113
cittavistara (S), 200
citta-visuddhi (P), 189
cittekaggatā. See *cittaikāgratā*
Cūḷa-Māluṅkya-sutta (P), Lesser Discourse to Māluṅkyaputta, 126
Cūḷavedalla-sutta (P), Lesser Discourse of the Miscellany, 74
Culla-vagga (P), Small Group, 84
Cunda (S, P), 94

dāna-pāramī. See *dāna-pāramitā*
dāna-pāramitā (S; *dāna-pāramī*, P), 28, 29
darśana (S; *dassana*, P), 186
darśana-bhūmi (S), 200
darśana-mārga (S), Way of View, 153, 191, 195, 196
dasa anussatiyo (P), 180
dasa asubha-saññā (P), 180
daśa-balāni (S), 62
Daśabhāṇavāra-vinaya (S), Vinaya in Ten Recitations, 81
daśa-bhūmi (S), 197, 198, 201
Daśabhūmika-vibhāṣā-śāstra (S), Commentary on the [first two of the] Ten Stages, 43
daśa-caryā (S), 197, 201
daśa jñānāni (S), 220 n. 6
dasa kasiṇa-āyatanāni (P), 180
dasa-pāramī. See *daśa-pāramitā*
daśa-pāramitā (S; *dasa-pāramī*, P), 29
daśa-pariṇāma (S), 197, 201
daśa-śraddhā (S), 199, 201
daśa-vihāra (S), 197, 198, 201
dassana. See *darśana*
daurmanasya (S; *domanassa*, P), 149
deśa (S), 101
Dhamma. *See* Dharma
dhamma-āyatana. See *dharma-āyatana*
Dhammacakkappavattana-sutta (P), Sūtra of the Turning of the Wheel of the Law, 218 n. 5
Dhammadassin (P), 215 n. 3
dhamma-dīpa (P), 128
Dhammaguttika. *See* Dharmaguptaka
Dhammapada (P), Verses on the Law, 71, 77, 78, 84, 128
Dhammasaṅgaṇi (P), Enumeration of Dhammas, 83, 84, 87
dhamma-saraṇa (P), 128
dhammavicaya. See *dharmavicaya*
dhammavicaya-sambojjhaṅga. See *dharmavicaya saṃbodhyaṅga*
Dhammuttarika. *See* Dharmottarīya
dhāraṇī (S), 46
Dharma (S; Dhamma, P), 32, 35, 53, 58, 68, 75, 76, 77, 82, 86, 87, 88, 92, 93, 94, 114, 128, 166, 180, 181, 185, 187, 192, 193, 205
dharma (S), 44, 58, 86, 87, 88, 89, 96, 97, 98, 100, 102, 103, 111, 112, 113, 115, 116, 119, 121, 122, 124, 125, 126, 130, 136, 156, 164, 217 n. 22, 218 n. 1
dharma-āyatana (S; *dhamma-āyatana*, P), 110, 112
dharma-āyatanikāni (S), 101

dharma-dhātu (S), 59, 114, 117, 185, 217 n. 2, 218 n. 6
Dharmaguptaka (S; Dhammaguttika, P), Those Who Are Protected by the Law, 36, 38, 40, 78, 80, 81, 83, 90, 103, 169, 170, 172
Dharmaguptaka Tripiṭaka (S), 86
dharma-jñāna (S), 220 nn. 1, 6
Dharmākara (S), 60
dharma-kāya (S), 57, 58, 116
dharmameghā-bhūmi (S), 201
dharma-mudrā (S), 121
dharma-nairātmya (S), 130
dharmānusārin (S), 193, 194, 202
Dharmapāla (S), 45, 145
Dharmarakṣa (S), 57
Dharmaskandha (S), Aggregate of Dharmas, 83
dharma-uddāna (S), Seals of the Law, 121. See also *dharma-mudrā*
dharmavicaya (S; *dhammavicaya*, P), 166, 187
dharmavicaya saṃbodhyaṅga (S; *dhammavicaya-sambojjhaṅga*, P), 166
Dharmottarīya (S; Dhammuttarika, P), 36, 38
dhātu (S, P), 54, 116, 119
dhātu-gabbha (P), 54
dhātu-[vavatthāna-]kammaṭṭhāna (P), 182
Dhātukathā (P), Discussion of Elements, 83, 84
Dhātukāya (S), Group on Mental Elements, 83
dhyāna (S; *jhāna*, P), 62, 165, 166, 168, 169, 170, 174, 175, 176, 177, 178, 179, 180, 183, 184, 190, 193, 206, 220 n. 3
dhyāna-pāramitā (S), 28
dhyāna-saṃvara (S), 169
dibbacakkhu. See *divyacakṣus*
dibbasota. See *divyaśrota*
Dīgha-nikāya (P), Collection of Long Discourses, 56, 72, 77, 78, 84, 91, 122, 174, 216 n. 10
Dīghiti, [King], 72
Dignāga (S), 45
Dīpaṃkara (S; Dīpaṅkara, P), 215 nn. 3–6
Dīpaṅkara. *See* Dīpaṃkara
Dīrgha-āgama (S), Long Discourses, 78
diṭṭhadhamma-sukhavihāra. See *dṛṣṭadharma-sukhavihāra*
diṭṭhi. See *dṛṣṭi*
diṭṭhi-parāmāsa. See *dṛṣṭi-parāmarśa*
diṭṭhi-visuddhi (P), 189
Divākara (S), 57
divyacakṣus (S; *dibbacakkhu*, P), 184
divyaśrota (S; *dibbasota*, P), 184
Divyāvadāna (S), Heavenly Stories, 72
domanassa. See *daurmanasya*
dṛṣṭadharma-sukhavihāra (S; *diṭṭha-dhamma-sukhavihāra*, P), 179
dṛṣṭi (S; *diṭṭhi*, P), 101, 186, 209, 211
dṛṣṭi-parāmarśa (S; *diṭṭhi-parāmāsa*, P), 212
dṛṣṭiprāpta (S), 193, 194
duggati. See *durgati*
duḥkha (S; *dukkha*, P), 149
duḥkha-duḥkhatā (S; *dukkha-dukkhatā*, P), 130
duḥkhāḥ sarvasaṃskārāḥ (S; *sabbe saṅkhārā dukkhā*, P), 130
duḥkha-jñāna (S), 220 n. 6
duḥkha-satya (S; *dukkha-sacca*, P), 155
duḥśīla (S; *dussīla*, P), 113
dukkha. See *duḥkha*

dukkha-dukkhatā. See *duḥkha-duḥkhatā*
dukkha-sacca. See *duḥkha-satya*
dūraṃgamā-bhūmi (S), 201
durāroha (S), 199
durgati (S; *duggati*, P), 176
durjaya (S), 200
dussīla. See *duḥśīla*
dutiyajjhāna (P), 190
Dvādaśamukha-śāstra (S), Treatise on the Twelve Gates, 43
dvaṅgula-kappa (P), 214 n. 7

Ekavyāvahārika (S; Ekabbohārika, P), 37, 39
Ekabbohārika. *See* Ekavyāvahārika
ekāyana-magga (P), 164
Ekottara-āgama (S), Discourses Treating Enumerations, 78, 121

gāmantara-kappa (P), 214 n. 7
gaṇa (S, P), 92
gandha-āyatana (S, P), 111
Gandhāra (S, P), 214 n. 11
gandharva (S), 61, 215 n. 9
gandha-viṣaya (S), 99, 101
gantha. See *grantha*
garuḍa (S), 61, 215 n. 9
gāthā (S, P), 68, 69, 70, 71, 73, 216 n. 14
Gautama (S; Gotama, P), 23, 56, 215 n. 3
geya (S; *geyya*, P), 68, 69, 70, 216 n. 14
geyya. See *geya*
ghana (S), 145
ghāna-āyatana. See *ghrāṇa-āyatana*
ghāna-indriya. See *ghrāṇa-indriya*
ghāna-viññāṇa-dhātu. See *ghrāṇa-vijñāna-dhātu*
ghrāṇa-āyatana (S; *ghāna-āyatana*, P), 109
ghrāṇa-indriya (S; *ghāna-indriya*, P), 99, 101, 109
ghrāṇa-vijñāna-dhātu (S; *ghāna-viññāṇa-dhātu*, P), 116
Gokulika. *See* Kaukkuṭika
Gotama. *See* Gautama
gotra-bhūmi (S), 200
grantha (S; *gantha*, P), 206
guṇa (P), 87, 89

Haimavata (S), Original Sthavira, 38
hetu (S, P), 87, 89
Himavanta (P), 214 n. 11
Hīnayāna (S), 24, 25, 26, 27, 28, 29, 31, 40, 43, 65, 68, 69, 85, 123, 172, 180, 213 n. 6, 218 n. 6
hirī. See *hrī*
hirottappa-samannāgata (P), 189
hrī (S; *hirī*, P), 99, 101, 219 n. 1

icchantika (S), 196
idaṃpratyayatā (S; *idappaccayatā*, P), 135
idappaccayatā. See *idaṃpratyayatā*
iddhividhā-ñāṇa. See *ṛddhividhi-jñāna*
Indra (S), 61, 75, 122, 123, 215 n. 9
Indradhvaja (S), 215 n. 4
indriya (S, P), 102, 109
indriyesu guttadvāra (P), 189
īrṣyā (S), 99, 101, 209
īryāpatha (S), 205
Isigili-sutta (P), 32
iṣu (S), 206
Īśvara (S), 61, 215 n. 9
itivṛttaka (S), 69, 72, 73
itivuttaka (P), 69, 72. See also *itivṛttaka*

Itivuttaka (P), "Thus-Said" Sūtras, 77, 78, 84

jāgariyam anuyutta (P), 190
jalogipātuṁ-kappa (P), 214 n. 7
Jambudhvaja (S), 215 nn. 4, 6
janmaja (S), 200
janmanideśa (S), 200
jarā (S), 99, 101
jarā-maraṇa (S, P), 149
jaṭā (S, P), 206
jātaka (S, P), 69, 72, 73
Jātaka (P), 73, 78, 84
Jātaka-atthakathā (P), 73
jātarūparajata-kappa (P), 214 n. 7
jāti (S, P), 99, 101, 149
Jaṭila (S), 215 n. 6
java (S), 101
jhāna. See *dhyāna*
jihvā-āyatana (S; *jivhā-āyatana*, P), 109
jihvā-indriya (S; *jivhā-indriya*, P), 99, 101, 109
jihvā-vijñāna-dhātu (S; *jivhā-viññāṇa-dhātu*, P), 116
jivhā-āyatana. See *jihvā-āyatana*
jivhā-indriya. See *jihvā-indriya*
jivhā-viññāṇa-dhātu. See *jihvā-vijñāna-dhātu*
jīvitendriya (S), 99, 101
jñāna (S; *ñāṇa*, P), 202, 216 n. 12
jñāna-pāramitā (S), 29, 185
Jñānaprasthāna (S), The Course of Knowledge, 83

Kakusandha. *See* Krakucchanda
kāla (S), 101
kalala (S), 145
kalpa (S), 29, 30, 57, 61
Kalpa-sūtra (S; Brahmanic), 70
kāmacchanda (P), 192
kāma-dhātu (S, P), 149, 175
kāma-taṇhā. See *kāma-tṛṣṇā*
kāma-tṛṣṇā (S; *kāma-taṇhā*, P), 148
kammaṭṭhāna (P), 180
Kāṇadeva. *See* Āryadeva
Kanakamuṇi (S; Koṇāgamana, P), 56, 215 nn. 2, 3, 5
Kaniṣka (S), 217 n. 17
kaṅkhāvitaraṇa-visuddhi (P), 189
Kapilavastu (S), 54
Kasmīra (P), 214 n. 11
Kassapa. *See* Kāśyapa
Kassapika. *See* Kāśyapīya
Kāśyapa (S; Kassapa, P), 56, 215 nn. 2–6
Kāśyapīya (S; Kassapika, P), 36, 38, 40
Kāśyapīya Tripiṭaka (S), 86
Kathāvatthu (P), Subjects of Discussion, 83, 84
Kaukkuṭika (S; Gokulika, P), 37, 39
kaukṛtya (S; [*kukkucca*, P]), 99, 101
Kauṇḍinya (S), 215 nn. 4, 6
kausīdya (S; *kosajja*, P), 99, 101, 165, 209, 212
kāya (S, P), 57, 58, 164
kāya-āyatana (S, P), 109, 112
kāya-indriya (S, P), 99, 101, 109
kāyasakṣin (S), 193, 194
kāya-vijñāna-dhātu (S; *kāya-viññāṇa-dhātu*, P), 116
kāya-viññāṇa-dhātu. See *kāya-vijñāna-dhātu*
khandha. See *skandha*
Khanda-vagga (P), 217 n. 18
Khandhaka. *See* Skandhaka
khanti-pāramī. See *kṣanti-pāramitā*
khīṇāsava. See *kṣīṇāsrava*
Khuddaka-nikāya (P), Collection of Minor Works, 56, 71, 72, 75, 77, 78, 79, 84

Khuddaka-pāṭha (P), Short Readings, 77, 84
kilesa. See *kleśa*
kiṃnara (S), 61, 215 n. 9
kiriyā (P), 205
kleśa (S; *kilesa*, P), 100, 203, 209
kleśa-mahābhūmika (S), 98
kodha. See *krodha*
Kokkulika. *See* Kaukkuṭika
Koṇāgamana. *See* Kanakamuṇi
Koṇḍañña (P), 215 n. 3
kosajja. See *kausīdya*
Krakucchanda (S; Kakusandha, P), 56, 215 nn. 2, 3, 5
krodha (S; *kodha*, P), 99, 101, 209
kṛtāvī-bhūmi (S), 201
kṣaṇa (S), 195
kṣaṇika (S), 145
kṣānti (S), 195, 220 n. 1
kṣānti-pāramitā (S; *khanti-pāramī*, P), 28, 29
kṣaya-jñāna (S), 220 n. 6
kṣīṇāsrava (S; *khīṇāsava*, P), 65, 193
Kṣudraka-āgama (S), Miscellaneous Discourses, 78, 79
Kṣudraka-piṭaka (S), Miscellaneous Basket, 78, 79
[*kukkucca*]. See *kaukṛtya*
kumāra-bhūta (S), 200
Kumārajīva (S), 123
kuśala (S), 100
kuśaladharma-saṃgrāhaka-śīla (S), 170
kuśala-mahābhūmika (S), 98
Kuśinagara (S; Kusinārā, P), 54, 75
Kusinārā. *See* Kuśinagara

Lakkhaṇa-suttanta (P), Sūtra on the Distinguishing Marks, 216 n. 10
lakṣaṇa (S), 61, 115
Lalitavistara (S), Detailed Narration of the Sport of the Buddha, 57
Laṅkāvatāra-sūtra (S), Sūtra of the Appearance of the Good Doctrine in [Sri] Lanka, 45
loka (S, P), 66, 176
lokāgradharma (S), 195
Lokakṣema (S; Chih Lou-chia-ch'ang, C), 49
lokanātha (S), 67
lokavid (S; *lokavidū*, P), 66
lokottara (S), 66, 176
lokavidū (P). See *lokavid*
Lokottaravāda (S), 39, 40, 56
Lokottaravādin (S), 57, 199
Lumbinī (S, P), [Garden], 54

macchariya. See *mātsarya*
mada (S, P), 99, 101, 209, 211
Madhyama-āgama (S), Medium-length Discourses, 72, 74, 78
Mādhyamika (S), Middle Way, 43, 44, 84
Mādhyamika-śāstra, also *Mūla-madhyamaka-kārikā* (S), Treatise on the Middle, 43
Magadha (S, P), 54
Māgadhī, 47
maggāmagga-ñāṇadassana-visuddhi (P), 189
magga-sacca. See *mārga-satya*
Mahā-assapura-sutta (P), Greater Discourse at Assapura, 189
Mahā-apadāna-suttanta (P), Sūtra of the Story of the Great Ones, 56
Mahābhārata (S), 134
mahābhūmika (S), 98, 107
Mahādeva (1) (S), 34, 214 n. 8
Mahādeva (2) (P), 214 n. 11
Mahādhammarakkhita (P), 214 n. 11

Mahāhatthipadopama-sutta (P), Greater Discourse on the Simile of the Elephant's Footprint, 218 n. 2
mahā-kalpa (S), 30
mahā-karuṇā (S), 63, 188
Mahākaruṇā-puṇḍarīka-sūtra (S), Sūtra of Great Compassion, 56
Mahā-Kassapa. *See* Mahā-Kāśyapa
Mahā-Kāśyapa (S; Mahā-Kassapa, P), 75, 76, 216 n. 16
Mahāpadāna-suttanta (P), Sūtra of the Story of the Great Ones, 72
Mahā-parinibbāna-suttanta (P), Sūtra of the Great Decease, 122, 125
Mahā-parinirvāṇa-sūtra (S), Mahāyāna Sūtra of the Great Decease, 44, 122
Mahā-prajñāpāramitā-śāstra (S), Treatise on the Great Perfection of Wisdom Sūtra, 43
Mahā-prajñāpāramitā-sūtra (S), Great Perfection of Wisdom Sūtra, 63
Mahārakkhita (P), 214 n. 11
Mahā-ratnakūṭa-sūtra (S), Sūtra of the Great Accumulation of Treasures, 45
Mahāraṭṭha (P), 214 n. 11
Mahāsāṃghika (S; Mahā-saṅghika, P), Great Assembly, 34, 35, 37, 39, 56, 80, 82, 199
Mahāsāṃghika Tripiṭaka (S), 86
Mahā-saṃnipāta-sūtra (S), Great Collection of Sūtras, 45
Mahāsaṅghika. *See* Mahā-sāṃghika
Mahā-vagga (P), Great Group, section of Khandhaka, 84, 217 n. 18
Mahāvairocana (S), 53, 58, 65
Mahā-vairocana-sūtra (S), Great Sun Sūtra, 46
Mahā-vaitulya-mahā-saṃnipāta-sūtra. See *Mahā-saṃnipāta-sūtra*
Mahāvastu (S), The Great Account, 56, 199
Mahāvedalla-sutta (P), Greater Discourse of the Miscellany, 74
Mahā-vibhaṅga (P), Great Analysis, 84
Mahāyāna (S), 23, 24, 25, 26, 27, 28, 29, 31, 32, 40–47, 48, 49, 57, 58, 63, 68, 69, 70, 74, 77, 82, 84, 85, 86, 88, 91, 116, 127, 129, 133, 145, 170, 171, 172, 180, 196, 198, 199, 200, 201, 213 n. 6
Mahāyāna-abhidharma-sūtra (S), Sūtra on Mahāyāna Abhidharma, 45
Mahāyāna-saṃgraha (S; *She-ta-ch'eng-lun-shih-ch'in-shih,* C), Comprehensive Treatise on Mahāyāna Buddhism, 45
Mahāyāna-śraddhotpāda-śāstra (S), Treatise on the Awakening of Faith in the Mahāyāna, 46
Mahāyāna-sūtrālaṃkāra (S), Treatise on the Adornment of Mahāyāna Sūtras, 45
Mahāyāna Tripiṭaka (S), 84–86
Maheśvara (S), 61, 215 n, 9
Mahiṃsāsaka. *See* Mahīśāsaka
Mahinda (P), 48, 214 n. 11
Mahisa-maṇḍala (P), 214 n. 11
Mahīśāsaka (S; Mahiṃsāsaka, P), 36, 38, 40, 80, 81
Mahīśāsaka Tripiṭaka (S), 86
mahoraga (S), 61, 215 n. 9
Maitreya (S; Metteyya, P), 56, 60, 215 n. 8

Maitreyanātha, or Maitreya (S), 45
Majjhantika (P), 214 n. 11
Majjhima (P), 214 n. 11
Majjhima-nikāya (P), Collection of Medium-length Discourses, 74, 77, 84, 116, 126, 189, 218 n. 2
Malla (S, P), 54
Māluṅkyaputta (P), 126, 127
māna (S), 99, 101, 193, 209, 210, 211
manas (S), 44, 106, 108, 109, 110, 119, 120
manasikāra. See *manaskāra*
manaskāra (S; *manasikāra*, P), 99, 101, 104, 107
manas-vijñāna (S), 106, 108
mānātimāna (S), 210
Maṅgala (P), 215 n. 3
mano (S, P), 106
mano-āyatana (S, P), 110, 119
mano-dhātu (S, P), 106, 120, 214 n. 9
mano-indriya (S, P), 109
mano-vijñāna-dhātu (S; *mano-viññāṇa-dhātu*, P), 116
mano-viññāṇa-dhātu. See *mano-vijñāna-dhātu*
mantra (S), 46
Māradhvaja (S), 215 nn. 4, 6
mārga-jñāna (S), 220 n. 6
mārgākāra-jñāna (S), 185
mārga-satya (S; *magga-sacca*, P), 158
mati (S), 99, 105, 107
mātsarya (S; *macchariya*, P), 99, 101, 209, 212
māyā (S, P), 99, 101, 209
medhā (S, P), 186
Medhaṅkara (P), 215 n. 3
mettā-pāramī (P), 29
Metteyya. *See* Maitreya
micchā-diṭṭhi. See *mithyā-dṛṣṭi*
micchāmāna. See *mithyāmāna*
middha (S, P), 99, 101
mīmāṃsā (S; *vīmaṃsā*, P), 165, 187
mithyā-dṛṣṭi (S; *micchā-diṭṭhi*, P), 192, 211
mithyāmāna (S, *micchāmāna*, P), 210
moha (S, P), 99, 101
mrakṣa (S), 99, 101, 209
Mṛgadāva (S), 54
mudrā (S), 46
Mūla-madhyamaka-kārikā. See *Mādhyamika-śāstra*
Mūla-Sarvāstivāda (S), Root Sarvāstivādins, 35, 80
Mūlasarvāstivāda-vinaya (S), 82, 84
Mūla-Sarvāstivādin (S), 57, 82, 84. *See also* Mūla-Sarvāstivāda
mūrdhan (S), 195
muṣitasmṛtitā (S), 101, 209

nāga (S), 61, 215 n. 9
Nāgamuni (S), 215 n. 6
Nāgārjuna (S), 43, 44, 63
naiḥsargika-prāyaścittika (S; *nissaggiya-pācittiya*, P), 80, 81
nairātmya (S), 116, 127
naivasaṃjñānāsaṃjñāyatana (S; *nevasaññānāsaññāyatana*, P), 177
Nālandā (S), 45, 84
nāma (S, P), 97
nāma-kāya (S), 99, 101
nāma-rūpa (S, P), 97, 147
ñāṇa. See *jñāna*
ñāṇadassana-visuddhi (P), 189
Nārada (P), 215 n. 3
nekkhamma-pāramī (P), 29
nevasaññānāsaññāyatana. See *naivasaṃjñānāsaṃjñāyatana*
nidāna (S, P), 69, 71–72
nidāna-kathā (P), 72
Nidāna-vagga (P), 217 n. 18

niddesa (P), 74, 75
Niddesa (P), Expositions, 74, 78, 84
niḥsvabhāva (S), 128, 187
nikāya (P), 77
Nikāya (P), 71, 77–78, 146
nikāya-sabhāgatā (S), 99, 101
nippapañca (P), 219 n. 1
nirmāṇa (S), 205
nirmāṇa-kāya (S), 58, 60
nirodha-jñāna (S), 220 n. 6
nirodha-sacca. See *nirodha-satya*
nirodha-samāpatti (S, P), 99, 101, 178, 184
nirodha-satya (S; *nirodha-sacca,* P), 157
nirupadhiśeṣa-nirvāṇa (S; *anupādisesa-nibbāna,* P), 133
nirvāṇa (S; *nibbāna,* P), 27, 28, 44, 63, 66, 87, 97, 114, 115, 121, 131, 132–34, 139, 140, 141, 142, 150, 154, 158, 164, 166, 182, 193, 216 n. 11, 218 n. 6, 220 n. 3
nirvikalpa-jñāna (S), 187
nissaggiya-pācittiya. See *naiḥsargika-prāyaścittika*
nissatta-nijjīvatā (P), 87, 88, 89, 126
niṣṭhā (S), 197
niṣyanda-kāya (S), 59
nivvāṇa (Ardha-māgadhī), 134
nivaraṇa (S), 206
nivṛta-avyākṛta (S), 204
Nyāya (S), 43

ogha (S, P), 206
omāna. See *avamāna*
ottappa. See *apatrāpya*

paccavekkhana. See *pratyavekṣaṇa*
pācittiya. See *prāyaścittika*
pada-kāya (S), 99, 101
Padmottara (S), 215 n. 4
Padmuttara (S), 215 nn. 3, 5, 6
Paduma (P), 215 n. 3
Paiśācī (S), 47, 48
pakkhiya. See *pakṣika*
pakṣika (S; *pakkhiya,* P), 164
[*paḷāsa*]. See *pradāsa*
Pāli (Buddhism), 23, 29, 35, 36, 47, 56, 68, 77, 79, 80, 82, 91, 94, 97, 105, 107, 110, 111, 113, 114, 116, 120, 122, 132, 145, 160, 180, 183, 204, 205
Pāli (language), 48, 49, 56, 72, 73, 74, 77, 108, 116, 124, 125, 214 n. 12, 220 n. 3
Pāli Abhidhamma, 83, 84
Pāli Nikāya, 78
Pāli Vinaya, 93
pamāda. See *pramāda*
pañca balāni (S, P), 165
pañca-dharma-kāya (S), 58
pañcanīvaraṇa-pahāna (P), 190
Pañcaviṃśatisāhasrikā-prajñāpāramitā (S), Perfection of Wisdom Sūtra in Twenty-five Thousand Lines, 42
pañcendriyāṇi (S; *pañcindriyāni,* P), 165
pañcindriyāni. See *pañcendriyāṇi*
paññā. See *prajñā*
pañña-pāramī. See *prajñā-pāramitā*
paññā-sikkhā. See *prajñā-śikṣa*
paññatti (P), 116
Paññattivāda. *See* Prajñaptivāda
paracitta-jñāna (S), 220 n. 6. See also *cetopariya-ñāṇa*
pārājika (S, P), 80, 81, 171
paramāṇu (S, P), 103
pāramitā (S, P), 29, 59, 66, 73, 185
Pāraṃgata (S), 215 n. 6
paratantra-svabhāva (S), 140, 219 n. 9
parideva (S, P), 149

parijñā (S; *pariññā*, P), 186
parikalpita-svabhāva (S), 140, 219 n. 9
parikkhā. See *parīkṣā*
parīkṣā (S; *parikkhā*, P), 187
parinibbāna. See *parinirvāṇa*
parinirvāṇa (S; *parinibbāna*, P), 133, 220 n. 3
pariniṣpanna-svabhāva (S), 140, 219 n. 9
pariññā. See *parijñā*
parisā. See *pariṣad*
pariṣad (S; *parisā*, P), 89
parisuddha-ājīva (P), 189
parisuddha-kāyasamācāra (P), 189
parisuddha-manosamācāra (P), 189
parisuddha-vacīsamācāra (P), 189
Parivāra (S, P), Accessory, 81, 84
pariyatti (P), 87, 89
pariyuṭṭhāna. See *paryavasthāna*
paryavasthāna (S; *pariyuṭṭhāna*, P), 203
[*passaddhi*]. See *praśrabdhi*
passaddhi-sambojjhaṅga. See *praśrabdhi saṃbodhyaṅga*
paṭhamajjhāna (P), 190
paṭicca-samuppāda. See *pratītya-samutpāda*
pāṭidesanīya. See *pratideśanīya*
paṭigha. See *pratigha*
pātimokkha. See *prātimokṣa*
Pātimokkha. See *Prātimokṣa*
paṭipadā-ñāṇadassana-visuddhi (P), 189
paṭisambhidā. See *pratisaṃvid*
Paṭisambhidā-magga (P), The Way of Analysis, 78, 84
paṭisandhi-viññāṇa (P), 219 n. 10
Paṭṭhāna (P), Book of Relations, 83, 84
pavāraṇā. See *pravāraṇā*,
pavivitta (P), 219 n. 1
peśī (S), 145
Petavatthu (P), Tales of Hungry Ghosts, 77, 84
phassa. See *sparśa*
phoṭṭhabba-āyatana. See *spraṣṭavya-āyatana*
phusana. See *sparśana*
Phussa (P), 215 n. 3
piṭaka (S, P), 68
Piṭaka (S, P), 25
pīti-sambojjhaṅga. See *prīti saṃbodhyaṅga*
Piyadassin (P), 215 n. 3
poṣadha (S; *uposatha*, P), 79
prabhākarī-bhūmi (S), 201
pradāsa (S; [*paḷāsa*, P]), 99, 101, 209
Pradyota (S), 215 nn. 4, 6
prajñā (S; *paññā*, P), 30, 101, 164, 165, 185, 186, 219 n. 1
prajñā-pāramitā (S; *pañña-pāramī*, P), 28, 29, 42, 185, 188
Prajñāpāramitā-hṛdaya-sūtra (S), Heart of Wisdom (or Heart) Sūtra, 42
Prajñāpāramitā-sūtra (S), 200
Prajñapti (S), Book of Manifestation, 83
Prajñaptivāda (S; Paññattivāda, P), 37, 39
prajñā-śikṣa (S; *paññā-sikkhā*, P), 167
prajñā-vimukta (S), 193, 194
Prakaraṇa (S), Treatise, 83
prākarṣika (S), 146
Prākrit, 47, 48
prakṛti-pariśuddha-nirvāṇa (S), 133
pramāda (S; *pamāda*, P), 99, 101, 209, 212
pramuditā-bhūmi (S), 201
praṇidhāna (S), 202, 213
praṇidhāna-pāramitā (S), 29

prāpti (S), 99, 101
praśākhā (S), 145
Prāsaṅgika (S), 44
praśrabdhi (S; [*passaddhi*, P]), 99, 101
praśrabdhi saṃbodhyaṅga (S; *passaddhi-sambojjhaṅga*, P), 167
Pratāpa (S), 215 n. 4
prathama-cittotpādika (S), 200
pratideśanīya (S; *pāṭidesanīya*, P), 80, 81
pratigha (S; *paṭigha*, P), 99, 101, 209
prātimokṣa (S; *pātimokkha*, P), 168
Prātimokṣa (*Prātimokṣa-sūtra*, S; *Pāṭimokkha*, *Pāṭimokkha-sutta*, P), Inventory of Offenses of Monks and Nuns, 70, 79
prātimokṣa-saṃvara (S), 169
pratiniyama (S), 101
pratisaṃkhyā-nirodha (S), 98, 101, 114
pratisaṃvid (S; *paṭisambhidā*, P), 187
pratītya-samutpāda (S; *paṭicca-samuppāda*, P), 135, 213 n. 5
prativedha (S), 197
pratyavekṣaṇa (S; *paccavekkhana*, P), 187
pratyekabuddha (S), 31, 32, 33, 55, 61, 62, 176, 184, 185, 196, 201, 215 n. 6
pratyekabuddha-bhūmi (S), 201
Pratyekabuddhayāna (S), 24, 31–33, 200
pravāraṇā (S; *pavāraṇā*, P), 81
pravṛtti (S), 101
prāyaścittika (S; *pācittiya*, P), 80, 81, 217 n. 20
prayoga (S), 195, 196, 197
prīti saṃbodhyaṅga (S; *pīti-sambojjhaṅga*, P), 166
pṛthagjanatā (S), 101
Pubbaseliya. *See* Pūrvaśaila
pubbenivāsānussati-ñāṇa. See *pūrvanivāsānusmṛti-jñāna*
pudgala-nairātmya (S), 130
Puggalapaññatti (P), Description of Individuals, 83, 84
puñña-khetta. See *puṇya-kṣetra*
puṇya-kṣetra (S; *puñña-khetta*, P), 65
purisadamma-sārathi. See *puruṣadamya-sārathi*
puruṣadamya-sārathi (S; *purisadamma-sārathi*, P), 67
Pūrva-mīmāṃsā (S), 43
pūrvanivāsānusmṛti-jñāna (S; *pubbenivāsānussati-ñāṇa*, P), 184, 190
Pūrvaśaila (S; Pubbaseliya, P), 37
pūrvayoga-sampanna (S), 200
puṣpamaṇḍita (S), 200
Puṣya (S), 215 nn. 4–6

rāga (S), 99, 101, 209
Rājagirika (P), 37
Rājagṛha (S), 65, 75
Rakkhita (P), 214 n. 11
rākṣasa (S), 122, 123
rasa-āyatana (S, P), 111
rasa-viṣaya (S), 99, 101
ratana-ttaya. See *tri-ratna*
Rathavinīta-sutta (P), Discourse on the Relays of Chariots, 189
Ratnagotravibhāga-mahāyānôttaratantra-śāstra (S), Treatise on the Jewel-nature, 46
ratna-traya. See *tri-ratna*
ṛddhividhi-jñāna (S; *iddhividhā-ñāṇa*, P), 184
Revata (P), 215 n. 3
rucira (S), 200
rūpa (S, P), 97, 98, 100, 102, 103, 203
rūpa-āyatana (S, P), 110

rūpa-dhātu (S, P), 149, 175
rūpa-kāya (S), 58
rūpavatī (S), 200
rūpa-viṣaya (S), 99, 101

sabba-dhamma. See *sarva-dharma*
Sabbatthivāda. *See* Sarvāstivāda
sabbe dhammā anattā. See *anātmanaḥ sarvadharmāḥ*
sabbe saṅkhārā aniccā. See *anityā sarvasaṃskārāḥ*
sabbe saṅkhārā dukkhā. See *duḥkhāḥ sarvasaṃskārāḥ*
śabda-āyatana (S; *sadda-āyatana*, P), 110
śabda-viṣaya (S), 99, 101
sacca-abhisamaya (P), 202
sacca-pāramī (P), 29
ṣaḍ-āyatana (S; *saḷāyatana*, P), 147
sadda-āyatana. See *śabda-āyatana*
saddhā. See *śraddhā*
Saddharma-puṇḍarīka-sūtra (S), Lotus Sūtra, 43
Saddharma-puṇḍarīka-sūtra-upadeśa (S), 75
sādhumatī-bhūmi (S), 201
ṣaḍ-vijñāna (S; *cha-viññāṇa*, P), 106
Sagātha-vagga (P), 217 n. 18
śaikṣa (S; *sekha*, P), 92, 94, 191
śaikṣa-dharma (S; *sekhiya-dhamma*, P), 80, 81
sakkāya-diṭṭhi (P), 192, 217 n. 1
sakṛdāgāmin (S), 191
sakṛdāgāmi-pratipanna (S), 191
Śākya (S; Sākya, P), 23, 76
Śākyamuni (S; Sākyamuni, P), historical Buddha, 23, 25, 26, 32, 33, 40, 41, 42, 48, 53, 54, 56, 57, 58, 59, 60, 64, 72, 73, 76, 92, 102, 105, 115, 122, 125, 151, 154, 174, 186, 215 n. 8
Śākyamuni (S), a Buddha of the Past, 59
Śākyamuni (S), fundamental, or original, buddha, 56, 215 nn. 3–6
śāla (S), 75
saḷāyatana. See *ṣaḍ-āyatana*
Śalistamba-sūtra (S), Sūtra of the Rice Stem, 218 n. 3
Saḷāyatana-vagga (P), 217 n. 18
samādhi (S, P), 62, 99, 101, 105, 107, 164, 165, 174, 177, 178, 179, 183, 184
samādhi saṃbodhyaṅga (S; *samādhi-sambojjhaṅga*, P), 167
samādhi-sambojjhaṅga. See *samādhi saṃbodhyaṅga*
samādhi-sikkhā. See *samādhi-śikṣa*
samādhi-śikṣa (S; *samādhi-sikkhā*, P), 167
sāmagrī (S), 101
samāhita (S, P), 179, 219 n. 1
sāmaṇera. See *śrāmanera*
sāmaṇerī. See *śrāmaṇerī*
Samantagupta (S), 215 n. 4
samāpanna (S, P), 179
samāpatti (S, P), 178, 180, 220 n. 3
samatā-jñāna (S), 120
samatha. See *śamatha*
śamatha (S; *samatha*, P), 177, 178, 179
śamatha-vipaśyanā (S), 179, 186
samaya (S, P), 173
Samayabhedoparacanacakra (S), Treatise on the Principles of Different Schools, 38
sāmbandhika (S), 145
sambhāra (S), 195, 196, 197
saṃbhoga-kāya (S), 58, 59
sambodhi. See *saṃbodhi*
saṃbodhi (S; *sambodhi*, P), 166, 187, 205

Saṃdhinirmocana-sūtra (S), Sūtra of Profound Understanding, 45
saṃghāvaśeṣa (S; *saṅghādisesa*, P), 80, 81, 217 n. 19
saṃgīti (S), 76
Samitāvin (S), 215 nn. 4, 6
saṃjñā (S; *saññā*, P), 97, 99, 101, 104, 107
saṃjñā-vedayita-nirodha (S), 101, 114
Samkantika. *See* Sānkrāntika
Sāṃkhya (S), 43
saṃkhyā (S), 101
sammā-ājīva. See *samyag-ājīva*
sammā-diṭṭhi. See *samyag-dṛṣṭi*
sammā-kammanta. See *samyak-karmānta*
sammā-ñāṇa. See *samyag-jñāna*
sammā-samādhi. See *samyak-samādhi*
sammā-sambodhi. See *samyak-saṃbodhi*
sammā-sambuddha. See *samyaksaṃbuddha*
sammā-saṅkappa. See *samyak-saṃkalpa*
sammā-sati. See *samyak-smṛti*
Saṃmatīya (S; Sammitika, P), 35, 36, 38
Saṃmatīya Tripiṭaka (S), 86
sammatta-niyata-rāsi. See *samyaktva-niyata-rāśi*
sammā-vācā. See *samyag-vācā*
sammā-vāyāma. See *samyag-vyāyāma*
sammā-vimutti. See *samyag-vimukti*
Sammitika. *See* Saṃmatīya
sampajāna. See *samprajāna*
sampayoga. See *saṃprayoga*
samprajāna (S; *sampajāna*, P), 186
saṃprayoga (S; *sampayoga*, P), 107
saṃsāra (S), 25, 27, 133, 153, 154, 218 n. 6
saṃskāra (S; *saṅkhāra*, P), 95, 97, 105, 106, 113, 124, 147, 149
saṃskāra-duḥkhatā (S; *saṅkhāra-dukkhatā*, P), 131
saṃskṛta (S; *saṅkhata*, P), 95, 124, 149
saṃskṛta-dharma (S; *saṅkhata-dhamma*, P), 96, 98, 112
samudaya-jñāna (S), 220 n. 6
samudaya-sacca. See *samudaya-satya*
samudaya-satya (S; *samudaya-sacca*, P), 156
saṃvara (S, P), 113, 169
saṃvara-śīla (S), 170
saṃvṛti-jñāna (S), 220 n. 6
samyag-ājīva (S; *sammā-ājīva*, P), 159
samyag-dṛṣṭi (S; *sammā-diṭṭhi*, P), 159
samyag-jñāna (S; *sammā-ñāṇa*, P), 161
samyag-vācā (S; *sammā-vācā*, P), 159
samyag-vimukti (S; *sammā-vimutti*, P), 161
samyag-vyāyāma (S; *sammā-vāyāma*, P), 160
samyak-karmānta (S; *sammā-kammanta*, P), 159
samyak-samādhi (S; *sammā-samādhi*, P), 160
samyaksaṃbuddha (S; *sammā-sambuddha*, P), 33, 66
samyak-saṃkalpa (S; *sammā-saṅkappa*, P), 159
samyak-smṛti (S; *sammā-sati*, P), 160
samyaktvaniyata-rāśi (S; *sammatta-niyata-rāsi*, P), 192, 202
saṃyojana (S, P), 205

Saṃyukta-āgama (S), Grouped Discourses, 78, 154, 164, 218 nn. 1, 4
Saṃyuktābhidharma-hṛdaya-śāstra (S), Expanded Treatise on the Essence of Abhidharma, 44
Saṃyuktāvadāna (S), Various Stories, 72
saṃyutta (P), 217 n. 18
Saṃyutta-nikāya (P), Collection of Grouped Discourses, 77, 78, 84, 142, 149, 152, 164, 217 n. 18, 218 nn. 1, 4, 5
Saṅgha (P), the Order, 53, 55, 82, 89–94, 180, 181
saṅgha (P), 34, 89, 92, 171
saṅghādisesa. See *saṃghāvaśeṣa*
Saṅgītiparyāya (S), Section for Recitation, 83
Saṅgīti-suttanta (P), Sūtra of the Recital, 174
saṅkhāra. See *saṃskāra*
saṅkhāra-dukkhatā. See *saṃskāra-duḥkhatā*
saṅkhata. See *saṃskṛta*
saṅkhata-dhamma. See *saṃskṛta-dharma*
Sānkrāntika (S; Samkantika, P), 36
saññā. See *saṃjñā*
Saṇṇāgārika (S; Chandāgārika, P), 36, 38
Sanskrit, 48, 49, 50, 56, 57, 72, 74, 85, 108, 121, 123, 124, 179
śāntaṃ (S; *santaṃ*, P), 132
santaṃ nibbānaṃ. See *śāntam nirvāṇam*
śāntam nirvāṇam (S; *santaṃ nibbānaṃ*, P), 132
santuṭṭha (P), 219 n. 1
sapta bodhyaṅgāni (S; *satta bojjhaṅgā*, P), 166
Sāramati (S), 45
Saraṇaṅkara (P), 215 n. 3
Śāriputra Abhidharma (S), 83, 84, 103
sarīra. See *śarīra*
śarīra (S; *sarīra*, P), 54
Sarvābhibhu (S), 215 n. 5
sarva-dharma (S; *sabba-dhamma*, P), 88, 96
sarvajña-jñāna (S), 185
sarvajñatā-jñāna (S), 185
Sarvāstivāda (S; Sabbatthivāda, P), Those Who Hold the Doctrine That All Exists, 35, 36, 38, 40, 80
Sarvāstivādin (S), 35, 62, 69, 71, 72, 81–82, 96–97, 103, 105, 107, 110, 112, 113, 114, 136, 145, 182, 194, 203, 204, 205, 206, 209, 211, 216 n. 17, 218 n. 6. *See also* Sarvāstivāda
Sarvāstivādin Abhidharma (S), 83, 84, 86
Sarvāstivādin Tripiṭaka (S), 86
sarvatraga (S), 100
śāstā-devamanuṣyānām (S; *satthā devamanussānaṃ*, P), 67
Śatasāhasrikā-prajñāpāramitā-sūtra (S), Perfection of Wisdom Sūtra in One Hundred Thousand Lines, 42
Śata-śāstra (S), Treatise in One Hundred Verses, 43
śāṭhya (S), 99, 101, 209
sati. See *smṛti*
sati-sambojjhaṅga. See *smṛti saṃbodhyaṅga*
sati-sampajaññena samannāgata (P), 190
satkāya-dṛṣṭi (S; *sakkāya-diṭṭhi*, P), 211

ṣaṭ-pāramitā (S), 28
satta bojjhaṅgā. See *sapta bodhyaṅgāni*
sattānaṃ cutūpapāta-ñāṇa (P), 190
Sattapaṇṇa-guhā. *See* Saptaparṇa-guhā
satthā devamanussānaṃ. See *śāstā-devamanuṣyānām*
sattva (S), 26
sattvaloka (S), 66
sattvārthakriyā-śīla (S), 171
Sautrāntika (S; Suttavāda, P), 36, 38, 44
saupādisesa-nibbāna. See *sopadhiśeṣa-nirvāṇa*
savikalpa-jñāna (S), 187
sekha. See *śaikṣa*
sekhiya-dhamma. See *śaikṣa-dharma*
Siddhattha (P), 215 n. 3
Siddhattika (P; [Siddhārthika, S]), 37
Sikhin. *See* Śikhin
Śikhin (S; Sikhin, P), 56, 215 nn. 2, 3, 5
sikkhamānā. See *śikṣamāṇā*
śikṣamāṇā (S; *sikkhamānā*, P), 90, 91
sīla. See *śīla*
śīla (S; *sīla*, P), 113, 164, 168, 169, 172, 219 n. 1
sīlabbata-parāmāsa. See *śīlavrata-parāmarśa*
sīla-pāramī. See *śīla-pāramitā*
śīla-pāramitā (S; *sīla-pāramī*, P), 28, 29, 171
sīla sikkhā. See *śīla-śikṣa*
śīla-śikṣa (S; *sīla sikkhā*, P), 167
śīla-vinaya (S), 172
sīla-vipatti. See *śīla-vipatti*
śīla-vipatti (S; *sīla-vipatti*, P), 113. See also *duḥśīla*, *dussīla*
sīla-visuddhi (P), 189
śīlavrata-parāmarśa (S; *sīlabbata-parāmāsa*, P), 192, 212
śilpa-sthāna (S), 205
sirigiloṇa-kappa (P), 214 n. 7
Śiva (S), 215 n. 9
skandha (S; *khandha*, P), 96
Skandhaka (S; Khandhaka, P), Chapters, 81, 84, 170
smṛti (S; *sati*, P), 99, 101, 105, 107, 165
smṛti saṃbodhyaṅga (S; *sati-sambojjhaṅga*, P), 166
Sobhita (P), 215 n. 3
soka. See *śoka*
śoka (S; *soka*, P), 149
Soṇa Uttara (P), 214 n. 11
sopadhiśeṣa-nirvāṇa (S; *saupādisesa-nibbāna*, P), 132
sota-āyatana. See *śrota-āyatana*
sota-indriya. See *śrota-indriya*
sota-viññāṇa-dhātu. See *śrota-vijñāna-dhātu*
sparśa (S; *phassa*, P), 99, 101, 105, 107, 147
sparśana (S; *phusana*, P), 187
sparśa-viṣaya (S), 99, 101
spraṣṭavya-āyatana (S; *phoṭṭhabba-āyatana*, P), 111
śraddhā (S; *saddhā*, P), 99, 101, 165, 219 n. 1
śraddhādhimukta (S), 193, 194
śraddhānusārin (S), 193, 194, 202
śrāmaṇera (S; *sāmaṇera*, P), 73, 90
śrāmaṇerī (S; *sāmaṇerī*, P), 90
śrāvaka (S; *sāvaka*, P), 25, 26, 30, 32, 55, 61, 62, 65, 176, 184, 185, 191, 196
Śrāvakayāna (S), 24, 25, 32, 40, 200
Śrīmālādevī-siṃhanāda-sūtra (S), Śrīmālā (or Queen of Śrīmālā) Sūtra, 44

Śrīvijaya (S), 51
srotāpanna (S), 191
srota-āpatti-pratipanna (S), 191
śrota-āyatana (S; *sota-āyatana*, P), 109
śrota-indriya (S; *sota-indriya*, P), 99, 101, 109
śrota-vijñāna-dhātu (S; *sota-viññāṇa-dhātu*, P), 116
śruta (S; *suta*, P), 219 n. 1
sthavira (S), 213 n. 7
Sthavira, [Original]. *See* Haimavata
Sthaviravāda (S; Theravāda, P), Those Supporting the Teaching of the Elders, 34, 35, 36, 38
Sthaviravāda Tripiṭaka (S), 86
Sthiramati (S), 45
sthiti (S), 99, 101
stūpa (S), 54
styāna (S; *thīna*, P), 99, 101, 209, 212
śuddhādhyāśaya (S), 200
sudurjayā-bhūmi (S), 201
sugata (S, P), 66
sugati (S, P), 176
Sujāta (S, P), 215 n. 3
Sukhāvatī (S), 60
Sukhāvatī-vyūha-sūtra (S), [Larger], Sūtra of Infinite Life, 43, 51
Sukhāvatī-vyūha-sūtra (S), [Smaller], Amitābha Sūtra, 51
Sukhāvatī-vyūha-sūtra-upadeśa, [Larger], 75
Sumana (P), 215 n. 3
Sumedha (P), 215 n. 3
suññata (P), 220 n. 5
śūnya (S), 102, 112, 127
śūnyatā (S), 30, 31, 42, 44, 86, 116, 127
Suprabhāsa (S), 215 nn. 4, 6
Susiddhikara-sūtra (S), Sūtra of Good Accomplishment, 46
śuṣkavidarśanā-bhūmi (S), 200
suta. See *śruta*
sūtra (S; *sutta*, P), 68, 69–70, 71, 216 n. 14
Sūtra-piṭaka (S; Sutta-piṭaka, P), 34, 35, 68, 69, 71, 75, 77–79, 82, 84, 85
Sūtra-vibhaṅga (S; Sutta-vibhaṅga, P), Analysis of the Sūtra, 70, 79, 84, 170
sutta. *See* sūtra
Sutta-nipāta (P), Collection of Suttas, 74, 77, 78, 84, 94
Sutta-piṭaka. *See* Sūtra-piṭaka
Suttavāda. *See* Sautrāntika
Sutta-vibhaṅga. *See* Sūtra-vibhaṅga
Suvaṇṇabhūmi (P), 214 n. 11
Suvarṇaprabhāsottama-rāja-sūtra (S), Golden Light Sūtra, 45
svabhāva-kāya (S), 58
Svātantrika (S), 44

Tambapaṇṇī (P), 214 n. 11
taṇhā. See *tṛṣṇā*
Taṇhaṅkara (P), 215 n. 3
tanu-bhūmi (S), 201
tārā-kalpa (S), 57
tathāgata (S, P), 43, 58, 60, 64–65, 126, 211
tathāgata-garbha (S), 44, 45, 86, 116, 136
Tathāgata-garbha-sūtra (S), Sūtra of the *Tathāgata*-Embryo, 44
tathatā (S), 64, 87, 101, 114, 188, 218 n. 2, 219 n. 8
tatiyajjhāna (P), 190
te-vijjā (P), 190
Theragāthā (P), Verses of the Elder Monks, 71, 77, 78, 84
Theravāda (P), 23, 29, 34, 35, 36,

38, 47, 48, 87. *See also* Sthaviravāda
Theravādin. *See* Theravāda
Therīgāthā (P), Verses of the Elder Nuns, 71, 78, 84
thīna. See *styāna*
tīni saṃyojanāni (P), 192
tīṇi vimokkhā-mukhāni (P), 220 n. 5
Tipiṭaka. *See* Tripiṭaka
tiracchānayoni. See *tiryag-yoni*
ti-ratana. See *tri-ratna*
Tissa (P), 215 n. 5
tisso sikkhā. See *trīṇi śikṣāṇi*
Tiṣya (S), 215 n. 5
Triṃśikā-vijñaptimātratā-siddhi (S), Thirty Verses on the Doctrine of Consciousness Only, 45
trīṇi śikṣāṇi (S; *tisso sikkhā,* P), 167
trīṇi smṛtyupasthānāni (S), 62
trīṇy ārakṣyāṇi (S), 216 n. 13
tripiṭaka (S), 85
Tripiṭaka (S; Tipiṭaka, P), 25, 35, 49, 50, 68, 69, 77, 84, 85, 214 n. 12
tripiṭaka-dhara (S), 85
tri-ratna (*ratna-traya,* S; *ti-ratana, ratana-ttaya,* P), 53
tṛṣṇā (S; *taṇhā,* P), 148, 209
tyāga (S; *cāga,* P), 219 n. 1

ubhayato-bhāga-vimukta (S), 193, 194
Udāna (P), Solemn Utterances of the Buddha, 71, 77, 78, 84
udāna (S, P), 69, 71
Udāna-varga (S), Solemn Utterances of the Buddha, 71
uddesa (P), 74
upādāna (S, P), 148
upādāya-rūpa (S, P), 112
upadeśa (S), 69, 74–75, 216 n. 14
upakleśa (S), 100
upakleśa-bhūmika (S), 98
Upāli (S, P), 76
upanāha (S, P), 99, 101, 209, 210
upāsaka (S, P), 90
upāsikā (S, P), 90
upaṭṭhita-sati (P), 219 n. 1
upāya (S, P), 188, 194, 202
upāya-pāramitā (S), 29
upāyāsa (S, P), 149
[*upekkhā*]. See *upekṣā*
upekkhā-pāramī (P), 29
upekkhā-sambojjhaṅga. See *upekṣā saṃbodhyaṅga*
upekṣā (S; [*upekkhā,* P]), 99, 101
upekṣā saṃbodhyaṅga (S; *upekkhā-sambojjhaṅga,* P), 167
ussada. See *utsada*
uposatha. See *poṣadha*
uṣmāgata (S), 195
utsada (S; *ussada,* P), 206
Uttaraśaila (S), 39

vagga (P), 77, 217 n. 18
Vaibhāṣika (S), 44
vaipulya (S), 69, 74
Vairocana (S), 59, 215 n. 8
Vaiśeṣika (S), 43
Vaiśravaṇa (S), 61
Vajjiputtika. *See* Vātsīputrīya
Vajracchedikā-prajñāpāramitā-sūtra (S), Diamond Wisdom (or Diamond) Sūtra, 42
vajrapāṇi (S), 215 n. 9
vajraratna (S), 172
Vajraśekhara-sūtra (S), Diamond Peak Sūtra, 46
Valabhī (S), 45
vana (S; *vanatha,* P), 206
vanatha. See *vana*

Vanavāsa (P), 214 n. 11
Varanasi (Bārāṇasī, S, P), 54, 92, 152
vārṣika (S), 81
vastu (S), 115
Vasubandhu (S), 44, 45, 46, 133
Vātsīputrīya (S; Vajjiputtika, P), 36, 38
Vaṭṭagāmanī (S), 216 n. 17
vedalla (P), 69, 74
vedanā (S, P), 97, 99, 101, 104, 107, 148, 164
Vedānta (S), 43
Vedānta- or Brahma-sūtra (S; non-Buddhist), 70
vepulla (S). See *vaipulya*
Vessabhu. *See* Viśvabhu
vetulla (S). See *vaipulya*
veyyākaraṇa. See *vyākaraṇa*
Vibhaṅga (P), Distinctions, 83, 84
vibhava (S, P), 157
vibhāṣā (S), 75. See also *vyākhyā*
vibhava-taṇhā. See *vibhava-tṛṣṇā*
vibhava-tṛṣṇā (S; vibhava-taṇhā, P), 148
vicāra (S), 99, 101
vicikicchā (P), 192
vicikitsā (S), 99, 101, 209, 212
vidyā (S; *vijjā*, P), 166, 186
vidyācaraṇa-saṃpanna (S; *vijjācaraṇā-sampanna*, P), Perfect in Knowledge and Conduct, 66, 105, 186
Vigraha-vyāvartanī (S), Treatise on the Transcendence of Controversy, 43
vihiṃsā (S), 99, 101, 209, 210
vijjā. See *vidyā*
vijjācaraṇa-sampanna. See *vidyācaraṇa-saṃpanna*
viññāṇa. See *vijñāna*
vijñāna (S; *viññāṇa*, P), 97, 106, 107, 110, 147
Vijñānakāya (S), Group on Consciousness, 83
Vijñānavāda (S), 44, 145, 186, 198
vijñānānantyāyatana (S; *viññāṇānañcāyatana*, P), 177
vijñapti-karman (S), 203
vijñaptimātratā (S), 44
Vijñaptimātratāsiddhi-śāstra. (S), Treatise on the Establishment of the Doctrine of Consciousness Only, 45
vikṣepa (S), 101, 209
vimalā-bhūmi (S), 201
Vimalakīrti-nirdeśa-sūtra (S), Vimalakīrti Sūtra, 42
vīmaṃsā. See *mīmāṃsā*
Vimānavatthu (P), Tales of Heavenly Palaces, 77, 84
Viṃśatikā-vijñaptimātratā-siddhi (S), Twenty Verses on the Doctrine of Consciousness Only, 45
vimukti (S; *vimutti*, P), 62, 166
vimutti. See *vimukti*
Vinaya (S, P), 68, 70, 72, 75, 76, 77, 79, 80, 81, 82, 170, 172
vinaya (S, P), 172
vinaya (S, P), 172
Vinaya-piṭaka (S, P), 33, 34, 35, 75, 77, 79–82, 84, 85, 92, 93, 218 n. 5, 219 n. 1. *See also* Vinaya
viniyata (S), 100
viññāṇa. See *vijñāna*
viññāṇānañcāyatana. See *vijñānānantyāyatana*
vipāka (S, P), 205
vipariṇāma-duḥkhatā (S; *vipariṇāma-dukkhatā*, P), 131

vipariṇāma-dukkhatā. See *vipariṇāma-duḥkhatā*
vipassanā. See *vipaśyanā*
Vipassin. *See* Vipaśyin
vipaśyanā (S; *vipassanā,* P), 179, 183, 186
Vipaśyin (S; Vipassin, P), 56, 215 nn. 2, 3, 5
viriya. See *vīrya*
viriya-pāramī. See *vīrya-pāramitā*
viriya-sambojjhaṅga. See *vīrya saṃbodhyaṅga*
vīrya (S; *viriya,* P), 99, 101, 165
vīrya-pāramitā (S; *viriya-pāramī,* P), 28, 29
vīrya saṃbodhyaṅga (S; *viriya-sambojjhaṅga,* P), 166
visuddhi (P), 168, 189
Visuddhimagga (P), The Path of Purity, 189, 220 n. 4
Viśvabhu (S; Vessabhu, P), 56, 215 nn. 2, 3, 5
vītarāga-bhūmi (S), 201
vitarka (S), 99, 101
vivitta-senāsana (P), 190
vyākaraṇa (S; *veyyākaraṇa,* P), 68, 69, 70
vyākhyā (S), 75. See also *vibhāṣā*
vyañjana (S), 61
vyañjana-kāya (S), 99, 101
vyāpāda (P), 192

yakṣa (S), 61, 75, 215 n. 9
Yamaka (P), Book of Pairs, 83, 84
yāna (S, P), 24
Yasa. *See* Yaśas
Yaśas (S; Yasa, P), 92, 217 n. 23
Yaśottara (S), 215 n. 5
yauvarājya (S), 200
yauvarājyatā (S), 200
Yoga (S), 43, 85, 172
yoga (S, P), 101, 179, 206
Yogācāra (S), Yoga Practice, 44, 45, 46, 85, 106, 120, 219 n. 9. *See also* Vijñānavāda; Yogācārin
yogācāra (S), 179, 200
Yogācārabhūmi-śāstra (S), Treatise on the Stages of Yoga Practice, 45
Yogācārin (S), 45, 69, 97, 100, 106, 108, 113, 114, 128, 136, 140, 204, 208, 209, 211. *See also* Yogācāra
yogācārya (S), 179
Yoga-sūtra (S; non Buddhist), 70
Yona (P), 214 n. 11
Yonaka Dhammarakkhita (P), 214 n. 11

General Index

Abhidharmakośa-śāstra (S), 44, 57, 113, 169, 185–86, 194
Abhidharma-mahāvibhāṣā-śāstra (S), Great Commentary, 44, 57, 63–64, 217 n. 17
Abhidharma-nyāyānusāra-śāstra (S), Treatise Following the True Teachings of the Abhidharma, 44
absolute pure faith in the four imperishables (*avetyaprasāda*, S), 173–74. *See also* four imperishables
absolute, or sacred, good (*anāsava-kusala*, P), 87–88
absolute Truth (*tathatā*, S), or Thusness, 64, 87, 114, 123, 217 n. 2–218, 219 n. 8; realm of, 188. *See also* unconditioned *dharmas*
Accessory (the third section of the Vinaya). *See* Parivāra
Acchariya-abbhutadhamma-sutta (P), Discourse on Wonderful and Marvelous Qualities, 74
action itself (*kiriyā*, P). *See* moral neutrality, two kinds of
actions (*saṃskāra*, S), 106, 142, 143, 147, 150, 204; becoming and, 149; grasping and, 148. *See also* mental constituents; twelve links
Acts of the Buddha, The. See *Buddhacarita*
Adhyardhaśatikā-prajñāpāramitā-sūtra (S), Sūtra of the Advancement Toward Truth, 42
afflictions (*āsrava*, S), 168
Āgamas (Āgama, S, P), 35, 75, 82, 184, 188, 206; Chinese, 78, 91, 105, 121, 146; fifth, 79; four, 77, 78–79; origin of, 33, 41; six *dhātus* of, 119; twelve links of, 146, 147
Aggregate of Dharmas. *See* Dharmaskandha
aggregates (*skandha*, S), 96, 107; nonself of, 102. *See also* five aggregates
Ājñāta-Kauṇḍinya (S), 186
ālaya, or storehouse, consciousness (*ālaya-vijñāna*, S), 106, 108, 128, 136
all *dharmas* (*sarva-dharma*, S), 96, 97, 124, 126, 185, 218 n. 3; mind and six consciousnesses and, 119; suffering and, 156

all phenomena (*saṃskāra,* S), 105. *See also* actions; all *dharmas;* mental constituents
altruistic practice, 27, 28, 29
ambrosia (*amṛta,* S), 132, 133, 134. *See also* nirvāṇa, synonyms for
Amida (J; Amitābha, Amitāyus, S), 24, 173. *See also* Buddha of Infinite Life; Buddha of Infinite Light
Amitābha Sūtra. *See* Smaller *Sukhāvatī-vyūha-sūtra*
analysis of the four great elements (*dhātu-[vavatthāna-]kammaṭṭhāna,* P), 182, 183
Analysis of the Sūtra. *See* Sūtra-vibhaṅga
Ānanda (S, P), 76, 216 n. 16
ancillary practice, 182, 183
anger (*pratigha,* S), 148, 171, 182, 190, 209. *See also* fundamental defilements
anger (*vyāpāda,* P), 119, 129, 192, 210. *See also* five lower fetters; "greed, anger, and folly (ignorance)"
Aṅguttara-nikāya (P), Collection of Discourses Treating Enumerations, 74, 77, 78–79, 84, 91, 168
An Shih-kao (C), 49
Apadāna (P), Stories of the Lives of Certain Monks and Nuns, 78, 84
appendix of the Vinaya, 81, 82. *See also* Parivāra
application (*prayoga,* S), 196. *See also* five stages leading to enlightenment; realization of [the four] good roots
appropriate means, 67. *See also* expedient ways; skillful means (*upāya*)
arhat, 30, 65–66, 75–76, 178, 184, 193; defilements and, 205, 207; enlightenment, 92, 94, 102, 161, 189–90; stage of attainment of, (*arhattva,* S), 191; stage of effort of, (*arhat-pratipanna,* S), 191. *See also* ten epithets of a buddha
arhat stage, 188, 191, 193; final, (*aśaikṣa-phala,* S), 153, 195, 196
"a road leading to one place" (*ekāyana magga,* P), 164
arrogance (*mada,* S), 99, 101, 209, 211. *See also* auxiliary defilements
arts and crafts (*śilpa-sthāna,* S). *See* nonimpedimentary moral neutrality, four types of
Āryadeva (S), also known as Kāṇadeva, 43
ārya, or noble, stage (of practice), 192, 194, 195, 196, 197, 202
aśaikṣa stage, 193
asaṃkhyeya kalpa (S), 30, 57. *See also* eon (*kalpa*)
Asaṅga (S), 44, 45, 133
ascetic practices, adherence to, 212
Asiatic Researches, Calcutta journal, 50
Aśoka (S), 34, 48, 214 n. 11
Aśokāvadāna (S), Story of Emperor Aśoka, 72
aspects of nonself, 122
aspiration to enlightenment (*bodhicitta,* S, P), 26–27, 43–44, 86, 173
assembly (*gaṇa,* S, P), 92. *See also* Saṅgha

associated mental functions (*cittasaṃprayukta-saṃskāra*, S), 98, 100, 105, 107, 112, 113, 208. *See also* mental attributes
associations (*saṃprayoga*, S), theory of, 107
Aṣṭasāhasrikā-prajñāpāramitā (S), Perfection of Wisdom Sūtra in Eight Thousand Lines, 42, 85
Aśvaghoṣa (S), 46, 105
ātman (S), absolute Self, 116, 126, 130
attachment, 108, 145, 167.
attachment to the five aggregates, suffering inherent in, 152, 155, 156
attachment to heretical practices (*sīlavrata-parāmarśa*, S), 148, 192, 206, 212
attachment to self (*ātma-grāha*, S), 108, 120, 125, 204, 210
attainment (*samāpatti*, S, P), 178. *See also* eight *samāpattis*; terms denoting concentration
attention (*manaskāra*, S), 99, 101, 105, 107. *See also* ten basic mental functions
auxiliary defilements (*anukleśa*, S), 208, 209–10, 212
avadāna (*apadāna*), 72. *See also* "heroic feats"
Avadānaśataka (S), One Hundred Stories, 72
Avalokiteśvara (S), 61, 215 n. 8
Avataṃsaka-sūtra (or *Buddha-avataṃsaka-nāma-mahā-vaipulya-sūtra*, S), Flower Garland Sūtra, 42, 74, 85, 140–42, 185, 197; ten meritorious acts in, 171, 172; ten perfections in, 29; ten stages of bodhisattva in, 201; Three Treasures and, 55
awakening (*buddhi*, S, P), 186. *See also* synonyms for *prajñā*

becoming (*bhava*, S, P), 143, 145, 149, 150, 204. *See also* afflictions (*āsrava*); existence (*bhava*)
becoming (*pravṛtti*, S), 101. *See also* functions dissociated from mind
benevolence, perfection of, (*mettā-pāramī*, P), 29
benevolence and compassion. *See* great compassion
Bhaiṣajyaguru (S), Buddha, or Tathāgata, of Healing, 59–60, 65. *See also* reward-body of a buddha
Bhikkhunī-vibhaṅga (P), Nuns' Analysis, 84
birth (*jāti*, S), 143, 145, 149, 204; and rebirth, 155; suffering inherent in, 155
birth-body of a buddha (*rūpa-kāya*, S), 57–58. *See also* buddha bodies
birth and death (*saṃsāra*, S), 29, 66, 133. *See also* rebirth; transmigration
birth and death, cycle of, (*saṃsāra*, S), 88, 114, 131, 153–54, 157, 218 n. 6; nirvāṇa and, 133, 134; release from, 25, 27, 92, 126, 139
Birushana Butsu (J; Vairocana, S), 59. *See also* Law-body of a buddha
bliss of mind and body. *See* merits of concentration; terms denoting concentration

bodhisattva (S), 29, 42, 44, 176, 184, 188; concept, 26–27; four universal vows of, 27, 213 n. 1; highest wisdom of, 185; *pārājika* offense of, 171; practice, stages of, 196–202; reward-body and, 59–60; vehicle of, 24, 25. *See also* doctrine of the ten realms
bodhisattva-*avadāna* (S). See *avadāna* (*apadāna*)
Bodhisattva-bhūmi (S; *P'u-sa-shan-chieh-ching,* C), Treatise on the Conduct of a Bodhisattva, 85
bodhisattva knowledge, 185
bodhisattva practice, 27, 28, 31, 32, 42, 196–99; fifty-two stages of (T'ien-t'ai), 197, 199; forty-one stages of (Fa-hsiang), 197, 199. *See also* ten stages of bodhisattva practice
bodhisattva precepts, 172, 173
bodhisattva stage (*bodhisattva-bhūmi,* S), 197, 201. *See also* ten abodes
bodhisattva vows (*praṇidhāna,* S), 26, 28, 59, 202, 213 n. 1
body (*kāya,* S, P), 57–58, 164; contemplation of (*see* four fields of mindfulness); mindfulness of (*see* ten states of mindfulness)
body for others' enjoyment, [buddha's], 58. *See also* buddha bodies
bonds (*paryavasthāna,* S), 203, 205. *See also* synonyms for the defilements
Book of Manifestation. *See* Prajñapti
Book of Pairs. *See* Yamaka
Book of Relations. *See* Paṭṭhāna
Brahmā (S, P), Hindu deity, 32–33, 75, 151, 215 n. 9
Brahmajāla (Brahma Net) precepts, 85, 171, 172
Brahmajāla-sūtra (S; *Fan-wang p'u-sa-chieh-ching,* C), Sūtra of the Brahma Net, 59, 85, 171
brahman (S), cosmic, or ultimate, reality, 116, 126
"broad and wide" (*vaipulya,* S), 74. *See also* expanded sūtras; *vaipulya* and *vedalla*
Buddha (buddha, S, P), 33, 53, 135, 142, 153, 176; defined, 23; Dharma and, 73, 74, 75, 114; discussion of, 55–68; historical (*see* historical Buddha); nirvāṇa and, 132, 133; realm of (*see* doctrine of the ten realms); vehicle of, (Buddhayāna, S), 24, 25, 200. *See also* Eternal Buddha; fundamental buddha; *term by name* (as Śākyamuni)
buddha bodies (*buddha-kāya,* S), 44, 57–61, 214 n. 10
Buddhacarita (S), The Acts of the Buddha, 105
Buddhagayā (S, P), 54
Buddhaghosa (S, P), 87, 88, 189, 220 n. 4
Buddhagotra-śāstra (S), Treatise on the Buddha-nature, 45–46
buddhahood: attainment of, 26, 28, 59, 60, 70, 196, 202; Śākyamuni's, 54; stage of, 198; way of, 93. *See also* predictions of buddhahood
Buddha of Infinite Life (Amitāyus, S), 24, 43, 53, 60, 173
Buddha of Infinite Light (Amitābha, S), 24, 43, 53, 59–60, 65, 173
buddha knowledge, 185. *See also*

buddha wisdom; three kinds of wisdom
buddha-nature (*buddhagotra*, S), 44, 46, 67, 86, 116, 133; all sentient beings and, 26, 196, 197. *See also* potential to become buddhas
buddha-nature (*buddhagotra*) precepts, 172. *See also* Mahāyāna precepts in China and Japan
buddha-nature tradition, treatises in, 45–46
Buddhapiṭaka-nirgraha-sūtra (S), Superior Sūtra of the Buddha Treasury, 57
buddha realms (*buddha-kṣetra*, S), 44, 214 n. 10. *See also* three periods and ten directions, buddhas of
Buddha's first discourse, 54, 92, 102, 152. *See also* "setting the wheel of the Law in motion"
Buddhas of the Past, 56–57, 60, 72, 73, 215 nn. 2–6. *See also* seven Buddhas of the Past
buddha stage (*buddha-bhūmi*, S), 201
Buddha, or Tathāgata, of Healing (Bhaiṣajyaguru, S), 59–60, 65
Buddha-treasure, 53, 54, 56, 64
Buddhavaṃsa (P), Lineage of the Buddhas, The, 56, 78, 84
buddha wisdom, 58, 184, 186, 197. *See also* buddha knowledge; wisdom
Buddhism: Abhidharma (sectarian), 23, 25, 26, 32, 34–40, 47, 70, 105, 132–33, 143, 191; Chinese, 47, 49, 85, 136, 172, 173, 197–99; defined, 23; East Asian, 91; Esoteric (or Tantric), 46; Hīnayāna, 68; Indian, 23, 40, 172, 173, 197, 199; Japanese, 136, 172, 173; Mahāyāna, 24, 33, 40–47, 50, 57, 70, 84, 127, 133, 196, 197, 199; Northern, 24, 47, 49–51, 110, 204; Pāli (Southern or Theravāda), 23, 47, 68–69, 97, 105, 107, 110, 114, 120, 180, 183, 204; primitive (presectarian), 23, 33–34, 56, 70, 86, 96, 97, 110, 124, 130, 173, 202; Pure Land, 24; Southern, 24, 47–49, 110; Theravāda, 47, 48; in Sri Lanka, 47, 48; Tibetan (or Lamaism), 46–47, 49–50, 197; Vietnamese, 49; Zen, 125
Buddhist community. *See* monastic communities
Buddhist Hybrid Sanskrit, 48, 49. *See also* Sanskrit
Buddhist theory (rational, ethical, and religious), 66
Buddhology, 40, 136
Burnouf, Eugène, 50

Cakkavattisīhanāda-suttanta (P), Sūtra on the Preaching of the Wheel-rolling King, 56
calm, or tranquillity, (*śamatha*, S), 167, 176, 177, 178–79; mindfulness of (*see* ten states of mindfulness); of nirvāṇa, 182
"calm and contemplation" (*śamatha-vipaśyanā*, S), 179, 186
Cariyā-piṭaka (P), Collection Concerning Conduct, 73, 78, 84, 105
catalogues of canonical works, 85–86
Catuḥśataka (S), Treatise in Four Hundred Verses, 43
causality (dependent origination),

135, 136, 145, 151, 192, 218 n. 6; components of, 140; doctrine of, 30, 32, 135, 137, 139; four varieties of, 145–46; general (external, physical), 137–39, 140, 142; law of, 30, 32, 137; religious (internal, mental), 137–39, 140, 142; theories of, 136–37; three categories of, 142; two types of, 137
cause (*hetu*, P), 87, 89. See also *dharma*, four characteristics of
cause and effect in the three periods, 143, 145, 147, 204
causing injury (*vihiṃsā*, S), 99, 101, 119, 209. *See also* associated mental functions; auxiliary defilements
cessation of perception and feeling (*nirodha-samāpatti*, S, P), 99, 101, 178, 184; concentration of, 178.
Chachakka-sutta (P), Discourse on the Six Sixes, 116–17
ch'an (C; *zen*, J), a type of concentration practice, 179
Ch'an (C; Zen, J) sect, 65, 180
Chang-shou-wang pen-ch'i-ching (C), Sūtra of the Heroic Deed of King Dīghīti, 72
"chanting the title of the Lotus Sūtra," 173
Ch'an-yüan-chu-ch'uan-chi (C), collection of famous sayings of Ch'an masters, 179–80
Chapters. *See* Skandhaka
Chen-yen (C; True Word) sect, 117. *See also* Shingon
Chien-chen (C), 172
chih-hui (C). See *prajñā* and *jñāna*
Chih Lou-chia-ch'ang. *See* Lokakṣema
Chinese Āgamas. *See* Āgamas, Chinese
Chinese Buddhism. *See* Buddhism, Chinese
Chinese canon, 49–50, 69, 72, 74, 77, 78, 121
Chinese translations of the scriptures, 49, 79
Chinese Tripiṭaka, 49, 50
chi-pieh (C; *vyākaraṇa*, S), 70. *See also* predictions of buddhahood
ch'ung-sung (C; *geya*, S), verse added to prose, 70
classical Sanskrit, 48. *See also* Sanskrit
clear mirror or still water. *See* right concentration
clear understanding (*ājñā*, S), 186. *See also* synonyms for *prajñā*
code of precepts (*prātimokṣa*, S), 168, 172
code of precepts governing behavior (*prātimokṣa-saṃvara*, S), 169
cognition, 106, 117, 147, 148. *See also* consciousness
Collection Concerning Conduct. See *Cariyā-piṭaka*
Collection of Discourses Treating Enumerations. *See* Aṅguttara-nikāya
collection of famous sayings of Ch'an masters. See *Ch'an-yüan-chu-ch'uan-chi*
Collection of Grouped Discourses. *See* Saṃyutta-nikāya
Collection of Long Discourses. *See* Dīgha-nikāya
Collection of Medium-length Discourses. *See* Majjhima-nikāya
Collection of Minor Works. *See* Khuddaka-nikāya

collections of monastic regulations (Vinaya-piṭakas), 33
Collection of Suttas. See *Sutta-nipāta*
commentaries on *abhidharmas,* scholastic, (*vibhāṣā, vyākhyā,* S), 75. See also *upadeśa*
Commentary on the [first two of the] Ten Stages. See *Daśabhūmika-vibhāṣā-śāstra*
Commentary on the *Jātaka.* See *Jātaka-atthakathā*
common stage (of practice), 194, 195, 196, 197. See also *ārya,* or noble, stage (of practice)
community of believers (*pariṣad,* S), 89. *See also* monastic communities
community of ordained men (*bhikṣu-saṃgha,* S), 89
community of ordained women (*bhikṣuṇī-saṃgha,* S), 89
compassion, 28, 29, 63, 129, 184, 188, 202
complete nirvāṇa (*parinirvāṇa,* S), 133, 220 n. 3
Comprehensive Treatise on Mahāyāna Buddhism. See *Mahāyāna-saṃgraha*
concentration (*cittaikāgratā,* S), 179. *See also* terms denoting concentration
concentration (*samādhi,* S, P), 62, 105, 107, 167, 168, 190; discussion of, 174–84; five roots of emancipation and, 165, 166; synonyms for, 179; threefold practice and, 160–61, 164. *See also* seven factors of enlightenment
concentration (*samāhita,* S), 179, 219 n. 1
concentration of the formless realm, 175–76, 178, 179
concentration of the realm of desire, 175, 178
concentration of the realm of form, 175, 176
concentration on breathing (*ānāpāna-smṛti,* S), 166. *See also* five meditations for settling the mind; ten states of mindfulness
concentration on the infinity of space, 178. *See also* four formless concentrations
concentration on the three subjects. *See* three gates to liberation
concentration, practice of, (*samādhi-śikṣa,* S), 63. *See also* threefold practice
condition (as specific term), 117, 123, 137, 183
conditioned (*saṃskṛta,* S), 95, 97, 124, 149
conditioned, or phenomenal, *dharmas* (*saṃskṛta-dharma,* S), 96, 97, 98, 112, 115, 122, 128; three aspects of, 122
conditions leading to nirvāṇa, 139, 140, 141, 142, 150, 153–154
conditions leading to transmigration, or rebirth, 139, 140, 141, 142, 150, 153, 154
confessional ceremony of *pravāraṇā,* 81
confession ceremonies, semimonthly, (*poṣadha,* S), 79
conscience (*apatrāpya,* S), 99, 101, 219 n. 1. *See also* associated mental functions; five and seven treasures
consciousness (*vijñāna,* S), 44, 110,

117, 142–43, 178, 204; five aggregates and, 97, 102, 107; mental constituents and, 105; storehouse, 106, 108; three kinds of, 147. *See also* eight consciousnesses; six consciousnesses
Consciousness Only (Vijñānavāda) school. *See* Fa-hsiang; Hossō; Yogācāra; Yogācārins
consciousness only (*vijñaptimātratā,* S), 44, 45, 140
consecutive (*sāmbandhika*) causality, 145, 146. *See also* four varieties of causaltiy
consideration, or viewing, (*anupaśyanā,* S), 186. *See also* synonyms for *prajñā*
contact (*sparśa,* S), 99, 101, 105, 107, 142–43, 145, 147–48, 204; mental constituents and, 105. *See also* twelve links
contact (*sparśana,* S), 187. *See also* synonyms for *prajñā*
contact with what we hate, suffering inherent in, 152, 155, 156
contemplation, 46, 164, 188, 193
contemplation of causes and conditions, 187
contemplation of impermanence, 125
contemplation of the five aggregates, 164, 184
contemplation of the four *dhyāna* stages, 183
contemplation of the Four Noble Truths, 184
contemplation of the loathsomeness of food (*āhāre paṭikūla-saññā,* P), 182
contemplation of the ten impurities, 180, 182
contemplation [of the virtues] of the Buddha, 46, 183
contemplation, or insight, (*vipaśyanā,* S), 179, 183–84, 186
continual awareness of faults, 64. *See also* eighteen unique virtues of a buddha
Controller of Humans (*puruṣadamya-sārathi,* S), an epithet of a buddha, 64, 67
Council of Rājagṛha. *See* First Council
Course of Knowledge, The. *See* Jñānaprasthāna
craving (*tṛṣṇā,* S), 143, 145, 149–50, 158, 204, 209; two aspects of, 206
craving for existence (*bhava-tṛṣṇā,* S), 148, 152, 156–57. *See also* six cravings; three cravings
craving for nonexistence (*vibhava-tṛṣṇā,* S), 148, 152, 156–57
craving for sensuous desires (*kāma-tṛṣṇā,* S), 148, 152, 156–57
craving for the formless realm, 193
craving for the realm of desire, 192
craving for the realm of form, 193
Cūḷa-Māluṅkya-sutta (P), Lesser Discourse to Māluṅkyaputta, 126
Cūḷavedalla-sutta (P), Lesser Discourse of the Miscellany, 74
Cunda (S, P), 94
cycle of birth and death. *See* birth and death, cycle of

Daśabhāṇavāra-vinaya (S), Vinaya in Ten Recitations, 81–82
Daśabhūmika-vibhāṣā-śāstra (S), Commentary on the [first two of the] Ten Stages, 43

death, mindfulness of. *See* ten states of mindfulness
Deer Park (Mṛgadāva, S), 54, 152
defilements (*kleśa*, S), 62, 87, 93, 127, 132, 163, 192; concept of, 203–6; Sarvāstivādin theory of, 206–8; suffering and, 150, 157, 158; Yogācārin theory of, 208–12. *See also* synonyms for the defilements
defilements of practice, 207–8. *See also* delusions of volition
defilements of view, 207–8. *See also* five false views
deliverance, 86, 87
delusion, 24, 27, 62, 65, 107, 115; defilements and, 204, 205, 207; morality and, 169; suffering and, 131, 140
"delusion, karma, and suffering," 204
delusions of volition, 207. *See also* defilements of practice
dependent nature (*paratantra-svabhāva*, S). *See* three-natures theory
dependent origination (*pratītya-samutpāda*, S), 138, 151, 155, 210, 213 n. 5; doctrine of, 30, 134, 135–37, 150. *See also* causality; Twelve-linked Chain of Dependent Origination
Derge edition (Tibetan Tripiṭaka, pub. around 1730), 50
derivatives (*upādāya-rūpa*, S, P), 102, 103, 111–12. *See also* four great elements
"derived concept." *See* transitory *dharmas*
Description of Individuals. *See* Puggalapaññatti
desirable realms [of rebirth] (*sugati*, S, P), 176
desire (*chanda*, S, P), 99, 101, 107, 119, 182, 206; concentration and, 175, 177–78; craving and, 148, 156–57
desire, affliction of, 168
desire for existence, 206
Detailed Narration of the Sport of the Buddha. See *Lalitavistara*
determination, perfection of, (*adhiṭṭhāna-pāramī*, P), 29. *See also* ten perfections, Pāli Buddhist
Dhammacakkappavattana-sutta (P), Sūtra of the Turning of the Wheel of the Law, 152, 156, 157–58, 218 n. 5, 219 n. 1
Dhammapada (P), Verses on the Law, 71, 77, 78, 128
Dhammasaṅgaṇi (P), Enumeration of Dhammas, 83, 84, 87
Dharma (*dharma*, S), the Buddha's teachings, or Law, 32–33, 35, 53, 128, 187, 205; discussion of, 68–89; eight stages of effort and attainment and, 192; eight types of attainment and, 193; faith and practice of, 94; Law-body and, 58; Mahāyāna, 86; primitive Buddhist definition of, 86; Saṅgha and, 92–93; ten states of mindfulness and, 180; truth and, 114; and Vinaya, 75, 76, 82
dharma (S), 89, 96, 107, 108, 115, 119; four characteristics of, 87–89. See also *dharmas by term*
Dharma Eye (initial enlightenment), 102, 136, 153, 186, 202
Dharmaguptaka (S), 40, 78, 80, 83, 103; Four-Part Vinaya, 81, 172;

on ordained monks and nuns, 90, 169, 170; Tripiṭaka, 86
Dharmakāra (bodhisattva), 60. *See also* Buddha of Infinite Light (Amitābha)
Dharmapāla (S), 45, 145
Dharmarakṣa (S), 57
Dharma realm (*dharma-dhātu*, S), 59, 115, 185, 217 n. 2, 218 n. 6
dharmas as objects of consciousness (*dharma-āyatanikāni*, S), 101. *See also* form (*rūpa*)
dharmas dissociated from mind, 97. *See also* functions dissociated from mind
Dharmaskandha (S), Aggregate of Dharma, 83
dharmas not subject to change. *See* unconditioned *dharmas*
dharmas of form, 103, 110, 111, 112, 113. *See also* form (*rūpa*); material *dharmas*
dharmas of mental attributes, 113. *See also* associated mental functions; mental attributes
Dharma-teaching lord, 53
Dhātukathā (P), Discussion of Elements, 83, 84
Dhātukāya (S), Group on Mental Elements, 83
dhyānas of the realm of form, 177
Diamond, or Diamond Wisdom, Sūtra. See *Vajracchedikā-prajñāpāramitā-sūtra*
Diamond Peak Sūtra. See *Vajraśekhara-sūtra*
diamond (*vajraratna*) precepts, 172. *See also* Mahāyāna precepts
Dīgha-nikāya (P), Collection of Long Discourses, 56, 72, 77, 78, 84, 216 n. 10; concentration and, 174–75; Saṅgha and, 91; threefold practice in, 167–68; "verse of impermanence" in, 122
Dignāga (S), 45
Dīrgha-āgama (S), Long Discourses, 78. *See also* Dīgha-nikāya
disciple (*śrāvaka*, S), 25, 191, 196. *See also* five groups of sentient beings; *śrāvaka*
Discourse on the Relays of Chariots. See *Rathavinīta-sutta*
Discourse on the Six Sixes. See *Chachakka-sutta*
Discourse on Wonderful and Marvelous Qualities. See *Acchariya-abbhutadhamma-sutta*
discourses (*sūtra*, S), 68, 69, 70, 71, 216 n. 14. See also *sūtra* (*sutta*)
Discourses Treating Enumerations. *See* Ekottara-āgama
discriminating nature (*parikalpita-svabhāva*, S), 140, 142, 219 n. 9. *See also* three-natures theory
discriminating wisdom (*savikalpa-jñāna*, S), 187
"discriminating wisdom attained after nondiscriminating wisdom," 188
discrimination of true from false (*dharmavicaya*, S), 187. *See also* investigation of the Dharma
discursive thought (*vitarka*, S), 99, 101, 175. *See also* associated mental functions
Discussion of Elements. *See* Dhātukathā
disregard of the precepts (*asaṃvara*, S), 113. *See also* unmanifested form
Distinctions. *See* Vibhaṅga
distraction (*vikṣepa*, S), 101, 180,

181, 182–83, 209; elimination of, 63. *See also* associated mental functions; auxiliary defilements
Divākara (S), 57
Divyāvadāna (S), Heavenly Stories, 72
doctrine of consciousness only, 44, 45
doctrine of dependent origination, 30, 32, 137
doctrine of inner witness, 151
doctrine of karmic retribution, 176
doctrine of nonself, 126
doctrine of the Four Noble Truths, 134, 150, 151
doctrine of the interpenetration of the ten realms, 177
doctrine of the stages of enlightenment, 197
doctrine of the ten realms, 176–77. *See also* ten realms of existence, or ten realms
doctrine of the Twelve-linked Chain of Dependent Origination, 157
Dōgen (J), 55, 87, 173
donation, 29, 31, 65, 91, 176, 213 n. 3.
donation, perfection of, (*dāna-pāramitā*, S), 28, 29, 31
doubt about the teachings (*vicikitsā*, S), 99, 101, 183, 190, 192; defilements and, 206, 207, 209, 212. *See also* fundamental defilements
"dull defilements." *See* defilements of practice
Dvādaśamukha-śāstra (S), Treatise on the Twelve Gates, 43

early Mahāyāna, 84, 197, 200
sūtras and treatises, 42–43
ease, 93, 122, 131, 154
effort, 160, 183, 207. *See also* right effort
effort. *See* seven factors of enlightenment
effort, perfection of, (*vīrya-pāramitā*, S), 28, 29
eight *ārya* (noble) stages of effort and attainment, 86, 191, 192, 194, 196, 205; first stage of enlightenment and, 202; Saṅgha and, 91, 92, 93
eight consciousnesses, 86, 101, 106–7. *See also* mind (*citta*)
eighteen elements of existence (*aṣṭādaśa dhātavaḥ*, S), 86, 88, 96, 103, 114, 116–20; consciousness and, 106, 110
eighteen or twenty schools of Buddhism, 34–35. *See also* Buddhism: Abhidharma (sectarian)
eighteen unique virtues of a buddha (*aṣṭādaśa āveṇika-buddha-dharmāḥ*, S), 26, 62, 63
Eightfold Path (*ārya-aṣṭāṅgika-mārga*, S), 28, 102, 150, 152, 164, 186; concentration and, 174; discussion of, 158–60; threefold practice and, 160–61
eight forms of recognition (*kṣānti*, S), 208, 220 n. 1
eight forms of wisdom, 208, 220 n. 1
eighth consciousness. See *ālaya*, or storehouse, consciousness
eight kinds of suffering, 155
eight precepts, 90, 170
eight qualities of *śrāvakas*, *pratyekabuddhas*, and bodhisattvas (*aṭṭha mahāpurisa-vitakka*, P), 163, 219 n. 1

eight *samāpattis*, 178, 180, 220 n. 3
eight stages of mastery of the senses (*aṭṭhābhibhāyatanāni*, P), 184
eight types of attainment, 191, 193, 194, 202
eighty-four thousand teachings, 87, 163
eighty secondary marks (of a buddha), 26, 60, 64, 216 n. 10. *See also* thirty-two primary marks (of a buddha)
Ekottara-āgama (S), Discourses Treating Enumerations, 78, 121
elements of existence (*dhātu*, S, P), 83, 116, 119. *See also* eighteen elements of existence
elements of existence (*dharmas*), 88, 125; discussion of, 95–120; fivefold classification for, 96. *See also* all *dharmas;* one hundred *dharmas* in five categories
eleven forms of knowledge, 186. See also *prajñā* and *jñāna*
elimination of all residue of the defilements, 64. *See also* eighteen unique virtues of a buddha
emancipation, or liberation, (*vimukti*, S), 58, 63, 67, 91, 102, 205; from cycle of birth and death, 64, 134; five roots of, 166; ten powers and, 62. *See also* release
emancipation through wisdom (*prajñā-vimukta*, S). *See* eight types of attainment
emptiness (*śūnyatā*, S), 31, 44, 89, 102, 127, 178; concept of, 42, 116; Mahāyāna concept of, 88; non-self and, 128; two kinds of, 129–30; of wisdom, 30
emptiness of the *dharmas*, 130
emptiness of the self, 130
empty (*śūnya*, S), 102, 112, 127, 129
endeavor (*vīrya*, S), 99, 101, 165, 166. *See also* associated mental functions; five roots of emancipation
endeavor. *See* seven factors of enlightenment
endeavor (*vīrya, viriya*) to attain *dhyāna*. *See* four psychic powers
endless mutual influence of all things, 139
enjoyment-body of a buddha (*saṃbhoga-kāya*, S), 58, 59, 60. *See also* homogeneous-body (*niṣyanda-kāya*, S); reward-body
enlightened one, 23, 55. *See also* Buddha (buddha)
enlightenment (*bodhi*, S, P), 62, 164, 165, 205; attainment of, 127, 211; first stage of, 153, 174, 184, 186, 192, 202 (*see also* Dharma Eye); four degrees of, 200; as ideal of Buddhism, 87; *śaikṣa* (S, *sekha*, P), 92; Śākyamuni's, 32, 151; undefiled and supramundane, 153; wisdom of, 179, 184, 185, 186, 187; world of, 140. See also *term by name* (as world of enlightenment)
enmity (*upanāha*, S, [P]), 99, 101, 209. *See also* auxiliary defilements
Enumeration of Dhammas. *See* Dhammasaṅgaṇi
eon (*kalpa*, S), 29–30, 57, 61
equanimity. *See* seven factors of enlightenment
equanimity (*upekṣā*, S), 99, 101, 119, 175. *See also* four *dhyānas*

equanimity, perfection of, (*upekkhā-pāramī*, P), 29
Esoteric teachings, 24. *See also* Buddhism: Esoteric (or Tantric)
Eternal Buddha, 53
"evidential [turn of the wheel]." *See* "three turns of the wheel"
evil (*akuśala*) defilements, 204
existence (*bhava*, S, P), also becoming, 30, 88, 95, 97, 112, 114; becoming as, 149; causality and, 139, 140; defined, 96, 115. *See also* elements of existence
Exoteric teachings, 24
expanded sūtras (*vaipulya*, S), 69. See also *vaipulya* and *vedalla*
Expanded Treatise on the Essence of Abhidharma. See *Saṃyuktābhidharma-hṛdaya-śāstra*
expedient ways, 87. *See also* appropriate means; skillful means (*upāya*)
explanatory discourses (*upadeśa*, S), 69, 74–75, 216 n. 14
expositions (*niddesa*, P). See *upadeśa*
Expositions. See *Niddesa*
external sense fields (*bāhira-āyatana*, S, P), 109
extinction and nonreproduction owing to lack of a productive cause (*apratisaṃkhyā-nirodha*, S), 98, 101, 114. *See also* unconditioned *dharmas*, three
extinction of defilements through wisdom (*pratisaṃkhyā-nirodha*, S), 98, 101, 114. *See also* unconditioned *dharmas*
extinction of feeling and perception (*saṃjñā-vedayita-nirodha*, S), 101, 114. *See also* unconditioned *dharmas*
extinction of pleasure and pain (*āniñjya*, S), 101, 114. *See also* unconditioned *dharmas*
extreme views (*antagrāha-dṛṣṭi*, S), 211. *See also* false views; fundamental defilements
eye, the, (*cakṣu*, S). *See* synonyms for *prajñā*
Eye Storehouse of the True Law. See *Shōbōgenzō*

faculty, or ability, (*indriya*, S, P), 109
faculty of sight (*cakṣur-indriya*, S), 99, 101, 109
Fa-hsiang (C; Vijñānavāda) sect, 145, 196, 197, 219 n. 9
faith (*śraddhā*, S), 66, 67, 99, 101, 202, 219 nn. 1, 2; absolute pure, 173–74; in Buddhism, 93; concentration and, 180–81; Dharma Eye and, 153; Eightfold Path and, 159, 161; eight types of attainment and, 192, 193, 194; five excellent powers and, 166; five roots of emancipation and, 165; focus of, 58; object of, 53, 54, 60 (*see also* Buddha-treasure); and practice, 31, 42, 53, 89, 92, 94, 163; stage of *arhat* and, 188
false views (*dṛṣṭi*, S), 101, 171, 186, 205–6, 207, 208, 209, 211, 217 n. 1; five, 113, 207, 208, 209, 211; sixty-two, 211; twenty, of self, 102, 217 n. 1
false views about a permanent self (*sakkāya-diṭṭhi*, P), 192, 206, 217 n. 1
Fan-wang p'u-sa-chieh-ching (C; *Brahmajāla-sūtra*, S), Sūtra of the Brahma Net, 59, 85, 171

farseeing wisdom, 62–63. *See also* three types of equanimity
feeling (*vedanā,* S, P), 97, 99, 101, 102, 105, 164; causality and, 142–43, 145; classification of, 104, 148; contemplation of (*see* four fields of mindfulness); mental functions and, 107–8, 113. *See also* five feelings; six feelings; three feelings
fei-wo (C), "without ego," 127
female lay believer (*upāsikā,* S, P), 90, 172. *See also* four groups [of believers]
female novice, single, (*śrāmaṇerī,* S), 90, 169, 172. *See also* seven groups [of believers]
fetters (*saṃyojana,* S, P). *See* synonyms for the defilements
field for planting merit (*puṇya-kṣetra,* S), an epithet of an *arhat,* 65
fifty-two stages of bodhisattva practice, 197, 199
"final knowledge." See *prajñā* and *jñāna*
First Council, 65, 75–76, 79, 82
five aggregates (*skandha,* S), 86, 88, 96, 122, 130, 156; contemplation of, 164, 184; discussion of, 97–108; nature of truth and, 114, 116; twelve links and, 143–45
five and seven treasures (system of practice), 163, 219 n. 1
five ascetics, 92, 102, 152, 153, 186
five attributes, Law-body equated with, (*pañca-dharma-kāya,* S), 58, 67, 91. *See also* Unsurpassed (*anuttara*)
five attributes of *dhyāna,* 183
five classes of disciples, 220 n. 7; degrees of, 197
five collections (*nikāya,* P). *See* five Nikāyas
five desires, 157, 183
five excellent powers (*pañca balāni,* S), 164, 165–66
five false views, 113, 207, 208, 209, 211–12. *See also* defilements of view; false views
five feelings, 104. *See also* feeling (*vedanā*); six feelings; three feelings
five forms of wisdom. See *prajñā* and *jñāna*
five groups of sentient beings, 196
five higher fetters, 193, 206, 207. *See also* synonyms for the defilements
five hindrances (*pañca nivaraṇāni,* S), 183, 190, 206
five kinds of parsimony, 212. *See also* auxiliary defilements
five kinds of *zen,* 179–80. *See also* five meditations for settling the mind
five lay precepts, 90, 170
five lower fetters, 192, 206, 207. *See also* synonyms for the defilements
five meditations for settling the mind, 182–83. *See also* meditation on the five gateways; Sarvāstivādin stages of practice
five merits of *samādhi.* *See* merits of concentration
five Nikāyas, 77. *See also* Nikāyas
Five-Part Vinaya (of Mahīśāsakas), 81. *See also* seven complete Vinayas

five realms of existence, 61. *See also* realms of existence
five [physical] sense organs (*indriya*, S, P), 102, 111. *See also* sense organs
five roots of emancipation (*pañcendriyāṇi*, S), 164, 165, 166
five sense objects (*āyatana*, S, P), 102, 111
five senses, 120, 157
five stages leading to enlightenment, 196, 198
five supernormal powers, 184, 186, 193. *See also* six supernormal powers
five theses deprecating the *arhat*, 34, 214 n. 8
five types of *zen*, 180
Flower Garland sect. *See* Hua-yen; Kegon
Flower Garland Sūtra. See *Avataṃsaka-sūtra*
Fo-i-chiao-ching (C), Sūtra of the Teachings Left by the Buddha, 58
folly, or ignorance (*avidyā*), 131, 158, 180, 181, 182, 206, 207. *See also* "greed, anger, and folly (ignorance)"
Fo-pen-hsing-chi-ching (C), Sūtra Stories of Deeds of the Buddha, 56
forbearance [or patience], perfection of, (*kṣānti-pāramitā*, S), 28, 29
force of purpose, perfection of, (*bala-pāramitā*, S), 29
"foremost in hearing many teachings." *See* Ānanda
forgetfulness (*muṣitasmṛtitā*, S), 101, 209. *See also* auxiliary defilements
form (*rūpa*, S, P), 97, 98, 100, 110, 183, 203; basic definition of, 103; formless concentrations and, 177–78; three categories of, 110; traditional definition of, 102
form (*rūpa-āyatana*, S, P), three categories of, 110
form (*lakṣaṇa*), 61, 115
"Form is identical with emptiness," 102, 129
formless concentrations (*ārūpya-samāpatti*, S), 177, 178; four, 177–78
formless realm (*ārūpya-dhātu*, S), 67, 149, 177–78, 204, 208; all defilements of, 207; concentration of, 175–76, 179 (*see also* "fundamental concentration"); heavens of, 176; rebirth in, 184, 192–93. *See also* three realms of existence
formula for taking refuge in the Three Treasures, 55
forty-eight minor prohibitions, 170, 171
forty-one stages of bodhisattva practice, 197, 199
forty subjects of concentration, 180–82, 220 n. 4
foundation for inducing the six consciousnesses, 120
four absolute purities (*catasraḥ sarvākāra-pariśuddhayaḥ*, S), 64, 216 n. 12. *See also* eighteen unique virtues of a buddha
four Āgamas. *See* Āgamas, four
four *anvaya-jñāna* (S). *See* eight forms of wisdom; ten forms of knowledge

four-body doctrine (of buddha bodies), 58. *See also* buddha bodies
four Brahmā abodes (*cattāro brahma-vihārā* or *cattasso appamaññāyo*, P), 181, 182. *See also* four immeasurable contemplations
four *dharma-jñāna* (S). *See* eight forms of wisdom; ten forms of knowledge
four *dhyāna* heavens, 176, 184
four *dhyānas* (meditational states), 160, 168, 170, 174–75, 220 n. 3; of realm of form, 177, 178, 190
four *dhyāna* stages, 183
four divisions (*āgama*, S, P), 78. *See also* Āgamas, four
four fields of mindfulness (*catvāri smṛty-upasthānāni*, S), 164, 166, 186, 195
four formless concentrations (*ārūpya-samāpatti*, S), 177–78
four forms of wisdom. See *prajñā* and *jñāna*
four good roots (Sarvāstivādin stage of practice), 195, 196, 198
four great elements, 102, 103, 111, 112, 119. *See also* derivatives; six great elements
four groups [of believers], 90. *See also* seven groups [of believers]
four holy ways, 194. *See also* Sarvāstivādin stages of practice
four immeasurable contemplations, 182. *See also* four Brahmā abodes
four imperishables, 202. *See also* absolute pure faith in the four imperishables
four kinds of fearlessness (*catvāri vaiśāradyāṇi*, S), 62, 64. *See also* eighteen unique virtues of a buddha
four kinds of grasping. *See* grasping (*upādāna*)
four kinds of unhindered understanding (*pratisaṃvid*, S), 187. *See also* synonyms for *prajñā*
four kinds of wisdom (*prajñā*, S), 186. See also *prajñā* and *jñāna*
four means (*catvāri saṃgraha-vastūni*, S), 28, 213 n. 3
four noble realms of enlightenment. *See* doctrine of the ten realms
Four Noble Truths (*catvāri ārya-satyāni*, S), 28, 30, 86, 102, 114, 168; causality and, 139, 140; contemplation of, 184; discussion of, 151–61; doctrine of, 155, 156; four good roots and, 196; meditation on, in sixteen aspects, 195
four outflows. *See* synonyms for the defilements
Four-Part Vinaya (of Dharmaguptakas), 81, 82, 172; sect of, 82
four *pratisaṃvids* (four kinds of unhindered understanding). *See* synonyms for *prajñā*
four psychic powers (*catvāra ṛddhipādāḥ*, S), 164, 165, 187
four right efforts (*catvāri samyakprahāṇāni*, S), 164–65
Four Seals of the Law, 86, 121–24, 134, 135, 139, 140; formula of, 121. *See also* Seals of the Law; Three Seals of the Law
fourth *dhyāna* (S), 168, 175, 179, 190. *See also* four *dhyānas*; meditation

four ties (*grantha*, S). *See* synonyms for the defilements
four types of monks, 94
four types of nonimpedimentary moral neutrality, 205
four universal vows of the bodhisattva (*praṇidhāna*, S), 27, 213 n. 1. *See also* bodhisattva; bodhisattva vows
four varieties of causality, 145–46. *See also* causality (dependent origination)
four yokes (*yoga*, S, P). *See* synonyms for the defilements
freedom, unhindered, 129; from all hindrances, 55
frivolity (*auddhatya*, S), 99, 101, 193, 206, 209, 212; and regret, 183, 190, 206. *See also* associated mental functions; auxiliary defilements; five higher fetters
fully accomplished, or true, nature (*pariniṣpanna-svabhāva*, S), 140, 219 n. 9. *See also* three-natures theory
fully enlightened being (*tathāgata*, S, P), 23, 43
function of wisdom, 187–88
functions dissociated from mind (*cittaviprayukta-saṃskāra*, S), 98, 100, 105, 112, 113–14. See also *dharmas* dissociated from mind
fundamental buddha, 58. *See also* Buddha (buddha); Eternal Buddha; Śākyamuni
"fundamental concentration," 175, 178
fundamental defilements (*kleṣa*, S), six and ten, 207–12
future *kalpa* of adornment (*alaṃkāra-kalpa*, S), 57. *See also* eon (*kalpa*)

Gautama (S), Śākyamuni's clan, Śākyamuni, 23, 56, 215 n. 3
general causality. *See* causality, general (external, physical)
general teachings (*uddesa*, P). *See* explanatory discourses; *upadeśa*
generosity (*tyāga*, S). *See* five and seven treasures
geya (*geyya*), 70. *See also* twelve divisions, the teachings in
Gilgit, manuscript from, 82
Golden Light Sūtra. See *Suvarṇaprabhāsottama-rāja-sūtra*
good and evil, 27, 88, 89, 178, 192; defined, 165. *See also* absolute, or sacred, good; relative, or mundane, good
Gotama. *See* Gautama
grasping (*upādāna*, S, P), 143, 145, 148, 149, 150, 204
Great Account, The. See *Mahāvastu*
Great Assembly (Mahāsāṃghika, S), 34, 35, 37, 39, 80, 82, 199; lists of buddhas in, 56
Great Collection of Sūtras. See *Mahā-saṃnipāta-sūtra*
Great Commentary. See *Abhidharma-mahāvibhāṣā-śāstra*
great compassion (*mahā-karuṇā*, S), 62, 63, 64, 133, 188
Greater Discourse at Assapura. See *Mahā-assapura-sutta*
Greater Discourse of the Miscellany. See *Mahāvedalla-sutta*
Greater Discourse on the Simile of

the Elephant's Footprint. See *Mahāhatthipadopama-sutta*
great *kalpa* (*mahā-kalpa*, S), 29, 30, 57, 61. *See also* eon (*kalpa*)
great mirror wisdom. *See* four forms of wisdom
great, or superior, vehicle. *See* Mahāyāna
Great Perfection of Wisdom Sūtra. See *Mahā-prajñāpāramitā-sūtra*. *See also* Perfection of Wisdom sūtras
great self, 129
Great Sun, the cosmic buddha (Mahā-vairocana, S), 53, 58–59, 65
Great Sun Sūtra. See *Mahā-vairocana-sūtra*
"great sūtra store," 69
Great Way, 55
great wisdom, 133, 188
greed (*rāga*, S), 99, 101, 102, 129, 148, 190; concentration and, 181; overcoming, 182; of realm of desire, 209. *See also* defilements of practice; fundamental defilements
"greed, anger, and folly (ignorance)," 180, 206, 207, 208; extinction of, 132, 158
greed in the formless realm, 206, 209. *See also* five higher fetters
greed in the realm of desire, 206, 209. *See also* five lower fetters
greed in the realm of form, 206, 209. *See also* five higher fetters
grief (*śoka*, S), 143, 149
grief (*daurmanasya*, S), 149
Grouped Discourses. *See* Saṃyukta-āgama. *See also* Āgamas, four; Saṃyutta-nikāya
Group on Consciousness. *See* Vijñānakāya
Group on Mental Elements. *See* Dhātukāya

harmony (*yoga*, S). *See* functions dissociated from mind
Harvard Oriental Series (Cambridge, Mass.: Harvard University Press), 214 n. 12
Heart of Wisdom, or Heart, Sūtra. See *Prajñāpāramitā-sūtra; Prajñāpāramitā-hṛdaya-sūtra*
heavenly beings, realm of. *See* doctrine of the ten realms
Heavenly Stories. See *Divyāvadāna*
heavens of the formless realm, 176
hells (*naraka*, S). *See* doctrine of the ten realms
"heroic feats" (*avadāna*, S), 69, 72. See also *avadāna* (*apadāna*)
heterodox views. *See* false views
heterogeneous result (*vipāka*, S). *See* nonimpedimentary moral neutrality, four types of
Hīnayāna (S), small, or inferior, vehicle, 24–25, 65, 69, 85, 123, 218 n. 6; differences between Mahāyāna and, 26, 27, 213 n. 6; division of, into two vehicles, 31–32
Hīnayāna precepts, 172. *See also* Four-Part Vinaya
Hīnayāna *zen*. *See* five types of *zen*
historical Buddha, 23, 54, 56, 60, 65, 196; death of, 132; direct teaching of, 41. *See also* Buddha (buddha); Gautama; Śākyamuni
Hodgson, Brian H., 50
holy way of goodness and purity, 66

homogeneous-body of a buddha (*niṣyanda-kāya*, S), 59. *See also* enjoyment-body of a buddha; reward-body of a buddha
"hortative [turn of the wheel]." *See* "three turns of the wheel"
Hossō (J; Vijñānavāda) sect, 145. *See also* Fa-hsiang (C)
hsing (C; *saṃskāra*, S), actions, or mental constituents, 105
Hsüan-tsang (C), 35–40, 85–86, 185
Hua-yen (C), Flower Garland sect, 136, 137, 139, 197, 218 n. 6, 219 n. 9

I-ching (C), 35–40, 85
ideal state, 27, 115, 154–55, 163. *See also* nirvāṇa
ideal wisdom (*bodhi*, *saṃbodhi*, S), 205
ignorance (*avidyā*, S), 60, 119, 142–43, 148, 150, 193, 204; affliction of, 168; concept of, 147, 210; craving and, 149, 157. *See also* folly; "greed, anger, and folly (ignorance)"
ignorance (*moha*, S). *See* associated mental functions
illusion that there is a real self, 120
immorality (*duḥśīla*, *śīla-vipatti*, S), 113
immortal nirvāṇa (*amṛta-nirvāṇa*, S), 66
impartial wisdom. *See* four forms of wisdom
impedimentary moral neutrality (*nivṛta-avyākṛta*, S), 204–5
impermanence (*anityatā*, S), 104, 124–25, 126, 131, 134, 140; all things and, 117, 121, 123, 124, 125, 140; and nonself, 130. *See also* functions dissociated from mind
"impermanence, suffering, and nonself," 97, 102, 109, 122, 124, 160, 164. *See also* three aspects of conditioned *dharmas*
impurity, 104, 131, 164, 182. *See also* contemplation of the ten impurities; four fields of mindfulness
inability to attain enlightenment (*pṛthagjanatā*, S). *See* functions dissociated from mind
inclination (*adhimokṣa*, S), 99, 101, 107. *See also* associated mental functions
"indicative [turn of the wheel]." *See* "three turns of the wheel"
indolence (*pramāda*, S), 99, 101, 209, 212. *See also* auxiliary defilements
Indra (S), Hindu deity, 61, 75, 122–23, 215 n. 9
inducing cause (*āvajjana*, P), 120. *See also* foundation for inducing the six consciousnesses
infinitely successive (*prākarṣika*) causality, 146. *See also* four varieties of causality
infinitesimal particles (*paramāṇu*, S, P), 103. *See also* form (*rūpa*)
initial enlightenment. *See* Dharma Eye; enlightenment (*bodhi*), first stage of
initial organization of the canon, 69
insight, or contemplation, (*vipaśyanā*, S), 179, 186, 193
instantaneous (*kṣanika*) causality,

145, 146. *See also* four varieties of causality
interdependent origination, 139
intermediate auxiliary defilements, 208, 209, 212
internal sense fields (*ādhyātmika-āyatana*, S), 109
Introduction à l'histoire du Bouddhisme Indien (Introduction to the History of Indian Buddhism), 50
introductions (*nidāna-kathā*) to *jātaka* tales, 72
introductory narratives relating the circumstances of a work (*nidāna*, S, P), 69, 71–72. *See also* twelve divisions, the teachings in
Inventory of Offenses of Monks and Nuns (*Prātimokṣa*, *Prātimokṣa-sūtra*, S), 70, 79
investigation (*parīkṣā*, S), 187
investigation (*vicāra*, S), 99, 101, 175. *See also* associated mental functions
investigation (*mīmāṃsā*, S), 165, 187. *See also* four psychic powers; synonyms for *prajñā*
investigation of the Dharma (*dharmavicaya*, S), 187. *See also* discrimination of true from false; seven factors of enlightenment
"invoking the buddha Amida," 173
Isigili-sutta (P), 32
itivṛttaka and *itivuttaka*, 72–73
Itivuttaka (P), "Thus-Said" Sūtras, 72, 77, 78

jātaka (S, P), stories of former lives of the Buddha, 69, 72, 73
Jātaka (P), Tales of the Buddha's Former Lives, 78.
Jātaka-atthakathā (P), Commentary on the *Jātaka*, 73
jealousy (*īrṣyā*, S), 129, 206. *See also* auxiliary defilements
Jñānaprasthāna (S), The Course of Knowledge, 83–84
Jōdo Shin (J) sect, 173
joy. *See* seven factors of enlightenment; six *dhātus*
joy in the Dharma, 166
"just sitting" form of Zen meditation. See *shikan taza*

Kāṇadeva. *See* Āryadeva
Kaniṣka (S), 217 n. 17
Kapilavastu (S), 54
karma (*karman*, S), 27, 62, 128, 133, 143, 145, 150, 192; *avadāna* and, 72; becoming and, 149; defilements and, 203, 204, 205; dependent origination and, 136; false views and, 211, 212; *saṃskāra* and, 106. *See also* "delusion, karma, and suffering"; manifest karma; mental karma; nonmanifest karma
karmic existence. *See* becoming (*bhava*)
karmic retribution, 27, 72, 88, 108, 146, 176, 192. *See also* three periods of karmic retribution
karmic ties, 93
Kāśyapīya, 40; Tripiṭaka, 86
Kathāvatthu (P), Subjects of Discussion, 83, 84
keeping the precepts, 174, 176, 183. *See also* Six Perfections
Kegon (J) sect, 117. *See also* Huayen

Khuddaka-nikāya (P), Collection of Minor Works, 56, 75, 77–78, 79, 84; *Itivuttaka* section of, 72–73; *Jātaka* section of, 73; Solemn Utterances of the Buddha in, 71
Khuddaka-pāṭha (P), Short Readings, 77, 84
"Kie Buppōsō-hō" (J), Taking Refuge in the Three Treasures, 55
knowledge (*jñāna*, S), 185, 186, 202, 216 n. 12, 220 n. 6
knowledge (*vidyā*, S), 166, 186
knowledge, perfection of, (*jñāna-pāramitā*, S), 29, 185. *See also* ten perfections, Mahāyāna
knowledge of all things in every aspect and relationship (*sarvajñatā-jñāna*, S). *See* three kinds of wisdom
knowledge of everything to do with salvation (*mārgākāra-jñāna*, S). *See* three kinds of wisdom
knowledge of reality, 186
knowledge that all the *dharmas* are empty (*sarvajña-jñāna*, S). *See* three kinds of wisdom
Kṣudraka-āgama (S), Miscellaneous Discourses, 78, 79
Kṣudraka-piṭaka (S), Miscellaneous Basket, 78, 79
Kuan-p'u-hsien-p'u-sa-hsing-fa-ching (C), Sūtra of Meditation on the Bodhisattva Universal Virtue, 59
Kūkai (J), 24
Kumārajīva (S), 123–24
Kuśinagara (S), 54, 75

lack of anger, 119
lack of desire, 119
lack of modesty (*anapatrāpya*, S), 99, 101, 209, 212. *See also* associated mental functions; auxiliary defilements
lack of self, 88
Lalitavistara (S), Detailed Narration of the Sport of the Buddha, 57
Lamaism. *See* Buddhism: Tibetan (or Lamaism)
lamentation (*daurmanasya*, S), 119, 143, 149, 175
languor (*styāna*, S), 99, 101, 190, 209, 212. *See also* associated mental functions; auxiliary defilements
languor and drowsiness, 183, 190, 206. *See also* five hindrances
Laṅkāvatāra-sūtra (S), Sūtra of the Appearance of the Good Doctrine in [Sri] Lanka, 45
Larger *Sukhāvatī-vyūha-sūtra* (S), Sūtra of Infinite Life, 43, 51, 75, 85. See also *upadeśa*
Larger *Sukhāvatī-vyūha-sūtra-upadeśa* (S), a treatise on the Sūtra of Infinite Life, 75
late Mahāyāna, 46–47
latent acts. *See* nonmanifest karma; unmanifested form
Law (the Buddha's teachings), 40, 41, 53, 54, 58, 68, 93, 129; Buddhas of the Past and, 56; dependent origination and, 135; nature of truth and, 114, 127; reward-body and, 59. *See also* Dharma
Law-body of a buddha (*dharma-kāya*, S), 57, 58–59, 116. *See also* buddha bodies
Law-treasure, 53, 54
Le Lotus de la bonne loi (F), the Lotus Sūtra, 50

Lesser Discourse of the Miscellany. See *Cūḷavedalla-sutta*
Lesser Discourse to Māluṅkya-putta. See *Cūḷa-Māluṅkya-sutta*
Lineage of the Buddhas, The. See *Buddhavaṃsa*
Liu-tu-chi-ching (C), Sūtra of the Collection of the Practices of the Six Perfections, 73
Lokakṣema (S; Chih Lou-chia-ch'ang, C), 49
Lokottaravāda, 40, 56, 57, 199
Lokottaravādins. *See* Lokottara-vāda
Long Discourses. *See* Dīrgha-āgama
lord of the world (*lokanātha,* S), 67–68. *See also* World-honored One (*bhagavat*)
Lotus Sūtra, the, (*Saddharma-puṇḍarīka-sūtra,* S), 43, 53, 59, 75, 85, 215 n. 8, 219 n. 8; Sanskrit, 50, 123; "Tactfulness" of, 69; translation by Kumārajīva of, 123
Lotus universe, 59
Lumbinī Garden, 54
Lü (C; Vinaya, S, P) sect, 79, 172. *See also* Ritsu sect

Madhyama-āgama (S), Medium-length Discourses, 72, 74, 78
Mādhyamika-śāstra, or *Mūla-madhyamaka-kārikā* (S), Treatise on the Middle, 43, 44
Magadha (S, P), 54
Mahā-apadāna-suttanta (P), Sūtra of the Story of the Great Ones, 56, 72
Mahā-assapura-sutta (P), Greater Discourse at Assapura, 189
Mahābhārata, Hindu epic, 134
Mahādeva (1) (S), 34, 214 n. 8
Mahāhatthipadopama-sutta (P), Greater Discourse on the Simile of the Elephant's Footprint, 218 n. 2
Mahākaruṇa-puṇḍarīka-sūtra (S), Sūtra of Great Compassion, 56
Mahā-Kāśyapa (S), 75, 76, 216 n. 16
Mahā-parinibbāna-suttanta (P), Sūtra of the Great Decease, Pāli, 122, 125, 167–68, 220 n. 3
Mahā-parinirvāṇa-sūtra (S), Mahāyāna Sūtra of the Great Decease, 44, 122, 123
Mahā-parinirvāṇa-sūtra (S), Sūtra of the Great Decease, Mahāyāna, 44, 122, 132
Mahā-prajñāpāramitā-śāstra (S), Treatise on the Great Perfection of Wisdom Sūtra, 43, 63
Mahā-prajñāpāramitā-sūtra (S), Great Perfection of Wisdom Sūtra, 63. See also *Prajñāpāramitā-sūtra*
Mahā-ratnakūṭa-sūtra (S), Sūtra of the Great Accumulation of Treasures, 45
Mahāsāṃghika, 35; Tripiṭaka, 86
Mahā-saṃnipāta-sūtra, or *Mahā-vaitulya-mahā-saṃnipāta-sūtra* (S), Great Collection of Sūtras, 45, 74
Mahā-vagga, Great Group, section of Khandhaka, 84, 217 n. 18
Mahāvairocana (S), Great Sun, the cosmic buddha, 53, 58–59, 65
Mahā-vairocana-sūtra (S), Great Sun Sūtra, 46
Mahāvastu (S), The Great Account, 56; ten stages [of bodhisattva] in, 199–200

Mahāvedalla-sutta (P), Greater Discourse of the Miscellany, 74
Mahāyāna (S), great, or superior, vehicle, 33, 49, 68, 74, 75, 197; differences between Hīnayāna and, 28; discussion of, 25–26, 40–47; doctrines of ten stages and, 199–201; eighteen unique virtues of, 63; emptiness and, 88, 129–30; lay and ordained believers and, 91; nirvāṇa and, 133; Tripiṭaka, 84–86
Mahāyāna-abhidharma-sūtra (S), Sūtra on Mahāyāna Abhidharma, 45
Mahāyāna Buddhism. *See* Buddhism: Mahāyāna
Mahāyāna precepts, 82, 170–72
Mahāyāna precepts in China and Japan, 172–73
Mahāyāna-saṃgraha (S), Comprehensive Treatise on Mahāyāna Buddhism, 45, 133. See also *She-ta-ch'eng-lun-shih-ch'in-shih*
Mahāyāna-śraddhotpāda-śāstra (S), Treatise on the Awakening of Faith in the Mahāyāna, 46, 136
Mahāyāna-sūtrālaṃkāra (S), Treatise on the Adornment of Mahāyāna Sūtras, 45, 121
Mahāyāna Sūtra of the Great Decease. See *Mahā-parinirvāṇa-sūtra*
Mahāyāna *zen*. *See* five types of *zen*
Mahinda (P), 48, 214 n. 11
Mahīśāsaka, 40; Tripiṭaka, 86
Maitreya (S), buddha of the future, 56, 60, 215 n. 8
Maitreyanātha, (S), 45
Majjhima-nikāya (P), Collection of Medium-length Discourses, 74, 77, 78, 84, 116–17, 126, 189, 218 n. 2
major auxiliary defilements, 208, 209, 212
"Make the Dharma your island," 128
male lay believer (*upāsaka*, S, P), 90
male novice (*śrāmaṇera*, S), 73, 90, 169, 170, 172
Malla (S, P), ancient Indian kingdom, 54
Māluṅkyaputta (P), 126, 127
manas consciousness (*manas-vijñāna*, S), 44, 106, 108, 119; mind and, 119–20. *See also* seventh consciousness
manifest-body of a buddha (*nirmāṇa-kāya*, S), 58, 59, 60–61, 215 n. 8; superior and ordinary aspects of, 60. *See also* buddha bodies
manifest karma (*vijñapti-karman*, S), 203. *See also* nonmanifest karma; unmanifested form
mantras (mystical incantations), 46. *See also* Three Secrets
manuscripts, 82; palm-leaf, 51, 86; Sanskrit, 50
married female novice (*śikṣamāṇā*, S), 90–91, 169, 170, 172
Master of the Tripiṭaka. See *san-tsang-shih*
material *dharmas*, 97, 102, 103, 112–13. See also *dharmas* of form
meditation (*dhyāna*, S), 32, 62, 125, 151, 165, 174–75, 196. *See also* four *dhyānas*; terms denoting concentration

meditation on breathing, 183. *See also* concentration on breathing
meditation on compassion, 182, 184. *See also* five meditations for settling the mind
meditation on the five gateways, 183
meditation on the Four Noble Truths in sixteen aspects, 195
meditation, perfection of, (*dhyāna-pāramitā*, S), 28. *See also* Six Perfections
medium *kalpa*. *See* eon (*kalpa*)
Medium-length Discourses. *See* Madhyama-āgama
mental attributes (*caitta-* or *caitasika-dharmāḥ*, S), 107, 108, 120. *See also* associated mental functions; *dharmas* of mental attributes; mental *dharmas*
mental constituents (*saṃskāra*, S), 95, 97, 102, 107, 108, 126; associated mental functions and, 113; becoming and, 149; defilements and, 204; discussion of, 105–6. *See also* actions
mental *dharmas*, 97, 102. *See also* associated mental functions; mental attributes
mental faculty (*mano-indriya*, S, P), 109–10
mental karma, 203
mental objects (*dharma-āyatana*, S), 109, 110, 112, 117
mental objects (*dharma-dhātu*, S), 59, 114; four and ten, 117
mental suffering felt because of destruction or loss (*vipariṇāma-duḥkhatā*, S), 130–31, 155–56. *See also* suffering, three types of
merit, 65, 73, 202
merits of concentration, 183–84
metaphysics, 88, 95, 115, 127, 128. *See also* ontology
methods of practice, 82, 154, 163, 167, 180
methods of practicing concentration, 180–83
middle Mahāyāna, 43–46, 50
Middle Way (Mādhyamika, S) school, 43, 44, 85
mind (*citta*, S, P), 98, 100, 110, 142, 164, 216 n. 12; associated mental functions and, 113; concept of, 106–7; consciousness and, 147; four psychic powers and, 165
mind (*manas*, S), 44, 106, 108, 109, 110, 119
mind free from defilements and delusions (*citta-vimukta*, S). *See* eight types of attainment
mind, purity of, (*citta-visuddhi*, P). *See* seven purities
mind to attain *dhyāna*. *See* four psychic powers
mindfulness. *See* seven factors of enlightenment
mindfulness (*smṛti*, S), 99, 101, 107, 175, 183, 196; of calm, 182; of death, 181; five roots of emancipation and, 165; four fields of, 164, 166; mental constituents and, 105
mindfulness of the breath. *See* concentration on breathing
"mind realm" (*mano-dhātu*, S, P), 106, 120, 214 n. 9
"mind ruler," 98, 107
mind seeking enlightenment, 167. *See also* aspiration to enlightenment
mind to seek religion, 125

minor auxiliary defilements, 208, 209–10, 211
Minor Works, Collection of. *See* Khuddaka-nikāya
minute particles, 124
miracle narratives (*adbhutadharma*, S), 69, 74
Miscellaneous Basket. *See* Kṣudraka-piṭaka
Miscellaneous Discourses. *See* Kṣudraka-āgama
missionaries. *See* Aśoka
mixed prose and verse (*geya*, S), 68, 69, 70, 73. *See also* twelve divisions, the teachings in
mode of deportment (*iryāpatha*, S). *See* nonimpedimentary moral neutrality, four types of
monastic communities (*saṅgha*, P), 34, 48, 84, 89, 92, 171; Vinaya collections on, 79, 81. *See also* assembly (*gaṇa*); Order (Saṅgha); Order-treasure
monastic regulations (*saṃvara*, S, P), 33, 79, 113, 169. *See also* precepts; regulations (*vinaya*)
monastic regulations (Vinaya, S, P), 68, 72, 172. *See also* regulations (*vinaya*)
morality (*śīla*, S), 58, 67, 91, 113, 190, 219 n. 1; discussion of, 168–74; threefold practice and, 62, 160, 161, 164. *See also* precepts
morality applicable to the state of delusion, 169
morality applicable to the state of nondelusion (*anāsrava*, S). *See* precepts of nondelusion
morality, perfection of, (*śīla-pāramitā*, S), 28, 29, 171. *See also* Six Perfections; ten perfections
morality, practice of, (*śīla-śikṣa*, S), 63, 167. *See also* threefold practice
morality, purity of, (*sīla-visuddhi*, P). *See* seven purities
moral neutrality (*avyākṛta*, S), 107, 113, 115, 126, 204; two kinds of, 205. *See also* neutral (*avyākṛta*) defilements; three moral categories
mudrās (symbolic hand gestures), 46. *See also* Three Secrets
Mūla-Sarvāstivāda (Root Sarvāstivāda), 35
Mūla-Sarvāstivādin Vinaya (*Mūla-sarvāstivāda-vinaya*, S), 82, 84.
Müller, Max, 51
mundane *dharmas*, 88
mundane knowledge, 185, 186. *See also* ten forms of knowledge
mundane wisdom, 184, 185
mystical verses (*dhāraṇī*, S), 46

Nāgārjuna (S), 43, 44, 63
Nālandā monastic university, 45, 84
name (*nāma*, S, P), 97
"name and form" (*nāma-rūpa*, S, P), 97, 142, 143, 145, 147, 204
narratives of former matters (*itivṛttaka*, S), 69, 72, 73. *See also* twelve divisions, the teachings in
neutral (*avyākṛta*) defilements, 204
Nichiren (J) sect, 173
Niddesa (P), Expositions, 74, 78, 84. *See also* Nikāyas
Nikāyas, 71, 77–78
nine divisions, the teachings in, 68–69, 70, 72
nine fetters, 206. *See also* synonyms for the defilements
nine kinds of pride, 210. *See also*

fundamental defilements; pride
nine *samāpattis* (*anupūrva-samāpatti,* S), 178
ninth *samāpatti* (*nirodha-samāpatti,* S, P). *See* cessation of perception and feeling
nirvāṇa (S), 114, 121, 122, 140, 142, 164, 166; complete, 133, 220 n. 3; contemplation of calm of, 182; defined, 132, 205; deliverance of, 87; as *dharma* of enlightenment, 115; discussion of, 132–34; [in Hua-yen doctrine], 218 n. 6; other shore of, 29; in primitive Buddhism, 97 (*see also* unconditioned *dharmas*); or release from *saṃsāra,* 154 (*see also* truth of the extinction of suffering); state of, 27, 131, 158; state of enlightenment in, 139; synonym for (*see* unconditioned); synonyms for, 133–34; theory concerning, 44
nirvāṇa, immortal, (*amṛta-nirvāṇa,* S), 66
nirvāṇa innately as pure as self-nature (*prakṛti-pariśuddha-nirvāṇa,* S), 133
nirvāṇa insight into suffering, 190, 193. *See also* six supernormal powers
Nirvāṇa Sūtra (Sūtra of the Great Decease). See *Mahā-parinibbāna-suttanta; Mahā-parinirvāṇa-sūtra*
nirvāṇa without fixed abode (*apratiṣṭhita-nirvāṇa,* S), 63, 133, 216 n. 11
nirvāṇa without residue (*nirupadhiśeṣa-nirvāṇa,* S), 133. *See also* perfect tranquillity
nirvāṇa with residue (*sopadhiśeṣa-nirvāṇa,* S), 132–33
no backsliding, 200
noble (*ārya,* S), 153
Noble Eightfold Path. *See* Eightfold Path
noble truth of suffering, 152. *See also* Four Noble Truths; truth of suffering
noble truth of the cause of suffering, 152. *See also* truth of the cause of suffering
noble truth of the termination of suffering, 152. *See also* truth of the extinction of suffering
noble truth of the Way to the termination of suffering, 152. *See also* truth of the Way to the extinction of suffering
"no ego" (*wu-wo,* C), 127
"no more backsliding" (*avinipāta-dhamma,* P), 202
nonattachment (*anupalambha,* S), 205
nonattachment (*aprāpti,* S), 89, 99, 129. *See also* functions dissociated from mind
nonattachment to craving, 152
nonbeing (*wu,* C), 127
nonbelief (*āśraddhya,* S), 99, 101, 209. *See also* auxiliary defilements
non-Buddhist *zen. See* five types of *zen*
noncovetousness (*alobha,* S), 99, 101, 219 n. 1. *See also* associated mental functions
nondelusion (*anāsrava,* S), 133, 153, 169. *See also* precepts of nondelusion; synonyms for nirvāṇa
nondiscernment (*asaṃprajanya,* S). *See* auxiliary defilements

nondiscriminating wisdom (*nirvikalpa-jñāna,* S), 187. *See also* function of wisdom
nonexistence (*vibhava,* S, P), 112, 115–16, 140, 157, 186, 211; defined, 116. See also *wu* (C), "nonbeing"
nonhindrance (*anāvaraṇa,* S), 129
nonimpedimentary moral neutrality (*anivṛta-avyākṛta,* S), 204; four types of, 205
nonmanifest karma (*avijñapti-karman,* S), 203
nonreturner (*anāgāmin,* S, P), 178, 184, 191, 194, 195, 201; five lower fetters and, 192–93, 206, 207
nonself (*nairātmya,* S), 86, 89, 116, 134, 205; all things and, 88, 112, 117, 121, 140, 164; of the aggregates, 102; concept of, 129; craving and, 157; discussion of, 125–30; emptiness and, 128–29; impermanence and, 130; impermanence, suffering, and, 97, 102, 109, 122, 124, 160, 164; two kinds of, 129–30. *See also* Four Seals of the Law; "that which is intrinsically devoid of self"
nonself of sentient beings (*pudgala-nairātmya,* S), 44, 86, 129–30
nonself of the *dharmas* (*dharma-nairātmya,* S), 44, 86, 130
nonsuffering, 53, 132
no retrogression from the *ārya* stage, 202
"no self," 88
"no self-nature" (*niḥsvabhāva,* S), 128, 187
nothingness (nihilism), 115–16, 127, 157, 178; concept of, 177. See also *wu* (C), "nonbeing"
novices, three types of, 90–96, 170

obedient hearing (*śruta,* S), 219 n. 1. *See also* five and seven treasures
objects of mind (*dharma,* S), 164
objects of sight (*rūpa-āyatana,* S, P), 103, 112
objects of the body (*kāya-ātayana,* S, P), 109, 112
observing the precepts, perfection of. *See* morality, perfection of
odors (*gandha-āyatana,* S, P), 109, 111, 183
offenses, 79, 217 nn. 19, 20; and regulations, 71–72
old age and death (*jarā-maraṇa,* S, P), 131, 143, 145, 149–50, 204
Old Māgadhī (S), 47–48
olfactory nerves (*ghrāṇa-indriya,* S), 99, 101, 109. *See also* form (*rūpa*); six sense organs
omniscience, 63
Omniscient (*samyaksaṃbuddha,* S), an epithet of a buddha, 64, 66
once-returner (*sakṛdāgāmin,* S), 191, 194, 195, 201
"one encounter, once in a lifetime," 125
one hundred *dharmas* in five categories, 97
one hundred seventy *dharmas* in four categories, 97
One Hundred Stories. See *Avadānaśataka*
"One is all, all is one," 139
one true Buddhist Law, 43
One Vehicle, 43
one who has achieved right con-

firmation (*samyaktvaniyata-rāśi,* S), 192, 202
one who has extinguished all delusions (*kṣīṇāsrava,* S). *See* Worthy of Respect (*arhat*)
one who has nothing more to learn (*aśaikṣa,* S), 65, 191, 193, 194, 195, 207
one who is perfectly enlightened (*samyaksaṃbuddha,* S), 66, 115. *See also* Omniscient; perfectly enlightened buddha
one who lives by the path. *See* four types of monks
ontology, 95, 112, 115, 126, 127, 128, 133; defined, 30; unconditioned *dharmas* and, 114
ordained man, [fully], (*bhikṣu,* S), 90
ordained woman (*bhikṣuṇī,* S), 90
Order (Saṅgha, P), 53, 54, 55, 82, 89–94, 180; of ordained sages, 92
Order-treasure, 53, 54, 92
ordinary people's *zen. See* five types of *zen*
"the organ aiding the senses," 109
"organ, object, and consciousness," 117
original Buddhism, 33
outflows (*āsrava,* S), three and four. *See* synonyms for the defilements

pagoda, 54
pain, 96, 104, 119. *See also* suffering
Paiśācī (Middle Indo-Aryan Prākrit), 47, 48
Pāli, 47, 48
Pāli Abhidhamma, seven treatises of, 83, 84
Pāli Buddhism. *See* Buddhism: Pāli
Pāli Nikāya, 78, 146. *See also* five collections (*nikāya*); five Nikāyas
Pali Text Society translation series, 214 n. 12
Pāli Vinaya, 93
palm-leaf manuscripts, 51, 86
palpables (*spraṣṭavya-āyatana,* S), 109, 111–12. *See also* six objects [of cognition]
Pañcaviṃśatisāhasrikā-prajñāpāramitā (S), Perfection of Wisdom Sūtra in Twenty-five Thousand Lines, 42, 85
parable of the poisoned arrow, 126–27
pārājika offense of bodhisattvas, 80, 81, 171
pāramitā practice, 29
Parivāra (S, P), The Accessory, 81
parsimony (*mātsarya,* S), 99, 101, 206, 209, 212. *See also* auxiliary defilements
parting from what we love, suffering inherent in, 152, 154, 155, 156
past *kalpa* of constellations (*tārā-kalpa,* S), 57. *See also* eon (*kalpa*)
Path of Purity, The. See *Visuddhimagga*
Paṭisambhidā-magga (P), The Way of Analysis, 78
Paṭṭhāna (P), Book of Relations, 83, 84
Peking edition (Tibetan Tripiṭaka, pub. 1411), 50
people who still have more to learn (*śaikṣa,* S), 191
perception (*saṃjñā,* S), 97, 99, 101, 102, 107–8, 113; discussion of,

104; mental constituents and, 105
perfect enlightenment (*saṃbodhi,* S), 55, 166, 187. *See also* ideal wisdom; six stages of enlightenment
perfecting wisdom. *See* four forms of wisdom
Perfect in Knowledge and Conduct (*vidyācaraṇa-saṃpanna,* S), an epithet of a buddha, 64, 66, 105, 186
perfection (buddhahood), 25
perfection (*pāramitā,* S, P), 29, 59, 66, 73, 185. *See also* Six Perfections; ten perfections
Perfection of Wisdom, or Wisdom, sūtras. See *Prajñāpāramitā-sūtra*
Perfection of Wisdom Sūtra in Eight Thousand Lines. See *Aṣṭasāhasrikā-prajñāpāramitā*
Perfection of Wisdom Sūtra in One Hundred Thousand Lines. See *Śatasāhasrikā-prajñāpāramitā-sūtra*
Perfection of Wisdom Sūtra in Twenty-five Thousand Lines. See *Pañcaviṃśatisāhasrikā-prajñāpāramitā*
perfect knowledge of all things past, present, and future, 64. *See also* eighteen unique virtues of a buddha
perfect knowledge of the state of emancipation, 58, 67, 91. *See also* five attributes, Law-body equated with
perfectly enlightened buddha (*samyaksaṃbuddha,* S), 33. *See also* Omniscient
perfect tranquillity (*parinirvāṇa,* S), 133, 220 n. 3. *See also* complete, or final, nirvāṇa; nirvāṇa without residue
periodic (*āvasthika*) causality, 145–46. *See also* four varieties of causality
"permanence, ease, ideal self, and purity," 133. *See also* buddha-nature; self-nature
personality types, 182, 183, 191, 194; six, 180
perverse views (*mithyā-dṛṣṭi,* S), 192, 211. *See also* five false views
Petavatthu (P), Tales of Hungry Ghosts, 77
phenomena (*dharma*), contemplation of. *See* four fields of mindfulness
phenomenological suffering (*saṃskāra-duḥkhatā,* S), 131, 155. *See also* suffering, three types of
phenomenon (*vastu,* S). *See* existence, defined
physical suffering (*duḥkha-duḥkhatā,* S), 130, 155, 156. *See also* suffering, three types of
place of enlightenment (*bodhi-maṇḍa,* S, P), 31
"place of entry (*āyatana,* S, P). *See* sense fields
placing of the self at the center of all things (*ātma-māna,* S), 108, 120
polluter of the path. *See* four types of monks
power of habit, 103, 108, 110, 113, 170, 204; becoming and, 145; twelve links and, 147, 149. *See also* unmanifested form
practice, 31, 32, 66, 73, 82, 87, 154; discussion of, 163–202. *See also*

practices *by term* (as bodhisattva practice)
prajñā and *jñāna*, 185–86
Prajñāpāramitā-hṛdaya-sūtra (S), Heart of Wisdom, or Heart, Sūtra, 42, 51, 102, 129. See also *Prajñāpāramitā-sūtra*
Prajñāpāramitā-sūtra (S), Perfection of Wisdom, or Wisdom, sūtras, 42, 85, 123, 171–72, 200, 219 n. 8
Prajñapti (S), Book of Manifestation, 83
Prakaraṇa (S), Treatise, 83
Prākrit, (vernacular), 47, 48
Prāsaṅgika (S), 44. *See also* middle Mahāyāna
pratyekabuddha (S), 55, 61, 62, 176, 196, 201, 215 n. 6; concept of wisdom and, 184, 185; discussion of, 31–33; two categories of, 32. *See also* solitary buddhas, vehicle of
pratyekabuddha knowledge. *See* three kinds of wisdom
pratyekabuddhas, realm of. *See* doctrine of the ten realms; ten realms of existence
pratyekabuddha stage (*pratyekabuddha-bhūmi*, S), 201
preacher of the path. *See* four types of monks
precepts, 76, 92, 113, 202; five lay, 90, 148, 170; Mahāyāna, 170–73. *See also* morality; precepts *by term* (as *samaya* precepts)
"precepts and regulations" (*śīla-vinaya*, S), 76, 172
Precepts Basket (Vinaya-piṭaka, S, P), 33–35, 75, 77, 84, 85, 92–93, 218 n. 5, 219 n. 1; discussion of, 79–82
precepts for creating good, 170
precepts for full and immediate enlightenment. *See* Tendai precepts
precepts for restraining evil (*saṃvara*, S, P), 169, 170
precepts for the practice of benefiting others (*sattvārthakriyā-śīla*, S), 171
precepts for the promotion of good (*kuśaladharma-saṃgrāhaka-śīla*, S), 170, 171, 174. *See also* "to do only good"
precepts for the restraint of evil (*saṃvara-śīla*, S), 170, 172, 174. *See also* "to do no evil"
precepts of nondelusion (*anāsrava-saṃvara*, S), 169, 170
precepts (restraints) as meditation (*dhyāna-saṃvara*, S), 169, 170
predictions of buddhahood (*vyākaraṇa*, S), 68, 69, 70
preparation (*sambhāra*, S). *See* five stages leading to enlightenment
"present insight into the noble truth" (*sacca-abhisamaya*, P), 202
present *kalpa* of sages (*bhadrakalpa*, S), 57. *See also* eon (*kalpa*)
pride (*māna*, S), 125, 193, 206, 207, 208; kinds of, 210–11. *See also* fundamental defilements
primitive (presectarian) Buddhism. *See* Buddhism: primitive (presectarian)
profound observing wisdom. *See* four forms of wisdom
Puggalapaññatti (P), Description of Individuals, 83
Pure Emerald Light, eastern realm of. *See* Bhaiṣajyaguru
Pure Land Buddhists, 53

Pure Land sect, 137
purity of knowledge and insight (*ñāṇadassana-visuddhi,* P). *See* seven purities
purity of views. *See* seven purities
Pūrva-mīmāṃsā (S), Hindu school of philosophy, 43
P'u-sa-shan-chieh-ching (C; *Bodhisattva-bhūmi,* S), Treatise on the Conduct of a Bodhisattva, 85

Queen of Śrīmālā, or Śrīmālā, Sūtra. See *Śrīmālādevī-siṃhanāda-sūtra*

raging streams (*ogha,* S, P). *See* synonyms for the defilements
rainy-season retreat (*vārṣika,* S), 81
Rājagṛha (S), 65, 75
Rathavinīta-sutta (P), Discourse on the Relays of Chariots, 189
Ratnagotravibhāga-mahāyānôttaratantra-śāstra (S), Treatise on the Jewel-nature, 46
reaching the other shore (*tao-pi-an,* C), 29. *See also* nirvāṇa, synonyms for; perfection (*pāramitā*)
"real aspect of all things," 114, 123–24, 136–37, 183
realization of the four good roots (*prayoga,* S), 196. *See also* five stages leading to enlightenment
realm of defilements, 186
realm of delusion, 115
realm of desire (*kāma-dhātu,* S, P), 67, 149, 169, 170, 176, 179, 201; concentration of, 175, 178; defilements and, 204, 207, 208; stages of effort and attainment and, 191, 192; wisdom and, 184. *See also* three realms of existence
realm of enlightenment, 66, 88, 115, 176; wisdom of, 185. *See also* doctrine of the ten realms; supramundane realm, or world
realm of form (*rūpa-dhātu,* S, P), 67, 149, 169, 170, 175, 177; concentration of, 176; defilements and, 204, 207, 208; four *dhyānas* of, 178, 179; fundamental concentration of, 175; stages of effort and attainment and, 193. *See also* four *dhyānas;* three realms of existence
realm of formlessness. *See* formless realm
realms of existence. *See* five realms of existence; six realms of existence; ten realms of existence, or ten realms; three realms of existence
rebirth, 132–33, 145, 176, 191, 211, 212; birth and, 155; craving and, 152, 157; karma and, 27; Pure Land Buddhism and, 24. *See also* birth and death, cycle of; transmigration
receptacle world (*bhājanaloka,* S), 66. *See also* world of sentient beings
Record of the Western Regions. See *Ta-T'ang hsi-yü-chi*
regulations (*vinaya,* S, P), 33, 72, 77, 79–81, 84, 93, 172
relative, or mundane, good (*āsava-kusala,* P), 87, 88
release, 56, 127, 131, 139, 152, 212; from adherence to concept of self, 120; from cycle of birth and death (*saṃsāra*), 25, 27, 92, 126, 154; from all the delusions, 93; from delusion, 67; from future

rebirth, 132; from suffering, 27, 53, 93. *See also* nirvāṇa, synonyms for
release from the world of delusion, perfection of, (*nekkhamma-pāramī*, P), 29. *See also* ten perfections, Pāli Buddhist
relics (*śarīra*, S), 54. *See also* Buddha-treasure
religious causality. *See* causality, religious (internal, mental)
residue (*anuśaya*, S), 203, 205. *See also* synonyms for the defilements
retributive existence. *See* becoming (*bhava*)
reward-body of a buddha (*saṃbhoga-kāya*, S), 58, 59–60. *See also* enjoyment-body of a buddha; homogeneous-body of a buddha
right action (*samyak-karmānta*, S), 152, 159, 167, 174, 189. *See also* Eightfold Path
right concentration (*samyak-samādhi*, S), 152, 160, 167
right effort (*samyag-vyāyāma*, S), 152, 160, 167, 190
right knowledge (*samyag-jñāna*, S), 161
right knowledge (*samprajāna*, S), 186–87. *See also* synonyms for *prajñā*
right liberation (*samyag-vimukti*, S), 161
right livelihood (*samyag-ājīva*, S), 152, 159, 167, 174, 189
right mindfulness (*samyak-smṛti*, S), 152, 160, 164, 167, 190
right mindfulness (*upaṭṭhita-sati*, P), 219 n. 1
right speech (*samyag-vācā*, S; *sammā-vācā*, P), 152, 159, 167, 174, 189
right thought (*samyak-saṃkalpa*, S), 152, 159, 161, 167, 189
right view (*samyag-dṛṣṭi*, S), 147, 152, 159, 161, 167, 174, 186, 200
Rinzai (J), Zen sect, 173, 215 n. 8
Ritsu (J; Lü, C) sect, 79, 172–73
rules for admission to the community, 81
rules for rituals and ceremonies, 46
Rushana Butsu (J; *Vairocana*, S), 59, 215 n. 8. *See also* Birushana Butsu

Sacred Books of the Buddhists series, 214 n. 12
Sacred Books of the East series, 51, 214 n. 12
sage (*ārya*, S), 23, 113, 131, 153, 170, 185, 193; *arhat* as supreme, 65; Eightfold Path of, 158; five excellent powers and, 166; four right efforts and, 165; nature of Saṅgha and, 91, 92; suffering and, 131. *See also* noble (*ārya*)
Saichō (J), 173
Śākyamuni (S), historical Buddha, 23, 25, 56, 58, 65, 115; *avadāna* and, 72; biography of, 105; as Buddha-treasure, 53; deification of, 26; epithet of, 154; enlightenment under the *bodhi* tree, 32, 151; final instructions to his disciples, 125, 128; first discourse, 92, 102 (*see also* "setting the wheel of the Law in motion"); Mahāyāna Buddhism and, 40, 42; as manifestation-body, 60;

primitive Buddhism and, 33; sites of the four great events of his life, 54; Southern Buddhism and, 48; as transformed-body, 59. *See also* buddha bodies; Gautama
Śākyamuni (S), a Buddha of the Past, 56, 174, 215 nn. 3–6
Śākyamuni (S), fundamental, or original, buddha, 59. *See also* Eternal Buddha
Śalistamba-sūtra (S), Sūtra of the Rice Stem, 218 n. 3
salvation, 60, 63, 202
Samayabhedoparacanacakra (S), Treatise on the Principles of Different Schools, 38
samaya precepts, 173
Saṃdhinirmocana-sūtra (S), Sūtra of Profound Understanding, 45, 219 n. 9
Saṃmatīya (S), 35; Tripiṭaka, 86
saṃskāra (S). *See* actions
Saṃyukta-āgama (S), Grouped Discourses, 78, 154, 164, 218 nn. 1, 4
Saṃyuktabhidharma-hṛdaya-śāstra (S), Expanded Treatise on the Essence of Abhidharma, 44
Saṃyuktāvadāna (S), Various Stories, 72
Saṃyutta-nikāya (P), Collection of Grouped Discourses, 77, 78, 84, 217 n. 18, 218 nn. 1, 4, 5; dependent origination and, 142–43; five aggregates and, 97–102; four fields of mindfulness and, 164; Four Noble Truths and, 152; twelve links and, 147, 149
San-ch'ien-fo-ming-ching (C), three Sūtras of the Names of Three Thousand Buddhas, 57
saṅgha (P). *See* monastic communities
Saṅgha (P): functions of, 92–94; standard definition of, 91. *See also* Order; Order-treasure
Saṅghīti-suttanta (P), Sūtra of the Recital, 174–75, 177
Saṅgītiparyāya (S), Section for Recitation, 83
San-lun (C; Three Treatises) sect, 137, 219 n. 8
Sanskrit, 48, 49, 50, 51, 56
san-tsang-shih (C; *tripiṭaka-dhara,* S), Master of the Tripiṭaka, 85
Sāramati (S), Mahāyāna philosopher, 45
Śāriputra Abhidharma (S), 83, 84, 103
Sarvāstivāda (S), 35, 36, 38, 40, 80. *See also* Sarvāstivādins
Sarvāstivādin Abhidharma (S), 83, 84, 86; seven treatises of, 83, 84
Sarvāstivādins, 35, 62, 81–82, 136, 207, 216 n. 17; *dharma* categories of, 96–97, 103, 105, 107; *dharma* theory of, 112–14; five meditations and, 182; four varieties of causality of, 145; moral neutrality and , 205; twelve divisions and, 69
Sarvāstivādin stages of practice, 194–96
Sarvāstivādin Tripiṭaka (S), 86
Śatasāhasrikā-prajñāpāramitā-sūtra (S), Perfection of Wisdom Sūtra in One Hundred Thousand Lines, 42
Śata-śāstra (S), Treatise in One Hundred Verses, 43

Sautrāntika (S), 44
scholarly commentaries and treatises. *See* treatises (*abhidharma*)
Seals of the Law (*dharma-mudrā*, or *dharma-uddāna*, S): discussion of, 121–34. *See also* Three Seals of the Law; Four Seals of the Law
Second Council, 34.
sectarian schism, 26, 33, 77,
Section for Recitation. *See* Saṅgītiparyāya
sect of the Four-Part Vinaya, 82
seed (*bīja*, S), 108. *See also* storehouse consciousness
"seed syllable" (*bīja*, S), 46. *See also* Three Secrets
seeing (*darśana*, S). *See* synonyms for *prajñā*
self, 120, 126, 127–28, 129, 148; false idea of, 97–102, 108
self-enjoyment-body of a buddha, 58. *See also* four-body doctrine (of buddha bodies)
self-enlightenment, doctrine of, 151
selfishness (*asmīti-chanda*, S), 108. *See also* storehouse consciousness
self-nature, 133. *See also* buddha-nature; "no self-nature"
self-reliant teachings, 24
semblance of enlightenment, 197. *See also* six stages of enlightenment
semimonthly confession ceremony (*poṣadha*, S), 79
sense fields (*āyatana*, S, P), 112; defined, 108–9; internal and external, 109–10. *See also* twelve sense fields
sense organs (*indriya*, S, P), 102, 109. *See also* five [physical] sense organs; form (*rūpa*); six sense organs
"setting the wheel of the Law in motion," 54, 152. *See also* Śākyamuni, historical Buddha: first discourse
seven Buddhas of the Past, 56, 174, 215 n. 2. *See also* Buddhas of the Past
seven complete Vinayas, 81
seven expedient degrees, 194. *See also* Sarvāstivādin stages of practice
seven factors of enlightenment (*sapta bodhyaṅgāni*, S), 164, 166–67
seven groups [of believers], 90, 172. *See also* four groups [of believers]
seven kinds of pride, 210. *See also* fundamental defilements; pride; synonyms for the defilements
seven purities (*visuddhi*, P), 168, 189, 191
seventeen stages of *arhat* practice, 168, 189–90, 191
seventh consciousness (*mano-dhātu*, S, P), 106. See also *manas* consciousness
seven treatises of the Pāli Abhidhamma, 83
seven treatises of the Sarvāstivādin Abhidharma, 83
seventy-five *dharmas* in five categories, 97, 130
Shakuson (J), Śākyamuni the World-honored One, 23
shame (*hrī*, S), 99, 101, 189, 219 n. 1. *See also* five and seven treasures
shamelessness (*āhrīkya*, S), 99, 101,

209, 212. *See also* auxiliary defilements
"sharp defilements," 207. *See also* defilements of view
Sheng-ching (C), Stories of Former Incarnations, 73
She-ta-ch'eng-lun-shih-ch'in-shih (C), Vasubandhu's commentary on the *Mahāyāna-saṃgraha,* 133
shikan taza (J), 173
Shingon (J; True Word) sect, 24, 46, 58–59, 119, 136, 137. *See also* Chen-yen
Shinran (J), 24
Shōbōgenzō (J), Eye Storehouse of the True Law, 55
Short Readings. See *Khuddaka-pāṭha*
sites of the four great events of Śākyamuni's life, 54
six consciousnesses (*ṣaḍ-vijñāna,* S), 44, 96, 110, 120, 142; discussion of, 106, 147; eighteen elements of existence and, 116, 117; mind and, 119
six contacts (*cha-phassā,* P), 117, 148. *See also* six sixes (*cha-chakka*)
six cravings (*cha-taṇhā,* P), 117, 148
six *dhātus* (*dhātu,* S, P), 119
six feelings (*cha-vedanā,* P), 117, 148
six great elements, 86, 119, 219 n. 7
six investigations (*cha-vicārā,* P), 117
six objects [of cognition], 96, 103, 109, 116, 117, 142, 147; discussion of, 110–12
six orthodox schools of Hindu philosophy, 43
six perceptions (*cha-saññā,* P), 117
Six Perfections (*ṣaṭ-pāramitā,* S), 26, 31, 32, 86, 179; Eightfold Path and, 28–29; wisdom and, 184, 185, 188, 201. *See also* perfection (*pāramitā*)
six precepts, 91, 170
six realms of existence, 27, 67, 131
six reflections (*cha-vitakkā,* P), 117
six sense organs (*ṣaḍ-āyatana,* S), 96, 103, 109, 147, 148, 204; dependent origination and, 142, 143, 145; eighteen elements of existence and, 116, 117
six sixes (*cha-chakka,* P), 117
six stages of enlightenment, 197. *See also* bodhisattva practice, fifty-two stages of
six supernormal powers, 193
sixteen mental states of the stage of the Way of View, 208
six types of feeling, 104. *See also* six feelings
six volitions (*cha-cetanā,* P), 117
Skandhaka (S), Chapters, 81, 84, 170
skillful means (*upāya,* S, P), 188, 194, 201–2; seven types of (*see* seven expedient degrees). *See also* appropriate means; expedient ways
skillful means, perfection of, (*upāya-pāramitā,* S), 29
sloth (*kausīdya,* S), 99, 101, 165, 209, 212. *See also* auxiliary defilements
Smaller *Sukhāvatī-vyūha-sūtra* (S), Amitābha Sūtra, 51
small *kalpa,* 30. *See also* eon (*kalpa*)
small, or inferior, vehicle. *See* Hīnayāna
Solemn Utterances of the Buddha. See *Udāna*; *Udāna-varga*
solitary buddhas, vehicle of,

(Pratyekabuddhayāna, S), 24, 31–33. See also *pratyekabuddha*
sorrow (*parideva*, S, P), 143, 149
Sōtō (J) sect, 173, 215 n. 8
soul, metaphysical self or, 128. *See also* self
sounds (*śabda-āyatana*, S), 109, 110, 183. *See also* six objects [of cognition]
Southern Tripiṭaka (S), 214 n. 12
space (*ākāśa*, S), 97, 98, 101, 114, 119, 178. *See also* unconditioned *dharmas*
spurious sūtras, 197–99
śrāvaka (S), 25, 26, 65, 184, 196; enlightenment of, 26, 191; practice of, 32; realm of, 176
śrāvaka knowledge, 185. *See also* three kinds of wisdom
Śrīmālādevī-siṃhanāda-sūtra (S), Queen of Śrīmālā, or Śrīmālā, Sūtra, 44
stage at which there is nothing more to be learned (*aśaikṣa-phala*, S), 153, 195, 196. *See also* one who has nothing more to learn
stage of neither perception nor nonperception (*naivasaṃjñānā-saṃjñāyatana*, S), 177
stage of nothingness (*ākiṃcanyāyatana*, S), 177
stage of the infinity of consciousness (*vijñānānantyāyatana*, S), 177
stage of the infinity of space (*ākāśānantyāyatana*, S), 177
state of balance between calm and contemplation, 179
Sthaviravāda (S), 34, 35; Tripiṭaka, 86. *See also* Theravāda
Sthiramati (S), 45
storehouse consciousness (*ālaya-vijñāna*, S), 44, 45, 106, 108, 128, 136, 218 n. 6
Stories of Former Incarnations. See *Sheng-ching*
stories of former lives of the Buddha (*jātaka*, S, P), 69, 72, 73. See also *Jātaka*
Stories of the Lives of Certain Monks and Nuns. See *Apadāna*
Story of Emperor Aśoka. See *Aśokāvadāna*
streamwinner: stage of attainment of (*srota-āpanna*, S), 191, 201; stage of effort of (*srota-āpatti-pratipanna*, S), 191, 192, 200, 201, 202
stubborn, perverted views (*dṛṣṭi-parāmarśa*, S), 212. *See also* five false views
studies on the Vinaya (*abhivinaya*, S), 82
stūpa (S), or relic tower, 54
Subjects of Discussion. *See* Kathāvatthu
substance, 95, 109, 115, 126, 128. *See also* metaphysics; ontology
substantial-body of a buddha (*svabhāva-kāya*, S), 58
subtle. *See* nirvāṇa, synonyms for
suffering (*duḥkha*, S), 109, 140, 143, 149, 150–51, 154; all things and, 121, 130, 131, 132, 140; cause of, 156–57; discussion of, 130–32, 155–56; extinction of, 157–58; release from, 27, 53, 60, 93; three types of, 130–31, 155. *See also* Four Noble Truths
śūnyatā. *See* emptiness

Superior Sūtra of the Buddha Treasury. See *Buddhapiṭaka-nirgraha-sūtra*
supernatural knowledge (*abhijñā,* S), 166, 186
supernormal powers (*abhijñā,* S), 74, 165, 179, 184, 186, 193, 205
supramundane realm, or world (*lokottara,* S), 66, 107, 115, 169, 176, 178. *See also* realm of enlightenment
supreme and perfect enlightenment (*anuttara-samyaksaṃbodhi,* S), 66
"supremely rich field," 91, 92, 93
"supreme, perfectly enlightened one" (*anuttara-samyaksaṃbuddha,* S), 55. *See also* Ominiscient; perfectly enlightened buddha (*samyaksaṃbuddha*)
supreme wisdom. *See* four kinds of fearlessness
"surpassing organ, the," 109
Susiddhikara-sūtra (S), Sūtra of Good Accomplishment, 46
sūtra (*sutta*), 69–70. *See also* discourses (*sūtra*); twelve divisions, the teachings in
Sūtra Basket (Sūtra-piṭaka, S), 34–35, 68, 69, 71, 75, 82, 85; discussion of, 77–79
Sūtra of Adornments. See *Ying-luo-pen-yeh-ching*
Sūtra of Good Accomplishment. See *Susiddhikara-sūtra*
Sūtra of Great Compassion. See *Mahākaruṇa-puṇḍarīka-sūtra*
Sūtra of Infinite Life. *See* Larger *Sukhāvatī-vyūha-sūtra*
Sūtra of Meditation on the Bodhisattva Universal Virtue. See *Kuan-p'u-hsien-p'u-sa-hsing-fa-ching*
Sūtra of Profound Understanding. See *Saṃdhi-nirmocana-sūtra*
Sūtra of the Advancement Toward Truth. See *Adhyardhaśatikā-prajñāpāramitā-sūtra*
Sūtra of the Appearance of the Good Doctrine in [Sri] Lanka. See *Laṅkāvatāra-sūtra*
Sūtra of the Brahma Net. See *Brahmajāla-sūtra; Fan-wang p'u-sa-chieh-ching*
Sūtra of the Collection of the Practices of the Six Perfections. See *Liu-tu-chi-ching*
Sūtra of the Great Accumulation of Treasures. See *Mahā-ratnakūṭa-sūtra*
Sūtra of the Great Decease, Mahāyāna. See *Mahā-parinirvāṇa-sūtra*
Sūtra of the Great Decease, Pāli. See *Mahā-parinibbāna-suttanta*
Sūtra of the Heroic Deed of King Dīghīti. See *Chang-shou-wang pen-ch'i-ching*
Sūtra of the Recital. See *Saṅghīti-suttanta*
Sūtra of the Rice Stem. See *Śalis-tamba-sūtra*
Sūtra of the Story of the Great Ones. See *Mahā-apadāna-suttanta*
Sūtra of the *Tathāgata*-Embryo. See *Tathāgata-garbha-sūtra*
Sūtra of the Teachings Left by the Buddha. See *Fo-i-chiao-ching*

Sūtra of the Turning of the Wheel of the Law. See *Dhamma-cakkappavattana-sutta*
Sūtra on Mahāyāna Abhidharma. See *Mahāyāna-abhidharma-sūtra*
Sūtra on the Preaching of the Wheel-rolling King. See *Cakkavattisīhanāda-suttanta*
Sūtra Stories of Deeds of the Buddha. See *Fo-pen-hsing-chi-ching*
Sūtra-vibhaṅga (S), Analysis of the Sūtra, 70, 79, 84, 170
Sutta-nipāta (P), Collection of Suttas, 74–75, 77, 78, 84, 94
Suvarṇaprabhāsottama-rāja-sūtra (S), Golden Light Sūtra, 45
Svātantrika (S), 44. *See also* middle Mahāyāna
synonyms for nirvāṇa, 133–34
synonyms for *prajñā*, 185, 186–87
synonyms for the defilements, 205–6

tactile nerves (*kāya-indriya*, S, P), 109. *See also* form (*rūpa*); six sense organs
Takakusu, Junjirō (J; 1866–1945), 214 n. 12
taking refuge in the Three Treasures, 53, 173; formula for, 55. *See also* "Kie Buppōsō-hō"; three refuges
tale of the young ascetic of the Himalayas, 122–23
Tales of Heavenly Palaces. See *Vimānavatthu*
Tales of Hungry Ghosts. See *Petavatthu*
Tales of the Buddha's Former Lives. See *Jātaka*
Tao-hsüan (C), 82
tao-pi-an (C; *pāramitā*, S), "reaching the other shore," 29. *See also* nirvāṇa, synonyms for
taste buds (*jihvā-indriya*, S), 109. *See also* form (*rūpa*); six sense organs
tastes (*rasa-āyatana*, S, P), 111, 183. *See also* six objects [of cognition]
Ta-T'ang hsi-yü-chi (C), Record of the Western Regions, 86
Tathāgata (S), an epithet of a buddha, 64–65
tathāgata-embryo (*tathāgata-garbha*, S), 44, 86, 116, 136, 218 n. 6
tathāgata-embryo tradition, 45
Tathāgata-garbha-sūtra (S), Sūtra of the *Tathāgata*-Embryo, 44
Tathāgata of Healing (Bhaiṣajyaguru, S), 59–60, 65
tathatā (S). *See* absolute Truth
Teacher of Gods and Humans (*śāstā-devamanuṣyānām*, S), an epithet of a buddha, 64, 67
teaching for the instruction of others, 151
teaching of the Tripiṭaka or Piṭaka (T'ien-t'ai term for non-Mahāyāna sects), 25
teachings (*pariyatti*, P). See *dharma*, four characteristics of
teaching that relies on the strength of another, 24
ten abodes (*daśa-vihāra*, S), 197, 200, 201
ten *aśaikṣa dharmas*, 161, 163, 184
ten basic [associated] mental functions (*mahābhūmika*, S), 107. *See also* associated mental functions
Tendai (J; T'ien-t'ai, C), sect, 59, 173
Tendai precepts, 173

ten defilements of practice, 208
ten directions (in Buddhist cosmology), 57, 60, 215 n. 7
ten disputed practices, 34, 214 n. 7
ten epithets of a buddha, 64–68
ten fetters, 206. *See also* synonyms for the defilements
ten forms of knowledge (*daśa jñānāni*, S), 185–86, 220 n. 6
ten good precepts, 170, 171, 172, 173, 176
ten grave prohibitions, 170, 171, 173
ten impurities, contemplation of, 180, 182
ten meritorious acts, 171–72
ten merits of the regulations, 93
ten perfections (*daśa-pāramitā*, S), Mahāyāna, 29
ten perfections (*dasa-pāramī*, P), Pāli Buddhist, 29
ten perverse views, 211. *See also* five false views
ten powers [of a buddha] (*daśa-balāni*, S), 62, 64
ten precepts [for novices], 90, 170. *See also* precepts; ten good precepts
ten realms of existence, or ten realms, 124, 176–77, 218 n. 2; interpenetration of, 177, 218 n. 3
ten stages of bodhisattva practice (*daśa-bhūmi*, S), 29, 59, 60, 61, 86, 197; discussion of, 199–202
ten stages of developing buddha wisdom. *See* ten stages of bodhisattva practice
ten stages of faith (*daśa-śraddhā*, S), 197, 201
ten stages of practice (*daśa-caryā*, S), 197, 201
ten stages of transference of merit (*daśa-pariṇāma*, S), 197, 201
ten states of mindfulness (*dasa anussatiyo*, P), 180–82
ten suchnesses, 123–24, 137, 218 nn. 1, 3. *See also* "real aspect of all things"
ten universals (*dasakasiṇa-āyatanāni*, P), 180
terms denoting concentration, 178–80
"that which is about the Dharma" (*abhidharma*, S), 35, 82. *See also* treatises
"that which is about the Vinaya" (*abhivinaya*, S), 82
"that which is intrinsically devoid of self" (*nissatta-nijjīvatā*, P), 87, 88, 89, 126
theories of dependent origination, 136–37
theories of the ten stages, 199–200
theory and practice, 66, 153
theory of associated mental functions. *See* associated mental functions
theory of associations (*saṃprayoga*, S), 107
theory of consciousness, 106
theory of dependent origination, 114; Yogācārin, via the storehouse consciousness, 136
theory of dependent origination of the six great elements, 119, 136
theory of eight consciousnesses, Yogācārin, 108
theory of impermanence, 124
[theory of] innumerable buddhas of the present, 57
theory of karmic retribution, 108
theory of "real aspect," 136, 137

theory of the "real aspect of all things," 136–37
theory of the six consciousnesses, 44
theory of two kinds of nirvāṇa, 133
"the other shore," 24, 29, 66, 133. *See also* nirvāṇa, synonyms for; "this shore"
Theragāthā (P), Verses of the Elder Monks, 71, 77–78
Theravāda (P), 23, 34, 35, 47, 48–49
Theravāda Buddhism. *See* Buddhism: Pāli
Therīgāthā (P), Verses of the Elder Nuns, 71, 78
thirty-seven practices conducive to enlightenment (*bodhipākṣika-dharma,* S), 86, 163, 164–67, 217 n. 18
thirty-three forms (of Avalokiteśvara), 61
thirty-two primary marks (of a buddha), 26, 60, 64, 216 n. 10
Thirty Verses on the Doctrine of Consciousness Only. See *Triṃśikā-vijñaptimātratā-siddhi*
"this shore," 24, 29
thorough consideration (*pratyavekṣaṇa,* S), 187. *See also* synonyms for *prajñā*
thorough knowledge (*parijñā,* S), 186. *See also* synonyms for *prajñā*
Those Supporting the Teaching of the Elders. *See* Theravāda
those with no potential for enlightenment at all (*icchantika,* S). *See* five groups of sentient beings
thoughtless trance (*asaṃjñi-samāpatti,* S). *See* functions dissociated from mind
three actions that need not be guarded against (*trīṇy ārakṣyāṇi,* S), 64, 216 n. 13
three aspects of conditioned *dharmas,* 122
Three Baskets (Tripiṭaka, S), 25, 35, 49, 50, 68, 69, 77; Mahāyāna Tripiṭaka, 84–86. *See also* Chinese Tripiṭaka; Southern Tripiṭaka; Tibetan Tripiṭaka
three-body doctrine (of buddha bodies), 58
three cravings, 148, 152, 156, 157. *See also* craving (*tṛṣṇā*); six cravings
three feelings, 104, 107, 148. *See also* feeling (*vedanā*); five feelings; six feelings
three fetters (*tīni saṃyojanāni,* P), 192, 205–6, 207. *See also* synonyms for the defilements
three fires, 206. *See also* synonyms for the defilements
threefold practice (*trīṇi śikṣāṇi,* S), 62, 67, 86, 163–64, 191; discussion of, 167–88; Eightfold Path and, 160–61
three gates to liberation (*tīṇi vimokkhā-mukhāni,* P), 184, 220 n. 5
three impurities, 206. *See also* synonyms for the defilements
three insights (*te-vijjā,* P), 190, 193
three kinds of pride, 210–11. *See also* pride
three kinds of wisdom, 185. See also *prajñā* and *jñāna;* wisdom (*prajñā*)

three moral categories, 107
three natures of existence. *See* three-natures theory
three-natures theory, 86, 140–42, 219 n. 9
three outflows (*āsrava*, S). *See* synonyms for the defilements
three periods and ten directions, 60; buddhas of, 57
three periods of karmic retribution, 146
three poisons, 206. *See also* synonyms for the defilements
three pure causes, 194. *See also* Sarvāstivādin stage of practice
three pure precepts (Yoga precepts), 85, 170, 171, 172, 173
three realms of existence, 67, 107, 115, 129, 131,149, 193; concentration and, 178; defilements and, 205, 208, 211; discussion of, 175–76; ten stages and, 201. *See also* realms of existence
three refuges, 53, 173; precepts of, 173. *See also* taking refuge in the Three Treasures
Three Seals of the Law, 86, 121, 123, 124. *See also* Seals of the Law; Four Seals of the Law
Three Secrets, 46, 86
three stages of *arhat* practice, 193. *See also* Sarvāstivādin stages of practice
three Sūtras of the Names of Three Thousand Buddhas. See *San-ch'ien-fo-ming-ching*
"three thousand realms in one thought," 124, 218 n. 3
Three Treasures (*tri-ratna, ratna-traya*, S): denial of, 211; not to disparage, 171; as objects of faith, 54; and pure precepts, 173, 202; taking refuge in, 53, 173
Three Treatises school. *See* San-lun
"three turns of the wheel" [of the Four Noble Truths], 153
three types of equanimity (*trīṇi smṛtyupasthānāni*, S), 62–63, 64
three types of suffering, 130–31, 155. *See also* suffering
three vehicles, 23, 24, 32, 200
three wise degrees, 196. *See also* Sarvāstivādin stages of practice
Thusness. *See* absolute Truth; unconditioned *dharmas*
"thus-said" narratives (*itivṛttaka*, S; *itivuttaka*, P), 69, 72, 73. See also *itivṛttaka* and *itivuttaka*
"Thus-Said" Sūtras. See *Itivuttaka*
Tibetan Buddhism (Lamaism). *See* Buddhism: Tibetan, (or Lamaism)
Tibetan Tripiṭaka, 50
Tibetan Vinaya, 81
T'ien-t'ai (C; Tendai, J) sect, 25, 117, 124, 137, 183, 219 n. 8; Fa-hsiang sect and, 196, 197; ten realms of existence and, 176
ties (*grantha*, S), four. *See* synonyms for the defilements
"to be parted from what is loved." *See* parting (separation) from what we love, suffering inherent in
"to be united with what is hated." *See* contact with what we hate, suffering inherent in
"to confer benefits on all sentient beings." *See* precepts for the practice of benefiting others

"to do no evil" (*saṃvara-śīla*, S), 170, 172, 174
"to do only good" (*kuśaladharma-saṃgrāhaka-śīla*, S), 170, 174
tranquil (*śāntam*, S), 132, 133. *See also* synonyms for nirvāṇa
tranquillity (*praśrabdhi*, S), 53. *See also* seven factors of enlightenment
tranquillity, or calm, (*śamatha*, S), 121, 131, 177, 178–79, 220 n. 3; of nirvāṇa, 27
tranquillity, perfect. *See* nirvāṇa, complete; perfect tranquillity
transformations (*nirmāṇa*, S). *See* nonimpedimentary moral neutrality, four types of
transformed-body of a buddha (*nirmāṇa-kāya*, S), 58, 60, 61. *See also* manifest-body of a buddha
transitory *dharmas* (*paññatti*, P), 88, 112, 116
transmigration (*saṃsāra*, S), 27, 127, 128, 140, 149–50, 157; nirvāṇa and, 114; three-natures theory and, 142. *See also* birth and death, cycle of; rebirth
Treatise. *See* Prakaraṇa
Treatise Basket (Abhidharma-piṭaka, S), 35, 68, 82–84, 85
Treatise Following the True Teachings of the Abhidharma. See *Abhidharma-nyāyānusāra-śāstra*
Treatise in Four Hundred Verses. See *Catuḥśataka*
Treatise in One Hundred Verses. See *Śata-śāstra*
Treatise on the Adornment of Mahāyāna Sūtras. See *Mahāyāna-sūtrālaṃkāra*
Treatise on the Awakening of Faith in the Mahāyāna. See *Mahāyāna-śraddhotpāda-śāstra*
Treatise on the Buddha-nature. See *Buddhagotra-śāstra*
Treatise on the Conduct of a Bodhisattva. See *Bodhisattva-bhūmi; P'u-sa-shan-chieh-ching*
Treatise on the Establishment of the Doctrine of Consciousness Only. See *Vijñaptimātratāsiddhi-śāstra*
Treatise on the Great Perfection of Wisdom Sūtra. See *Mahā-prajñāpāramitā-śāstra*
Treatise on the Jewel-nature. See *Ratnagotravibhāga-mahāyānôttaratantra-śāstra*
Treatise on the Middle. See *Mādhyamika-śāstra*
Treatise on the Principles of Different Schools. See *Samayabhedoparacanacakra*
Treatise on the Stages of Yoga Practice. See *Yogācārabhūmi-śāstra*
Treatise on the Transcendence of Controversy. See *Vigraha-vyāvartanī*
Treatise on the Twelve Gates. See *Dvādaśamukha-śāstra*
treatises (*abhidharma*, S), 30, 35, 68, 74, 75, 82, 84, 109
Triṃśikā-vijñaptimātratā-siddhi (S), Thirty Verses on the Doctrine of Consciousness Only, 45
true Dharma, 93
true *dharmas* (*bhūta*, S), 88, 112, 116
true nature. *See* fully accomplished, or true, nature; three-natures theory

True Pure Land (Jōdo Shin, J) sect, 173
true words (mantra, S), 46
True Word sect. *See* Chen-yen; Shingon
Truth, 114–16. *See also* absolute Truth; Dharma
truth, 87, 114–16. *See also* Dharma; nirvāṇa, synonyms for; ten perfections, Pāli Buddhist
truth of the cause of suffering (*samudaya-satya,* S), 153, 154, 156–57
truth of suffering (*duḥkha-satya,* S), 131, 152, 153, 154, 155. *See also* Four Noble Truths
truth of the extinction of suffering (*nirodha-satya,* S), 153, 154, 157–58
truth of the Way to the extinction of suffering (*mārga-satya,* S), 153, 154, 158
truth, perfection of, (*sacca-pāmamī,* P), 29. *See also* ten perfections, Pāli Buddhist
Tsung-mi (C), 180
tu (C; *pāramitā,* S), "crossing over," 29
tu-wu-chi (C; *pāramitā,* S), "reaching the limitless," 29. See also *tao-pi-an*
twelve divisions, the teachings in, 68–75
Twelve-linked Chain of Dependent Origination, 30, 32, 86, 105–6, 140, 151; discussion of, 142–50; five meditations and, 182; individual links and, 204; modern interpretations of, 146; religious causality and, 139; suffering and, 131
twelve links, 143, 145, 146–50
twelve sense fields (*āyatana,* S, P), 86, 88, 96, 102, 119; discussion of, 108–16
twenty false views of self (*ātma-dṛṣṭi,* S), 102, 217 n. 1. *See also* false views
twenty-five ancillary practices (T'ien-t'ai meditational practices), 183
Twenty Verses on the Doctrine of Consciousness Only. See *Viṃśatikā-vijñaptimātratā-siddhi*
two-body doctrine (of buddha bodies), 57–58
two kinds of emptiness, 129–30. *See also* emptiness
two kinds of nonself, 86, 129–30. *See also* nonself
two vehicles, 23, 24

Udāna (P), Solemn Utterances of the Buddha, 71, 77, 78, 84
Udāna-varga (S), Solemn Utterances of the Buddha, 71
ultimate, or cosmic, reality (*brahman,* S), 116, 126
ultimate truth of the universe (Dharma, S), 58. *See also* truth
unattained aims, suffeing of, 152, 155, 156
unconditioned (*asaṃskṛta,* S), 96, 97, 114, 133. *See also* nirvāṇa, synonyms for
unconditioned *dharmas* (*asaṃskṛta-dharma,* S), 96, 97, 112, 114, 115; three, 114
undefiled consciousness (*amala-vijñāna,* S), 106
Understander of the World (*lokavid,* S), an epithet of a buddha, 64, 66–67

understanding (*mati*, S), 105, 107. *See also* ten basic [associated] mental functions
undesirable realms of rebirth (*durgati*, S), 176, 202
undetermined, the. *See* associated mental functions; five groups of sentient beings
unfailing effort (*āraddhaviriya*, P), 219 n. 1
unhindered understanding, or knowledge, (*pratisaṃvid*, S), 187
unmanifested form (*avijñapti-rūpa*, S), 103, 110, 112–13, 170. *See also* conditioned *dharmas;* form (*rūpa*)
unpremeditated evil, 113. *See also* unmanifested form
Unsurpassed (*anuttara*, S), an epithet of a buddha, 64, 67
upadeśa, 74–75. *See also* explanatory discourses
Upāli (S, P), an eminent disciple of Śākyamuni, 76
utterances (*udāna*, S, P), 68–69, 71

Vaibhāṣika (S), Sarvāstivādin offshoot, 44
vaipulya and *vedalla*, 74
Vairocana (S), a Buddha, 59, 215 n. 8. *See also* Mahāvairocana
Vajracchedikā-prajñāpāramitā-sūtra (S), Diamond, or Diamond Wisdom, Sūtra, 42, 51, 85, 89
Vajraśekhara-sūtra (S), Diamond Peak Sūtra, 46
Various Stories. See *Saṃyuktāvadāna*
Vasubandhu (S), 44, 45, 46, 133
Vaṭṭagāmanī (S), 216 n. 17
Vedanta- or Brahma-sūtras (non-Buddhist), 70
vehicle (*yāna*, S), 24
vehicle of the bodhisattvas (Bodhisattvayāna, S), 24, 25
vehicle of the buddhas (Buddhayāna, S), 24, 25, 200
vehicle of the hearers (Śrāvakayāna, S), 24, 25, 40
vehicle of the solitary buddhas (Pratyekabuddhayāna, S), 24, 31–33
vehicle, two and three: discussion of, 24–33
"verse of commandment of the seven Buddhas," 174
"verse of impermanence," 122, 123
verses (*gāthā*, S, P), 68, 69, 70, 71, 73, 216 n. 14
Verses of the Elder Monks. See *Theragāthā*
Verses of the Elder Nuns. See *Therīgāthā*
Verses on the Law. See *Dhammapada*
Vibhaṅga (P), Distinctions, 83, 84
victor of the path, 94. *See also* four types of monks
view (*dṛṣṭi*, S), 186. *See also* false views; right view; seven purities
viewing or consideration (*anupaśyanā*, S), 186. *See also* synonyms for *prajñā*
Vigraha-vyāvartanī (S), Treatise on the Transcendence of Controversy, 43
Vijñānakāya (S), Group on Consciousness, 83
Vijñānavāda (S; Consciousness Only) school, 44. *See also* Yogācāra (Yoga Practice) school, Yogācārins
Vijñaptimātratāsiddhi-śāstra (S),

Treatise on the Establishment of the Doctrine of Consciousness Only, 45
Vimalakīrti-nirdeśa-sūtra (S), Vimalakīrti Sūtra, 42
Vimalakīrti Sūtra. See *Vimalakīrti-nirdeśa-sūtra*
Vimānavatthu (P), Tales of Heavenly Palaces, 77
Viṃśatikā-vijñaptimātratā-siddhi (S), Twenty Verses on the Doctrine of Consciousness Only, 45
Vinaya in Ten Recitations. See *Daśabhāṇavāra-vinaya*
Vinaya of the Mahāsāṃghikas, 82
Vinayas, 79, 170. *See also* morality; Precepts Basket; regulations (*vinaya*)
Vinaya sect. *See* Lü; Ritsu; sect of the Four-Part Vinaya
Vipassin. *See* Vipaśyin
Vipaśyin (S; Vipassin, P), one of seven Buddhas of the Past, 56, 215 nn. 2, 3, 5
virtue (*guṇa*, P), 87, 89
Visuddhimagga (P), The Path of Purity, 189, 220 n. 4
volition (*cetanā*, S, P), 99, 101, 105, 106, 107. *See also* mental constituents; ten basic mental functions
vows (*praṇidhāna*, S), 26, 28, 60, 202; four universal, of the bodhisattva, 27, 213 n. 1
vows, perfection of, (*praṇidhāna-pāramitā*, S), 29. *See also* ten perfections, Mahāyāna
Vulture Peak, 53, 59

walking, standing, sitting, and lying down. *See* nonimpedimentary moral neutrality, four types of
Way, the, 91, 93, 158–61. *See also* Buddha's Way
Way of Analysis, The. See *Paṭisambhidā-magga*
way of buddhahood, 93
Way of Practice (*bhāvanā-mārga*, S), 192, 193, 196, 207; stage of, 153
way of the sage (*ārya*), 158, 165
Way of View (*darśana-mārga*, S), 191, 193, 196, 197, 207; stage of, 153, 208
Well Departed (*sugata*, S), an epithet of a buddha, 64, 66
western realm of Sukhāvatī, 60. *See also* Buddha of Infinite Light (Amitābha)
wheel-rolling kings (*cakravartin*, S), 61, 73
will (*chanda*) to attain *dhyāna*, 165. *See also* four psychic powers
wisdom (*medhā*, S, P), 186. *See also* synonyms for *prajñā*
wisdom (*prajñā*, S): aspects and degrees of, 184; benefit of, 168; bringing, into action, 183; defilements and, 205; discriminating, 187, 188; emptiness of, 30; of enlightenment, 166, 179, 184, 185; four forms of, 185; four kinds of, 186; great, 133, 188; highest, of a bodhisattva, 185; nondiscriminating, 187, 188; perfect and unfailing, 63; right view and, 159; supreme, 62; of supreme enlightenment, 188; true, 160, 183; unfailing, 63 (*see also* buddha wisdom). See also *term by name*
wisdom, perfection of, (*prajñā-pāramitā*, S), 28, 29, 185, 188, 201.

See also Six Perfections; ten perfections
wisdom, practice of, (*prajñā-śikṣa,* S), 62, 67, 161, 164, 167, 190; discussion of, 184–88. *See also* threefold practice
wisdom free from defilements, 186
wisdom of regarding all things equally (*samatā-jñāna,* S), 120
wisdom of the embodied nature of *dharma-dhātu. See* five forms of wisdom
wisdom of the realm of defilements, 185
Wisdom sūtras. See *Prajñāpāramitā-sūtra*
without ego (*fei-wo,* C), 127
World-honored One (Bhagavat, S), an epithet of a buddha, 23, 64, 67–68
world of delusion [or defilements] (*loka,* S, P), 29, 66–67, 140, 142, 176, 178, 185; realms in (*see* six realms of existence). *See also* world of the three realms
world of enlightenment, 142. *See also* realm of enlightenment; supramundane realm, or world
world of sentient beings (*sattva-loka,* S), 66. *See also* receptacle world
world of the three realms (*loka,* S, P), 66–67, 176
worry (*pradāsa,* S). *See* auxiliary defilements
Worthy of Respect (*arhat,* S), an epithet of a buddha, 30, 64, 65–66. See also *arhat;* ten epithets of a buddha
wrath (*krodha,* S), 209. *See also* auxiliary defilements
Wright, Daniel, 50
wrong views, affliction of, 168
wu (C), "nonbeing," 127
wu-wo (C), "no ego," 127

Yamaka (P), Book of Pairs, 83, 84
Yasa. *See* Yaśas
Yaśas (S), 92, 217 n. 23
Ying-luo-pen-yeh-ching (C), Sūtra of Adornments, 197–99, 201
ying-sung (C; *geya,* S), verse corresponding to prose, 70. *See also* mixed prose and verse
Yoga (S), Hindu school of philosophy, 43
yoga (S, P), a concentration practice, 179
yoga adept (*yogācārya,* S), 179. *See also* terms denoting concentration
Yogācāra (S), 44, 45, 46, 85, 106, 120, 219 n. 9. *See also* Vijñānavāda (S; Consciousness Only) school; Yogācārins
Yogācārabhūmi-śāstra (S), Treatise on the Stages of Yoga Practice, 45, 63–64, 121
Yogācāra center at Valabhī, 45
Yogācārins (Yogācārin, S), 45, 113, 114, 136, 208, 211; consciousness and, 106, 108, 128; defilements and, 204, 209; one hundred *dharmas* in five categories of, 97, 100–101; three-natures theory and, 140; twelve divisions and, 69. *See also* Yogācāra (Yoga Practice) school
yoga practice (*yogācāra,* S), 45, 179

Yoga precepts, 85, 172. *See also* three pure precepts
Yoga-sūtras (non Buddhist), 70
yokes (*yoga*, S, P), four, 206. *See also* synonyms for the defilements
young ascetic of the Himalayas, 122–23

zen (J; *ch'an*, C), 179; five kinds of, 179–80
Zen (J; Ch'an, C) sect, 59, 65, 137, 173
Zen Buddhism. *See* Buddhism: Zen (Ch'an)
Zen master, 55
Zen meditation, 173
zen of the highest vehicle (also *zen* of the patriarchs, or *zen* of the *tathāgatas*), 180. See also *zen*, five kinds of